Praise for
*Twilight at Monticello*

"So skillfully written and well-researched that the book held my interest until the final page . . . Like all people, famous or almost unknown, Jefferson was a mass of contradictions. Crawford explores them masterfully, thus indeed presenting a new Jefferson for a new generation."
—*Houston Chronicle*

"A worthy addition to the already enormous body of Thomas Jefferson scholarship. Crawford did his homework well, using literally dozens of sources to give us an unvarnished picture of the human side of one of America's greatest leaders in an entertaining, fast-moving narrative. You might never look at Monticello in quite the same way again after reading this book."
—*Free Lance-Star* (Fredericksburg, Va.)

"In *Twilight at Monticello*, Alan Pell Crawford treats his subject with grace and sympathetic understanding, and with keen penetration as well, showing the great man's contradictions (and hypocrisies) for what they were. And he brings alive a milieu. . . . Drawing on new

archival sources, Mr. Crawford reconstructs daily life at Monticello and depicts a colorful supporting cast of eminent personages, family members and retainers."
—*The Wall Street Journal*

"A brave, even courageous book."
—*Daily Progress* (Charlottesville, Va.)

"Alan Crawford's beautifully written, evocative portrait of 'the sage of Monticello' in his retirement years is a welcome addition to the Jefferson bookshelf. Juxtaposing affecting scenes of Jefferson's domestic life with fresh and illuminating perspectives on his subject's late-life political, philosophical, and spiritual preoccupations, Crawford's fine book should engage and reward a wide readership. This is a wonderful introduction to one of the most fascinating—and one of the most generally misunderstood—figures in American history."
—PETER ONUF, Thomas Jefferson Professor of History, University of Virginia

"Broader in focus than its title suggests, *Twilight at Monticello* covers the entirety of Jefferson's life and explores an abundance of subjects, including his stances on religion, slavery and federalism as well as Jefferson's relationship with his slave Sally Hemings. It's an intimate, well-researched look at Jefferson, and even readers with only a passing interest in our third president will find it fascinating."
—*Richmond Times-Dispatch*

"Elegant [and] elegiac . . . Even those who have studied Jefferson closely will learn a great deal from this well-written, authoritative look at Jefferson's last years."
—*Crisis Magazine*

"Land-rich, cash-poor, the two-time president struggled until his death in 1826 with debts, droughts, squabbling progeny and a leaky roof. How this most remarkable man persevered, sometimes desperate enough to engage in dubious transactions, is the melancholy story historian Alan Pell Crawford tells with great subtlety and charm in *Twilight at Monticello*."    —Bloomberg.com

Also by Alan Pell Crawford

*Unwise Passions: A True Story of a Remarkable Woman—and
the First Great Scandal of Eighteenth-Century America*

*Thunder on the Right: The "New Right" and the Politics of Resentment*

# TWILIGHT AT MONTICELLO

*He exhibited "an extraordinary degree of health, vivacity and spirit"*
*(Daniel Webster, 1824). Portrait by Thomas Sully, 1821.*

ALAN PELL CRAWFORD

# Twilight at Monticello

THE FINAL YEARS *of* THOMAS JEFFERSON

RANDOM HOUSE TRADE PAPERBACKS

*New York*

*For James F. Curran*

2009 Random House Trade Paperback Edition

Copyright © 2008 by Alan Pell Crawford

All rights reserved.

Published in the United States by Random House Trade Paperbacks,
an imprint of The Random House Publishing Group,
a division of Random House, Inc., New York.

RANDOM HOUSE TRADE PAPERBACKS and colophon are
trademarks of Random House, Inc.

Originally published in hardcover in the United States by
Random House, an imprint of The Random House Publishing Group,
a division of Random House, Inc., in 2008.

LIBRARY OF CONGRESS CATALOGING-IN-PUBLICATION DATA
Crawford, Alan Pell.
Twilight at Monticello: the final years of Thomas Jefferson/by Alan
Pell Crawford.
p. cm.
Includes bibliographical references and index.
ISBN 978-0-8129-6946-7
1. Monticello (Va.)—History—19th century. 2. Jefferson, Thomas,
1743–1826—Homes and haunts—Virginia—Albemarle County.
3. Jefferson, Thomas, 1743–1826. 4. Presidents—Retirement—
United States—Case studies. 5. Jefferson, Thomas, 1743–1826—
Family. 6. Jefferson, Thomas, 1743–1826—Friends and associates.
7. Albemarle County (Va.)—Social life and customs—19th century.
8. Plantation life—Virginia—Albemarle County—History—19th
century. 9. Presidents—United States—Biography.
10. Ex-Presidents—United States—Biography. I. Title
E332.74.C73 2008
973.4'6092—dc22 2007019602

Printed in the United States of America

www.atrandom.com

2 4 6 8 9 7 5 3 1

Book design by Simon M. Sullivan

Nature intended illusions for the wise as well as
for fools lest the wise should be rendered too
miserable by their wisdom.

CHAMFORT

# Thomas Jefferson and His Descendants

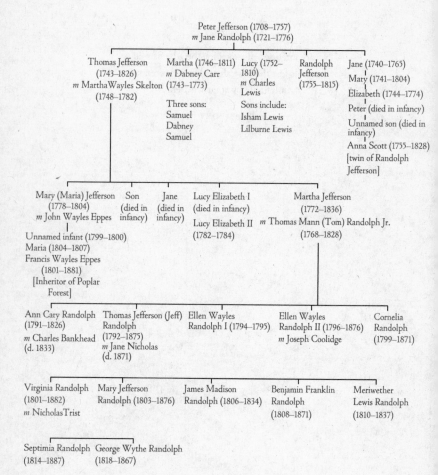

Peter Jefferson (1708–1757)
*m* Jane Randolph (1721–1776)

Thomas Jefferson (1743–1826) *m* Martha Wayles Skelton (1748–1782)

Martha (1746–1811) *m* Dabney Carr (1743–1773)

Three sons:
Samuel
Dabney
Samuel

Lucy (1752–1810) *m* Charles Lewis

Sons include:
Isham Lewis
Lilburne Lewis

Randolph Jefferson (1755–1815)

Jane (1740–1765)
Mary (1741–1804)
Elizabeth (1744–1774)
Peter (died in infancy)
Unnamed son (died in infancy)
Anna Scott (1755–1828) [twin of Randolph Jefferson]

Mary (Maria) Jefferson (1778–1804) *m* John Wayles Eppes

Unnamed infant (1799–1800)
Maria (1804–1807)
Francis Wayles Eppes (1801–1881) [Inheritor of Poplar Forest]

Son (died in infancy)

Jane (died in infancy)

Lucy Elizabeth I (died in infancy)
Lucy Elizabeth II (1782–1784)

Martha Jefferson (1772–1836) *m* Thomas Mann (Tom) Randolph Jr. (1768–1828)

Ann Cary Randolph (1791–1826) *m* Charles Bankhead (d. 1833)

Thomas Jefferson (Jeff) Randolph (1792–1875) *m* Jane Nicholas (d. 1871)

Ellen Wayles Randolph I (1794–1795)

Ellen Wayles Randolph II (1796–1876) *m* Joseph Coolidge

Cornelia Randolph (1799–1871)

Virginia Randolph (1801–1882) *m* Nicholas Trist

Mary Jefferson Randolph (1803–1876)

James Madison Randolph (1806–1834)

Benjamin Franklin Randolph (1808–1871)

Meriwether Lewis Randolph (1810–1837)

Septimia Randolph (1814–1887)

George Wythe Randolph (1818–1867)

# Contents

Monday, February 1, 1819, began quietly, as did most days at Monticello during the ten years in which Thomas Jefferson had been retired from public life. It would end far differently.

Jefferson, as usual, rose at dawn. Perhaps singing softly to himself, as he often did when engaged in some pleasurable pursuit, he laid the hearth with his own hands, recorded the temperature, and bathed his feet in cold water, a practice to which he attributed his long life. He was seventy-five now, and while his once red hair was gray, and he stooped a bit, he could still do most things for himself, and—this was a point of pride with Jefferson—he still possessed all his teeth.

Jefferson could also ride again, which he had been unable to do a few months ago when, after a visit to the mineral springs in the Blue Ridge, he suffered from an extremely painful "system of boils" on his backside, the treatments for which—an ointment of sulfur and mercury—seemed only to make matters worse. For weeks, he was brought low by blood poisoning, which almost killed him. Some New York newspapers reported that he had died.

During the worst of it, in August and September, if he had the energy to make the two-mile trip into Charlottesville or wished to visit a neighbor's plantation, he was bounced about in horse-drawn carriages over the rough roads of hilly Albemarle County, Virginia. For weeks, the pain was such that he couldn't sit up. When he wrote letters—a major part of his daily routine for many years but one that he was beginning to find irksome—he had to do so lying down. Now he could once again move about in the saddle or on foot, but he was not as strong as he had been before, and would never be again.

After breakfast—tea or coffee with warm muffins, served in the dining room at eight—he would leave the house, on some occasions helped by his butler and valet, a slave named Burwell Colbert, who grew up at Monticello and, as a child, had worked in Jefferson's nail-making shop. Together, they would make their way toward the kitchen garden a hundred feet or so southeast of the pavilion that jutted out from Jefferson's private chambers on Monticello's first floor. With Burwell at his side, he picked his way cautiously along the red clay path that led past the rank-smelling privy vent and down a short but sharp decline to the gate in the ten-foot-high paling fence built alongside Mulberry Row. That was where the workshops stood, one after another in a line that intersected the path from the house to the garden and led to the old family graveyard.

Jefferson loved order, symmetry, and balance, and there was no place on the mountaintop more orderly, symmetrical, and balanced than the garden, which he had designed many years ago and worked to perfect for half a century. Jefferson had started the garden in 1769, a year before he even began to build his house. Inside the fence, whose boards were set close together "so as not to let even a young hare in," the garden stretched for a thousand feet; the two-acre enclosure was itself neatly subdivided into twenty-four squares, each devoted to a different plant.

This being February, the ground in some spots was still hard from winter's chill, muddy in others. Even when the weather was raw, Jefferson would in-

*"No place on the mountaintop more orderly, symmetrical, and balanced."*
*Jefferson's vegetable garden at Monticello, looking southeast.*

spect with boyish glee the condition of the vegetables and medicinal herbs that grew, pale green to a ghostly gray, in winter. There were turnips and leeks and broccoli for the table, but much of what was planted in the garden was intended for medicinal use. The more incapacitated Jefferson became from headaches, rheumatism, and chronic diarrhea, the more dependent he became on his "garden pharmacy."

There was French lavender, which his copy of the *Edinburgh New Dispensary* recommended for "disorders of the head," and thyme, prescribed by *Culpeper's Complete Herbal* for stomach ailments, which "expels wind." If thyme did not do the trick, Jefferson could try home remedies made with rosemary and wormwood. To treat his rheumatism, he turned to various topical medications that used pepper plants.

For most vegetables, he would, of course, have to wait. When spring returned in another month or two, the next season's produce would be ready for the consumption of Jefferson's large family and for the many visitors who showed up at the plantation, expecting to be fed. The *Spinacia oleracea,* or spinach, he had planted the week before, on January 26; peas went in the next day. By the first week in February, directing the activities of the slaves who worked in the garden, he would see to it that the celery seeds were properly sown. The slaves would have to be closely supervised: if they weren't watched, he thought, they could be careless in their duties, or deceitful.

Such conclusions did not come easily to Jefferson, who worried about slavery—and about individual slaves—his entire life. Some slaves could be quite trustworthy. This was true, for example, of the members of the Hemings family who served as maids and waiters at Monticello or were craftsmen in the workshops near the garden. Others Jefferson considered less reliable. Two weeks earlier, on January 17, Jefferson had written to tell Joel Yancey, the overseer at Poplar Forest—a plantation he owned about ninety miles south of Monticello in Bedford County—to be especially careful when assigning tasks to a slave there named Dick.

The previous year, Dick had brought a wagonload of produce from the Bedford County plantation that, at first inspection, seemed to contain everything Jefferson expected. He learned later, however, that the slave "did not deliver a bag containing a bushel of dried peaches which he said had dropped thro a hole in the bottom of his waggon; altho' no hole was seen which could have let such a mass through." More recent than that, Jefferson noticed that Dick delivered a load of soap that weighed thirty-eight pounds rather than, as should have been the case, forty-five; "and the barrel of apples [he brought] is a little more than half full." Such "repeated accidents cannot but excite suspicions of him, sufficient to make us attentive in future." Eternal vigilance may have been the price of liberty; it was most assuredly a cost of owning slaves.

Overseers had to be watched as well. Some of them drove the slaves too hard. The deaths of five slave children in the last four years made Jefferson wonder whether the white men in his employ were allowing the mothers sufficient time to care for their infants. Too many overseers rushed the women back into the fields as quickly as possible, which was shortsighted. Jefferson concurred in the belief widely held among planters that slave women were of greater value than slave men: women bore children and therefore added to the labor force; male field hands, by contrast, consumed as much as they produced. "I consider the labor of a breeding woman as no object," he reminded the overseer, "and that a child raised every 2 years is of more profit than the crop of the best laboring man." While the labor of a slave woman is important, it is "their increase, which is the first consideration with us."

Until the overseers understood that fact, needless inefficiencies would result. There was nothing complicated in the matter, though Jefferson found something wonderful in it. Here, as in so many areas of life, Nature had made it agreeable for man to do what was virtuous. It was proper to allow the slave women to look after their babies, and the master was repaid many times over when he permitted them to do so. In this, "as in all other cases," Jefferson had decided, "providence has made our interests & our duties coincide perfectly."

On these morning walks in the garden, Jefferson loved to reflect on the happy economies of the natural order. The older he got, the more he appreciated the sublime pleasures of the life of the mind, to which he now sought to devote himself almost exclusively.

He also took great delight in sharing his enthusiasm for Nature with others. Many times on these garden walks, he would be accompanied by his grandchildren—Meriwether Lewis Randolph, perhaps, who had just turned nine, or the boy's sister, Septimia, who was five. In earlier years, Jefferson's favored companion on these outings had always been their much older sister, Ann Cary Randolph, now Ann Bankhead. Jefferson's first grandchild, Ann was a delicate woman whose love of garden plants had been almost as ardent as his own.

*"His able assistant in the garden."*
*Jefferson's granddaughter Ann Cary Randolph Bankhead.*

But Ann was grown up now, married, with children of her own, living on a plantation on the western slope of the mountain, half a mile away.

Deprived of Ann's company, but enjoying that of her younger siblings, Jefferson would make his way, hand in hand with Meriwether Lewis and Septimia, between the neat rows of plantings in this ninety-thousand-square-foot Eden. Along the way, in his soft, somewhat reedy voice, Jefferson discoursed on Nature and its splendors and, for reasons the children never quite understood, insisted on using important-sounding Latin names for perfectly ordinary things, such as squash and wooly worms. He would explain, with great patience, exactly what had been planted where, when it would come up, and how soon it would be brought to the table.

Jefferson would speculate, too, about the trees and the flowers and the animals on the property. His observations in past years indicated that the red maples would bloom as early as February 18, three weeks away. The cherry trees would begin to display their fragile blossoms in the second week of March; a week later, the asparagus would be ready for picking. He would hear the first whippoorwill, crying plaintively in the night, by April 2, the first robin three weeks after that. Ticks would show up in mid-March, but the family would not have to contend with houseflies until late April. By then—when Jefferson would turn seventy-six—all the songbirds would bring their music to the mountaintop.

But it was still winter on the mountain, and Jefferson often found himself "shivering and shrinking" from the cold, as he told Charles Thomson, an old friend from revolutionary days. When the chill got to him, as it surely did on this morning, he left the near barren garden and returned to the house, where the fireplaces smoked, and the house slaves would be tending to their chores.

Then, bidding the little ones to be about their lessons or their play, Jefferson disappeared into his private chambers. Putting on his glasses, he sat at his writing table and answered letters. The physical act of writing had become painful, thanks to a stiff right hand caused thirty years earlier in a rare moment of romantic abandon for which he would pay the rest of his life. In September 1786, on a walk along the Seine with the beautiful (and married) Maria Cosway, Jefferson, then U.S. minister to France, tried to leap a fence. He came crashing to the ground, fracturing his wrist, which never healed. ("How the right hand became disabled," he wrote to a friend in the American legation in London shortly after the embarrassing mishap, "would be a long story for the left to tell. It was one of those follies from which good cannot come but ill may.")

These days, writing was nearly as wearisome as it had been when the wrist was first injured and he had taught himself to write with his left. More than that, Jefferson found that he had less patience than he once had with the inquiries of strangers. When his hand was too tired to write anymore, he turned to reading. He had canceled his subscriptions to the out-of-state newspapers, but he still took the *Richmond Enquirer* for the advertisements, which he considered "the only truths to be relied on in a newspaper."

He retained an insatiable appetite for books, however, as he told John Adams the year before, when Adams sent him a copy of John Pickering's essay on the pronunciation of the Greek language, which Jefferson read "with great pleasure." He would soon receive from his old friend in Massachusetts a copy of the Nathaniel Bowditch translation of Laplace's *Mécanique céleste,* with commentaries. Until then, Jefferson was once again losing himself in Thucydides' account of the Peloponnesian War—in Greek, of course. Now that he had long since retired from politics, Jefferson told Nathaniel Macon of North Carolina on January 12, 1819, he could "slumber without fear, and review in my dreams the visions of antiquity."

This willful escape into such pleasing reveries made life's harsher realities endurable in ways that they otherwise were not. Enthroned at Monticello, where the clouds themselves seemed to shroud the mountaintop in an agreeable if ghostly intangibility, Jefferson professed to ignore events beyond the walls of his own bed chamber or, at most, the gates of Monticello, but this was disingenuous. Jefferson kept abreast of political developments, largely through correspondence with such friends as his Albemarle County neighbor James Monroe, who had succeeded James Madison of adjacent Orange County in the presidency, or with Madison himself.

Jefferson would never cease to fret about the future of the republic at whose birth he had played such a significant role. The survival of this exercise in self-government—the first in the history of the world, he believed—could never be taken for granted, as each day brought new dangers. The country's economy had never fully recovered from the War of 1812, and the news out of Washington had been discouraging for months. This was especially so for the honest and independent farmers whom Jefferson considered the backbone of this historic experiment in political liberty.

Even now, in February 1819, these farmers had good reason to fear that their future—as well as that of republicanism itself—was at stake. As winter gave way to spring and rain turned Virginia's roads into mud wallows, the planters' sleep—and much of the nation's—would be haunted by two developments that very few southerners were prepared to cope with, or even understand. These two issues, intertwined in many ways, would haunt Jefferson throughout his retirement; his family would wrestle with their implications for long years after their patriarch had departed. The nation itself would struggle with them for the next half-century and never put them fully to rest even then.

The first involved the form of the American economy, a question forced to the forefront by actions of the Second Bank of the United States, a Hamiltonian institution that Jefferson regarded as unconstitutional and had opposed. The second issue concerned the future of the slave system on which the southern economy was based. The settlers of Missouri had applied for statehood, and factions in the North were attempting to prohibit slavery within the new state's borders. This attempt Jefferson also considered unconstitutional. How these two dramas played out over the months and years to come would have enormous implications for the planters, their families, and their way of life. Jefferson himself could not yet fathom their enormity, though within a matter of months, no American, north or south, would be able to escape their consequences. By January and February 1819, however, everyone knew this much: the price of tobacco, wheat, and corn had been falling for several years, hit hard by competition from the cheaper and more fertile farms south and west of the

Appalachians, where ambitious and energetic men had been moving in great numbers since Jefferson left the presidency.

For decades now, even the biggest planters had been getting by on credit extended on the presumed value of next year's crop. The planters lived on hope—and no small measure of self-delusion—borrowing wherever they could, including from one another. Just twelve days ago, on January 21, Jefferson himself, strapped for cash, had borrowed $50 from James Leitch, a Charlottesville storekeeper.

The first signal that such habits could not be sustained indefinitely had come six months earlier, in the summer of 1818. About the time the peaches at Monticello ripened and the Indian corn was ready for harvest, the Second Bank of the United States, having mismanaged its own affairs, curtailed its lending and put pressure on its branch banks in the states to curtail theirs. Suddenly many planters found it impossible to renegotiate their loans and, in some cases, had to pay them back in full. By December 1818, a shortage of paper money left Virginia planters with few assets but land and slaves, which they already possessed in surplus.

What Jefferson did not know—no one could—was that by the end of February, the whole country would be in the grip of a severe economic depression. In the coming Panic of 1819, banks would go under, unemployment in the towns of the North would reach all-time highs, and shops, apothecaries, and taverns would close their doors. In the easygoing South, bankruptcy laws would suddenly be taken seriously for the first time in memory, and the courts began to enforce these laws, as was routinely done in New England. Once wealthy and respected gentlemen with venerable genealogies were forced off their ancestral plantations. Crops, land, and slaves were sold for whatever price the planters could get.

As more energetic Virginia planters struggled mightily to save themselves, and as far too many of their less vigorous neighbors merely looked on in helpless, horrified, sometimes drunken disbelief, rancorous debate raged in the Congress over what to do about Missouri. In February, amendments were offered to the Missouri statehood bill prohibiting the further introduction of slavery into the Louisiana Territory, acquired in 1803, during Jefferson's first term. The amendments would also free, at age twenty-five, all slaves who were born in Missouri after it became a state.

These amendments passed the House, where the northerners enjoyed a narrow majority, but they lost in the Senate, where the South still held sway. When Congress adjourned in March, the slavery question was left unresolved and would not, of course, be settled once and for all for another forty-six years, at Appomattox Court House, a day's carriage ride southeast of Charlottesville.

Although Jefferson had been critical of slavery, he also believed that the federal government had no constitutional authority to tell a state whether it could or could not allow slavery to exist within its borders. Still, he counseled calm forbearance. Yes, he told his neighbors, the northern states were playing a dangerous game. This attempt to impose their will on their southern brethren—dangerous to southern property holders, it went without saying—was dangerous as well to the interests of the North. The plantations of the South, he reminded his neighbors, provided the "bread and butter" on which the rising "manufacturing and navigating" interests of the North depended. As reasonable men, Jefferson believed, the northerners would realize their folly soon enough, and when they did, their better, more rational nature would reassert itself. When their passions cooled, the northerners would "return to the embraces of their natural and best friends."

On this first day of February 1819, Jefferson felt increasingly worried about the planters' financial plight, and his own. Money was tight, but this difficulty, Jefferson told himself, was surely temporary. He and his family, at Monticello and at other farms within a few miles—plantations called Carlton, Tufton, and Edgehill—might need to cut back on their expenditures, but not forever. Jefferson had been saying as much for several years. Yes, the seas looked stormy right now, he had written in 1815, when his family first began to be hard pressed. But they would "live as long, eat as much and drink as much, as if the wave had already glided under the ship. Somehow or other these things find their way out as they come in, and so I suppose they will now."

Jefferson himself was deeply in debt. He had borrowed considerable sums from a number of banks and cosigned loans for friends, but he never kept track of how much debt he carried at any time. Whatever the sum, he operated in the belief that he could rescue his family from these obligations with minimal inconvenience. All he had to do was sell some of his undeveloped acreage in Bedford County, near his Poplar Forest plantation. Profits from the sale would enable him to pay back everything he owed, and once this was done, "I shall be for ever at ease." His family, he believed, would be taken care of for the rest of his life and beyond.

Jefferson did not want to sell his land—no self-respecting planter did—but if that was required to provide for those he loved, he would try to find the strength to do it. In time, he trusted, the great plantations would be productive again, and the times of hardship would pass. Provided the country's diplomats performed their jobs rationally and with due care, and provided that foreign governments did not act rashly, there would always be markets for Virginia's tobacco and wheat. If only Jefferson's neighbors could be made to adopt more scientific agricultural methods so the soil was not depleted so rapidly, prosperity would return.

Wishing would make it so, Jefferson believed—that and purposeful activity. A lifetime of practice had taught Jefferson that the secret of happiness was the diligent avoidance of despair, and despair was most efficiently avoided by keeping busy. No matter how bleak one's external circumstances might be—and they seemed bleak, indeed, to many Virginia planters in the first months of 1819—facing them with a resolutely optimistic frame of mind was half the battle. In the unlikely event that this approach failed and life's difficulties seemed insurmountable, the challenge was to bend as cheerfully as possible to Nature's will. Remaining cheerful, however, would soon become more difficult than Jefferson imagined.

When his reading was done and he was ready for his morning ride, Jefferson still had much to feel hopeful about. His plans to establish a new university for Virginia were being debated in the state legislature in Richmond, and he might well receive news this very day that a dream many years in the making was about to come true.

Eager to embark on his morning's exercise, Jefferson was helped into the saddle, took the reins, and urged his horse down the path leading away from the gates that sealed off the house and yard from the rest of the plantation. For the next two or three hours, he rode about the property, applying, whenever necessary, the small whip that he carried.

In warmer months, when the red clay fields were being worked, he would inspect the farms. Should he come upon a group of slaves who did not appear to be laboring as hard as they might, Jefferson would pull his horse to a halt and shake the whip at them, a bit of play-acting that a French visitor, the Comte de Volney, had observed at Monticello.

Jefferson also enjoyed riding through the dense wilderness of red cedars and willow oaks that covered the mountain. On long summer days, he could enjoy the inspiring views to the west—the Peaks of Otter might be the highest in all of North America, he believed—and, to the east, the oceanic immensity of fields and pastures and woodlands that command "all the neighbouring heights as far as the Chesapeake," in the words of another French visitor.

On winter nights, when the weather was clear, Jefferson could see Castor and Pollux, Canis Major, and the Pleiades. His enjoyment of the science of astronomy was impossible, of course, without proper instruments. So, tomorrow, on February 2, he would send $10 to William Davenport in Philadelphia. Davenport, an instrument maker in the former national capital, was repairing Jefferson's telescope. This telescope would enable him to study the heavens more carefully, and to observe the ongoing construction at Charlottesville of the new University of Virginia, to which—provided the state came up with the money—Jefferson would devote so much of his energy in the seven years of life left to him.

Even before the legislature had committed itself to the project, Jefferson and the other members of the prospective school's board of trustees had ordered construction to begin. Ever since his earliest days in the Virginia legislature, Jefferson had dreamed of establishing in his own home county an institution of higher learning to rival Harvard or the College of New Jersey at Princeton. The lawmakers in Richmond had been debating the matter of funding the university for several weeks, and, as Jefferson told John Adams on January 19, 1819, we "are all atiptoe here in the hourly expectation of what our legislature decides."

By three or four o'clock, when the dinner bell rang at Monticello, Jefferson was back on the mountaintop, weary from his ride and hoping for a favorable report from Richmond. Instead, he received news of a far different and very distressing nature.

Sometime that afternoon, near the Charlottesville courthouse, there had been a fight. His beloved grandson Jeff Randolph had been stabbed. The wounds were serious. No one knew whether he would survive.

Thomas Jefferson Randolph, born at Monticello in September 1792, was the first son of Martha Jefferson Randolph, Jefferson's only surviving daughter. Jeff

*"The greatest of God-sends which heaven has granted to me."*
*Thomas Jefferson (Jeff) Randolph, 1808.*

was now twenty-six years old, and, at six feet, four inches, taller even than Jefferson, who towered over most men. A model son and grandson, Jeff was a hardworking, conscientious young man who, each year, assumed greater responsibility for managing the plantations. Jeff had married three years ago, in 1815, and now had three children of his own.

Sometime around 1818, Jefferson had turned over all of his farmland to this steady, dependable man, who had a special claim on Jefferson's affections—as Jefferson had on his. As a small boy, Jeff had shown a peculiar aversion to dust, which seems to have prevented his playing outdoors the way most boys did. Jefferson was eager to help and, even though he despised dogs himself, got the boy a puppy. Frolicking with the puppy seemed to cure Jeff, and he soon came to love plantation life, which was nothing if not dusty. For years, he refused to wear shoes, even in cold weather, so Jefferson personally hand-stitched the boy a pair of moccasins.

Before long, this once frail child had grown big for his age and was spending half the night with the older slaves, hunting possums and seeking out bee trees, which they would knock over to steal the honey. When little Mars Jeff grew sleepy on these outings, one of the men would put him on his own broad back, carry him to the slave quarters, and deposit the drowsy form in his own wife's bed. Hours later, when the men returned from their roistering, they would rouse Jeff for coffee, fried meat, eggs, and honey. Then, as the white overseer was just beginning his day and the men were steeling themselves for the hard work to come, the bleary-eyed boy would be toted back to the big house.

There, at his mother's knee and in the refined company of his sisters, Jeff learned to read and to write. These were matters of great urgency to his grandfather, though they did not come as quickly to the boy as they did to his sisters. Jeff had never become a keen scholar like his grandfather, or even an enthusiastic botanist and scientific farmer like his father, the high-strung and erratic Thomas Mann Randolph, Jr.

But Jeff possessed qualities the other two men lacked, which his grandfather recognized and encouraged. He was steady and hardworking, capable of spending endless hours on the farm without signs of fatigue and without complaint. In practical matters, Thomas Jefferson could not have wished for a more worthy heir. He would one day tell this dogged, dutiful grandson that he was "the greatest of the God-sends which heaven has granted to me." Jefferson not only loved this young man; he also needed him.

People who had witnessed the fight in which Jeff Randolph was stabbed reported that his assailant was his brother-in-law Charles Lewis Bankhead. Bankhead was also a member of the family. Ten years earlier, in September 1809, he had married Jeff's elder sister Ann Cary Randolph, the same young woman who shared her grandfather's love of gardening. Ann had just turned twenty-eight.

The people who sent word up the mountain that Bankhead had stabbed Jeff also said that Bankhead had been drinking when the fight broke out. This would have surprised no one: Bankhead drank so often and so heavily that the household at Monticello, Jefferson included, was well aware of it. That he could be dangerous when intoxicated was no secret either. He had caused ugly scenes before, sometimes at Monticello itself, but mostly, it seemed, when Jefferson was away. These confrontations had involved other family members and, on at least one occasion, the slave Burwell, Jefferson's butler, valet, and personal "body-servant." How Bankhead treated his wife when they were at their own plantation just down the mountain, no one could say for certain, though he had apparently beaten her, as Jefferson had been told.

But on such emotionally charged matters, empirical, observable facts that enabled a rationalist like Jefferson to make sense of the world could be difficult to establish. About all he could determine with anything akin to certainty was that a fight had occurred, that Jeff had been wounded, and that Bankhead was alleged to have been his attacker. Beyond that, people said that Jeff had been taken to a room in the back of Leitch's store (the same Leitch from whom Jefferson, twelve days ago, had borrowed $50) across from the jail and the courthouse, next to the slave auction house.

By the time Jefferson had learned only this much, the sun had gone down, and the women at Monticello insisted that it was too late and too dark for Jefferson to set out. Ignoring their admonitions, he ordered another horse to be brought back to the terrace. When the women again objected, Jefferson repeated the order "in a tone which brooked no further opposition." When his mount arrived, and he was helped back into the saddle, Jefferson struck the horse, which bounded forward at a gallop. The women watched in grim anticipation as the horse approached "the notch," a gap in the dark woods where the mountain begins its sudden descent. Then, "with a clatter of hoofs," horse and rider disappeared over the mountainside, leaving the moonlit dome of Monticello far behind.

Within the hour, Jefferson had ridden the four miles to Leitch's store, dismounted, and made his way to the back room. There he found his grandson lying on a makeshift bed of blankets that covered a baling crate. Then this most self-possessed of men knelt at his grandson's bedside and wept.

*Part One*

---

MORNING AND MIDDAY

# Chapter 1

## A Society of Would-be Country Squires

The Virginia Piedmont, to which Thomas Jefferson returned upon his retirement from the presidency early in 1809, had not changed much since his birth there on April 13, 1743. Jefferson was born at his father's tobacco plantation, Shadwell, on the Rivanna River, which flows through a gap in a small range called the Southwest Mountains. A few miles west of Shadwell, on the far side of the Southwest Mountains, the town of Charlottesville would be established. Just past Charlottesville stood the Blue Ridge Mountains, beyond which lay the Shenandoah Valley, walled off by the more imposing Alleghenies. On the other side of the Alleghenies stretched the great American West.

This was rugged territory in 1734, when Peter Jefferson received his first land grant in what would become Albemarle County, and it would remain

*"A dreary region of woods and wretchedness." Sketch of*
*Monticello Mountain from Edgehill, 1844.*

rugged for decades to come. As late as the American Revolution, a half century after Shadwell was built, Albemarle was a "dreary region of woods and wretchedness," in the words of Thomas Anburey, a British officer held prisoner near Monticello but, as a gentleman, given considerable freedom of movement. Wild horses roamed at will, "and have no proprietors, but those on whose lands they are found," Anburey observed. Hogs ran wild, and packs of wolves preyed on the deer as well as on any sheep the planters kept. Even in Jefferson's time, a Monticello slave would recall, "you could see the wolves in gangs runnin' and howlin', same as a drove of hogs." The Indians that had once lived there and left traces of their existence—an abandoned burial mound stood near Peter Jefferson's property—had moved south and west or vanished altogether by the time the Englishmen began to build their houses.

The countryside where Peter Jefferson established his family was unlike that of the Virginia Tidewater, where wide and deep rivers—the James, Potomac, York, Rappahannock, and Appomattox—cut through vast expanses of fertile flatlands. Forty or fifty miles west of Richmond, as the Blue Ridge comes into view, the land becomes hilly; the valleys between the hills are cobwebbed with creeks, a geography that presented a greater agricultural challenge than the planters of the Tidewater were accustomed to, as Peter Jefferson and other settlers would soon discover.

These settlers, unlike the Jeffersons, were not all of English derivation. There were also scores of Scots-Irish and Germans who had come down from Pennsylvania through the Shenandoah Valley. These were farmers who made tidy livings from small but well-tended plots of ground, as John Hammond Moore has written in his history of Albemarle County, "doing their own work, with the help of sons, relatives, and hired hands." Having never depended upon slaves to labor for them, these hardworking men (and women) either had little patience for the pretensions of the lordly slaveholders—or were intimidated by them.

Two years after Thomas Jefferson's birth, when the first list of Albemarle County "tithables," or white males eighteen and older, was compiled, there were only 1,394 taxpayers in the entire county. The total population of Albemarle—male and female, young and old, white and black, was about 4,250. About half of the people of Albemarle were enslaved, many just brought over from Africa.

The smallest group, though they wielded by far the greatest influence, were the self-styled gentlemen who had come from the East, bringing their slaves, their liquor, and sometimes their libraries. The most influential of the English settlers were the Jeffersons and the future president's maternal relatives, the Randolphs.

To clear Albemarle's hilly land and grow crops on it proved challenging to all the settlers, lowborn and high. Much of this land, cut deep with gullies, bristled with the stumps and lifeless trunks of trees that had been killed rather than chopped down. To save time and trouble, the settlers merely hacked off a strip of bark all around the trunk, leaving the tree to wither and die, usually within a couple of years. Although trees might put out a spindly growth of leaves the next season, Anburey wrote, they would soon stand skeletal and bare against the sky, giving the landscape a "very singular, striking, and dreadful appearance." Eventually, the rotting trees toppled over "with a most horrible crash," but until they fell, farming went on as if they were not there at all. The underbrush was either burned away or dug out with hoes. The soil "was scratched with plows," according to Anburey, "and the first crop was planted under the canopy of dead branches."

A Virginia farm field "should seem dangerous to walk in . . . for the trees are of a prodigious magnitude and height, from which are impending in awful ruins vast limbs, and branches of an enormous size, which are continually breaking off." The fences that enclosed these farmlands and kept livestock from wandering off were constructed in a zigzag arrangement so haphazard that New Englanders made a joke of it: when a man was drunk, they would say he was "making Virginia fences."

Very little of the acreage to which the planters held title was under cultivation at any one time, and farming anywhere except in the bottomlands along the river proved arduous. When tobacco was ready for transport, farmers rolled their hogsheads to the riverbanks and waited until a "freshet" swelled the streams, which enabled them to get their crops to the Tidewater on canoes and batteaux.

After such a storm, Anburey noted, the waters rolled down from the mountains, overflowed the banks for miles on end, and washed away the earth, "which being of a red cast, appeared like a torrent of blood." When the water was high, boats could move all the way to Richmond. For much of the year, however, the Rivanna, being either iced over in winter or too shallow in summer, was not navigable at all.

Virginia farmers relied on fires as well as floods. In the spring and fall, planters eager to rid their fields of weeds, fallen leaves, and stubble set fires "which traverse whole counties," Thomas Jefferson wrote in his book *Notes on the State of Virginia*. Fires "are very frequent," Anburey reported, "and at Charlottesville I have seen the mountains on a blaze for three or four miles in length."

The fields were plowed "not more than two inches deep," in Jeff Randolph's words, and the few nutrients left in the soil after tobacco, wheat, and corn had been grown on a given field were washed away by the same thundershowers that allowed farmers to get their crops to market. This erosion contributed to the soil's depletion with astonishing speed. Eventually, entire fields were "abandoned to gullies[,] broom, and briers," Randolph observed. By 1804, "nine tenths of the cleared land in [the area around Shadwell and Monticello] was in this condition," its owners "having sold it at low rates and moved west."

Most Virginians, black and white, lived in cabins or shacks, but here and there, on the hills overlooking the Rivanna, stood crude manor houses that their builders called mansions, surrounded by unpainted wooden outbuildings, stables, and slave quarters. These plantations were, for the most part, self-contained, self-supporting communities and the closest approximations of towns or cities for miles around.

Travel between these plantations and to the towns back east—sixty miles east to Richmond, say, or a hundred forty to Williamsburg—could be perilous. The dirt roads and carriage trails that connected the plantations were often impassable. Finished goods, like crops, moved mostly by boat. So, quite often, did the settlers. Whether they went by boat or made their way along the crude roads, people traveling to visit neighbors frequently found themselves facing vast clouds of black smoke from the farmers' fires.

Because Virginians lived at such distances from one another, they took every opportunity to socialize. They endured considerable hardship to attend barbecues, fish fries, and horse races, and at all of these events drunkenness was commonplace. The society into which Thomas Jefferson was born aspired to gentility but rarely achieved it. Taverns predated houses of worship, which, although established by the Church of England, were attended but grudgingly by the colonials they had been built to serve.

Under English common law, which prevailed through the colonial period,

Virginians could be fined for missing church once, flogged for a second infraction, and put to death for a third. Until Thomas Jefferson, as a member of the Virginia legislature, recommended revisions to the penal code, "free-thinkers" could find their children taken away. During Jefferson's childhood such laws, though rarely, if ever, enforced, remained on the books.

This was not a pious culture, nor an especially law-abiding one, but it was convivial. As soon as work was done, when holidays rolled around, or when there was business to attend to at the courthouse, the leading men of the county entertained themselves in raucous fashion, playing cards, dice, and billiards, often for high stakes. Violence frequently followed, "it not being the fashion of the day," in Jeff Randolph's words, "for men to restrain their tempers."

In 1748, five years after Jefferson's birth, fighting had gotten so vicious that Virginia's colonial legislature passed a general statute against maiming, making it a felony to cut out another person's tongue, put out his eye, or bite his nose or lip; thirty years later, just before the Revolution, the lawmakers added a prohibition against "gouging, plucking or putting out an eye, biting, kicking or stomping upon" a fellow subject of the British crown.

At horse races, competition was often restricted "to the better sort of Virginians only," Anburey found, and the planters, serving as their own jockeys, were uninhibited in the use of the whip, which they applied to one another as readily as to their mounts. Fox hunting, though viewed in some Tidewater circles as vulgar, remained popular in the Piedmont, where the sportsmen not only chased their prey with the help of dogs but shot at it as well. These would-be country squires seldom turned their weapons on one another, and murder was rare. Dueling, however, was an accepted practice, associated with an aristocratic way of life that ambitious English settlers were determined to transplant in the New World.

# CHAPTER 2

## An Upcountry Prince

Thomas Jefferson's first memory, he used to tell his family, was of being "handed up to a servant on horseback [and] carried on a pillow." This experience suggests an exalted social position, which Jefferson would probably have enjoyed even if his father, often depicted by historians as a mere yeoman farmer, had not married into the highest levels of Virginia's landed gentry.

Thomas Jefferson came from Welsh stock that had settled on royal land grants in Henrico County, east of Richmond, sometime in the late seventeenth century. These early Jeffersons held important posts as "gentlemen justices" in the county courts, posts secured through appointment by the royal governors. In 1749, Thomas Jefferson's father, Peter Jefferson, a surveyor by trade, worked with Joshua Fry, an Oxford-educated Englishman who taught mathematics at the College of William and Mary, to survey the boundary line between Virginia and North Carolina. The two men also completed one of the first and best maps of the Virginia Colony. Peter Jefferson's knowledge of Virginia's interior equipped him to select promising acreage along the Rivanna River in what would become Albemarle County; his earnings enabled him to establish himself there as a planter, naming his plantation Shadwell, after the parish in London where his wife had been baptized.

Peter Jefferson was a large, powerfully built man who commanded the respect of his neighbors and whose feats of strength inspired tall tales. This backcountry Hercules could simultaneously grab two hogsheads of tobacco, "weighing nearly 1,000 pounds apiece," people claimed, and hoist them, arms extended at right angles to his body, to an upright position. (Similar feats were attributed to Augustine Washington, George's father. By one account, Augustine could "raise up and place in a wagon a mass of iron that two ordinary men could barely raise from the ground.") Although Peter Jefferson received little or no formal schooling, he valued education, kept a library, and passed down to his eldest son his copies of Addison and Steele's *Spectator* and the works of Jonathan Swift.

In October 1739, Peter Jefferson improved his already enviable position by marrying the socially prominent Jane Randolph, a daughter of the lordly Isham Randolph of Dungeness plantation on the James River west of Richmond. Isham Randolph was the seventh son of William Randolph, a Warwickshire cavalier who, around 1660, established the Randolph clan in Virginia. William Randolph and his sons soon amassed considerable fortunes from tobacco, built baronial estates along the Tidewater rivers, and married off their daughters to men of position or promise who could safeguard the existing family fortunes and produce additional wealth on their own.

Isham Randolph was a sea captain as well as a planter, and after being widowed, he had sailed back to England around 1718 to seek a second wife. Jane Randolph, a product of this second marriage, was born in England. The Randolphs, Thomas Jefferson would observe with slight sarcasm, "trace their pedigree far back to England and Scotland, to which let everyone ascribe the faith and merit he chooses."

Further burnishing their credentials as early settlers, the Randolphs took great pride in their ancestral link to Pocahontas and her father, Chief Powhatan, who were New World royalty. Richard Randolph of Curles plantation, an uncle of Jane Jefferson's, had married Jane Bolling, a granddaughter of Pocahontas through her marriage to John Rolfe.

Thomas Jefferson attached greater importance to matters of lineage than he would sometimes admit. When he was about to marry, he asked an associate in London to obtain a set of the family's coat of arms, "having [Laurence] Sterne's word for it that a coat of arms may be purchased as cheap as any other coat." Either kind of coat can make what later generations would call a fashion statement, establishing social rank. Jefferson's democratic sympathies may have led him to mock the aristocratic aspirations of Virginia's first families, but some of them he nonetheless shared.

Thomas Jefferson's relationship with his parents poses problems for biographers because so little is known about it. If he ever wrote an affectionate word about his mother or his father, it is lost to history, along with other information from which it might be possible to reach firm conclusions about the nature of his childhood and adolescence. Any such documents perished on February 1, 1770, when the house at Shadwell "was burnt to the ground," as the *Virginia Gazette* reported. No lives were lost in the fire, Jefferson told a friend, but "every paper I had in the world, and almost every book" was destroyed.

The absence of documentary evidence is thus accounted for. The lack of anecdotal material—family stories, passed on by Jefferson's descendants—is less readily explained. That he told his children and grandchildren almost nothing about his own parents seems unusual, especially for a man who, while hardly introspective, was not just verbal but voluble. His "autobiography," begun in 1821 when he was seventy-seven, may be the least personal work of its kind in the sweep of western literature, recording little more than the barest facts of his parents' existence, with most of the book devoted to political events.

This reticence with respect to his father might be easily explained. Thomas Jefferson simply did not know his father as well as most boys do. As a surveyor, Peter Jefferson was often away from the plantation on assignment, and because he wanted to be sure his son received the best education available in Virginia, Thomas Jefferson spent much of his childhood at the eighteenth-century equivalent of boarding schools. These were in every case far from the two plantations at which he grew up, Shadwell and Tuckahoe. (The latter was a Randolph family estate near Richmond that Peter Jefferson managed for several years.)

In 1752, when Thomas Jefferson was nine and the rest of the family returned from Tuckahoe to Shadwell, he remained behind to attend school in the Richmond area. Some time later, when he came home to Shadwell, he was promptly enrolled in a second school, also some miles from home, where the Reverend William Douglas, a Scots clergyman, instructed him in French, Greek, and Latin. At Douglas's school, Jefferson began to perfect his political and diplomatic skills. Seeking changes in the curriculum, but reluctant to confront the teacher directly, Jefferson sent another student in his stead. "For his temerity," the historian John Chester Miller has written, "the hapless accomplice was roundly rebuked by the clergyman-pedagogue while Jefferson himself remained undetected and unscathed. Jefferson, one of the great managers of men, began his career as a manager of children."

In 1757, Thomas was packed off to a third school, this one fourteen miles from home. In all cases, he lived near the school or with his instructors, returning to Shadwell only on vacations. By the time that Thomas would have been old enough to work closely with his father on the farm, Peter Jefferson was dead.

Scholars who have compared the childhoods of colonists who grew up to rebel against the British crown to those of Tory loyalists have developed useful hypotheses. Drawing upon psychoanalytic theory, biographers have also offered fascinating suppositions about Jefferson's relationships with his parents and the effect on his psychological development. The paucity of information about Jefferson's childhood casts any conclusions about his particular case, however plausible, into the realms of theory and conjecture. Kenneth S. Lynn noted in his discussion of Jefferson's childhood that, in families of the revolutionary generation, there existed

> a considerable tension between mothers and sons, which caused the latter to view the former as sharp-tongued termagants to be avoided wherever possible, or as hopeless ignoramuses who could not talk intelligently about anything important. The very fact that we have no evidence at all about the mothering of most patriots may also tell us something about the quality of mother-son relations in the Revolutionary generation.

Jefferson's upbringing, Lynn speculates, was much like George Washington's. Their fathers died when their sons were quite young: George Washington's father, Augustine, died at forty-nine, when George was eleven, and Peter Jefferson at fifty, when Thomas was fourteen. Both boys then became the oldest males in their respective households—independent-minded young men whose desire to control their own affairs seemed to have bumped up against the determination of their strong-willed mothers to remain in charge. Even after the deaths of their fathers, "whom they admired enormously," Lynn writes, Washington and Jefferson "did not draw any closer to their mothers."

That Jefferson's feelings for his mother were complicated seems beyond dispute. That whatever affection he felt for her was tempered by hostility is highly likely, considering that he lived under her roof when he enjoyed other options and that he never seems to have spoken fondly of her even to his own children. That he would regard her as a "hopeless ignoramus" seems unlikely, for, like many Randolph women, Jane Jefferson was probably highly intelligent and capable.

After Peter Jefferson died, his property became his widow's, and their children—Thomas and seven siblings—continued to live at Shadwell. For six years after he turned twenty-one, had inherited his own property, and was earning his own living as a lawyer, Jefferson lived at home. Even after Shadwell burned and the family moved into the dependencies on the plantation, Jefferson continued to live with his mother for almost a year. He would not move to his own house at Monticello until he was twenty-seven.

Life at Shadwell surely had its attractions for this eldest son of the plantation gentry, doted on by older sisters and admired by younger siblings of decidedly inferior intellectual gifts.

"It is curious to remark the unequal distribution of talent in this family— each gifted member seeming to have been made so at the expense of the others," wrote Sarah N. Randolph, one of Jefferson's great-granddaughters, in 1858. This may put the matter kindly. Jefferson was especially close to a sister, Jane, four years his senior, who shared Jefferson's love of books and music, never married, and may have devoted much of her energy to encouraging her promising younger brother.

His other siblings, however, probably offered less in the way of companionship. Elizabeth Jefferson, a year younger than Thomas, "was rather deficient in intellect," Sarah Randolph wrote, and Jefferson's account books show that he looked after this unfortunate sister well into her adulthood (Elizabeth drowned in the Rivanna at thirty), making sure she "should be well dressed."

For many years biographers have asserted that Randolph Jefferson, Thomas Jefferson's only brother, was also mentally retarded, though Randolph's own correspondence demonstrates that this was not the case. Randolph Jefferson would never write elegant prose like his brother, but compared with many Piedmont farmers, he was an educated man, literate if unsophisticated. He attended schools in Williamsburg, studied the violin in his student days, and might have taken classes at the College of William and Mary.

For most of his life, however, Randolph Jefferson was a muddy-boots farmer. He owned a plantation about twenty miles south of Monticello, married twice, and raised a family. He was not especially close to his more distinguished brother, however, and the disparity in their abilities was sufficiently obvious that local wags joked about Randolph Jefferson's clear inferiority. They said that he had once given a great deal of thought to a matter that had vexed both brothers in the management of their farms: the tendency of squirrels to eat the planters' corn right off the stalk.

"Tom, I'll tell you how to keep the squirrels from pillaging the corn," Randolph Jefferson supposedly said. "You see they always eat on the outside row. Well then, don't plant any outside row."

CHAPTER 3

## The Education of a Philosopher

In 1760, when Jefferson turned seventeen, he rode to Williamsburg to attend the College of William and Mary, accompanied by a "body servant," a slave named Jupiter.

Like many young Virginia gentlemen, Jefferson had developed a fondness for elegant clothes, evenings at the theater, and blooded horses. Whenever one of his mounts was led out for his enjoyment, Jefferson would inspect the animal to see that it had been properly groomed. Determined that his horse's coat shone "as faultlessly as a mirror," he would produce a white cambric handkerchief, drape it lightly over the animal's withers, and then remove it; if any dust appeared on the handkerchief, he would send the horse back for further grooming.

Despite a well-developed sense of entitlement, Jefferson managed to avoid the snares of "Devilsburg," as he called the colonial capital, which was notorious for the temptations it presented to young men of means. Although "thrown into the society of horse racers, card players [and] fox hunters," in Jefferson's words, he did not run up gambling debts, and there are no reports of drunkenness or debauchery.

A remarkably disciplined scholar, Jefferson spent money on books the way less purposeful young men spent it on whiskey or women. By the time Shadwell burned, Jefferson had amassed a library of more than twelve hundred volumes, many of them obtained while he was a student at William and Mary. Most of these books were destroyed in the fire, but within three and a half years, Jefferson had purchased 1,256 volumes to replace those he lost. During this period, he bought books at a rate of roughly one a day, at a time when books were costly items.

◇   ◇   ◇

It was at William and Mary that Jefferson had the historic good fortune to make the acquaintance of three of the Virginia capital's leading intellectual lights. These were William Small, George Wythe, and Francis Fauquier.

The only member of the William and Mary faculty who was not an Anglican priest, Small was a professor of mathematics and philosophy, possessed of "an enlarged and liberal mind," as Jefferson put it. Influenced by Adam Smith, David Hume, Francis Hutcheson, David Reid, and other figures of the Scottish Enlightenment, this widower, educated at Marischal College, Aberdeen, made Jefferson "his daily companion when not engaged in the school." From Small, Jefferson received "my first views of the expansion of science and of the system of things in which we are placed."

Wythe taught and practiced law, served in the Virginia House of Burgesses and in the United States Congress, and signed the Declaration of Independence. Although deprived of a formal education, he was "the best Latin and Greek scholar in the state," Jefferson said, committed "to liberty and the natural and equal rights of man."

Fauquier was the Royal Governor, though he tended to take the colonists' side in disputes with the crown. A fellow of the Royal Society, London's prestigious fraternity of scientists, the genial and broad-minded Fauquier was popular with prominent Virginians, who saw him as a "compleat gentleman." A music lover and a musician himself, Fauquier held weekly concerts at the Governor's Palace, where Jefferson played his violin.

This foursome also met regularly for dinner, where Jefferson, an adolescent among mature men of learning and accomplishment, "heard more good sense, more rational and philosophical conversations, than in all my life besides."

Much effort has been expended over the last century to account for how Jefferson came to believe the things he did: which books he read, what philosophers he consulted, whether his influences were English, Scottish, French, or even Greek. Whatever the case, these views were fixed by the time he left the College of William and Mary, and his years among the French *philosophes* in the 1780s did more to strengthen his existing ideas than to shape new ones.

Jefferson's opinions were those of Small, Wythe, and Fauquier. In broadest outlines, Jefferson was a republican in politics, a deist in religion, and a classicist in his tastes. Optimistic about the fundamental nature of man and committed to the notion that reason would free mankind from the shackles of oppressive superstition, Jefferson believed in the possibility, if not the in-evitability, of human progress.

In this, Jefferson was an idealist, though he never thought of himself as such. Seeing himself as a scientist, though that term would not come into use until the 1830s, Jefferson was firmly convinced that he based his conclusions on observ-able phenomena—upon an empirical basis—unbiased by what he dismissed as the gothic "metaphysics" of the established church, Anglican or Roman Catholic. Jefferson was also, in his own mind, a rationalist, serenely unaware that the rationalism in which he would place so much faith was itself as abstract and theoretical as that which he found objectionable in the teaching of churchmen.

Jefferson's view of himself as an empiricist may also suggest how little self-knowledge he possessed, for the struggle between the life of the mind and the hard facts of material reality would form the tragic drama of his life. In the years to come, unpleasant realities would always intrude on his idealized existence.

A case in point: in 1762, when he was nineteen, Jefferson spent Christmas at Fairfield, the plantation of Lewis Burwell III. Fairfield was one of the great houses of the Virginia Tidewater, and Rebecca Burwell, the proprietor's daugh-ter, was one of its great beauties. Jefferson was courting her at the time of his visit, though without much success. Rebecca had thought highly enough of him, however, to give him a portrait in miniature, which he kept in his watchcase.

During this visit, Jefferson slept in an attic. On Christmas morning he awoke to discover that rats had chewed their way through his pocketbook, "which was in my pocket, within a foot of my head." The "cursed rats" had also carried off a pair of "jimmy-worked silk garters" that he had won as a prize at a holiday ball and had eaten into the sheet music for several minuets. Well, Jef-ferson reported with youthful good humor, "rats will be rats."

The other indignity Jefferson suffered that morning, however, was not to be shrugged off with quite so light a heart, much as Jefferson tried. He found his watchcase floating in water from a leak in the roof. Rainwater had seeped into the case, soaking the miniature of his beloved. When he tried to remove the picture in hopes of drying it, it ripped apart in his hands.

This disheartening loss could not be written off to mere rats, he said, nor to a drippy roof. In "my opinion," he concluded with a strained attempt at levity, ". . . the Devil came and bored a hole over [the watchcase] on purpose." The destruction that was done when Jefferson tried to remove the portrait, he said, "was the last stroke Satan had in reserve for me." If that proved true, Jefferson would live a happy life indeed.

# CHAPTER 4

## The Young Revolutionary

T homas Jefferson was a twenty-one-year-old law student in Williamsburg when Parliament passed the Stamp Act of 1765, requiring revenue stamps on every colonial newspaper and broadside as well as on legal and commercial documents. When the May session of the Virginia House of Burgesses debated how best to respond to this decision to tax the written word itself, Jefferson made his way to the colonial capital and stood attentively at the door of the burgesses' chamber.

There the young scholar listened with astonishment as Patrick Henry, a newly elected member from upcountry Hanover County, began to speak. An ambitious ex–tavern keeper with little formal schooling, Henry let loose with an intemperate but powerful speech—"torrents of sublime eloquence," Jefferson called it—that went well beyond challenging Parliament's right to tax the king's loyal subjects in America without their consent. Far more inflammatory, Henry invoked Caesar and Brutus, Charles I and Cromwell, and then named George III himself as perhaps the next in line to deserve assassination.

Although the oration provoked incensed cries of "Treason!" from the more conservative men in the hall, it stirred the "young hot and giddy members," as Governor Fauquier called them, who eventually carried the day. The Virginia legislature approved Henry's Stamp Act Resolves, which not only denied Parliament's authority over the colonists but also implicitly endorsed their right to armed resistance should Parliament not relent.

Repeated throughout the colonies and in Great Britain, Henry's "very indecent language," in Fauquier's words, fanned the flames of rebellion, which in time proved impossible to extinguish. Jefferson was impressed with Henry's "splendid display" of oratorical fireworks, but appalled by the absence of reason or rigor in his arguments. Jefferson's own powers of persuasion, as would be demonstrated in the cause of American liberty soon enough, would prove very different.

In 1767, after studying law for five years, Jefferson was admitted to the Virginia bar, where he distinguished himself by his meticulous preparation, not by oratory. Although he had a profound distaste for public speaking and never became comfortable before a jury, he maintained a reasonably successful law practice for the next several years. In 1768, he was elected to the House of Burgesses as a representative from Albemarle, serving diligently on committees, where his attention to detail, his tact, and his gentlemanly willingness to negotiate, to compromise, and to reach consensus impressed his fellow burgesses.

Jefferson also proved exquisitely sensitive to the limits of their tolerance for enlightened causes—and readily capitulated to majority opinion: Within months of taking his seat in the colonial legislature, Jefferson wrote a plan for the manumission of slaves, which was proposed by another burgess. The plan found almost no support in the legislature, and, unfortunately, its text has been lost to history.

Changes in Jefferson's domestic life soon enabled him to give up the practice of law and devote his time and talents to the cause of American independence. On January 1, 1772, he married Martha Wayles Skelton, a well-to-do widow from Charles City County, at The Forest, her father's plantation about halfway between Richmond and Williamsburg. The newlyweds moved to a small brick structure on a mountaintop overlooking Shadwell, where Jefferson had already begun to clear ground for the much larger house that he would call Monticello. There, on September 27, 1772, just shy of nine months after the wedding, Martha gave birth to a daughter, also named Martha, who would grow up to be her father's closest companion and, in many ways, his most trusted adviser.

The following May, upon the death of his father-in-law, John Wayles, Jefferson and his wife inherited eleven thousand acres, many of them at Poplar Forest in Bedford County. Although he promptly sold about half of this land to pay some of his father-in-law's debts, this still left Jefferson in possession of about ten thousand acres—his own and those that he had come into by marriage. He and his wife also inherited 135 slaves from Wayles, which, added to the 52 whom Jefferson already owned, brought the total to 187. The Wayles inheritance, more than doubling Jefferson's wealth, made it possible for him to retire from the law, which he did not enjoy, and concentrate on his legislative duties, at which he excelled.

In 1774, at the age of thirty-one, Jefferson achieved national prominence through his pen: his "Summary View of the Rights of British America" argued with considerable ingenuity and lawyerly precision that Parliament had no legal authority to abrogate the rights of loyal English subjects simply because they had taken up residence in the American colonies. The "Summary View" was published throughout America and in Great Britain, establishing its author as an effective advocate of the rights of Americans. In March 1775, in recognition of his rising status as a leader, Jefferson was appointed to serve in Virginia's delegation to the Second Continental Congress, then coordinating the resistance of all the colonies to British rule. He was now thirty-two, and would soon expand his sphere of activities far beyond Virginia—first to Philadelphia, and then to the courts and salons of Europe.

CHAPTER 5

## *The Crucible of Revolution*

---

In an elegant phaeton and accompanied by two slaves, Jefferson left for Philadelphia on June 11, 1775. A week later, when he had reached Annapolis, Maryland, the colonists inflicted heavy losses on the British at Bunker Hill (Breed's Hill) outside Boston, boosting American morale. By the time Jefferson settled into his duties as a delegate to the Continental Congress that summer, George Washington had assumed command of the Continental Army, and the movement toward complete independence rapidly gained momentum.

Jefferson's performance in the Congress showed characteristic diligence. His "reputation for literature, science, and a happy talent for composition," his new friend John Adams decided, was well deserved. Appointed to a committee to draft what he called a "manifesto" justifying both the armed resistance the colonies had now been engaged in for more than a year and the formal break with the mother country that would follow, Jefferson, with the blessing of Adams, Benjamin Franklin, and other fellow committeemen, worked in near isolation over two sweltering weeks. When he emerged, he had produced a statement that communicated not so much his own thoughts, he insisted, as the "sentiments of the day, whether expressed in conversation, in letters, printed essays, or in the elementary books of public right."

This "expression of the American mind," designed to tell the world why it had become necessary "to dissolve the political bands" with Great Britain, was the Declaration of Independence. In it, Jefferson asserted that "all men are created equal" and that they possess unalienable rights to "life, liberty and the pursuit of happiness," rights that King George III had denied them. Given the king's many "abuses & usurpations," and the colonists' patient but unheeded petitions for redress, it was their right and duty to "throw off such government" and institute a new one. The united colonies were, from this time forward, "free and independent States." And in support of this declaration, the signers, representing the separate colonies, pledged to one another "our lives, our fortunes & our sacred honor."

After much debate, the Declaration of Independence was adopted on July 4, 1776, without a dissenting vote, and on August 2 was signed by fifty-six members of the Continental Congress.

Jefferson's draft of the Declaration had been worked over by the committee, but the urbane and dignified yet stirring prose of the final document remained very much his own. Also Jefferson's was a "vehement philippic against Negro slavery," in Adams's words, that the other delegates deleted. In this passage, which bespoke Jefferson's lifelong concern over slavery, he held the British crown responsible for introducing the institution into the colonies. Jefferson also blamed George III for perpetuating slavery by repeatedly prohibiting the colonies from imposing duties on the importation of slaves. The basis for this ingenious if implausible charge was that the colonies had wanted to tax the slave trade as part of an effort to end it. In truth, most of the colonies merely wished to raise revenue from the slave trade; finding Jefferson's allegation against the crown not only unpersuasive but needlessly inflammatory, the Congress removed it.

This was not Jefferson's only effort during the revolutionary period to express disapproval of slavery. In September 1776, convinced the war would be a quick one, Jefferson returned home and took a seat in the Virginia House of Delegates. There he served, alongside George Wythe, on a committee appointed to revise antiquated state laws dating from colonial subjugation. As part of its final report, the committee hoped to include a provision for the gradual emancipation of the slaves, who, upon receiving their freedom, would be sent out of the country. Under the plan, slavery would continue to exist in Virginia for at least three more generations, but when Jefferson and Wythe's colleagues decided that the moral sense of their fellow legislators was not sufficiently "refined" to accept this plan, the two abandoned it.

Jefferson did strike one monumentally historic blow for individual liberty as a member of the House of Delegates, drafting the Bill for Establishing Religious Freedom. Although the legislation underwent some editorial revision at the hands of George Mason and did not pass until 1786, long after Jefferson left the Virginia legislature, it provided that no one shall be compelled to frequent or support any religious worship, place, or ministry whatsoever, nor shall be enforced, restrained, molested, or burthened in his body or goods, or shall otherwise suffer, on account of his religious opinions or belief; but that all men shall be free to profess, and by argument to maintain, their opinions in matters of religion, and that the same shall in no wise diminish, enlarge, or affect their civil capacities.

Next to the Declaration, Jefferson considered the Bill for Establishing Religious Freedom the single greatest accomplishment of his public life.

Jefferson would not have the luxury of spending the rest of the war years revising Virginia's laws. In late 1778, the British took the fight to the southern colonies, firing on Savannah and then Charleston; in June 1779, they marched north toward the Carolinas. That month, an alarmed Virginia General Assembly elected Jefferson to succeed Patrick Henry as governor.

Jefferson had just turned thirty-six. With the births of Mary, or Maria as the family called her, on August 1, 1778, and Lucy Elizabeth, on November 30, 1780, he was now the father of three daughters. On April 15, 1781, however, five-month-old Lucy Elizabeth died, and Jefferson's grieving wife remained in frail health. Domestic worries and the burdens of public office proved almost overwhelming.

Virginia's constitution gave the governor sharply limited powers, and Jefferson found it impossible to raise, supply, and pay an army sufficient to defend the state against invasion. For nearly a year, British forces raided eastern Virginia almost at will, burning plantations, stables, storehouses, barns, and farms. In May 1781, as the redcoats under Lord Cornwallis marched toward Richmond, the General Assembly abandoned the capital and agreed to meet two weeks later in Charlottesville. Jefferson sent his grieving wife and two surviving daughters to wait out the danger at a neighbor's house. The exhausted and besieged governor rode on to Monticello.

On June 2, 1781, as Jefferson worked from home and tracked the enemy's movements, his term in office that he insisted would be his last expired. On June 4, a British raiding party began its ascent of Monticello in hopes of seizing the acting head of state, and Jefferson escaped down the mountain, barely eluding his would-be captors. After the war, this escape, coupled with the fact that Jefferson had been unable to provide the state with an adequate defense against British invasion and had fled with the rest of the government from Richmond to Charlottesville, would lead to accusations of cowardice and dereliction of duty.

In July and August 1781, as the British invaders withdrew to Yorktown and a French fleet sailed into Chesapeake Bay to prevent their departure by sea, Jefferson lived in retirement with his family at Poplar Forest. There, in the heat of midsummer, he wrote *Notes on the State of Virginia*. A response to inquiries from the French statesman François Barbé-Marbois, the *Notes* provided the world with its first detailed and largely objective look at Virginia's history, culture, and natural resources. Work on the book helped Jefferson deal with grief over his daughter Lucy's death as well as his fear for his wife's health.

The project was also a welcome distraction from his deep resentment that critics in the legislature blamed him for failing to protect the state from enemy invasion. Within weeks of the siege of Yorktown, which brought the war to a successful conclusion, an official inquiry into Jefferson's conduct as wartime governor exonerated him of all charges, but the fact that they had been at all raised would haunt him for much of his life.

CHAPTER 6

## "*Whence He Might Contemplate the Whole Universe*"

The following spring, when visited at Monticello by the Chevalier de Chastellux, a member of the French Academy and officer in General Rochambeau's army, Jefferson was again in good spirits. Although his host seemed "grave and even cold" when Chastellux first arrived, the visitor had "no sooner spent two hours with [him] than I felt as if we had spent our whole lives together." Their conversation ranged wide over history, science, and belles lettres, and "it seems indeed as though, ever since his youth, he had placed his mind, like his house, on a lofty height, whence he might contemplate the whole universe."

There was much more Jefferson was eager to show his visitor, but marital responsibilities kept him close to home. Martha Jefferson, pregnant again, was nearing her confinement and Jefferson, "as good a husband as he is a philosopher and citizen," Chastellux said, cut short their visit to be with her. On May 8, 1782, Martha Jefferson gave birth to another daughter. They gave her the name Lucy Elizabeth, just as they had named the daughter who had died the year before. Martha never regained her strength after the birth, however, and died on September 6, 1782. On her deathbed, she told Jefferson that she "could not die happy if she thought her children were ever to have a stepmother brought in over them," and the healthy thirty-nine-year-old, left with the care of three young daughters, promised never to remarry.

A prolonged period of intense grief followed Martha's death, and it was not until June 1783 that Jefferson had recovered sufficiently from this "stupor of mind," as he described it, to reenter public life, this time as a member of the U.S. Congress. In May 1784, at forty-one, he accepted an appointment to help John Adams and Benjamin Franklin, already overseas, to negotiate treaties of commerce with the nations of Europe. The following August, leaving Maria and the second Lucy Elizabeth with relatives in Virginia, Jefferson and his old-est child, eleven-year-old Martha, arrived in Paris, fulfilling a lifelong dream to make the Grand Tour of the Old World.

There they would spend the next five years, while Jefferson pursued his diplomatic duties, befriended the French *philosophes,* and traveled extensively through France, Italy, and England. He visited great houses, gardens, and vineyards, bought wagonloads of books, furniture, paintings, and sculptures, and cultivated a taste for French and Italian cuisine.

However enriching, these were not altogether idyllic years. In January 1785, Jefferson learned that whooping cough had claimed the second Lucy Elizabeth back in Virginia. Her death made Jefferson determined to keep both of his sur-viving daughters close by; in October 1787, Maria arrived from Virginia, ac-companied by her maid, an eleven-year-old slave girl named Sally Hemings.

In the summer and fall of that same year, the forty-four-year-old widower carried on an intense, though perhaps unconsummated, love affair with Maria Cosway, an Italian-born beauty married to an English painter. It was while foolishly attempting to leap a fence during a walk along the Seine with Maria that Jefferson fell and injured his wrist. The pain that afflicted him for the rest of his life would always bring back memories of pleasant days in Maria Cosway's company. It would also remind him of the folly of impetuous acts.

# CHAPTER 7

# "The Hated Occupations of Politics"

On November 23, 1789, Jefferson and his entourage sailed into port at Norfolk. On leave from his diplomatic duties in Europe, Jefferson intended only to visit Monticello, then to return to France. Before he got home, however, he learned "with real regret" that in late September President Washington had nominated him as secretary of state, a new post combining responsibility for foreign affairs as well as all other operations of government save finance and war. Reluctant to give up hope of going back to Europe, dispirited by the idea of returning to the political fray, Jefferson waited until December 15 to tell the president he would accept.

Happily, there were pleasant domestic duties to perform before taking up his new post in the spring. On February 23, 1790, at Monticello, Jefferson gave eighteen-year-old Martha in marriage to her cousin Thomas Mann Randolph, Jr., who was twenty-two. Theirs was, on paper, a promising match. Recently returned from studies in natural history at the University of Edinburgh, the bridegroom was a "young man of genius, science, and honorable mind," in Jefferson's words. Tom Randolph was also from a good family, with which the Jeffersons had already intermarried. (His father, Thomas Mann Randolph I, had been the proprietor of Tuckahoe, which Peter Jefferson managed after the former's early death.)

Born on September 12, 1768, Tom was the son of Thomas Mann Randolph, Sr., of Tuckahoe, where Jefferson spent much of his childhood. As was apparent early on, Jefferson would be an attentive—perhaps too attentive—father to his married daughter. The closeness of their bond might have been trying to any young husband, and was especially so to one who would prove as sensitive as Tom Randolph.

Shortly after arriving at the new seat of government in New York in late March, Jefferson told Martha that he missed her profoundly and hoped that she and her husband would settle near him in Albemarle. Martha replied that she wished to live at Edgehill, a farm just across the Rivanna from Monticello. Edgehill, fortuitously, belonged to Tom Randolph's father. If Tom Randolph purchased the property, they would be neighbors. Jefferson hoped Martha and her husband would live with him at Monticello, or at least divide their time between his much finer house and theirs. Before long, Jefferson's conjecture continued, Martha would be spending so many more days and nights at Monticello than at Edgehill, that she would consider Monticello their home. With Martha's sister Maria, now fifteen, also living at Monticello, his family circle would be complete.

Jefferson also told Martha that pleasing her husband must take precedence over all other considerations, "even your love to me." In reply, she reassured her father that he still came first in her affections and that she regarded any concern other than keeping her husband happy "as secondary to that *except* my love for you."

No sooner had he begun his duties as secretary of state in New York than Jefferson observed with "wonder and mortification" the speed with which his countrymen had abandoned the republican, not to mention revolutionary, fervor they had exhibited in the cause of independence. At dinner parties, Americans spoke with "preference [for] kingly over republican government," and, in their pomp and pageantry, state functions mimicked "those of European courts."

Secretary of the Treasury Alexander Hamilton was eagerly exploiting this turn toward "monarchy," forging a national economic program that, in Jefferson's views, threatened republican government itself. Hamilton proposed, for example, that the federal government assume the wartime debts of the states, and to his later regret, Jefferson agreed to this plan in exchange for Hamilton's support for a cause that Virginia's political leaders supported: locating the national capital on the Potomac, closer to their plantations and only about fifteen miles from George Washington's own Mount Vernon.

Hamilton's program also included establishment of a Bank of the United States and taxes for roads, ports, and canals. Such schemes, Jefferson believed, extended federal authority over matters reserved, under the Constitution, to "the people and the states." The increase in patronage that went with this power, he feared, invited corruption on a massive scale. For months, Jefferson fought the treasury secretary and his financial program, often bitterly, without success and at great sacrifice of personal dignity.

Weary of losing, degraded by the "indecency" of seeing these clashes spill into the newspapers, in February 1792 Jefferson told President Washington that he wished to give up his post when Washington's first term in office ended in December of that year. Jefferson, who would turn fifty in the spring, had begun to suffer from spells of rheumatism, his farms at Monticello had suffered in his absence, and he was sick of politics.

Washington implored Jefferson to stay on for one year more, which he agreed to do. In July 1793 he submitted his resignation, effective December 31, 1793. As his last day in office drew near, Jefferson wrote to Angelica Church, a friend in London, that he was finally going home to Virginia. He would soon

> be liberated from the hated occupations of politics and . . . remain in the bosom of my family, my farm, and my books. I have my house to build, my fields to farm, and to watch for the happiness of those who labor for mine. I have one daughter married to a man of science, sense, virtue, and compe-tence. . . . If the other shall be as fortunate [Jefferson would feel] as blessed as the most blessed of the patriarchs.

Returning to Monticello in January 1794, Jefferson found that the five years in which he had been away had taken their toll on his plantation. He told Washington that the farms exhibited "a degree of degradation far beyond what I had expected." Because his overseers had failed to prepare the fields for cultivation, "little will be done this year towards rescuing my plantations from their wretched condition."

Nevertheless, Jefferson seemed content. Tom Randolph had bought Edge-hill from his father, as Jefferson had hoped he would. Randolph worked the land there but lived at Monticello most of the time, with Martha and her fa-ther. Best of all for the completion of Jefferson's happiness, there were grand-children, a girl and a boy. Ann Cary Randolph, born on January 23, 1791, celebrated her third birthday shortly after Jefferson's return. Jefferson himself had picked her name. Ann was "very pretty," in Maria's words, with "beautiful deep blue eyes."

Thomas Jefferson Randolph, "your little namesake," as Martha called him in a letter to her father, was born September 12, 1792. Although he was not yet two at the time that Jefferson came home, he was "little inferior to his sister in point of size," his mother said, seemed hardier than Ann, "and bids fair to be as lively." Jefferson was delighted to have grandchildren, and visitors would find him "in a retirement I doat on, living like an antediluvian patriarch among my children and grandchildren, and tilling my soil."

Jefferson was also busily tearing down his old house—a gracious, if conventional Virginia manor house—and building in its place a new one. "Monticello, according to its first plan, was infinitely superior to all other houses in America, in point of taste and convenience," the exiled Duc de La Rochefoucauld-Liancourt reported after visiting Jefferson during the autumn of 1796. At the time he designed it, however, Jefferson "had studied taste and the fine arts in books only." Having now seen Europe, he was erecting a new Monticello that would resemble an Italian villa, with its three stories disguised as one. When complete, the house was expected to rank "with the most pleasant mansions in France and England." (The farms that were to pay for these renovations seemed less promising. Much of what Jefferson knew of agriculture, Liancourt observed, also came from books, and he took "theory for [his] guide.")

At the time of Liancourt's visit, Washington announced that he would not seek a third term as president, setting off a scramble to succeed him. Eager for war with France, the Federalists favored Vice President Adams. Sympathetic to the French but anxious to stay out of European wars, the Democratic-Republicans supported Jefferson who, with reluctance, agreed to be their standard-bearer. He had stayed out of politics for more than two years and felt prepared once more for the vicissitudes of public service.

The times, he believed, demanded his participation. The country was divided into two factions that "accuse each other of perfidy and treason," Liancourt wrote. Washington had led a united people, but his successor "will be only the president of a party." After the exhilaration of victory, the winner may experience "the keenest pangs of grief in his remaining days."

When the venomous campaign concluded with the election on December 5, 1796, Adams won seventy-one votes, while Jefferson, striving to remain above the fray at Monticello, drew sixty-eight, making him the vice president. Both men took office in March 1797, by which time France, retaliating for the administration's favoritism toward Great Britain, had seized three hundred American merchant ships and broken off diplomatic relations.

As Adams and the Federalists prepared for war by establishing a standing army and increasing taxes on houses, property, and slaves, the political atmosphere grew poisonous. "Men who have been intimate all their lives cross the streets to avoid meeting," Jefferson lamented to Edward Rutledge in June 1797, "and turn their heads another way lest they should be obliged to touch their hats."

This generally unpleasant season was not without its happy moments, however. That same month, when Martha Randolph told him that her sister Maria had become engaged to her cousin John Wayles Eppes, Jefferson wrote of his "inexpressible pleasure" at the news. With Maria's future happiness assured, Jefferson foresaw years—no, decades—of domestic tranquillity for the entire family. "I now see our fireside formed into a group, no one member of which has a fibre in their composition which can ever produce any jarring or jealousies among us. No irregular passions, no dangerous bias, which may render problematical the future fortunes and happiness of our descendants."


That summer, the Federalists in Congress, with the enthusiastic support of the irascible Adams, passed the Alien and Sedition Acts, designed to rid the country of supposed French spies and to prohibit speech that exposed the administration to writings of a "false, scandalous and malicious" nature. Several critics of the thin-skinned president were arrested, tried, and jailed for seditious libel, among them the physician-philosopher Thomas Cooper, a man of genuine character and accomplishment, but also an itinerant scandalmonger named James T. Callender. Although he pretended to be above political intrigue, starting in 1797 Jefferson had discreetly sponsored Callender in his attacks on Federalist opponents, beginning with Hamilton and including, ultimately, Adams.

Such prosecutions incensed the Democratic-Republicans. Jefferson and Madison, then a congressman from Virginia, responded by (anonymously) drafting the Kentucky and Virginia Resolutions, which called upon all the states to declare the Alien and Sedition Acts null and void on constitutional grounds. As a creation of the states, the federal Congress possessed only those powers granted to it, Jefferson and Madison argued, and certainly no authority to restrict political speech.

Although the Kentucky and Virginia Resolutions failed to overturn the Alien and Sedition Acts, they did galvanize opposition to President Adams who, by now, was heartily disliked. The Republicans despised Adams, but so did many members of his own party, including the "bastard" Hamilton, as the president called him.

In the spring of 1800, the Federalists grudgingly renominated Adams, with Charles Cotesworth Pinckney as his running mate, while the Democratic-Republicans again selected Jefferson and, for the vice presidency, Aaron Burr of New York. The ensuing campaign was even more vicious than the last. Subjected to a nonstop din of "squibs, scoffs, and sarcasms," Adams encouraged his remaining supporters to respond in kind. With the deist Jefferson in power, "murder, robbery, rape, adultery, and incest will all be openly taught and practiced," the *Connecticut Courant* warned. The air "will be rent with the cries of the distressed, the soil will be soaked with blood, and the nation black with crimes." With "disciples of Voltaire" running the country, claimed Timothy Dwight, the president of Yale, churches would be turned into "temples of reason," Bibles would be "cast into a bonfire," children would chant "mockeries against God," and wives and daughters would be "victims of legal prostitution."

Dispirited by these accusations, Jefferson nevertheless had good reason to be optimistic about his chances for election. Burr delivered New York to the Democratic-Republicans, and Hamilton, outraged by the administration's clumsy attempts to appease the French, had decided that Adams was even worse than Jefferson, dividing the Federalists.

On November 28, Jefferson arrived at the new seat of government in Washington confident of victory. The day for the electors to cast their ballots in their home states was December 3. Each elector cast two votes, one presumably for president and the other for vice president. But when the votes were counted, Jefferson learned that he and Burr had tied with seventy-three votes each, although the Democratic-Republicans had clearly intended Jefferson to head the ticket. (Adams ran third, with sixty-five votes.)

This deadlock threw the election to the House of Representatives, where state delegations would cast one vote each. Because the House was in the hands of Federalists, many of whom believed they could deal more advantageously with the wily Burr than with the more principled Jefferson, the outcome was still very much in question.

On February 11, 1801, as snow clouds settled over Jenkins Hill and a nervous crowd gathered in the streets, members of the House of Representatives convened in the unfinished Capitol to decide the historic contest. In the one-state, one-vote system, Jefferson needed the votes of nine of the sixteen states to win. On the first ballot, he received only eight, with six for Burr, two split, and one abstaining. A second ballot produced the same result, as did the third and fourth.

For six more days, as a wet snow blanketed the streets, the congressmen voted thirty-two more times, each time with the same outcome. By now, congressmen in their nightcaps carried blankets and pillows into the chamber and slept fitfully between the balloting.

Finally, on the morning of Tuesday, February 17, a handful of Federalists who had voted for Burr, exhausted and eager to break the deadlock so the nation would have a president when Inauguration Day came on March 4, broke ranks by abstaining, which delivered the presidency to Jefferson. Other pro-Burr electors also defected, and the final tally gave Jefferson ten votes to his opponent's four.

Candles appeared in the windows of the row houses on New Jersey Avenue to honor the president-elect, and at nine that night, Democratic-Republicans gathered to celebrate. As the revelers offered sixteen toasts before losing count, Jefferson remained in dignified isolation at his boardinghouse, believing it his duty to be "passive and silent" in such contentious times. His supporters were less restrained. "Here ends the 18th Century," one wrote.

The 19th begins with a fine clear morning wind at S.W.; and the political horizon affords as fine a prospect under Jefferson's administration, with returning harmony with France—with the irresistible propagation of the Rights of Man, the eradication of hierarchy, oppression, superstition and tyranny over the world.

# Chapter 8

## The Revolutionary Takes Command

O n the morning of March 4, 1801, the fifty-eight-year-old president-elect stepped outside his boardinghouse dressed "in plain cloth," in the words of an English traveler unaccustomed to republican simplicity, and rode the short distance to the Capitol, "without a single guard or even servant in his train." After hitching his horse to the fence, Jefferson entered the Senate chamber and, in tones so soft that the crowd had to strain to hear him, delivered his first inaugural address. In it, he struck a conciliatory tone that, while galling to his opponents, reflected a sincere desire to put aside old resentments. He and his erstwhile adversaries, Jefferson said, would work together to make the country stronger by making it freer. No one would be thrown out of his job for being a Federalist; critics would not be jailed for voicing dissent.

After calling for "wise and frugal government which shall restrain men from injuring one another, which shall leave them otherwise free to regulate their own pursuits of industry and improvement, and shall not take from the mouth of labor the bread it has earned," Jefferson proceeded, in two years of extraordinary political accomplishment, to make good on his promises. Eschewing Adams's state coach with its six horses and outriders, Jefferson rode about the town unattended, and, famously, greeted callers at the President's Mansion in his slippers. He abolished levees and other ceremonial functions. He welcomed Federalist and Democratic-Republican alike to informal feasts, where he disarmed even political adversaries with his reassuring country-squire hospitality. As the wine flowed, his conversation ranged over every subject but one: politics was *verboten*. Few lawmakers of either party could resist the president's engaging manner, "and most returned to the congressional pit," the historian Forrest McDonald has written, "with renewed faith in his wisdom and virtue."

Jefferson's first several months in office were distinguished by a high degree of collaboration and consensus in the cause of governmental "retrenchment." They were also characterized by a continuation of the intense, behind-the-scenes political intrigue that Jefferson had mastered as leader of the opposition under his predecessor. Jefferson's knack for cutting a deal when expedient would mark him, then and now, in critics' eyes, as a supreme hypocrite. But it also demonstrated the extent to which he was a pragmatic politician in a democratic system that was only then discovering how to replace the European system of command and control with one of compromise and consent.

Congress abolished internal taxes and paid down the federal debt, which had swelled under Hamilton. The army was reduced in size, military expenditures were slashed, and construction of new warships ceased. Such measures would be unnecessary if America pursued "peace, commerce, and honest friendship with all nations," as Jefferson said in his inaugural address. Congress allowed the Alien and Sedition Acts to expire. No such abridgements of civil liberties would be needed in a country that avoided foreign entanglements. Where reason ruled, unfettered debate was to be encouraged.

An additional cause for celebration was preceded by moments of anxiety. In 1802, when Spain ceded New Orleans to France, Jefferson, fearing that the western territories' only outlet to the sea would be lost, authorized the payment of up to $10 million for the port city and the adjacent lands to the east. When Napoleon offered to sell the entire 828,000-square-mile Louisiana Territory for $15 million, Jefferson acted quickly and, by the end of 1803, the United States took possession of that immense expanse of land, which rolled northwest from the mouth of the Mississippi to the Rockies.

Painfully aware that the Constitution did not authorize the president to acquire foreign territory, Jefferson acknowledged committing an act "beyond the Constitution," as he put it. Even if this appeared to violate his own doctrine of strict construction, to which he held others, Jefferson said he acted as a faithful servant should when faced with a "fugitive occurrence," a judgment few of his countrymen then or since would dispute. For Jefferson, who believed that an agricultural country's wealth lay in land, any objections he or anyone else might raise were mere "metaphysical subtleties." A better practical politician than theoretical philosopher, Jefferson read his fellow Americans well. When the *National Intelligencer* broke the news of the Louisiana Purchase on July 4, 1803, the public rejoiced.

◇   ◇   ◇

That same month, Meriwether Lewis, on Jefferson's orders, left Washington to join William Clark near present-day Louisville, Kentucky, and, with a crew of about forty-five, set off on the Ohio River for the West. Their mission, as Jefferson had described it when he asked Congress to fund it, would be a "literary pursuit." They were merely to gather "information on the Indian tribes, the fauna and flora of the region."

By January 1804, when Lewis and Clark were encamped near St. Louis and the country they were to explore no longer belonged to Spain or France, Jefferson told them that they could drop the pretense that they were only scientists. Now they were free to make treaties with the natives, in preparation for the "immense swarm" of Anglo-Saxon settlers that would follow. They were to people a great empire: in time, Jefferson believed, all of the continent would be populated with and ruled by English-speaking whites.

When he returned to Washington on December 28, 1806, without Clark but accompanied by an entourage of Osage Indians, Lewis received a hero's welcome. On January 14, 1807, a banquet was held in the explorers' honor, by which time Jefferson had received Lewis and the Indians at the President's House, as the whitewashed executive residence was then known. (The mansion would not be officially designated the White House until 1901.)

Lewis presented the president with a map of the four-thousand-mile journey, and, when it was spread out on the floor, Jefferson dropped eagerly to his knees to peruse it.

Jefferson's reelection in December 1804, when he won 162 votes to the Federalist Charles Cotesworth Pinckney's 14, surprised no one. The Republic was "in the full tide of successful experiment!" as his kinsman and cousin John Randolph crowed. "Taxes repealed; the public debt amply provided for, both principal and interest; sinecures abolished; Louisiana acquired; public confidence unbounded."

Jefferson's first years in office had not been without periods of great personal anxiety and acute embarrassment. In September 1802, James T. Callender, the rabble-rousing journalist whose attacks on the Federalists Jefferson had once sponsored, alleged, in the Richmond *Recorder,* that his former patron kept at Monticello a mulatto "concubine" identified only as "Sally." Callender also reported that "Sally" had a son Thomas, who bore a "striking . . . resemblance to the President himself."

THE PRESIDENT
*AGAIN.*

IT is well known that the man, *whom it delighteth the people to honor*, keeps, and for many years past has kept, as his concubine, one of his own slaves. Her name is SALLY. The name of her eldest son is TOM. His features are said to bear a striking although sable resemblance to those of the president himself. The boy is ten or twelve years of age. His mother went to France in the same vessel with Mr. Jefferson and his two daughters. The delicacy of this arrangement must strike every person of common sensibility. What a sublime pattern for an American ambassador to place before the eyes of two young ladies!

*"Her name is SALLY. The name of her eldest son is TOM." James T. Callender's allegations against Jefferson first appear, the Richmond Recorder, September 1, 1802.*

Within weeks, more stories and satiric verse about Jefferson's "Dusky Sally" and "Black Sal" appeared in Federalist newspapers in other major cities, igniting a controversy that bedeviled Jefferson for the rest of his life. Although he never commented on the allegations publicly, in October 1802, Jefferson wrote to Robert Livingston, his minister to France, telling him that every "decent" Federalist "revolts at [Callender's] filth." The charges, while embarrassing, did not damage Jefferson politically.

By late 1803, Jefferson faced a more immediate personal crisis in the failing health of his daughter, twenty-five-year-old Maria, who had married her cousin John Eppes six years earlier and was now pregnant for the third time. Maria was a sensitive, somewhat introspective woman whose tendency "to withdraw from society" troubled Jefferson. Happiness "requires that we should continue to mix with the world," he told her in March 1802; withdrawing from the world leads to a "misanthropic state of mind."

Unlike her elder sister Martha, Maria was also physically frail, as their mother had been. In December 1804, as she neared her confinement, Jefferson reassured her that childbirth was "no more than a jog of the elbow" but, weakening dramatically, she knew better. On February 15, at Edgehill, she gave birth to a daughter, also named Maria. When Jefferson came home in March, the elder Maria was "barely able to stand." Her stomach was "so disordered as to reject almost every thing," and a breast had abscessed. Rushed to Monti-

MRS. THOMAS M. RANDOLPH.

*"My evening prospects now hang on the slender thread of a single life."*
*Martha Randolph, Jefferson's sole surviving daughter.*

cello, Maria Jefferson Eppes died on the night of April 17, 1804. Thinking toward his retirement, a grieving Jefferson told a friend:

> My evening prospects now hang on the slender thread of a single life. Perhaps I may be destined to see even this last cord of parental affection broken! The hope with which I had looked forward to the moment when, resigning public cares to younger hands, I was to retire to that domestic comfort from which the last great step is to be taken, is fearfully blighted.

Jefferson's presidential duties left little time for grief. A week after Maria's burial at Monticello, Vice President Aaron Burr lost his bid to become governor of New York; several weeks later, in July, he dueled with Hamilton, on whom he blamed his defeat, and killed him. Although Burr had been replaced on the Democratic-Republican ticket by his fellow New Yorker George Clinton, Burr's increasingly erratic and suspicious conduct tormented Jefferson for the rest of his presidency.

Also in July, developments on the international front occupied Jefferson's mind. Throughout his years in public service, Jefferson was determined to keep Americans out of European wars, though he did not attempt to keep them out of European waters. As events of the next several months demonstrated, Jefferson was a unilateralist, and a noninterventionist, perhaps—but not an isolationist.

For two hundred years, Morocco, Algiers, Tripoli, and Tunisia had demanded tribute from countries moving goods on the Mediterranean. Jefferson, however, refused to pay; in May 1803, he dispatched Commodore Edward Preble with seven warships to persuade "the Barbarians of Tripoli to the desire of peace . . . by the sufferings of war." This effort succeeded, and, in a treaty of June 1805, Tripoli renounced its demand for tribute and agreed to stop harassing American ships, which established U.S. maritime rights in the Mediterranean.

Jefferson's decision to send U.S. forces overseas did not violate his pledge to keep America out of European wars. In fighting the Barbary pirates, he sought only to secure American independence, and he remained committed to this policy, with decidedly mixed results, for the remainder of his presidency. So determined was he to avoid "entangling alliances," moreover, that he rejected French and Russian offers of assistance in the conflict with Tripoli. Any alliances that resulted from such aid would have defeated Jefferson's purpose in sending warships to the Mediterranean in the first place, which was to make the United States an autonomous world power, beholden to none.

The following year, just before the close of the first congressional session since his triumphant reelection, Jefferson faced the possibility of bloodshed much closer to home. Three years earlier, his son-in-law Tom Randolph had been elected to Congress from Albemarle and had moved into the President's

House. There he lived with Jefferson's other son-in-law, John Eppes, who had been elected to Congress that same year from a district near Richmond.

In sixteen years of marriage to Jefferson's daughter, Randolph had proved to be a morbidly sensitive man, prone to violent outbursts and prolonged sulking. In October 1802, in a plaintive letter showering effusive praise on Jefferson, Randolph told his father-in-law that he felt like a "silly bird" among the "swans" at Monticello. Assuring Randolph that he had no reason to feel "extraneous," Jefferson said he held "the virtues of your heart and the powers of your understanding in a far more exalted view" than Randolph himself did.

But, in truth, Randolph had done little to inspire confidence. He had decided, for example, to seek the congressional seat representing Albemarle without consulting Jefferson. That seat was then occupied by Samuel Cabell, a loyal Democratic-Republican who spent the disputed election of February 1801, he said, "lying two nights on a blanket to make [Jefferson] President." Jefferson remained neutral in the race, which Randolph narrowly won.

Randolph came to public attention only once during his otherwise uneventful four years in the U.S. House of Representatives. In April 1806, for reasons that no one at the time seems to have understood, Tom Randolph took offense at something said during a congressional debate by his cousin John Randolph. Springing to his feet, Jefferson's son-in-law informed his fellow Virginian "that lead and even steel make very proper ingredients in serious quarrels." When challenges were exchanged and the public expected the two Randolphs to "cut each other's throats," as Congressman John Taylor told Senator Wilson Cary Nicholas, the president intervened.

Jefferson wrote to remind his son-in-law that he had a "wife, and a family of children, all depending for their happiness and protection in this world on you alone." Martha had been sick, Jefferson added, and what would become of the family if Randolph were to be shot? "Seven children, all under the age of discretion and down to infancy, could then be left without guide or guardian, but a poor broken-hearted woman, doomed herself to misery the rest of her life." Urged to "suppress all passion," Randolph mumbled an apology on the floor of Congress, and, to Jefferson's great relief, the matter was dropped.

Besides the birth of a son, James Madison Randolph, at the President's House during a visit by his wife, Martha, in January 1806, the only other significant event of Randolph's congressional career was also more private than public. In early 1807, Tom Randolph decided that Jefferson "felt a preference" for Eppes and, without a word, moved out of the President's House. He took lodgings at a Federalist boardinghouse, where he remained until his term in office ended. Having decided against seeking reelection, he then went home to Edgehill.

The greatest disappointment of Jefferson's otherwise triumphant first term in the presidency was his unsuccessful attempt to reduce the power of the Supreme Court, "that battery [from which] all the works of Republicanism are to be beaten down and erased," as he described it to John Dickinson on December 19, 1801.

During Jefferson's presidency, Democratic-Republicans controlled both the executive and legislative branches of government. This left only the courts in Federalist hands, with genuine differences in constitutional interpretation at stake. In *Marbury v. Madison,* a case resulting from John Adams's appointment of Federalist judges in his last hours in office, Chief Justice John Marshall—a Virginian and a distant cousin of Jefferson's, but a Federalist first and foremost—had declared an act of Congress "repugnant to the Constitution" and therefore void. By this act, Jefferson told Abigail Adams on September 11, 1804, the court claimed authority "to decide what laws are constitutional and what not, not only for themselves" but for the legislature and executive as well. Such power, insulated from the people, "would make the judiciary a despotic branch."

Increasingly frustrated, in the spring of 1805, the Senate attempted a frontal assault on Federalist judges, voting to impeach Associate Justice Samuel Chase, an outspoken Federalist given to partisan harangues from the bench. If Chase could be removed from office, it was rumored, Marshall himself would be targeted. This effort failed miserably, however. The bitterness resulting from this attempt further damaged Jefferson in the summer of 1807, when a federal court in Richmond, presided over by Marshall, tried Burr on criminal charges stemming from his suspicious activities in the Southwest where, prosecutors charged, he conspired to establish an empire of his own.

After Jefferson, in a rare lapse of dignity and cool judgment, told Congress that Burr was guilty "beyond all question," Marshall narrowly defined the charges against the defendant, making it possible for Burr, like Chase before him, to be acquitted—and for Jefferson to suffer a humiliating defeat.

With the courts more solidly than ever in Federalist control, Jefferson faced a new crisis, this one of international importance.

# CHAPTER 9

# *"In a State of Almost Total Incapacity"*

On June 22, 1807, the roar of cannons off the Virginia coast near Norfolk brought the United States and Great Britain to the brink of war. When the thirty-nine-gun U.S.S. *Chesapeake* ignored a demand by the fifty-two-gun British *Leopard* to be searched, the *Leopard* opened fire, killing three Americans and wounding eighteen. The *Leopard* also impressed four sailors alleged to have deserted from the Royal Navy.

This was the latest and most violent in a series of confrontations in which British ship captains had stopped American ships to seize native-born Americans they claimed were deserters. Indignant Americans howled, and the country had never been "in such a state of excitement since the battle of Lexington," Jefferson noted.

This outrage was predictable. In their war with each other, Great Britain and Napoleonic France had shown no regard for the maritime rights of neutrals. Both belligerents claimed the authority to interfere with any ship suspected of trading with the enemy. The *Chesapeake* incident, because it took place so close to U.S. shores, brought home this European war, hitherto confined to the high seas.

Regarding the attack as an act of war, in July Jefferson ordered all British warships out of American waters, instructed the governors to call up 100,000 state militiamen, and directed the Army and the Marine Corps to be enlarged to the greatest extent authorized by law. While the *Leopard*'s squadron hovered off the coast, a British ship believed to be loading cargo to supply the British squadron was fired on and disabled.

By the time Congress reconvened in the fall, England had withdrawn its ships to a point just beyond the three-mile U.S. territorial limit. But it also announced its intention of searching American ships for deserters even more vigorously. Aware since the previous spring that secret diplomatic efforts to resolve the maritime issues peacefully had failed, on December 18, Jefferson presented the overwhelmingly Democratic-Republican Congress with what he believed was a credible alternative to war. An embargo on trade with all European powers, he hoped, would cripple the British and French economies by denying the two chief belligerents American produce and raw materials. It would also deprive European manufacturers and merchants of a market for their finished goods.

At the time that Jefferson presented his plan to Congress, about fifteen hundred American vessels were at sea, carrying $60 million in commercial cargo. By calling these ships home, Jefferson would not only deprive the European powers of trade with the United States; he would also remove these vessels from danger of being fired on or seized. When the British and French saw their folly, the president reasoned, they would cease preying on American shipping and thus end the crisis.

Jefferson knew that the embargo would require sacrifice on the part of Americans. Endured with patience, this hardship would ultimately work to their advantage by requiring them to turn to domestic products, encouraging "home manufactures," and stimulating small-scale industry.

This policy of "peaceable coercion," as Jefferson called it, would constitute the one initiative for which an entire generation or more would remember his entire presidency. The defeat of the Barbary pirates, the purchase of the Louisiana Territory, the expedition by Lewis and Clark—all would pale in importance when measured against the embargo.

This "experiment," as Jefferson called it, would teach a war-weary world a great lesson. Other countries would observe how they, too, could avoid war and would discover how the citizens of a free republic, united in defense of their rights, responded in a crisis. That, anyway, was the theory; and now that Jefferson exercised a level of power he had never known before, he intended to see this experiment through to its conclusion, with tragically little regard for its catastrophic effects. In the ordeal that followed, the astute democratic politician of the first term was replaced by the astonishingly obtuse would-be scientific theorist of the second.

Congress approved the plan, and, on December 22, 1807, Jefferson signed the first of five embargo acts (he signed the last on January 9, 1809). The policy, in its earliest incarnation, merely prohibited U.S. ships from sailing into foreign ports. Later versions would be designed to close loopholes in the original legislation. They would also impose ever steeper penalties on American

planters, merchants, and shipping interests determined to defy the embargo—
or, in time, merely to transport, by sea or land, goods that might possibly find
their way into enemy ports.

The embargo's pinch was felt almost immediately, though not where Jefferson
had hoped. Virginia planters were among the first to suffer. With European
markets closed, tobacco rotted, unsold, in warehouses. The glut caused tobacco
prices to collapse. Cash-poor planters were unable to make payments on their
loans, and courts of law in Virginia refused to hear cases involving unpaid debts.

In early 1808, moreover, Virginians who could afford to do so continued to
buy their finery from overseas, on the black market. When Ellen Randolph
told her grandfather of widespread defiance of his efforts to keep European
products out of American hands, Jefferson was sorely disappointed. "You give
a bad account of the patriotism of the ladies of Williamsburg who are not disposed to submit to the small privation to which the embargo will subject them,"
he wrote in February. "I hope this will not be general and that principle and
prudence will induce us all to return to the good old plan of manufacturing
within our own families most of the articles we need."

Virginians "never lived so comfortably" as they did during the Revolution,
he wrote, "because we soon learnt to supply all our real wants at home, and we
could not run in debt, as not an hour's credit was given for anything." Only
then did Virginians discover the wisdom of "never spending our money before
we had it."

This was a lesson that Jefferson seems never to have learned himself: during
his second term as president, when the crisis with Great Britain and France
began to simmer, he decided to build a second home for himself at his Poplar
Forest plantation in Bedford County. Construction began in 1805 and continued through the darkest days of the embargo, at a time when he could scarcely
afford to keep Monticello in proper repair.

Within weeks of the embargo's imposition, Congressman William Burwell of
Albemarle, who also represented tobacco-rich Mecklenburg County, assured
Jefferson of his personal loyalty but warned that, when Congress reconvened in
the fall of 1807, it would be "necessary to remove the Embargo."

By this time, demands for an end to the embargo were coming from every state, often in far less respectful language. In the first months of the trade ban, American exports fell from $108 million to $22 million. Ports closed, merchants were ruined, and thirty thousand sailors, dockworkers, and fishermen lost their jobs. Ships ostensibly sailing from one American port to another mysteriously found themselves "blown off course," all the way to Canada, to the West Indies, and to Liverpool. Enterprising souls also moved goods by boat and by wagon into Canada for shipment overseas, and government agents who tried to stop them were fired on, with bloodshed on both sides. Opposing the embargo themselves and fearing for their lives, revenue agents resigned their posts.

Jefferson's response was to order a crackdown on shipping between American ports, and, at his direction, Treasury Secretary Albert Gallatin instructed government agents to detain all "suspicious" vessels. Meanwhile, Great Britain and France, inconvenienced only mildly by the disruption in commerce, looked on with derision at Jefferson's attempt to bring them to their knees.

In the congressional boardinghouses of Washington, tensions ran high. Denunciations of the embargo and its architect grew sulfurous. When Gallatin, Secretary of State Madison, and other officials of Jefferson's increasingly beleaguered administration demanded from critics a policy other than war to replace the embargo, Democratic-Republican John Randolph asked, "Shall a man be refused to be cured of a cancer unless you will provide him with a *substitute*?"

A letter from an ordinary citizen of Boston must have cut deeper. "How much longer," the man wrote to Jefferson, "are you going to keep this damned Embargo on to starve us poor people one of my children has already starved to death of which I [am] ashamed and declared that it died of apoplexy?"


In March 1808, Jefferson was stricken by one of the violent headaches that afflicted him at irregular intervals for most of his adult life. Psychological stress affected Jefferson physically, and there were periods when this otherwise healthy man physically and mentally collapsed. The first of these "periodical head-aches" as he called them, seized Jefferson in 1764 when, at the age of twenty-one, his proposal of marriage to the "Belinda" of his early correspondence was rejected. This attack lasted only two days. Twelve years later, when Jefferson's mother died, he became "incapacitated," by his own description, for several weeks.

The next major psychological crisis occurred in September 1782, when his wife died. The exact nature of his physical response to this event is impossible to reconstruct, though it seems extreme. At the moment of Martha Jefferson's death, he had to be led from the room "in a state of insensibility." Then he fainted and remained unconscious for so long that his family feared for his life.

When he regained consciousness, he paced ceaselessly in his room day and night for three weeks, "only lying down occasionally, when nature was completely exhausted." Almost three months elapsed before this "stupor of mind," as he described it, finally passed. During that time, he had been "as dead to the world as she whose loss occasioned it."

In November 1782, hoping that a return to public life would speed his recovery, Jefferson's friends arranged for his appointment as a peace commissioner to Europe. Jefferson accepted the post and was in Annapolis in 1783, waiting to cross the Atlantic, when the next episode occurred. He had been in "very ill health" during this period, he said. An attack of his "periodical headach[e]" prevented him from "reading, writing and almost thinking."

Seven years later, in 1790, when Jefferson was secretary of state, his clashes with Treasury Secretary Alexander Hamilton brought on "an attack of my periodical headach[e]" that again left him immobile. A year later, a trip to New York and New England with James Madison freed him from "the *almost constant headach[e]*" that had plagued him for several weeks. The fact that the pain disappeared when he took a holiday from political intrigue persuaded Jefferson that it had been brought on by "the *drudgery of business.*"

Biographers have asserted for many years that Jefferson suffered from migraines, an assertion that Jefferson's own descriptions show to be erroneous. "Migraine" was a word in common use in Jefferson's time, appearing in medical books that Jefferson owned. But "migraine" was not the word that Jefferson applied to his own ailment, and some of the symptoms he describes are not those of migraines. Jefferson's "periodical headaches" persisted day and night and lasted from a few days to several weeks. Migraines typically last for about four hours, occasionally for as long as a week. Unlike migraines, Jefferson's headaches were not confined to one side of the head, and they were not accompanied by nausea or vomiting. (He did, however, experience the sensitivity to light that often marks migraine.)

A more accurate description seems to be stress headache, resulting from involuntary muscular contraction from nervous tension. Jefferson himself attributed the onset of his headaches to the pressures of work, and they were therefore—to borrow the language of a later era—psychosomatic in nature. This indicates that he knew better than his biographers the source of his affliction.

Two of the episodes occurred during the greatest trials of his presidency. The first was in the spring of 1807, when Jefferson learned that diplomatic efforts to resolve the impressment issue had failed. Around March 13, the attack came on, lasted morning until night, and did not abate for a week. During that time, he told Gallatin, there was "but a little moment in the morning" in which he could work. For much of the week, the pain was so intense that he was "shut up in a dark room from early in the forenoon until night."

The second episode, one of the most painful Jefferson ever experienced, took place the following year, beginning on Friday, March 25, when opposition to the embargo could be heard from every part of the country. By Sunday, the pain was "severe." It persisted until the following Sunday, April 3. By Tuesday, April 12, the discomfort had ceased.

Two weeks later, he confessed to U.S. Attorney General Caesar Rodney that he had been capable of conscious thought for only an hour a day during his illness. The contentious congressional session, he said, had worn him down "to a state of almost total incapacity for business." For days on end, when the nation's position in the world was endangered and his own legacy teetered on the brink of ruin, Jefferson, by his own admission, lay helpless and insensible.

On April 13, 1808, Jefferson emerged from his bedroom "entirely recovered," as he put it, and even more determined to see his experiment in "peaceable coercion" through to its conclusion. This man of science had developed a hypothesis, the validity of which he sought to examine and, if possible, to confirm.

Acting quickly, and with none of the indecisiveness that characterized his service as wartime governor of Virginia, Jefferson began to enforce the embargo with a zeal that struck even longtime allies as excessive. In mid-April, wielding executive power far beyond that which he had condemned in John Adams, Jefferson announced that smuggling on Lake Champlain amounted to armed insurrection "too powerful to be suppressed by the ordinary course of judicial proceedings." Jefferson ordered all military authorities in the region "by all means in their power, by force or arms or otherwise," to put down the insurrection.

In early May, Jefferson ordered Gallatin "to consider every shipment of provisions, lumber, flaxseed, tar, cotton, tobacco, &c ... as sufficiently suspicious for detention." When in doubt, he told the treasury secretary, "consider me as voting for detention." In July, Jefferson began to use the Navy to blockade ports, stop ships, and seize cargo. In August, Jefferson said that Congress "must legalize all *means* which may be necessary to obtain its *end,*" and in September, he urged prosecution for treason not only of anyone who defied the embargo, but also for those who expressed disapproval of it.

"Too many," he admitted, were guilty of treason "to be punished with death." That being the case, Jefferson hoped that "the most guilty may be marked as examples, and the less so suffer long imprisonment." The only treason trial associated with defiance of the embargo, however, ended in acquittal.

Treason was much on Jefferson's mind at this time—that, and the powers that governments can exercise when their will is thwarted. In October, Jefferson answered a letter from James Brown, the secretary of the Louisiana Territory. Some months earlier, Brown had written to deny rumors that he had participated in the military escapades of Aaron Burr, whose trial for treason in September had also ended in acquittal.

Ostensibly defending his zealous prosecution of Burr, Jefferson said that the government sometimes has no alternative but to exceed its legal authority. "Should we have ever gained our Revolution," he asked, "if we had bound our hands by manacles of the law, not only in the beginning, but in any part of the revolutionary conflict? There are extreme cases where the laws become inadequate even to their own preservation, and where, the universal resource is a dictator, or martial law."

The beliefs that Jefferson expressed in response to the Burr conspiracy applied equally well to his enforcement of the embargo. What began as a ban on trade with Great Britain and France had escalated into a prohibition against all shipping along the Atlantic coast, including routine commerce between American ports. The movement of vessels on lakes, rivers, and bays without approval was also prohibited, as was that of ships to and from ports adjacent to foreign territory—meaning Canada—unless they received special exemption from the president. Gunboats could stop at will any boat or ship suspected of unlawful commerce; such vessels would then be held until the president personally authorized their release.

And still the effect on the European powers was negligible. In *The American*

*Presidency,* the historian Forrest McDonald likened the effort to bend England and France to America's will to "a flea trying to break up a dogfight by threatening suicide." The embargo's domestic impact, however, had been enormous. In *Jefferson and Civil Liberties,* Leonard W. Levy observes that the embargo, "begun as a means of coercing and starving England and France into respect for American rights, rapidly became an instrument of coercion against American citizens." An irony of Jefferson's presidency is that his greatest failure occurred not because this advocate of political liberty exaggerated his countrymen's desire to be free from government interference, but because he underestimated it.

The embargo left in tatters the immense popularity that Jefferson enjoyed during his first term as president. Now, as his days in office dragged to an end, he was bitterly despised in many parts of the country, but especially in New England. A precocious thirteen-year-old, William Cullen Bryant of Massachusetts, captured the anti-Jefferson feeling in light verse that proved wildly popular when published in Boston in 1808. The poem dredged up the rumors about Jefferson's mulatto "concubine" that had first surfaced six years earlier, ridiculed the president's interest in the natural sciences, and demanded his retirement:

> Go wretch, resign the presidential chair,
> Disclose thy secret measures foul or fair,
> Go, search with curious eye, for horned frogs,
> 'Mongst the wild wastes of Louisianan bogs;
> Go where Ohio rolls his turbid stream,
> Dig for huge bones, thy glory and thy theme;
> Go, scan, Philosophist, thy Sally's charms,
> And sink sublimely in her sable arms;
> But quit to abler hands, the helm of state,
> No image ruin on thy country's fate.

The one happy interlude in this otherwise anxious time in Jefferson's life was his late summer return to Monticello. He arrived on July 23 and immediately set to work on a flower garden he had been designing when first notified of the *Leopard's* attack on the *Chesapeake.* He also planned for further leveling of the broad expanse of the kitchen garden and a semicircular walkway on the lawn, lined with flowers. "I find that the limited numbers of our flower beds will be too much to restrain the variety of flowers in which we might wish to indulge,"

Jefferson had written to his granddaughter Ann Cary Randolph the previous year, "& therefore I have resumed an idea, which I had formerly entertained, but had laid by, of a winding walk surrounding the lawn before the house, with a narrow border on each side."

Ann was seventeen now, a "perfectly lovely woman," in the words of Jefferson's overseer Bacon. Ann's marriage to Charles Lewis Bankhead of Port Royal, Virginia, took place at Monticello on September 18, 1808. For years now, Ann had been her grandfather's "active and useful assistant in the garden," as her sister Ellen Randolph described her. Their letters, even during his presidential years, discuss tuberoses, tulips, amaryllis, and hyacinths, and they would continue to correspond about botanical subjects after the new Mr. and Mrs. Bankhead rode away to visit the bridegroom's parents, more than a hundred miles northeast of Charlottesville, on the Rappahannock River near Fredericksburg. Jefferson hoped that the newlyweds would return to Monticello in the spring.

The son of John L. Bankhead, a respected physician, Ann's husband was a

A *"perfectly lovely woman."* Ann Cary Randolph Bankhead.

"fine-looking man," in Bacon's words, who showed considerable promise. At Monticello, Bankhead could prepare for a career in the legal profession among the law books that Jefferson kept in the south pavilion. "I do not think he can take a more advantageous stand for study," Jefferson told Ann. "I hope therefore that he will consent to it, and that you will both ever consider yourselves as a part of our family until you shall feel the desire of separate establishment insuperable."

As a wedding present, Tom Randolph, Ann's father, gave Charles Bankhead about 1,450 acres near Poplar Forest in Bedford County—land that Jefferson had given to Randolph in 1790, when he and Martha married. If the Bankheads wanted their own home, Jefferson hoped they would move near him in Bedford.

Jefferson's other chief non-presidential interest during this period was planning for the education of his grandson and namesake, Thomas Jefferson Randolph. Jeff, who turned sixteen a week before Ann's wedding, had been taught Latin and French at home and then attended schools in Milton and Charlottesville. Jefferson had recommended that he enroll at the University of Pennsylvania at Philadelphia, where he would attend lectures in anatomy, botany, and natural history. Jefferson also wished the young man to pursue a course in surgery, which was "a convenient acquisition for a country gentleman." There were few surgeons in the Virginia Piedmont, Jefferson pointed out. Planters were "apt to live beyond their income & then be reduced to bankruptcy," and the ability to perform surgery could bring in extra income.

After the boy completed his studies in Philadelphia, Jefferson said, he should attend the College of William and Mary, "for his mathematics, natural philosophy, & chemistry." While attending college in Williamsburg, he would benefit by "making acquaintances with his [contemporaries] of his own country." This would be "useful to him in his progress through life."

Jefferson left Monticello for Washington for the last time in his life on September 24, 1808, accompanied by his grandson. Jeff Randolph planned to spend a few days at the President's House and then proceed by stage to Philadelphia. Martha Randolph worried that her eldest son might lack sufficient maturity to do well in a school so far from home. He was "impatient of reproof and *at times* irritable." He also had a hot temper, and Martha said she saw "enough of the Randolph character in him to give me some uneasiness as to the future."

In mid-October, after Jeff Randolph left for Philadelphia, the President's House was a lonely place. In December, Jefferson's miseries were multiplied by an abscessed jaw so painful that he was unable to leave the house. The election that month of James Madison as his successor offered little comfort. Given up for dead a decade earlier, the Federalists captured 70 percent of congressional seats in every state north of the Potomac except Pennsylvania. The Federalists also either took or retained control of all the state legislatures of New England.

On January 24, 1809, Jefferson's longtime friend Wilson Cary Nicholas, who represented Albemarle County in Congress, introduced legislation ending the embargo. When Jefferson learned that the bill passed, Jefferson expressed surprise. "I thought Congress had taken their ground firmly for continuing their embargo," he told Tom Randolph on February 7. By calling it *"their"* embargo," Jefferson shifted blame for this greatest disaster of his public life from his shoulders to theirs.

*Part Two*

LATE AFTERNOON AND SUNSET

# CHAPTER 10

# "A Prisoner Released from His Chains"

On the morning of March 4, 1809, having politely turned down a request to accompany the president-elect in his carriage, Thomas Jefferson and Jeff Randolph rode their horses down Pennsylvania Avenue to Jenkins Hill. Jefferson and his grandson attempted to blend in with the crowd of citizens—thousands, by one account—who trooped in the train of James Madison's military escort.

When Jefferson and his grandson reached the Capitol a little before noon, they tied their horses to a fence post, passed through the crowd to take their places inside the House chamber, and waited for Madison's official entry. After Madison was ushered in, Jefferson stood with his successor as Chief Justice John Marshall administered the oath of office to the new president. Praising his predecessors, Madison offered special words of gratitude to Jefferson. He had earned his "rich reward," Madison said, "in the benedictions of a beloved country, gratefully bestowed for exalted talents zealously devoted through a long career to the advancement of its highest interest and happiness."

Madison and the rest of the party exited, the cavalry fired two rounds from its cannons, and the new president reviewed nine militia companies. After the ceremonies, Jefferson called on the Madisons at their F Street residence where, as his friend the Philadelphia-born socialite Margaret Bayard Smith observed, Jefferson "seemed in high spirits," beaming "with a benevolent joy."

That night, at Long's Hotel, Jefferson attended the country's first official inaugural ball, presided over by Dolley Madison, resplendent in buff-colored velvet and draped in pearls. Again, Jefferson hoped to pass as a "plain, unassuming citizen," he said, and it might indeed have been possible to get lost among the other merrymakers. Four hundred tickets had been sold, and the crowd, John Quincy Adams said, "was excessive." (The heat was also "oppressive," Adams grumbled, "and the entertainment bad.")

Jefferson again was in a sunny mood. "Am I too early?" he asked upon his arrival. "You must tell me how to behave for it is more than forty years since I have been to a ball."

"You look so happy and satisfied Mr. Jefferson," one of the other guests said, "and Mr. Madison looks so serious not to say sad, that a spectator might imagine that you were the one coming in, and he the one going out of office."

"There's a good reason for my happy and his serious looks," Jefferson replied. "I have got the burthen off my shoulders, while he has now got it on his."

Jefferson had been looking forward to this day for months, and, if he is to be taken at his word, for years. He had always insisted that he never desired public office, and the decades in which he had spent so much of his energy in political struggle had only confirmed him in his suspicion that the game was not worth the candle.

"I am tired of a life of contention, and of being the personal object for the hatred of every man, who hates the present state of things," Jefferson had written to Martha Randolph on November 23, 1807. "I long to be among you where I know nothing but love and delight, and where instead of being

*"I long to be among you where I know nothing but love and delight."*
*Watercolor of Monticello lawn, commissioned by Ellen Coolidge,*
*featuring George, Mary, and Cornelia Randolph.*

chained to a writing table I would be indulged as others are with the blessings of domestic society, and pursuits of my own choice."

He longed to be through with politics so he could return to "my family, my books and farms," he wrote to Pierre-Samuel du Pont de Nemours on March 2, 1809. His family, books, and farms formed a kind of trinity of which Jefferson had written wistfully for many years.

Having gained the harbor myself, I shall look on my friends still buffeting the storm with anxiety indeed, but not with envy. Never did a prisoner released from his chains feel such relief as I shall on shaking off the shackles of power. Nature intended me for the tranquil pursuits of science, by rendering them my supreme delight. But the enormities of the times in which I have lived, have forced me to take a part in resisting them, and to commit myself on the boisterous ocean of political passions. . . . I leave everything in the hands of men so able to take care of them, that if we are destined to meet misfortunes it will be because no human wisdom could avert them.

Over the next week, Jefferson made his final preparations for leaving Washington. After selecting new clothes for Jeff Randolph (he "examined my wardrobe as my mother would have done and sent me to his own tailor with a list of articles that he thought I required," Randolph said), he bade farewell to the boy and sent him back to Philadelphia.

Aided by the overseer Edmund Bacon, Jefferson then continued his packing, which had been going on now for some weeks. In the resulting wagonloads of bundles, boxes, and crates were a number of recent purchases—six new pairs of shoes, a set of eighteen dessert spoons, a silver pudding dish, a print of Madison, and a coverlet of mantua silk that Jefferson planned to line with furs. Before leaving town, he also had his watch cleaned by a clockmaker at Thirteenth and F Streets, visited his barber, and ordered three dozen bow-backed Windsor chairs, painted black and gold, for his new house at Poplar Forest.

On March 9, Bacon set off for Monticello with a cavalcade that included three wagons and Jefferson's carriage and carriage horses. Two of the wagons were drawn by six-mule teams. The third wagon, "pretty much loaded with shrubbery from Maine's nursery," in Bacon's words, was pulled by four horses. The slaves rode on the wagons, and Bacon, on horseback, trotted along behind the carriage and carriage horses. Still other belongings were sent down the Potomac to the Chesapeake Bay, from there to the James River, and thence by boat to Richmond and on to Albemarle on the Rivanna.

Jefferson, who would follow two days later, still had a number of business transactions to take care of as he prepared for his new life as a private citizen. His financial situation would soon change dramatically. Jefferson would be giving up his annual salary of $25,000, and as there was no presidential pension, he would need to support himself and his family largely from agriculture. He was throwing off the burdens of public office, but those of private debt remained. Jefferson's debts, as he was keenly aware, were considerable, and it was from his farm income that he hoped to pay these as well.

Some of these debts dated back to pre-revolutionary loans from the British; another was owed a Dutch banking house from which he had borrowed $3,000 in the 1790s. He had been unable to keep up his payments on the Dutch debt, and, with interest, these by 1815 would double. Jefferson also estimated that he had incurred another $11,000 in debt during his presidency. This, he said, had been unavoidable. To entertain diplomats and legislators and to maintain the President's House in properly dignified style—he served only the "finest and most costly wines," Margaret Bayard Smith observed—he had had no choice but to spend more than he was paid. He also had taken out loans with several banks in Washington and in Richmond, the terms of which were continually being altered or extended as his financial situation shifted.

By Jefferson's calculations—although how he arrived at these figures remains a mystery—the most that he might owe immediately on his various debts was about $4,500. Even this was far more money than he could readily lay hands on, yet he felt sure that his assets vastly exceeded his liabilities. At the time of his retirement from the presidency, Jefferson owned about ten thousand acres in Albemarle and Bedford Counties, and some two hundred slaves.

Jefferson also owned three mills of questionable economic value on the Rivanna near Milton and a few lots in Richmond. Finally, he owned 157 acres in southwest Virginia, but this was land he purchased because he admired Natural Bridge, a rock formation there, not because it had any agricultural value. His nail-making operation at Monticello, like his commercial operations on the Rivanna, also generated no income. He had to take out loans to buy iron for the shop and, rather than sell his nails, engaged in barter. He often paid merchants for his rum, brandy, coffee, and other "groceries" in nails.

In acreage alone, Jefferson believed his holdings were worth fifty times the $4,500 that he owed upon leaving the presidency, although Dumas Malone, in his six-volume biography of Jefferson, writes, rather cryptically, that one "need not conclude from this that he valued his property at $225,000." Jefferson's finances, which he himself did not fully understand, will forever baffle historians. However much land or however many slaves he owned, neither could be easily converted to cash, and the value of both would decrease rather than increase in the years to come.

A third of the slaves he owned were children, some were too old to work, and more were employed as domestic servants than was the case on most working farms. A number of slaves were also skilled craftsmen or had special duties involving the garden, for example, or winemaking. Perhaps only a third of the two hundred were field hands, engaged in farm work that produced income for the estate. The others, it is safe to say, consumed more than they produced.

How much Jefferson actually earned from farming is also difficult to establish, but he estimated that his Albemarle lands, which produced mainly wheat, brought in from $2,000 to $3,000 a year, while the Bedford farms, producing tobacco, earned roughly the same amount. In his initial planning for his retirement, he intended to dedicate the earnings from these Bedford holdings solely to the payment of his debts. The family would then live "within the income of my Albemarle possessions," which should be sufficient, he believed, as long as they controlled their spending.

The landholdings in both Albemarle and Bedford, when and if they were ever sold, would provide a substantial patrimony. "Our lands, if we preserve them," he told Martha Randolph in January 1808, "are sufficient to place all the children in independance." He was determined to hold on to this land "to leave [it] as a provision for yourselves"—meaning Martha and her husband—"and your family."

That, anyway, was the long-term plan. When, before leaving for Monticello, he began to pay a number of small debts incurred during his presidency, Jefferson realized his need for ready cash was much greater than he had guessed and prevailed upon his business agent in Richmond to arrange yet another loan. "My intervening nights will be almost sleepless," he wrote, "as nothing could be more distressing to me than to leave debts here unpaid, if indeed I should be permitted to depart with them unpaid."

The agent arranged for Jefferson to borrow $8,000 from an Amelia County widow, a Mrs. Tabb, for a term of six months. About the same time, Jefferson transferred a loan of $4,500, which he had borrowed from the Bank of the United States, to Thaddeus Kościuszko, his old compatriot from revolutionary days. Kościuszko, now living in Paris, agreed to assume the debt, asking only that Jefferson pay the interest. Getting out from under the loan from the Bank of the United States was a "beam of light beaming on my uneasy mind," Jefferson said, in large part because he had prevailed upon James Madison to cosign the note.

As always, Jefferson tried to put the best face possible on his situation. His debts were the inevitable result of republican virtue, he insisted, suggesting that any honest public official would find himself in similar straits. To retire from office in better financial condition than one was in when elected would be dishonorable, for it would indicate that he had put his private interests above those of the public, or, worse, was corrupt. He retired with the consolation, he told Count Diodati, a friend from his days in Paris, "of having added nothing to my private fortunes during my public service and of retiring with hands as clean as they are empty."

Still, Jefferson worried. "I have now the gloomy prospect of retiring from office loaded with serious debts, which will materially affect the tranquillity of my retirement," he had told Martha on January 5, 1808, more than a year before his return to Monticello. "However, not being apt to deject myself with evils before they happen, I nourish the hope of getting along." He could always sell the land at Poplar Forest and pay his debts in that way, he told his daughter, but to do so would wipe out his grandchildren's inheritance.

Ever the realist, Martha told him the only sensible thing to do was to sell the land and let the next generation fend for itself. "The impossibility of paying serious debts by crops, and living at the same time, has been so often proved that I am afraid you should trust to it," she wrote on January 16, 1808.

> If by any sacrifice of the Bedford Lands you can relieve your self from the pressure of debt I conjure you not to think of the children, your own happiness is alone to be considered. Let not the tranquility of your old age be disturbed and we shall do well. I never could enjoy happiness to see you deprived of those comforts you have allways been accustomed to and which habit has rendered necessary to your health and ease.

In February of the following year, as Jefferson's departure from Washington drew near, Martha reminded him of the happy domestic scenes that awaited him and of her eagerness for his return. Surrounded by children "with never less than three talking to me at once," she told him that the geraniums they had planted in a pot were flourishing, that the arborvitae was budding, and that five-year-old Mary would enjoy copies of *The Road to Learning Made Pleasant* and *Rhymes for the Nursery,* if he could buy them for her.

Then, with feeling she seems never to have expressed to her husband, Martha told her father that as the day of his return drew near, "My heart beats with inexpressible anxiety and impatience. Adieu again My ever Dear and honoured Parent. That the evening of your life may pass in serene and unclouded tranquility is the daily prayer, and as far as my powers [continue] will be the dearest and most sacred duty of your devoted child."

In his reply, Jefferson again mentioned his anxiety about his debts and promised to curtail his spending. "I look with infinite joy to the moment when I shall be ultimately moored in the midst of my affections, and free to follow the pursuits of my choice," he wrote on February 27, 1809. His "single uneasiness" was that "the necessary economies" would prove a hardship to the family. His sole desire, he insisted, was for Martha's happiness and for that of her children. He would ask nothing for himself.

"My own personal wants," he reassured his daughter, "will be almost nothing beyond those of a chum of the family."

On March 11, Jefferson seated himself in his phaeton and, accompanied by two slaves, rolled out of Washington. At Georgetown, they crossed the Potomac by ferry and spent the first night at a friend's plantation ten miles southwest of the capital.

The next day, snow began to fall, and for one eight-hour stretch, Jefferson rode "through as disagreeable" a blizzard as he had ever experienced. By the time he reached Culpeper Courthouse, seventy miles from Washington, the snow was knee-high. A large crowd had gathered on the porch of Shackleford's tavern where, waiting to greet Jefferson, they drank whiskey and became increasingly raucous. When Jefferson arrived, they put up a boisterous hurrah. Bacon, with the wagons, was also waiting at the tavern. Informed that Jefferson would spend the night, the proprietor had a fire blazing in one of the private rooms.

Bacon hustled Jefferson into the room and locked the door, but the noisiest reveler followed, banging on the door and demanding entry. Relenting, Jefferson had Bacon let the man in, and many more pushed forward until his lodgings, as the overseer recalled, were "as full as I ever saw a barroom." After order was restored, Jefferson made a short speech that seemed to satisfy the noisy well-wishers, ate dinner, and turned in for the night.

The next morning, he decided that the roads had become impassable by two-wheeled conveyance and, climbing into the saddle, rode on alone. The following afternoon, Jefferson arrived in Albemarle. A few days earlier, a storm had dumped nine inches of snow on his familiar mountains. A rain that followed had turned the roads into wallows. After his mount struggled up the mountain, Jefferson pulled it to a halt at Monticello. It was March 15. He was well ahead of his belongings and feeling "no inconvenience from the expedition," he told Madison, "but fatigue."

Jefferson would turn sixty-six in less than a month. The fact that he had come through the ordeal no worse for wear gave him "more confidence in my *vis vitae*," he told Madison, "than I had before entertained."

CHAPTER 11

## *"Elevated Above the Mass of Mankind"*

---

Spring came late during Jefferson's first year back home. Northwest winds kept temperatures in the low twenties during much of March, and Monticello remained gray and raw through the end of the month. At the farms in Albemarle, the winter wheat struggled, while, in Bedford County, the tobacco had just been planted. In most years, the slaves by this time would be transplanting the tobacco from the seedbed into the main farm fields. Such a late start threatened the whole crop.

April was also cold, and in May, long stretches of near drought were punctuated by brief spells of punishing rains. Early in the month, Jefferson reported to his business agent that frost had killed two thirds of his Bedford County tobacco, and as a result, he would be unable to keep up his payments to Mrs. Tabb, the widow from whom he had borrowed $8,000. The note would be due, in full, in eight weeks.

As aware of his debts as Jefferson was, and as dismayed that his farms had been allowed to deteriorate during his long absences, it is odd that he showed less interest in farming when he returned to Monticello than in his gardens. In the weeks that preceded his departure from Washington, he had written detailed instructions about which flowers to plant and where they should go, and how the "experimental" vegetable garden southeast of the house should be leveled and laid out. He wrote to his granddaughter Ann Bankhead of the curving walkway on Monticello's front lawn where flowers would grow, to Martha of his determination to grow tropical fruits in his glassed-in "piazza," and to Edmund Bacon of the urgency of making the kitchen garden a four-terraced affair, where 350 varieties of fruits, vegetables, and herbs, many new to Virginia, could be grown. Bacon dutifully reported that work on the garden was progressing as Jefferson wished, but only at the expense of the cornfields.

By the time Jefferson was home, the first of the garden terraces had been readied. Planting followed, but in April and May, he reported to Jeff Randolph in Philadelphia, "no seeds in the garden came up." The results of this ambitious project would almost always prove disappointing. Year after year, the garden would fail to produce. For everyday dining, the family would rely to a remarkable extent on vegetables purchased from their slaves, who grew them in far more modest garden plots alongside their cabins.

Understandably, Jefferson spent a great deal of time during his first months back at Monticello simply enjoying the company of his large and growing family. At his insistence, Martha Randolph had moved from Edgehill to Monticello upon her father's return, bringing her six youngest children with her. In January 1810, she would give birth to her tenth child, Meriwether Lewis Randolph.

Tom Randolph took his meals at Monticello and often slept there, but his wife's permanent residence in her father's house instead of his own "could not have been wholly congenial to this proud and sensitive man," as Dumas Malone described him.

The newlyweds Ann and Charles Bankhead also moved to Monticello after their wedding visit to the Caroline County home of Bankhead's parents. Ann's brother, Jeff Randolph, was still at school in Philadelphia, but when he came back to Virginia he, too, would live at Monticello. Other members of the household included Francis Eppes, the seven-year-old son of Jefferson's other daughter, the late Maria Eppes, and Martha Carr, Jefferson's widowed sister. Until her death in 1811, Martha Carr would live off and on at Monticello, bringing her three sons, Peter, Samuel, and Dabney, and two daughters with her.

Finally, there were visiting relatives, who, as was the custom on Virginia plantations, would stay for weeks. One of these relatives, a young man named Isham Lewis, appeared at Monticello in May.

Isham Lewis was the second son of Thomas Jefferson's sister Lucy, who was born at Shadwell in 1752 and married Charles Lilburne Lewis of Albemarle in 1769. For a time, the Lewises, living at Monteagle plantation near Monticello, had prospered, owning several farms and thousands of acres. Eventually, however, they lost everything and, in 1807, moved to Kentucky to start anew.

There, the family's difficulties continued, and in April 1809, on a visit to Virginia, Isham Lewis wrote to his uncle Thomas Jefferson at Monticello, asking for help.

Eager to learn a trade, Lewis said, he was nonetheless reluctant to impose on his distinguished uncle and assured him that the request was "produced from necessity, brought on not from my own imprudences but those of an unfortunate father." His father had not only made "promises of wealth" that he had not kept, Lewis complained, but had also failed to train his son "in any useful pursuit." Lewis closed by asking whether Jefferson might help him get a job surveying the Louisiana Territory.

Jefferson's response, dated May 1, expressed sympathy for his nephew's plight but said that he saw no way "in which I can propose to you any certain relief." If, however, Lewis knew "common arithmetic, say multiplication and division," and could come to Monticello, Jefferson would teach him surveying, which would afford him the opportunity "of doing something for yourself."

Lewis spent two weeks at Monticello. At the conclusion of this visit, Jefferson gave him two letters of introduction, the first of which described him as "a young man of excellent dispositions, correct conduct, & good understanding," though "little aided by education." The "shipwreck of the fortunes of his family" had thrown him back on his own resources and, having learned the rudiments of surveying, he wished "to try himself in that line." The second described Lewis as "possessing qualities which might render him useful and of value," including an eagerness to learn. Lewis "has the capacity and the desire" to advance himself, and, "if favored by proper opportunities, will make himself eminent."

Jefferson also gave his nephew money for his return to Kentucky, which he reached in midsummer. From there, after a brief illness, Lewis left for Natchez to find work.

Meanwhile, Jefferson also concerned himself with the progress of his grandson Jeff Randolph in his studies in Philadelphia. Far from home, "without a friend or guardian to advise" him, Randolph would face temptation, and the "dangers are great." Remembering how he had been "thrown into the society of horse-racers, cardplayers [and] Foxhunters" in Williamsburg, Jefferson urged Randolph to study hard, shun bad company, and avoid discussing politics. "I never yet saw an instance of one or two disputants convincing the other by arguments," Jefferson wrote. "I have seen many of [them getting angry], becoming rude, and shooting one another."

Tact, graciousness, and diligence—characteristics that had served Jefferson well through the years—would serve his grandson well, too. "Look steadily to the pursuits which have carried you to Philadelphia," Jefferson advised, "be very select in the society you attach yourself to; avoid taverns, drinkers, smoakers, and idlers and dissipated persons generally; for it is with such that broils and contentions arise, and you will find your path more easy and tranquil."

By all accounts, Jeff Randolph looked steadily indeed to his studies. One of his professors reported that the boy showed signs of becoming "incessantly studious," and Charles Willson Peale, in whose home he lodged, said he was often bent over his books until two or three o'clock in the morning and had to be told to go to bed.

Only once did he display the Randolph temper that worried his mother. That was when Peale, warning the boy to avoid disputes with hot-tempered students, expressed "much contempt" for dueling, and Randolph replied "with some warmth" that his own father had fought a duel. Such "filial affection" was

*"Avoid taverns, drinkers, smoakers, and idlers."*
*Jeff Randolph at sixteen, a schoolboy in Philadelphia.*

impressive, Peale told Jefferson. With this one forgivable exception, Randolph behaved "with prudence and respectability," Peale reported.

Prudence and respectability were not enough, apparently, to warrant keeping the boy in Philadelphia. Sometime in the spring of 1809, the family decided that Randolph was needed at home. Schooling in Philadelphia was costly, money was tight, and there was farming to be done. Back in Virginia, Jeff could work on the farms and, if he chose to continue his education, he could, perhaps, take classes in Richmond. This would be no great loss to science, his grandfather had concluded with some reluctance. Randolph was a hardworking young man, Jefferson told Benjamin Rush, but he "lacks the bright fancy which captivates."

So Randolph came home. He spent the summer working at Edgehill and Monticello and would not enroll in classes again until the fall, in a second-rate school in Richmond that he attended only sporadically. Randolph's schooling had effectively ended at sixteen, and for the rest of his life, he would lament his "neglected education."

Jeff Randolph was at Monticello in early July 1809, when his sister Ann Bankhead suffered a miscarriage. Illness of one sort or another swept through the household that summer, though, as Margaret Bayard Smith observed during an August visit, the family seemed determined to carry on cheerfully and without alarm.

Several years earlier, Jefferson had helped Samuel Harrison Smith, Margaret's husband, establish *The National Intelligencer,* a Washington newspaper of Democratic-Republican opinions, which he edited.

"We have quite a sick family," Jefferson told the Smiths upon their arrival. "My daughter has been confined to the sick bed of her little son; my granddaughter has already lost her's and still keeps to her room and several of the younger children are indisposed." For two weeks, Martha and Tom Randolph had sat up every night, attending to the ailing children, "until they are almost worn out."

The family's poor health would have "cast a gloom over our visit," Mrs. Smith recalled, but for the hospitality of their hosts. Jefferson beamed with "benignant smiles," and Martha, called from the sickroom of twelve-month-old Benjamin Franklin Randolph, displayed such "kind and cheerful manners" that gloomy thoughts seemed prohibited. Dinner that night was a festive affair. Madeira and a "sweet ladies' wine" were selected from Jefferson's "immense and costly variety of French and Italian wines," and dessert was "succeeded by agreeable and instructive conversation in which every one seemed to wish and expect Mr. J. to take the chief part."

Three days into the Smiths' visit, Martha Randolph herself joined the sick list. Her eyes hurt, and the "excessive inflammation and pain," Mrs. Smith said, prevented her from meeting the family for dinner. Afterward, Mrs. Smith went upstairs to sit with Martha, and soon Jefferson joined them, holding his daughter's hand for more than an hour. Martha was still sick the next morning, so Mrs. Smith again sat with her. They talked of Jefferson's political career, and Martha showed her letters that he had written to her when she was in Paris.

Later that morning, Jefferson took his guests on a leisurely tour along the curved walkway he had designed several months before, pausing at "spots from which the house appeared to most advantage." The valley to the west "was covered by a thick fog, which had the appearance of the ocean and was unbroken except when the wood covered hills rose above the plain and looked like islands. As the sun rose, the fog was broken and exhibited the most various and fantastic forms, lakes, rivers, bays, and as it ascended, it hung in white fleecy clouds on the sides of the mountains." By afternoon, when the clouds had rolled over the mountain, "you could scarcely believe it was the same scene."

As they walked, Mrs. Smith viewed her host on "the top of this mountain, as a being elevated above the mass of mankind." When Jefferson described the walks, seats, and "little temples" he wished to erect, she was grateful that "after forty years spent on the tempestuous sea of political life, he had now reached the haven of domestic bliss." While the storm of great events rumbled in the distance, he "could hear its roaring and be at peace."

Retirement from public life did not mean, however, that Jefferson lacked projects he wished to see through to completion. As they walked, it became clear to Mrs. Smith that the improvements he had planned for this "habitation of philosophy and virtue" would "require a whole life to carry into effect." Many of these, he believed, were for the benefit of his family.

A "young man might doubt of ever completing or enjoying" these additions to the house and grounds. "But he seems to have transposed his hopes and anticipations into the existence of his children," Mrs. Smith wrote. "It is in them he lives, and I believe he finds as much delight in the idea that they will enjoy the fruit of his present labours, as if he hoped it for himself."

One morning, Jefferson took Mrs. Smith on a carriage ride down the trails that had been carved along the summit. While Jefferson prattled merrily away, the trails became more treacherous, and "fear took from me the power of listening to him, or observing the scene, nor could I forbear expressing my alarm," as the carriage seemed about to overturn and send them tumbling down the mountainside.

"My dear madam," Jefferson said, "you are not to be afraid, or if you are you are not to show it; trust yourself implicitly to me, I will answer for your safety. . . . I know every step I take, so banish all fear."

This proved more easily said than done. When the carriage reached an alarmingly precarious mountain pass, Mrs. Smith jumped out and waited, while a slave helped to get the vehicle through. Mrs. Smith then got back into the carriage, and Jefferson continued to explain his plans for improvements.

When they returned to the house, a relieved Mrs. Smith found Martha Randolph sitting with her sick son, reading Charles Robert Maturin's *The Wild Irish Boy*. Ann Bankhead was reading, too, so Mrs. Smith retired to her own room with a "Grecian romance" from Jefferson's library. Late in the afternoon, when dinner was served, Martha again sent her regrets, saying her eyes hurt so that she had gone to bed.

After dinner, the party adjourned to the portico, where Jefferson supervised a footrace for the grandchildren. He arranged them by size, "gave the word for starting and away they flew," making a quarter-mile circle around the back lawn. The little girls "came panting and out of breath to throw themselves into their grandfather's arms, which were opened to receive them; he pressed them to his bosom and rewarded them with a kiss." Seated on the grass with the children, Jefferson happily consented to officiate at a second race, this one on the pavilion itself.

"What an amusement do these creatures afford us," Mrs. Smith said.

"Yes," Jefferson replied, "it is only with them that a grave man can play the fool."

# Chapter 12

# "When I Expect to Settle My Grandchildren"

On August 22, 1810, Thomas Jefferson and Charles Bankhead set off for Bedford County. There Jefferson could check on the progress of the new house he was building at Poplar Forest, while Bankhead, evidently for the first time, would inspect the property that he and Ann had received as a wedding present from her father. Jefferson had become a great-grandfather for the first time the previous December, when Ann gave birth to John Warner Bankhead. She would soon be pregnant again, and, with a growing family, she and her husband had begun to think of establishing their own home, away from Monticello.

This would be only the second time that Jefferson had spent the night at his new "retreat," as he called it. A work in progress like Monticello, Poplar Forest was habitable but far from complete. Jefferson would continue to work on it, adding embellishments and ornamentation as the materials he favored became available. Construction and renovation of both houses would continue for years, until Jefferson's death, and repairs to both Poplar Forest and Monticello would be required for another two decades after that.

The morning was clear when the two men left Monticello, but, by afternoon, clouds had gathered. The drought that had begun in March had persisted through early summer and left the roads parched. Only two inches of rain had fallen in May and June, but a tardy downpour in late July threatened the wheat, corn, and oats, which had come up late and were not as sturdy as they should have been. Tobacco, the cash crop at Poplar Forest, would not be cut until September, but the leaves were so parched by this point in the season that no amount of moisture would revive them.

Although Jefferson noted such developments as he and Bankhead made their way south, what he cared most about was the house at Poplar Forest and the progress made on its construction in his absence. During this visit, he would secure the services of Reuben Perry, an accomplished carpenter from

Lynchburg, to finish the work. In 1812, Jefferson called Poplar Forest "the best dwelling house in the state, except that of Monticello; perhaps preferable to that, as more proportioned to the faculties of a private citizen."

Jefferson's original reason for building the house was a simple and straightforward one—though nothing with Jefferson was as simple and straightforward as might first appear. He was counting on the earnings of the farms at Poplar Forest to pay his debts and would need a comfortable house there in years to come. Comfortable need not mean architecturally ambitious, however, and S. Allen Chambers, noting in his study of Poplar Forest how expensive the project would prove, refers to Jefferson's "completely irrational plan to

*"The best dwelling house in the state, except that of Monticello."*
*Poplar Forest, Jefferson's octagonal retreat.*

achieve financial independence while building a house that would eventually cost as much, if not more, than the amount of the debt he hoped to erase."

Because he needed to justify to himself the time and expense that such an undertaking required, the need for a place to live was eventually subsumed in the notion that he was not building the house so much for himself as for his descendants. And Jefferson did indeed have high hopes for this house and the land that surrounded it. It would, of course, be pleasant to have grandchildren nearby when he visited. But he clearly envisioned something more grandiose than assuring himself of companionship. Jefferson saw Poplar Forest, more than Monticello, as the entire family's future home. For reasons that are not altogether clear—he never said—Jefferson dreamed of establishing a kind of colony in Bedford County, peopled by members of his own family. In 1806, shortly before work on the house began, Jefferson told Elizabeth Trist, a family friend in whose house in Philadelphia he had lodged many years earlier, that Bedford was "where I expect to settle my grandchildren." In 1810, he informed Gideon Granger, who served as U.S. postmaster during Jefferson's presidency, that it is "the most valuable of my possessions, and will become the residence of the greater part of my family." The house Jefferson built there would merely be a magnet, drawing them to the property.

For the rest of his life, Jefferson would attempt to persuade the next generation, beginning with the Bankheads, to settle at Poplar Forest. In November 1808, he told Martha Randolph that the Bankheads "think of settling ultimately at Poplar Forest," and at the time of their visit in August 1810, Jefferson offered the incentive of fifteen hundred acres of his own land there and a note for $500 to help them build their own house.

This dream of settling his descendants at Poplar Forest, as farmers, reflected Jefferson's understanding of the importance of the land to man's moral development and to the nation's political destiny. His view of agriculture as the basis of society was rooted less in practical considerations than in philosophical ones. "Those who labor in the earth are the chosen people of God . . . whose breasts He has made His peculiar deposit for substantial and genuine virtue," he wrote in *Notes on the State of Virginia*. Farming taught virtue and independence, while commerce subverted them. "Corruption of morals in the mass of cultivators is a phenomenon of which no age nor nation has furnished an example," Jefferson wrote in the same book. "It is the mark set on those, who, not looking up to heaven, to their own soil and industry, as does the husbandman for their subsistence, depend for it on [the] caprice of customers."

The American people would be capable of self-government only to the extent that they "remain virtuous," he told James Madison in 1787. They would be so only as long as the country remained agricultural, which it would be while "there remains vacant land in any part of America. When we get piled upon one another in large cities, as in Europe, we shall become corrupt as in Europe." The future of Americans, as individuals and as a nation, was inseparable from agriculture. Self-government required virtue, virtue was taught and preserved through farming, and farming was possible only where there was an abundance of undeveloped land. North America offered vast tracts of such land, and it was the duty of Americans to claim and cultivate it. Settling his family in Bedford County was a way of furthering this grand scheme, contributing to the development of the North American continent and the American nation, and inculcating virtue in his descendants.

These were highly abstract reasons for relocating his family to Bedford County, but to visit Poplar Forest was and is, the architectural historian Hugh Howard has written, "to visit an idea." To live there would be to inhabit an axiom. The villa, as Jefferson called it, is without question an architectural achievement of some note. It is also, in its symmetry of design, as abstract a building as anyone could hope—or be condemned—to live in. Poplar Forest, again quoting Howard, "has the purity of a geometry lesson."

Jefferson was fascinated with circles and squares—the architectural historian Roger G. Kennedy calls him "obsessed"—and had been sketching plans for using these forms for many years when he began to design Poplar Forest. On the wild woodlands of Southside Virginia, he would impose a pleasing, if highly abstract order that makes Poplar Forest his most distinctively Jeffersonian structure, surpassing even Monticello.

Under the sway not only of the Italian Andrea Palladio, designer of villas for the nobles of Venice, but also influenced by the English renaissance architect Inigo Jones and by later English architects James Gibbs, William Kent, and Robert Morris, Jefferson had been drawing octagonal rooms since the 1760s. He had used half-octagonals at Monticello. "Jefferson derived a profound solace—a healing, one might say—from invoking the archetypal power of certain geometric forms, especially the octagon and circle, and from the mathematics associated with them," the architectural historian Fiske Kimball has written.

An octagonal house could make greater use of natural light, with windows in eight and not four directions. These windows Jefferson used to great effect throughout the house, at whose center was a perfect cube that functioned as a dining room, "twenty-feet wide, deep, and tall," in Jefferson's words, with a sixteen-foot-long skylight.

The house, which he described as an "octagon 50 f. in diameter," opened onto a south portico beyond which stretched, on an east–west axis, a two-hundred-foot-long sunken garden. One hundred feet in either direction from the house, two earthen mounds, perfectly conical and linked to the house visually by stands of trees, parallel to the garden, give the house a Palladian balance, echoing the pavilions at Monticello. Just beyond the conical mounds were octagonal privies.

From above, the geometry of the design becomes even more striking than when seen from the front or rear. A circular roadway led to an access road that "penetrates the circle like a vector, terminating at a smaller circle," a carriage turnaround at the front door, Howard writes. The house sat in the center of a larger circle, and, "together with its attendant structures, it bisects that circle." Within the circular drive, enclosing the house, was an octagonal fence. "It's an idealized set of figures—including circles, cones, and octagons—all of which extend out from the perfect cube that was the dining room at its center."

Problems were apparent early on. "Had the original plans been carried out," Chambers observes, Poplar Forest would have been "a totally impractical house in which to live." Jefferson "got so carried away with his abstract musings," in Howard's words, that he failed to provide stairways connecting the lower level to the main floor. To make the house habitable required the installation of two indoor staircases. The design presented even more serious problems, however. Because of the skylights and experimental building materials, the roof continually leaked, and the theoretical economy of having fifteen fireplaces feed into only four chimneys proved erroneous. One of the original chimneys, "its flue steeply corbeled from the dining room, was probably the cause of fire in 1845," Howard writes. "Flames consumed the roof, reducing [the house] to a roofless ruin."

How much if any of this architectural virtuosity impressed Bankhead is hard to say, but upon their return to Monticello in early September, Jefferson reported that his grandson-in-law "is so pleased with the place & neighborhood that his settlement [in Bedford County] is decided on. He brings his people"—meaning his slaves—"here this winter, and his family in the spring."

Spring came, and, although Bankhead had yet to move his slaves or his family to Bedford, Jefferson contented himself with thoughts of happy days he and his granddaughter and her young family would spend together when they lived so near to Poplar Forest. Perhaps they might even move in with him, as Martha and her family had done at Monticello. Back in Albemarle, in May 1811, in one of Jefferson's most lyrical letters, he wrote to Ann:

Nothing new has happened in our neighborhood since you left us. The houses and trees stand where they did. The flowers come forth like the belles of the day, have their short reign of beauty and splendor, and retire like them to the more interesting office of reproducing their like. The hyacinths and tulips are off the stage, the Irises are giving place to the Belladonnas, as this will to the Tuberoses &c. As your Mamma has done to you, my dear Ann, as you will do to the sisters of little John, and as I shall soon and chearfully do to you all in wishing you a long, long, goodnight.

The following month, in June 1811, Jefferson's hope that Ann and her family would settle near him in Bedford County was dashed when Charles Bankhead announced that he had decided not to move there after all. In fact, he wished to sell the land that he and his wife had received as a wedding present and settle at Carlton, a plantation about half a mile down the road from Monticello, but also a short ride from Charlottesville.

"I fancy it is a great disappointment to Mr. Jefferson who pleased himself with the idea of Anns [*sic*] living in Bedford," Elizabeth Trist wrote. Ann was disappointed by her husband's decision, too. Although Ann would miss her family if she moved away from Albemarle, Mrs. Trist speculated that "it will not be so much [in her and her husband's interest] to be so near Charlottesville."

Why Ann did not wish "to be so near Charlottesville" is impossible to say with certainty. But moving away from the town would put distance between her husband and the temptations of a saloon there. Bankhead had begun to spend his days and nights at this saloon, returning to Carlton and sometimes even showing up at Monticello drunk and, on occasion, violent. "I have seen him ride his horse into the barroom at Charlottesville," Edmund Bacon recalled in his memoirs. "I have seen his wife run from him when he was drunk and hide in a potato hole to get out of danger."

Ann's motives were complicated, surely, by the fact that she cared deeply what her grandfather, her parents, and her siblings thought of her husband

and their marriage. If the Bankheads were to move to less populous Bedford County, her husband's temptations to drink might be lessened. But it is also true that, if they lived farther from Monticello, his behavior might be more easily concealed.

This would be a season of disappointments and disturbances for Jefferson, who had turned sixty-eight in the spring. His summer trip to Poplar Forest had to be postponed when he was afflicted with what he called rheumatism, a term that has been abandoned as medically imprecise, but which was probably rheumatoid arthritis. He felt severe pain when he tried to move, he told Benjamin Rush, and suffered from a "total prostration of the muscles of the back, hips and thighs" that prevented him from walking.

Jefferson, who had begun to fret about his physical health, was also fearful of mental deterioration. He had "forgotten much" of his mathematical knowledge, Jefferson told Rush. He found that he could regain what he had lost, but with greater difficulty than when he had first learned it. It is strange "that old men should not be sensible that their minds keep pace with their bodies in the progress of decay," he wrote. Had nothing else impelled him to retire from public life, "the fear of becoming a dotard, and of being insensible of it, would of itself have resisted all solicitations to remain."

There were days that summer when it seemed that his entire family was sick. Martha Randolph, who at thirty-eight had already given birth to ten children and was again pregnant, suffered for nearly six weeks from dysentery, an illness not uncommon where, as at Monticello, supplies of fresh water are unreliable. No sooner had Martha recovered than she had a miscarriage. "My children have also been all of them sick," she reported. A sister-in-law, Harriet Randolph Hackley, visited Monticello that summer, and she, too, became ill.

In August, Jefferson was well enough to make his delayed journey to Poplar Forest, this time without Charles Bankhead. As a welcome rain soaked the fields, Jefferson, perhaps to exercise the mental faculties he feared he would lose, made elaborate geographical calculations of the latitude of Poplar Forest. This was the kind of abstract contemplation that he found so soothing but always felt compelled to tell himself and others had immediate practical application.

Such mental exercises kept worrisome realities at a manageable distance for only so long, however. On the last day of August, when Jefferson was back at

Monticello, he got word that his younger sister, the former Martha Jefferson and the widow of his boyhood friend Dabney Carr, was seriously ill. "Our dear mother is yeidling [*sic*] at length to the unconquerable force of her disease," Peter Carr wrote from Carrsbrook, their plantation on the far side of Charlottesville; "—she is perfectly helpless, knows no person, and is insensible to every thing. I did not think she could have lived through the last night—she cannot possibly survive many days."

Jefferson at once arranged to have his sister brought to Monticello. There, in the first week of September, as the last of the delphiniums and globe amaranths were in bloom, she "at last yielded to a wasting complaint which has for two or three years been gaining upon her," as he wrote to his brother, Randolph Jefferson. "Without any increase in pain, or any other than her gradual decay, she expired three days ago."

On September 5, Martha Jefferson Carr was buried next to her husband in the Monticello graveyard. Jefferson's grief was eased somewhat by the joy he felt at a new addition to the family. Within weeks of Mrs. Carr's death, Ann Bankhead gave birth to her second son, Jefferson's second great-grandchild. They named the boy Thomas Mann Randolph Bankhead, after Ann's father.

# CHAPTER 13

# "The Shock of an Earthquake"

At four A.M., on Monday, December 16, 1811, a sudden and violent shock awakened Jefferson in his Monticello bedchamber. The shudder that rumbled beneath him had originated almost eight hundred miles west, between Natchez and St. Louis. In Norfolk, the *New York Evening Post* reported, clocks "stopt, and doors, and things suspended from the ceilings of the shops and stores, oscillated violently."

Along the Mississippi River, the effects of what became known as the New Madrid earthquake were far more horrifying. An "awful noise resembling loud but distant thunder, but more hoarse and vibrating" was followed by "the complete saturation of the atmosphere, with sulfurious vapor, causing total darkness," one witness to the event recalled. "The screams of the affrighted inhabitants running to and fro, not knowing where to go, or what to do—the cries of the fowls and beasts of every species—the cracking of trees falling, and the roaring of the Mississippi—the current of which was retrograde for a few minutes . . . formed a scene truly horrible."

At first, the Mississippi seemed to recede from its banks, "its waters gathering up like a mountain," the same witness reported, leaving boats bound for New Orleans beached on bare sand. Then, after rising "fifteen to twenty feet perpendicularly, and expanding, as it were, at the same moment," the river overflowed its banks in a swift and massive wave. Groves of young cottonwood trees were ripped from the banks, and entire islands disappeared. Within hours, "the earth was horribly torn to pieces," with hundreds of acres "covered over, in various depths, by the sand which issued from the fissures."

In the series of aftershocks that continued for days, houses collapsed, people who had not fled their homes were trapped beneath them, "and blood was every where," one Louisville resident wrote. The Shawnees, who, the whites had thought, "were friendly[,] went crazy and them savages killed twenty four people. . . . A lot of people thinks that the devil has come here. Some thinks that this is the beginning of the world coming to a end. . . . If we do not get away from here the ground is going to eat us alive." The *New York Evening Post* reported that residents of Natchez feared "a mysterious visitation from the Author of all nature, on them for their sins."

The naturalistic explanations attempted by more sophisticated observers proved no more helpful. "The Comet has been passing to the westward since it passed its perihelion perhaps it has touched the mountain of California, that has give a small shake to this side of the Globe," the *Louisiana Gazette and Daily Advertiser* reported.

Jefferson attached no moral or spiritual significance to earthquakes or their destructive power. The grandeur of the natural order inspired his awe, but he regarded such awe as scientific rather than religious. The idea that there was divine retribution in an earthquake, flood, hurricane, or volcanic eruption, he considered superstitious. Nature is orderly, harmonious, and benevolent, he believed, working in all ways to create and sustain life rather than to destroy it. Examined with sufficient care, even forces that might appear destructive would ultimately be shown to be creative.

Jefferson's interest in earthquakes could not have been wholly impersonal, however. Nearly forty years earlier, he had witnessed the first recorded earthquake in Virginia history, and it must have taken on special significance through its effect on his own family. At just after 2:11 P.M., on February 21, 1774, he noted "a shock of an earthquake at Monticello" so violent that it shook the house, causing everybody inside to run out the door. About forty-five minutes later, another shock was felt, "as violent though not so long." The following afternoon, the earth rumbled again, the Rivanna overflowed its banks, and terrified slaves could scarcely be made to return to work. Perhaps unsettled by the earthquake, Jefferson's sister Elizabeth, the one "rather deficient in intellect," wandered off. Three days later, on February 24, her dead body was found in the swollen Rivanna.

Jefferson sought ways to reconcile his belief that nature was economical and benevolent not only with the natural order's destructive force but also with men's capacity for destroying one another. The conclusions that he reached in this attempt to explain the seemingly irreconcilable, however, made it difficult to render moral judgments about the deepest questions of human conduct. These conclusions also raised serious questions about ethics and how, or why, to reward virtue and punish vice. How virtue and vice might even be defined in this system of thought also became problematic.

Although Jefferson deplored war—his ill-fated embargo had been designed to avoid it—his assumptions about the natural order led him to conclude that war must have social utility. War between peoples, like predation among animals, for example, helped control population. "This pugnacious humor of mankind," he decided, was "provided [for] in the mechanism of the Universe."

Jefferson's belief that war served benevolent purposes did not prevent him from opposing it but did make it more difficult to justify this opposition. If man's destructive impulses were implanted by Nature's God for beneficial purposes, and war was one way in which these purposes were served, then by what rational calculation should it be opposed? And if such collective exercises in destruction as war served Nature's purposes, why not such acts by individuals? Why not murder? These were questions that Jefferson's philosophical system could never answer, so he wished them away. They were "metaphysical," and as such, beyond the interest of a scientist.

But even scientists are troubled when wars threaten to engulf them and their families and, in December 1811, another war seemed unavoidable. In early November, Jefferson had been expecting a visit from James and Dolley Madison, who were to be accompanied by Secretary of War William Eustis and Secretary of the Navy Paul Hamilton and their families, when a British sloop of war, in blatant defiance of law prohibiting British and French warships from entering U.S. territorial waters, refused to withdraw from Delaware Bay. This was only the most recent of a series of renewed provocations by Great Britain, which had refused to make restitution for the firing on the *Chesapeake* during Jefferson's presidency and had continued to harass American ships at sea, and, in the congressional elections of 1810, a group of "War Hawks," led by John C. Calhoun of South Carolina and Henry Clay of Kentucky, had swept into office, howling for revenge.

Canceling their trip to Monticello, Madison, Eustis, and Hamilton rode on to Washington, where the president told a special session of Congress of his "deep sense of the crisis" before them. "A person of perfect truth direct from Washington," Jefferson told John Eppes that same month, had informed him that the navy secretary swore to remove the British ships from Delaware Bay "by force if practicable." The British minister to the United States, Jefferson went on, "has explicitly and officially stated in writing that his government finds it necessary to take possession of the ocean and permit no commerce on it but thro the ports of Great Britain."

Jefferson had suspected for at least four years that the British were wedded to such a policy, he told Eppes. War, which he had hoped to prevent through his embargo, now "seems determined on their part & inevitable on ours."

Another war should have come as no shock to Jefferson, however. Nations had been too long accustomed to settling their differences by force rather than by reason, he had concluded. That this war would be waged against an Old World monarchy also was not shocking, because monarchies were inherently more belligerent than republics. France was "a conqueror roaming over the earth with havoc tumult and outrage," Jefferson had told Congressman Walter Jones, of Virginia, the year before, and England was "a pirate spreading misery and ruin over the face of the ocean." Fortunately for America, "the Mammoth cannot swim, nor the Leviathan move on dry land, and if we keep out of their way, they cannot get at us." A nation that could avoid war with either of these powers, remaining "afloat against the wreck of the world," he said, "will be immortalized in history."

America, Jefferson believed, would be able to show the rest of the world that there were rational ways to resolve disagreements, and independent farmers, tilling the soil of the vast North American territory, would point the way. The very act of settling these lands inculcated virtue, and on them alone would virtue be preserved.

The rumblings of the New Madrid earthquake ceased in Virginia on December 16, 1811. Except for disturbing the household in its sleep, the earthquake did not prevent life at Monticello from going on as it had before. Hundreds of miles to the west, however, the quake would play an eerie role in the lives of Isham Lewis, the nephew to whom Jefferson had taught surveying years earlier, and Isham's elder brother Lilburne Lewis, who had moved with their parents to Kentucky to start anew.

After visiting Monticello, Isham went to Natchez to seek employment as a surveyor but soon returned to Rocky Hill, Lilburne's farm. In Isham's absence, Lilburne's wife had died and he had begun a precipitous slide into bankruptcy accompanied by heavy drinking. On December 15, the day before the earthquake, Lilburne ordered a seventeen-year-old slave named George to fill a pitcher from a nearby stream. But when George dropped the pitcher and broke it, Isham and Lilburne hauled him into the plantation kitchen, tied him to the floor, and, assembling the other slaves, ordered them to build a fire in the fireplace. Announcing that he was going to teach the slaves a lesson about disobedience, Lilburne brought an ax down on George's neck. When the boy died, Lilburne ordered one of the other slaves to cut the body to pieces and throw it into the fire.

At two o'clock the next morning, whatever semblance of peace had returned to Rocky Hill was again shattered. The earthquake hit, and the fireplace into which George's body parts had been cast collapsed. When daylight came, Lilburne ordered the slaves to rebuild the chimney and directing their efforts, told them to seal up any unburned remains in the masonry, putting an end, it seemed, to the whole horrid ordeal.

Two months later, however, in February 1812, George's severed head was discovered being dragged about by one of the Lewises' dogs. In March, Jefferson's nephews were indicted for murder, spent the night in jail, and then were released on bail. In April, while awaiting trial, Lilburne and Isham entered into a suicide pact. The following day, when their plan was to be carried out, proved appropriately forbidding. Clouds covered the sky, and a few miles downriver, the Ohio overflowed its banks. Just before noon, the ground shook again, and for some ten minutes, witnesses swore, compass needles did not point north.

The brothers met in the Rocky Hill graveyard, leaving a note with the "request to be entered in the same coffin & in the same grave." Their plan was to shoot each other simultaneously, as combatants might in a duel. At some point in their frenzied last-minute discussions, Isham would testify, Lilburne's flintlock rifle accidentally discharged. Lilburne dropped to the ground and bled to death on his wife's grave.

Panicked, Isham fled. A few days later, this "young man of excellent dispositions, correct conduct, & good understanding," as Jefferson had once described him, was captured, indicted for aiding in a suicide—which was, legally speaking, murder—and jailed a second time. He then escaped.

Jefferson surely knew of these macabre events. He remained in contact with the sisters of Isham and Lilburne for several years afterward. As their poverty deepened, these nieces of Jefferson's tried to borrow money from him, without success. There is no evidence that Jefferson ever acknowledged his nephews' actions.

# CHAPTER 14

# Old Friends Reunited

On January 21, 1812, Jefferson awoke at Monticello to clear skies, mild temperatures, and the pleasant surprise, later that day, of a letter from John Adams.

This letter was the first that Jefferson had received from Adams since 1801, when Jefferson had just defeated the prickly Boston Federalist for president. Their once strong friendship had suffered greatly during the bruising campaign that resulted in Jefferson's victory and Adams's humiliating defeat. The two candidates represented contrasting ideas about the kind of country America should be, and it proved impossible during this venomous contest to separate the personal from the political.

Jefferson's supporters had claimed that Adams was a vain and petty monarchist whose presidency was "one continued tempest of *malignant* passions," whose support for the Alien and Sedition Acts revealed his desire for despotic power, and whose hostility to France would plunge the nation into war with America's ally in its struggle for independence from Great Britain. Exhibiting equal hostility to blacks, Native Americans, and Virginia aristocrats, Adams's supporters called Jefferson "the son of a half-breed Indian squaw, sired by a Virginia mulatto farmer," a swindler, and, as governor of Virginia, a coward. This devious atheist, too much influenced by his Jacobin friends in France, would have the Bible "cast into a bonfire" and children would be "chanting mockeries against God."

Enough "abuse and scandal" was unleashed in that contest, Abigail Adams complained, "to ruin and corrupt the minds and morals of the best people in the world." Adams, who took everything personally, held Jefferson responsible for what his surrogates said, and Jefferson's studied refusal to take anything personally only incensed his touchy opponent all the more. When the votes were counted, and Jefferson proved immensely more popular than Adams, a friendship begun when they met as delegates to the Continental Congress almost twenty-five years earlier had fallen victim to political antagonism, hurt feelings, and, on Adams's part, some measure of sheer spite. Their last meeting before Adams left Washington had been unpleasant, and neither had forgotten it.

Even so, that last letter, dated March 24, 1801, suggested the affection, respect, and fellow-feeling that could exist between fathers, if not between political opponents. Jefferson had passed along unopened a package intended for his predecessor. Adams expressed his gratitude, adding that had Jefferson opened the package, he might have felt "a moment of Melancholly or at least of Sympathy with a mourning Father." In the package was mentioned the death of Adams's son Charles, aged thirty, from causes "which have been the greatest Grief of my heart and the deepest affliction of my Life." Charles Adams had drunk himself to death. Because Jefferson had no son, it "is not possible that any thing of this kind should happen to you, and I sincerely wish you may never experience any thing in any degree resembling it."

Adams closed the 1801 letter by noting that New England "is in a state of perfect Tranquility and I See nothing to obscure your prospect of a quiet and prosperous Administration, which I heartily wish you."

That, for more than a decade, was the end of their friendship. As Jefferson worked to overturn the programs and policies for which Adams, as president, had labored, communication between the two ceased.

In the summer of 1811, an Albemarle neighbor and friend of Jefferson spent two days with John Adams during a visit to Massachusetts. This was Edward Coles, born at Enniscorthy plantation in 1786. A relative through marriage to James Madison and Patrick Henry and a graduate of the College of William and Mary, Coles was also Madison's private secretary. He had heard Jefferson's account of their last meeting, and during his trip to Massachusetts, he heard Adams's version.

When Jefferson first called on his defeated predecessor, Adams said, he felt Jefferson had come too soon, as if to gloat. This had not been Jefferson's intention, Coles responded. Recalling what Jefferson had told him of the meeting, Coles explained how, "knowing Mr. Adams' sensitiveness," Jefferson had deliberately sought to assuage his old friend's feelings. Figuring out what time might be least likely to offend, Jefferson had gone to the President's House but realized, from Adams's expression, that he had miscalculated. Adams approached Jefferson in "a hurried and agitated step," Coles said, crying, "You have turned me out, you have turned me out!"

In reply, Jefferson had been as high-minded and verbose as Adams was succinct. Rarely had plainspoken New England and the grandiloquent South revealed themselves so vividly, or so comically. "I have not turned you out, Mr. Adams," Jefferson replied. The voters had simply chosen between two contrasting approaches to government. The contest was "not one of a personal character, between John Adams and Thomas Jefferson, but between the advocates and opponents of certain political opinions and measures, and, therefore, should produce no unkind feelings between the two men who happened to be placed at the head of the two parties."

As Coles related Jefferson's version of this last meeting, Adams said that his visitor could "not have given a more accurate account."

"Mr. Jefferson said I was sensitive, did he?" Adams asked Coles. "Well, I *was* sensitive."

The more Coles talked about his Albemarle neighbor, the more Adams loosened up. "I always loved Jefferson, and still love him," he said finally.

"That is enough for me," Jefferson said when told of Adams's comment. "I only needed this knowledge to revive towards him all the affections of the most cordial moments of our lives." Adams was "an honest man, often a great one, but sometime incorrect and precipitate in his judgments." Anyone who ever heard Jefferson speak of Adams knew that he "defended him when assailed by others, with the single exception as to political opinions."

Benjamin Rush reported to Adams how their mutual friend responded to the news of Coles's visit and, on New Year's Day, 1812, Adams cast aside the accumulated grievances of a dozen years and wrote his friend a letter. Appealing once more to the bond the two men shared as conscientious fathers, Adams sent Jefferson two volumes of *Lectures on Rhetoric and Oratory* that his son John Quincy Adams had delivered as a professor at Harvard. These Jefferson pronounced a "mine of learning and taste." The ice had been broken.

A letter from you [Jefferson wrote] carries me back to the times when, beset with difficulties and dangers, we were fellow laborers in the same cause, struggling with what is most valuable to man, his right of self-government. Laboring always at the same oar, with some wave ever ahead threatening to overwhelm us and yet passing under our bark, we knew not how, we rode through the storm with heart and hand, and made a happy port.

They were both old men now, Jefferson allowed. "Of the signers of the Declaration of Independance I see now living not more than half a dozen on your side of the Potomak, and, on this side, myself alone." Both had been blessed with good health. Jefferson lived "in the midst of my grandchildren, one of whom"—Ann Bankhead—"has lately promoted me to be a great grandfather."

After requesting more news, Jefferson closed. "No circumstances," he wrote, "have lessened the interest I feel in these particulars respecting yourself; none have suspended for one moment my sincere esteem for you; and I now salute you with unchanged affections and respect."

With this exchange of pleasantries began one of the most learned and provocative correspondences—literary, philosophical, political, and scientific—in the history of the American republic. The two statesmen corresponded through sickness and loss, when both complained that answering most of the mail they received had become a burden. Adams provided most correspondents with "gruff, short, unintelligible, mysterious, enigmatical, or pedantical answers," but his letters to Jefferson, while feisty, were also thorough and forthright. Jefferson's to Adams, though fewer in number, were unfailingly thoughtful and affectionate. They would write to each other about world events, the books they were reading, the pleasures and heartbreaks of family life, and, as the years passed, death and what, if anything, lay beyond. The one subject they would discuss only once—many years later—was slavery.

Jefferson thought a great deal about slavery as an abstract political, social, philosophical, and economic question. But, as a slaveholder, he also dealt with slavery as a day-to-day reality. And in April 1812, when he and Adams began a lengthy discussion of the sociology of American Indians, Jefferson faced the unpleasant duty of deciding what to do about one of the black men he owned.

This was Jame Hubbard, a skilled craftsman who had worked in Jefferson's nail-making factory and later on construction of the house at Poplar Forest. In the spring of 1811, Hubbard had slipped away but was spotted in Lexington, Virginia, in the southwestern part of the state. Hubbard had run off once before, in 1805. That time he had been jailed at Fairfax Court House, and Jefferson had to pay $35 to secure his release and another $20 to have him hauled home. After Hubbard ran off the second time and was seen in Lexington, Jefferson again hired a man to recapture him. But by the time the slave-catcher

RANAWAY, from his plantation, in Albemarle, a negro man called JAMES HUBBARD of the property of the Subscriber, living in Bedford, a Nailor by trade, of 27 years of age, about six feet high, stout limbs and strong made, of daring demeanor, bold and harsh features, dark complexion, apt to drink freely and had even furnished himself with money and probably a free pass; on a former elopement he attempted to get out of the State Northwardly, and was taken and confined in Halifax Jail for some time, being then the property of Thomas Jefferson, and probably may have taken the same direction now; whoever apprehends the said slave, and delivers him to the Subscriber in Bedford county, or into the Jail of either Albemarle or Bedford, shall receive Forty Dollars in addition to what the law allows.

REUBEN PERRY.

April 12.                                              w4w

"*Ran away, from his plantation, in Albemarle, a negro man.*" *Jefferson seeks the return of a slave. The* Richmond Enquirer, *April 12, 1811.*

made it to Lexington, Hubbard had fled farther, to Pendleton County in what is now West Virginia. Again Jefferson dispatched the slave-catcher, and this time he brought Hubbard back in shackles, earning $70 for his services.

"I had him severely flogged in the presence of his old companions and committed to jail," Jefferson told Reuben Perry, the carpenter he had hired to supervise the construction at Poplar Forest. By now, however, Jefferson believed that the moment Hubbard was "out of jail and his irons off," he would escape again. He therefore wished Perry to sell Hubbard "out of the state."

Selling a slave "out of the state" almost always meant selling him to a cotton or rice planter from the Deep South, or to a slave trader who supplied labor to such a planter. The move from Virginia to, say, Louisiana, meant a harsh fate indeed. In the swamplands of the Deep South, field hands could be worked to death with chilling dispatch.

Jefferson rarely punished slaves this severely and, by the standards of his time and place, he was a humane master. He regarded black people as individuals—less intellectually advanced than whites, but individuals all the same—and, in his personal dealings with slaves, he treated them with respect. Although he eventually turned over the management of his farms to Jeff Randolph, he still established the broad policies by which the farms were run, which included recognition of the slaves' physical and emotional needs. Jefferson left it to his overseers, however, to administer whippings as they saw fit.

Jefferson's account books indicate that no matter how dire his own finances he never stinted in the provisioning of slaves. Year in and year out, in war and peace, through good harvest and bad, the slaves received new clothes and new blankets. When sick, they were not forced to work, and they received medical attention as needed. A few weeks before he expressed his desire that Hubbard be sold "out of the state," Jefferson found that trade with Great Britain had made it impossible to buy more clothes for the slaves. Determined that they not do without, he installed his own spinning jenny and loom at Monticello. From then on, the slaves' clothing was manufactured at home.

Whether Hubbard was ever sold "out of the state" is not known, though Jefferson and Perry entered into a complicated and mutually advantageous transaction involving the skilled, if undependable, slave. In April 1812, while Hubbard was still missing from Poplar Forest, Jefferson agreed to sell him to Perry for $300. If Hubbard returned, and Perry seems to have believed he would, the carpenter would owe Jefferson an additional $200. Then Perry could either continue to use Hubbard on construction projects, or he could sell him. A skilled slave in his mid-twenties might be worth twice or three times the price Perry would pay, meaning Perry could realize a sizable profit.

This represented a gamble on Perry's part, but a manageable one: because Perry, as a carpenter, would not be likely to lay hands on $300, much less $500, he agreed to work off the debt to Jefferson "in Carpentry or House-joinery." The benefit to Jefferson was clear as well. From now on, the troublesome Hubbard would be somebody else's problem. In effect, Jefferson agreed to pay for work on his house by selling a slave.

Jefferson was always more concerned with the culture of American Indians than with that of African-American slaves, an interest that he and Adams shared. Jefferson had excavated a mound built by Indians near his father's property, studied their languages, and collected examples of their weapons, clothing, and other artifacts, which he displayed at Monticello. In June 1812, Jefferson told Adams that he had become curious about the Indians as a youth. Shadwell, Jefferson's childhood home, was on the road from the Shenandoah Valley to Williamsburg, and when representatives of the Indian tribes journeyed to the colonial capital, they camped there.

Jefferson had heard "the great Outassete, the warrior and orator of the Cherokees," deliver a stirring oration to his people before departing for a mission to England. "The moon was in full splendor, and to her he seemed to address himself in his prayers for his own safety on the voyage, and that of his people during his absence. His sounding voice, distinct articulation, animated action, and the solemn silence of his people at their several fires, filled me with awe and veneration, altho' I did not understand a word he uttered." The Cherokees and Creeks are "far advanced in civilization," with their good cabins, enclosed fields, and herds of cattle and hogs. Some could read and write, and others were skilled craftsmen. As a people, he decided, the Cherokees and Creeks seemed capable of making still greater progress.

Adams "also felt an Interest in the Indians and a Commiseration for them from my Childhood," he told Jefferson. The Punkapaugs and Neponsits had visited Adams's boyhood home in Braintree. A large family of Indians lived in a wigwam within a mile of Peacefield, his current home, "and I in my boyish Rambles used to call at their Wigwam, where I never failed to be treated with Whortle Berries, Blackberries, Strawberries or Apples, Plumbs, Peaches, etc." All the Indian girls "went out to Service and the Boys to Sea, till not a Soul is left." The disappearance of his Indian neighbors was not an unhappy turn of events, Adams had decided. "I remember the Time when Indian Murders, Scalpings, Depredations and conflagrations were as frequent on the Eastern and Northern Frontier of Massachusetts as they are now in Indiana, and spread as much terror."

Neither Jefferson nor Adams allowed youthful encounters with the Indians to prevent him from believing that they were a problem to be dealt with, especially when another war with Great Britain loomed. Any such war was likely to be fought not only against the British, but also against their allies in Tecumseh's Indian confederacy. Convinced that British agents based in Canada were inciting the Shawnees under Tecumseh to slaughter whites in the old Northwest Territory, Jefferson and Adams agreed that the way to prevent such attacks was to have U.S. troops expel the British from Canada and seize it. The conquest of Canada, Adams wrote, "will quiet the Indians forever and be as great a Blessing to them as to Us."

Jefferson, who had taken such drastic measures to avoid war with Great Britain three years earlier, showed no reluctance to fight if that was what it took to subdue the Indians. Driving the British out of Canada was the least that would be required, Jefferson wrote. Indians who "have made any progress" would be unlikely to succumb to "English seductions," but "the backward . . . will relapse into barbarism and misery, lose numbers by war and want, and we shall be obliged to drive them, with the beasts of the forest into the Stony Mountains." Annexing Canada "secures our women and children for ever from the tomahawk and scalping knife, by removing those who excite them."

The "doors of Congress will re-open with a Declaration of war," Jefferson predicted. The order to take Canada probably had already been issued.

## CHAPTER 15
## *At War Again*

Jefferson's prediction proved true. On June 1, 1812, President Madison asked for a declaration of war against Great Britain. Congress, granting the request, authorized the call-up of a hundred thousand militiamen, and, by June 19, the nation was again at war.

Preparations had been well under way for some months. In the spring, Congress, at Madison's request, imposed a temporary embargo on trade with Great Britain that recalled Jefferson's own failed experiment in "peaceful coercion." But Jefferson had changed his mind about embargoes, just as he had about war: now he viewed restrictions on trade with Great Britain not as a national leader seeking to defend American maritime interests, but as a farmer with crops to sell.

Virginia planters hurried to unload their product as fast as they could, but, Jefferson told Madison, those in the Piedmont had been able to dispose of only about a third of their flour or wheat and about three quarters of their tobacco. Estimating that farmers throughout the state were equally victimized, Jefferson urged Madison to reconsider the policy.

He wrote to Madison to say that if the embargo was primarily defensive in nature—"merely to keep our vessels and men out of harm's way"—then the planters should not be prevented from moving their produce to British markets on British ships. Now Jefferson urged that trade should continue even in wartime. Unless Madison really believed that a shortage of flour "will starve Great Britain, the sale of the remaining produce will be rather desirable . . . even in war, and even to our enemies," Jefferson argued. Such trade would be "mutually advantageous to the individuals, and not to their injury as belligerents." Americans, he said, "would go thro' a war with much less impatience if they could dispose of their produce." If not, "they will soon become querulous and clamor for peace."

The question would very quickly be moot, for by late spring of 1812, the

British had blockaded the Delaware and Chesapeake Bays as well as the ports at Charleston and Savannah, and sealed off the mouth of the Mississippi. By mid-June, however, worsening economic conditions in England, exacerbated by the end of trade with America, led Great Britain to reconsider its own course. Unaware, owing to the slowness of communications, that the United States had declared war, Parliament suspended the Orders in Council that forbade neutral shipping to and from France and thus effectively abandoned its only justification for harassing American ships, which had been the casus belli. This time "peaceful coercion" had worked, only not soon enough.

Deprived of a great deal of his agricultural income during the war, Jefferson turned to other sources for money. Many years earlier, he had persuaded his friend Philip Mazzei, a Florentine horticulturist, to settle near Monticello, plant grapes, and attempt to introduce winemaking to Virginia. Mazzei purchased a plantation near Monticello and two lots in Richmond, on one of which a house was built. He then returned to Europe in 1785. Jefferson promised to look after these properties in his friend's absence, and, in 1796, he sold the plantation but held on to the lots. In 1813, he put the lots on the market and quickly found a buyer. By this time, they were worth much more than Mazzei had paid for them.

Profits from the sale came to more than $6,000, but the British blockade made it impractical, Jefferson said, to send the money to Mazzei in Italy. Rather than reinvest it—Jefferson did not trust banks, Dumas Malone explains in his account of these transactions—he loaned the money to himself at 6 percent interest, promising to send interest payments annually. If Mazzei asked for the principal, Jefferson would give himself two years to pay it.

Jefferson thus functioned in this transaction as both lender and borrower of another man's money from a sale that Jefferson had made at his own discretion. "Suffice it to say here," Malone concludes in his generous rendition of this questionable arrangement, "that in an abnormal time Jefferson eased his immediate difficulties by incurring another debt on the assumption that things would surely get better."

They did not. On learning that Jefferson had sold his property, Mazzei demanded immediate payment. It was not made, and in 1816, when Mazzei died unreimbursed, Jefferson told his friend's heirs that he would repay the entire amount in three annual installments, to begin the following year. Citing poor harvests, he failed to keep this promise, too, and proposed paying the interest each year and the principal as soon as he could. Mazzei's heirs accepted this arrangement.

In 1818, Jefferson paid what he owed in back interest, but by this time, the principal amounted to $7,400, with interest coming to $444 a year. Jefferson never made any payments on the principal. On his deathbed, he spoke of these debts to his grandson Jeff Randolph, who promised to pay them.

By the summer of 1813, when Jefferson sold Mazzei's Richmond property, the war with Great Britain was being fought on the Great Lakes, in the old Northwest Territory, and off coastal towns from Charleston to Mobile. In April, U.S. troops burned government buildings in York (now Toronto), the capital of Canada. This infuriated the British, who, as Jefferson and Adams had predicted, encouraged the Shawnees, Creeks, and other Indian tribes to wage war not only on American soldiers but also on American settlers.

These attacks led Jefferson to abandon long-held beliefs about the Indians and their position in American society, beliefs that he had begun to reconsider by the time he and Adams resumed their correspondence. His patience with the Indians and with their English sponsors, Jefferson wrote the naturalist Alexander von Humboldt in December 1813, had run out.

"We spared nothing to keep them at peace with one another, to teach them agriculture and the rudiments of the most necessary arts, and to encourage [them to engage in] industry." Had they adopted the ways of the settlers with greater dedication, Jefferson said, the Indians "would have mixed their blood with ours, and been amalgamated and identified with us within no distant period of time." Unfortunately, the British have

> defeated all our labors for the salvation of these unfortunate people. They have seduced the greater part of the tribes within our neighborhood, to take up the hatchet against us, and the cruel massacres they have committed on the women and children of our frontiers . . . will oblige us now to pursue them to extermination, or drive them to new seats beyond our reach.

Since the British were to blame for inciting the Indians, whatever bleak fate befell these unfortunate people would be Great Britain's fault. This was not the first time Jefferson had blamed Great Britain for America's treatment of a nonwhite race. In the Declaration of Independence, Jefferson also held the British responsible for the slave trade and, therefore, for slavery itself.

Faced with a problem not of their making, Jefferson decided, Americans would simply have to handle the matter as best they could. "The confirmed brutalization, if not the extermination of this race in America," he told Von Humboldt, "is therefore to form an additional chapter in the English history of the same colored man in Asia, and of the brethren of their own color in Ireland, and wherever else Anglo-mercantile cupidity can find a two-penny interest in deluging the earth with human blood."

By fall, Jefferson's patience with the deprivations of war was also wearing thin. Although he never realized the irony of his position, Jefferson began to sound much like a New England merchant at the time of his own embargo. Sometimes he wondered what was to become not only of his family but also of Virginia itself.

We can indeed make enough to eat, drink and clothe ourselves; But nothing for our salt, iron, groceries and taxes, which must be paid in money. For what can we raise for the market? Wheat? We can only give it to our horses, as we have been doing ever since harvest. Tobacco? It's not worth the pipe it is smoked in. Some say whiskey; but all mankind must become drunkards to consume it.

Still, he concluded, "we shall not flinch. We must consider now, as in the Revolutionary war, that although the evils of resistance are great, those of submission would be greater."

One man determined not to submit was Tom Randolph, Jefferson's son-in-law. In the spring of 1813, Randolph was seized, in Jefferson's words, by an attack of "military fever." If he did not fight in at least one battle, Randolph declared in June, he "would be unhappy for life." This desire for glory on the field of battle would have been understandable, Jefferson felt, in a younger man with fewer responsibilities; such patriotism was indeed admirable. Randolph, however, was forty-three and the father of eight, with a seventh daughter they named Septimia on the way. Randolph's financial situation was as precarious as Jefferson's, and military service meant he would not be at Edgehill to supervise the farming. "He will be a great loss to his family and no man in the world a greater one to his affairs," Jefferson told Mrs. Trist.

Undaunted, Randolph joined the Army of the United States, with the rank of colonel and command of the 20th Regiment of Infantry. In August, he was ordered with his soldiers to Sackett's Harbor on Lake Ontario, where they were to join a larger march down the St. Lawrence River to assault Montreal. The 20th reached Sackett's Harbor in October, only to find that the main army had already left. United in November with this larger force near the entrance to the St. Lawrence, Randolph participated in the successful assault on British-held Fort Mathilda, which the 20th torched. When the army went into winter quarters, Randolph, granted leave, headed home.

Over the next several months, while Randolph remained in Albemarle, Jefferson worried that his son-in-law might "try another campaign." In December 1813, Randolph declared that, although he remained "impatient to risk honor, fortune, life" to defend Virginia, he would not return to active duty unless offered the rank of brigadier general. The offer never came.

In February 1814, however, Colonel Randolph was ordered to report to Leesburg to begin preparations for a spring campaign. When he asked for a

*Seized at forty-three by an attack of "military fever."*
*Thomas Mann Randolph, Jr., Jefferson's impulsive, irrational son-in-law.*

delay, his superiors told him that they regarded such a request as a resignation, and his command of the 20th Regiment was withdrawn.

Throughout the war, Jefferson somehow managed to make sure that work continued on his new house at Poplar Forest. During four rainy weeks there in the summer of 1814, he supervised the construction of what he called a "wing of offices." By offices, Jefferson meant workrooms—a dairy, a kitchen, a cook's room, and a smokehouse. These offices were linked by a verandah, extending 110 feet from the house eastward.

Here again, Jefferson's astonishing ingenuity and architectural gifts were on display. As at Monticello, this service wing was built into the slope of a hill, so that, from the south, all that could be seen was a low stone wall running from the house to the eastern mound. From the north, however, the walkway was both clearly visible and easily accessible. Although the individual rooms varied in size, depending upon the use to which they would be put, their doors were equidistant from one another to give an impression of perfect symmetry, balance, and order, and to make the rooms appear to be of the same dimension.

The office wing made the structure more practical, but it also increased the cost of construction at a time when it was all Jefferson could do to maintain Monticello. Although he estimated that the office wing would make the house worth at least $10,000, an immense sum in those days, historians who have studied the costs of its construction agree that his income from the Bedford County farms alone would never had covered it. The only way that work at Poplar Forest could have gone forward during the war seems clear: Jefferson used some or all of the $6,000 that he received from the sale of his friend Mazzei's property.

However enormous the cost, work on the house at Poplar Forest served to distract Jefferson from the war which, by that summer, was going badly. With the British menacing towns along the Chesapeake Bay, state officials, fearing that Richmond might be attacked, called out the militia. Ordered back to active duty, Tom Randolph was assigned to the 2nd Regiment of Virginia Cavalry and told to report to Camp Fairfield, outside Richmond.

On August 19, while militiamen were still assembling at Camp Fairfield, the British landed 4,500 troops at Benedict, Maryland, on the Patuxent River southeast of Washington. In heat so intense some soldiers collapsed before firing a shot, the British brushed aside an American force at Bladensburg and, at twilight on August 24, marched into a silent and largely deserted Washington. That night, they knocked out the windows of the Capitol, broke the locks, and set the building ablaze. Before long, flames engulfed the President's House, the Treasury Building, the War Office, and the Navy Yard.

Building up the defenses of Richmond, state officials appointed Randolph to command a special mobile force of six hundred of the "finest youth in Virginia," as William Fitzhugh Gordon, one of the volunteers, put it, and gave Randolph the rank of lieutenant colonel. On September 7, he ordered his men to take up a defensive position at the head of the York River. Their ranks were soon strengthened by the arrival of a company of light artillery, which included Jeff Randolph, the camp commander's twenty-one-year-old son.

In the malarial swamps near the old battlefield at Yorktown, the men had little to do but drill. Lieutenant Colonel Randolph, "with all his chivalry about him," as Gordon observed, put the troops through maneuvers until their horses were worn out. The drinking water soon went bad, fever swept through the muddy camp, and provisions ran low. Struggling to feed their own families, farmers were not eager to share their meager produce, and Randolph was able to obtain food for his men only "by force and after a painful search." Even then, he told Jefferson, he had to pay "a price that was sometimes half again more than [the food was] worth." (Writing to his grandfather on September 9, Jeff Randolph reported that the troops "have nothing in abundance, but ticks and musketoes.")

In mid-September, when the British had been repulsed at Baltimore and no longer posed a threat to Virginia, the American forces disbanded. Back in Albemarle, Jeff Randolph and his father read in the newspapers that before setting fire to the U.S. Capitol, the British had entered the upper floor of the Senate. There they destroyed the congressional library of three thousand volumes that Jefferson, during his years as a diplomat in Europe, had devoted much time and care to assemble.

# CHAPTER 16

# "This Enterprise Is for the Young"

In early August 1814, just after American and British troops clashed at Lundy's Lane near Niagara Falls, Jefferson received a letter from Edward Coles, the same young Albemarle neighbor who had helped reconcile Jefferson and Adams three years earlier.

Coles, now twenty-seven, faced a moral crisis and, believing that Jefferson would be sympathetic to his plight, sought the older man's counsel. At the College of William and Mary, Coles had come under the influence of one of his instructors, a cousin of President Madison's also named James Madison. The Episcopal bishop of Virginia, this James Madison was a man of enlightened views who envisioned the United States as a "New Jerusalem." This "New Jerusalem," however, was threatened from within by the sin of slavery, which was not only unjust to the slaves but also corrupted their owners. This was a view that Coles had come to share and that he believed Jefferson shared as well. Upon his father's death, Coles had inherited a plantation and the twenty-three slaves attached to it. Convinced that slavery was evil, Coles was determined not to be a slaveholder himself and to do justice to the black people he now owned. But he saw no realistic way to accomplish these goals. He could sell his slaves, but that meant they would become the property of men who, not sharing his opposition to slavery, would be less likely than he to treat them well. He could free them, but under Virginia law, they would be required to leave the state within a year of their emancipation. Once they were gone, they would presumably have to fend for themselves, without money, property, or political rights.

As he struggled with his dilemma, Coles came to the unhappy realization that he hated slavery more than he loved Virginia, which opened up a third possibility. If Virginia did not soon adopt more humane laws regarding slaves or did not outlaw slavery outright, Coles might feel it necessary to leave the state himself, taking his slaves with him. On July 31, 1814, eager to avoid such a drastic step, Coles wrote to Jefferson, urging him to take up the cause of abolition himself and rallying younger men like Coles around him. "I never took up my pen with more hesitation, or felt more embarrassment," Coles began, "than I do in addressing you on the subject of this letter."

> The fear of appearing presumptuous distresses me, and would deter me from venturing thus to call your attention to a subject of such magnitude, and so beset with difficulty as that of a general emancipation of the slaves of Virginia, had I not the highest opinion of your goodness and liberality, in not only excusing me for the liberty I take, but in justly appreciating my motives for doing so.

Coles would not belabor Jefferson on moral and political implications of slavery, which "are better understood by you than by me." But he would "beseech you to exert your knowledge and influence in devising and getting into operation some plan for the great gradual emancipation of slavery." Such an effort

> devolves particularly on you, from your known philosophical and enlarged view of subjects, and from the principles you have professed and practiced through a long and useful life, pre-eminently distinguished as well by being foremost in establishing on the broadest basis the rights of man, and the liberty and independence of your country, as in being throughout honored with the most important trust by your fellow citizens, whose confidence and love you have carried with you into the shades of old age and retirement.

In his retirement, Jefferson might, "with much addition to your own fame," advance even further "those hallowed principles contained in that renown[ed] Declaration of which you were the immortal author." Even if his efforts did not meet with immediate success, Jefferson's glory would be that much greater when they did prevail. Imagine then "what influence . . . the opinions and writings of Thomas Jefferson [will] have in all questions connected with the rights of man."

At the very least, Jefferson could leave mankind with a plan of how best to end slavery, "so that the weight of your opinion may be on the side of emancipation when that question shall be agitated, and that it will be sooner or later is most certain. That it may be soon is my most ardent prayer—that it will be, rests with you."

Coles offered one final explanation for addressing Jefferson so boldly. Since he had been old enough to think about slavery, Coles had found the institution so "repugnant" that he could not in good conscience keep the slaves that he inherited. If he remained in Virginia, he would have to sell his slaves or free them, and, because neither selling them, nor freeing them in Virginia, seemed a realistic course, Coles had begun to consider leaving the state, "and with it all my relations and friends." Taking his slaves with him, he could move to free territory, where, together, they could settle as free men. As bold as such a move was, and as ripe with glorious possibility, it was also one that Coles was reluctant to make. He loved Virginia, yet he also wanted to do right by his slaves, a dilemma he asked Jefferson to help him resolve.

"This I hope will be deemed by you some excuse for the liberty of this intrusion, of which I gladly avail myself to assure you of the very great respect and esteem for which I am, my dear Sir, your very sincere and devoted friend, Edward Coles."

Almost three weeks later, on August 25, 1814, Jefferson answered, in a letter that was characteristically thorough, thoughtful, and more revealing than he probably intended. While Coles was concerned, ultimately, with action—how a real slaveholder could free real slaves—Jefferson confined himself to philosophical, political, historical, and sociological abstraction.

The "sentiments breathed through [Coles's letter] do honor to both the head and heart of the writer," Jefferson began. His own opposition to slavery was well known, and the passage of time had only strengthened this conviction.

> The love of justice and the love of country plead equally the cause of these people, and it is a mortal reproach to us that they have pleaded it so long in vain, and should have produced not a single effort, nay I fear not much serious willingness, to relieve them and ourselves from our present condition of moral and political reprobation.

But Jefferson's early efforts in the Virginia House of Burgesses to end slavery had met such resistance that he had concluded that "nothing was to be hoped" from the present generation. To so much as even question slavery subjected the most blameless of men to unendurable social indignities. "Nursed and educated in the daily habit" of slaveholding, most Virginians in the 1770s considered black people "as legitimate subjects of property as their horses or cattle." Anyone attempting to persuade Virginia slaveholders otherwise was "denounced as an enemy to his country, and was treated with the grossest indecorum."

In the years since his service in the House of Burgesses,

I had always hoped that the younger generation, receiving their early impressions after the flame of liberty had been kindled in every breast, and had become as it were the vital spirit of every American; that the generous temperament of youth . . . would have sympathized with oppression wherever found, and proved their love of liberty beyond their own share of it.

This hope had been dashed. "Your solitary but welcome voice," he told Coles, "is the first which has brought this to my ear, and I have considered the general silence which prevails on this subject as indicating an apathy unfavorable to every hope." Even so, "the hour of emancipation is advancing on the march of time," whether by "the generous energy of our own minds, or by the bloody process of St. Domingo." There, some ten years before, the slaves under Toussaint L'Ouverture had risen up against their French masters and thrown off their oppressors.

A similar uprising could happen in America, especially now that the country was again at war with Great Britain. Whether the British would begin "offering asylum and arms to the oppressed, is a leaf our history has not yet turned over," Jefferson wrote. For that reason, driving out the invaders must take precedence, for now, over other considerations.

The method by which the slaves would be freed, "if permitted to be done by ourselves," had yet to be determined. Jefferson favored a program under which all slaves "born after a certain day" would be taught a trade and, "at a proper age," be expatriated, either to a territory of their own within the borders of the United States or to a foreign soil that they could colonize. This would allow time for a gradual replacement of slave labor with free labor, "and lessen the severity of the shock which an operation so fundamental cannot fail to produce."

Removal of these emancipated slaves was necessary, Jefferson believed, because blacks could never live as free people in the society that white Americans had established, without harm to the whites. To Jefferson's thinking, the idea that blacks might be assimilated into the larger society could appeal only to those who had no direct experience with Negroes, "or men probably of any

*"Like bidding old Priam to buckle on the armor of Hector."*
*Jefferson, at sixty-three, by Bass Otis.*

color." The "amalgamation [of blacks and whites] produces a degradation to which no lover of his country, no lover of excellence in the human character, can innocently consent." Black people "brought up from their infancy without necessity for thought or forecast, are by their habits rendered as incapable as children of taking care of themselves." Left to their own devices, they lacked even the capacity to care for their own offspring, "wherever industry is necessary for raising the young."

Jefferson was honored that Coles viewed him as the one person who could take on the "salubrious but arduous work" of leading a movement toward abolition. But this was "like bidding old Priam to buckle on the armor of Hector." "No," Jefferson wrote, "this enterprise is for the young, for those who can follow it up and bear it through to its consummation. It shall have all my prayers, and these are the only weapons of an old man."

For now, Coles should reconsider his desire to "abandon" Virginia if his native state did not conduct its business on the timetable he had established for it. Until more could be done for the blacks, "we should endeavor, with those whom fortune has thrown on our hands, to feed and clothe them well, protect them from ill usage, require such reasonable labor only as is performed voluntarily by freemen and be led to no repugnancies to abdicate them, and our duties to them."

Coles was correct that to sell his slaves would be "to commit them to those whose usage of them we cannot control." So he really had little choice but to "reconcile yourself to your country, and its unfortunate condition." Jefferson hoped, finally, that he would not diminish Virginia's population of antislavery men by leaving. Instead, he should "come forward in the public councils, become the missionary of this doctrine truly Christian, insinuate and inculcate it softly but steadily thro' the medium of writing and conversation." In time, Coles and those who thought as he did would succeed because "no good measure was ever proposed which, if duly pursued, failed to prevail in the end."

Jefferson closed on a note of mild encouragement. "That your success may be as speedy and complete, as it will be of honorable and immortal consolation to yourself, I shall as fervently and sincerely pray, as I assure you of my great friendship and respect."

Coles was not going to let the older man off this easily, however. Within the month, he responded, acknowledging that he felt "very sensibly your remarks on the propriety of yielding to my repugnancies in abandoning my property in slaves"—a course Coles never intended—"and my native State."

If there existed the slightest chance that he could transform public opinion, as Jefferson suggested, or by his own example as a slaveholder "ameliorate the condition of these oppressed people," Coles would not leave Virginia. Having never considered either as a real possibility, Coles in fact had devised a plan of his own, which required no man's encouragement, cooperation, or approval.

His plan was to move to the territory that is now Illinois, taking his slaves with him. There, across the Mississippi River from St. Louis, Coles would purchase land for "those who had been my slaves" and set them up as farmers and free men. Slaveholders who were serious about taking action to weaken slavery—action that might not free all slaves but could certainly free those who belonged to them—did not have to wait until everyone else agreed. They could act on their own. Such had been Coles's plan all along, and nothing Jefferson said had persuaded him to act otherwise.

As for Jefferson's prayers, Coles hoped that they would "not only be heard with indulgence in Heaven, but with influence on Earth." But he could not agree "that they are the only weapons of one your age; nor that the difficult task of cleansing the escutcheon of Virginia of the foul stain of slavery can best be done by the young." Eager to advance in life, young men too readily flowed "with the current of popular feeling" to take an independent and, indeed, controversial course. It was precisely because the antislavery position would be resisted so strongly that it could be advanced only "by those whose previous course of useful employment [gave them] the firmest footing in the confidence and attachment of their country." Only such men "have it in their power effectively to arouse and enlighten the public sentiment."

Even if the cause of emancipation were not controversial, it would require effort, energy, adjustment, and sacrifice on the part of those whose livelihood depended on slavery. Because the proponents of change would "contend against the weighty influence of habit and interest," only those "who have acquired a great weight of character" could lead this fight. This is why Coles had "looked to you, my dear Sir, as the first of our aged worthies to awaken our fellow-citizens from their infatuation to a proper sense of justice, and to the true interest of their country."

Was Jefferson really too old and feeble to undertake this cause?

Your time of life I had not considered as an obstacle to the undertaking. Doctor Franklin, to whom, by the way, Pennsylvania owes her early riddance of the evils of slavery, was as actively and as usefully employed on as arduous duties after he had past your age as he had ever been at any period of his life.

With apologizing for having given you so much trouble on this subject, and again repeating my thanks for the respectful and flattering attention you have been pleased to pay to it, I renew the assurances of the great respect and regard which makes me most sincerely yours.

There is no evidence that Jefferson replied to this second letter, and in all likelihood he did not. Coles was surely disappointed by the outcome of his efforts to elicit Jefferson's support, and he was certainly not persuaded by the older man to confine his efforts to "the public councils" and "the medium of writing and communications."

He could act, even if Jefferson would not. And if the younger man had trouble understanding Jefferson's immobility, there should be little surprise that Americans two centuries later would also find it difficult to comprehend or accept.

# CHAPTER 17

# *"When I Reflect That God Is Just"*

However much Thomas Jefferson's reply to Edward Coles's letters on slavery must have disappointed its recipient, and surely disappoints readers today, the reasoning behind the argument is more subtle than might appear.

Developed over years of practical political experience and scholarly study, Jefferson's approach to the problem of ending slavery, and of effecting radical social change of any kind, is at once more searching than has generally been granted, less self-serving than might be supposed, and yet nearly as imprisoning to thought and inhibiting to action as the political and economic realities that it attempted to explain. Jefferson's opinions on the subject are rooted in his understanding of human psychology—in, that is, his beliefs about ethics—and in his philosophy of history, which informed his attitudes about political and social change.

On August 30, 1814, five days after responding to Coles's first letter, Jefferson answered a letter from another friend who also sought advice. Hoping to help his son prepare for a career in law, the man asked Jefferson to recommend a course of study. In reply, Jefferson included a list of books under the heading "Ethics & Natl Religion." These included works by John Locke, Dugald Stewart, and Lord Kames, luminaries of the British and Scottish Enlightenment who believed that men possess an innate "moral sense."

This sense is much like the other senses, and one could learn more about it by studying the physiology of sight, for example, than by listening to "soothsayers and necromancers," as Jefferson had called clergymen in a letter the previous year. However much remained to be discovered about man's "moral sense," Jefferson said that it equipped men for life in community, for the Creator "would indeed have been a bungling artist," as he told Thomas Law on June 13, 1814, "had he intended man for a social animal, without planting in him social dispositions." It is through living in community that the moral sense is refined, and the test of whether an act is ethical is in its utility—to the individual, certainly, but more importantly, to the group.

It is a truism that Jefferson believed in human progress, but his was not a naïve belief that man's moral improvement over time was inevitable, or that it could be rushed. Jefferson believed that mankind progressed not, as Coles believed, through the acts of heroic individuals who set examples of moral excellence for others to imitate, but through the shared experience of the group as it inched its way toward a more enlightened society. Moral refinement advances by degrees, over time, and in response to specific historical circumstances.

And the great common experience of the settlers along the Atlantic coast was their break with Great Britain and—this had special meaning for Jefferson— the Declaration of Independence that, as he always insisted, distilled collective, rather than individual, aspirations. The achievement of American independence marked a significant moment in the history of human progress, and through it, the settlers had reached a new level of moral development. The continued existence of the republic established after the break with Great Britain could not be taken for granted. Even as Jefferson corresponded with Coles, British troops swarmed into Washington and burned the Capitol, while their warships menaced American waterways.

But Jefferson was encouraged that Virginia's young men had left their families and farms to resist the British, just as their fathers had done a generation earlier, moving ever closer to the republican ideal. The effort to protect their gains brought out in them the virtues on which self-government depended.

That the settlers who made this revolution were white was a fact of history—unfortunate, Jefferson believed, for those who were not white, but undeniable nonetheless. The settlers' refining experience, because it was an experience, could not be artificially transferred to blacks who, through no fault of their own, were not participants in it.

To Jefferson, who saw the crimes against blacks as national rather than individual in nature, blacks were not really Americans at all. They were Africans who had been dragged to this country against their will by Englishmen whose moral sense had not progressed as far as that of the more enlightened gentlemen of Jefferson's day. To whatever degree some black people might have adopted the ways of their white owners, or formed some agglomeration of English and African cultures, they nonetheless constituted a captive nation within U.S. borders. Whatever country a black man might choose to call his own, "it must be any other than one in which," Jefferson wrote in *Notes on the State of Virginia*, "he is born to live and labour for another."

Just as American whites had created their own nation along the Atlantic coast, African blacks in bondage within that nation would have to forge their own civilization, through unique historical experiences of their own. Only "as a free and independant people," Jefferson said, could they develop the virtuous habits of mind that would lift them up from that pitiable state into which they had been cast, and render them, too, capable of self-government.

This process could not be made easier than Nature had intended it to be. Their liberation would be a precondition of the development of blacks "as a free and independant people," but simply releasing them into the general population would surely create more problems than it would solve. Diffusion—populating the western territories with blacks and awaiting their assimilation into the white population—would not solve the problem either, because it would mean the extermination of the black race with no benefit to the whites. Considering the vast disparity in their levels of civilization, Jefferson believed, intermarriage between the two races would only hold back the whites. As he wrote in *Notes on the State of Virginia*, the "deep rooted prejudices" of the whites and "ten thousand recollections . . . of the injuries [blacks] have sustained" at their hands meant that coexistence on equal terms would "produce convulsions which will probably never end but in the extermination of the one or the other race."

The only sensible solution, Jefferson believed, lay in the expatriation of blacks to another land where they could participate in their own unique experience of self-determination and so forge their own national identity. Other advocates of "colonization" supported the transport of blacks from American soil simply to get rid of them. Sharing the racial prejudices of his day, Jefferson, too, wished to remove blacks from American soil. But he also believed that only settling on land of their own would enable them, too, to progress as a people, and he was sincere in his desire that they would do so.

Jefferson wanted to see slavery abolished voluntarily, by the free men of Virginia themselves. This would occur when, as a group, they came to see slavery for the crime against humanity that it was, but they could not be rushed to this conclusion. The refinement of the moral sense could not be enforced from without—opinions could not be compelled—and a decision that slavery must end should not be imposed, from without, against the will of Virginians or any other free people.

For others to force this decision upon them was to betray the Declaration of Independence and the American experiment in self-government that Jefferson believed was not only the great accomplishment of his own life, but also one of the great achievements of human history. The principles that this achievement established should not be violated, and the achievement itself threatened, because passionate people could not exercise patience.

"Truth advances," Jefferson observed, "and error recedes by steps only, and to do our fellow man the most good in our power, we must lead where we can, follow where we cannot, and still go with them, watching always the favorable moment for helping them to another step." On this basis, Jefferson chose what the historian John Chester Miller has called "the unheroic but eminently prudent policy of biding his time, awaiting the 'ripening' of public opinion." But as the blood-soaked breastworks, trenches, and rifle pits of Virginia would bear grim witness thirty-five years after Jefferson's death, these more enlightened attitudes would be long in coming.

That Jefferson could not act when urged to do more to end an institution that he acknowledged to be a moral wrong indicates the extent to which he was lacking in moral imagination. Trained up in the early forms of utilitarianism, Jefferson believed for most of his life that the proper subject of ethics was the maximization of human happiness. Happiness consists of tranquillity of soul, which is achieved not by the heroic gesture but through prudent conduct.

Ethics, to Jefferson, was little more than the process by which the rational individual chooses the most commonsense course from among a finite set of options. By reducing morality to a matter of rational selection and removing it from the "Gothic" influences of religious faith and practice, Jefferson ruled out the bold, the adventurous, and the imaginative, by which great challenges, such as ending slavery, might be accomplished. Reducing morality in this way also affords no place in the universe for the greatest mysteries of human existence—for good and evil, love, hate, tragedy, and inspiration.

This seems a surprisingly constricted view of the moral universe, especially from the author of the Declaration of Independence, with its soaring sense of human possibility. It is nonetheless the one by which Jefferson lived, even if he seems never to have been completely comfortable with it. He could always insist, as he did throughout his life, that the time to end slavery had not arrived.

But, tragically, that was so in part because Jefferson had resolutely chosen not to hasten its coming.

Although he himself did not act, it nonetheless saddened Jefferson that his countrymen were not progressing in their moral understanding as rapidly as he hoped they would. Their failure to realize that they should end slavery, he believed, only postponed a Day of Judgment that he considered inevitable. The possibility of a race war had haunted Jefferson at least since 1781, when he wrote in *Notes on the State of Virginia:*

> I tremble for my country when I reflect that God is just: that his justice cannot sleep forever: that considering numbers, nature, and natural means only, a revolution of the wheel of fortune, an exchange of situations, is among possible events: that it may become probable by supernatural interference. The Almighty has no attribute which can take side with us in such a contest.

# CHAPTER 18

# A Library for "the American Statesman"

On September 21, 1814, almost as soon as Jefferson found that the British had burned the U.S. Capitol, he wrote to his longtime friend Samuel Harrison Smith, the commissioner of federal revenue, offering to replace the books housed therein with ones of his own. Smith, who had edited the friendly *National Intelligencer* during Jefferson's presidency and was married to Margaret Bayard Smith, was now better connected in Washington than Jefferson, and probably more likely to know how best to effect the sale.

After deploring the "destruction of the public library with the noble edifice in which it was deposited," Jefferson turned immediately to the subject at hand. "I presume it will be among the early objects of Congress to re-commence their collection," he wrote. This would be difficult during wartime, since most of the books would have to be procured in Europe, and shipping them back would be risky.

"You know my collection, its condition and extent," he went on. "I have been fifty years making it, and have spared no pains, opportunity or expense." Many years earlier, he had spent every spare afternoon over two summers visiting Parisian bookstores, "turning over every book with my own hand" in search of works useful to Americans in public life. He had also established relationships during this period with booksellers in Amsterdam, Frankfurt, Madrid, and London to purchase "such works relating to America as could not be found in Paris."

As a result, his library included many works that "pertained particularly to whatever belongs to the American statesman." In the years since his return, Jefferson had diligently continued to collect books "related to the duties of those in the high concerns of the nation. In the diplomatic and parliamentary branches, it is particularly full." More than thirteen hundred volumes dealt with government and political economy. In these areas, so important to political leaders, such a collection "can never again be effected, because it is hardly probable that the same opportunities, the same time, industry, perseverance and expense," would return. The books were all well bound—some elegantly so—and in superb condition.

Jefferson had already decided to make this valuable collection available to the Congress upon his death, "at their own price." Events had persuaded him to offer the library now, when the need was immediate. He enclosed a catalogue of the books and asked Smith to forward it to the appropriate lawmakers on the Joint Library Committee of the Congress, "not knowing myself of whom the committee consists."

Jefferson offered to allow Congress to set the price, based on the assessment of its value "by persons named by themselves," although he meanwhile found a dealer in books to appraise the collection for him. Considering the unusual circumstances under which such a sale would take place, Jefferson was prepared to accept compensation on a schedule "convenient to the public." He would be agreeable to payment in annual installments to begin, if necessary, upon a return to "days of peace and prosperity." So that the legislators could make immediate use of the collection, he was prepared to send the books as soon as Congress agreed to its purchase. Eighteen or twenty wagons "would place it in Washington in a single trip of a fortnight."

Beyond that, all Jefferson asked was that he be allowed to keep a few books "to amuse the time I have yet to pass." These would be works of mathematics, mainly, and some classics. Even these could be counted with the rest of the collection, though payment for them would not be necessary until his death. Then these books, too, would be sent to Washington. If Congress wanted the books he wished to hold back for his own enjoyment, he would be willing to part with them as well.

In the meantime, he would compile an alphabetical index of their authors.

Jefferson's desire that Congress have his library at its disposal was motivated in part by public-spiritedness. He clearly believed that a knowledge of history, geography, philosophy, and political economy was critical to the preservation of the republic, and he knew his collection to be one the nation's finest and most comprehensive. But he was also in dire need of money.

At the time he made his offer, he was in the middle of what he would describe as "two years of embargo and non-intercourse, 3 of war, and 2 of disastrous drought." Severe weather in the spring had destroyed much of his wheat, and, as he told President Madison, the corn and tobacco in their part of Virginia had also suffered. In early August 1814, a month before the British burned the Capitol, Jefferson asked his business agent in Richmond to sell four hundred barrels of Monticello flour "for whatever he could get for it in cash."

Jefferson had held his wheat off the market since Christmas of 1813, hoping the price would go up. In late August 1814, he was told that it would not "sell at all for ready money," and that winter he was feeding his horses with it. Taxes, meanwhile, were "coming on us," he told Elizabeth Trist, "as an approaching wave in a storm."

Still he could not restrain his spending. Within a week of his writing to Mrs. Trist, he bought a new carriage horse for himself, a bright bay that he called Bedford. The price was $100, "payable in a year." (The following March, Bedford died.)

In October 1814, President Madison wrote to tell Jefferson that he thought the Library Committee "would report favorably on your proposition," which will "prove a gain to them, if they have the wisdom to replace it by such a collection as yours." This was encouraging news indeed.

# CHAPTER 19

# Jeff Randolph Takes a Wife

B y the fall of 1814, Jeff Randolph was home from the war. Five years had come and gone since Randolph had went to work on his grandfather's farms, and, at twenty-two, he was becoming eager for a home, family, and plantation of his own. Earlier in the year, Jefferson told Elizabeth Trist that Randolph had "found a lodestone at Warren," a plantation fifteen miles south of Monticello that belonged to Virginia governor Wilson Cary Nicholas. Nicholas lived there with his wife, the daughter of a well-to-do Baltimore merchant, and their family. Randolph's "lodestone" was their sixteen-year-old daughter, Jane. Jefferson believed "the attraction of the two bodies [to be] mutual," and their courtship was conducted over the next several months.

For reasons that are not altogether clear, Martha Randolph and her daughters were at first "unfavorably impressed" with Jane Nicholas. Their feelings, Randolph later wrote cryptically, had been influenced "by others." Who these unnamed others might have been is impossible to know with certainty, but a three-page statement dated June 21, 1814, and signed by Ann Bankhead, sheds some light on a situation that must have been as unpleasant as it was complicated.

Whatever the various motives of the women involved in this disagreeable episode might have been, they almost certainly involved money—or the distrust that can develop when money is tight. Such suspicions can be especially corrosive when people who are accustomed to having money find that they no longer do, which is the situation Ann Bankhead and the other Randolphs found themselves in during the sweltering summer of 1814.

Ann, who had spent her younger years in comfort at Monticello, by this time had been married for more than five years to Charles Bankhead and had borne him three children. Bankhead had yet to establish himself in any trade or profession, however, and Ann, like the other Randolphs, had become keenly aware of the family's precarious situation and quick to take offense at slights, real or imagined.

In her statement, Ann asserted that all the female members of the Monticello household opposed Jeff Randolph's choice of Jane Nicholas from the moment Charles Bankhead informed them of it. (Tom Randolph and Thomas Jefferson, Jeff's father and grandfather, "knew nothing of the affair.") The women believed that Mrs. Nicholas, Jane's mother, had spoken disrespectfully of Martha Randolph and Ann Bankhead, saying that she had no interest in befriending the Randolphs or visiting Monticello. Martha Randolph, Mrs. Nicholas supposedly said, was "a very vulgar looking woman," and Ann was a "poor stick." Mrs. Nicholas "hoped that none of her daughters would bury themselves in Virginia," as she had, by marrying a land-rich, cash-poor planter.

She certainly did not want them marrying a farmer with such meager prospects as Jeff Randolph, who owned nothing but "a small tract of land & five negroes—two of them worse than nothing." Jane's mother also considered it "very strange that so prudent a young man" who "always complained of how badly off he had been, that he was now in debt, &c &c.," would think of taking a wife. Considering how Mrs. Nicholas felt about the Randolphs, Ann Bankhead considered it "impossible there could ever be any cordiality between the families."

Although Martha Randolph insisted that if her son did marry Jane Nicholas, she would treat her new daughter-in-law "with affection" and that his sisters would be "civil," they wished that Randolph's wife "should be one they could love as one of themselves, and intimated strongly that this could never be the case with Miss N." If one could "judge the daughter from the mother," they feared that he would regret marrying her, especially when he had other options. For a time, they believed that he was in love with another girl, one who was "beautiful," while Jane Nicholas was regarded by most young men as "very homely."

Ann Bankhead did not say why her brother would court a "very homely" young lady he did not love. The obvious answer—for her money—occurred to both the Randolphs and the Nicholases. All Jeff needed to do to put everyone's mind at ease, Ann Bankhead said, "was to give Miss N. a full statement of his fortune and expectations," and his prospective in-laws would prevent the marriage.

Jeff Randolph made just such a "full statement of his fortune and expectations," not to Jane Nicholas but to her father. On February 4, 1815, he informed Governor Nicholas that his daughter had agreed to "confer on me, that inestimable boon, her hand; if I should be so fortunate as to find it meet with your approbation."

Randolph was well aware that he brought little, materially, to the marriage. "It has been a source of unavailing regret to me, that my pecuniary circumstances were such as will place your daughter in a situation far below that which she has been accustomed to, and had a right to expect," he wrote. "With the warmest feelings and highest sense of the sacrifice, which she is about to make to me, to her prospects to ranks and wealth; I have nothing to offer in return but a bare competency and a most enthusiastic and devoted attachment."

Counting land and slaves, Randolph estimated that he was worth no more than $12,000, and could expect nothing from his family. "My prospects from my father I consider as blank," he wrote. His grandfather would not be able to help, either. Jefferson's "estate is large, but unprofitable and unless judiciously managed will probably consume itself."

What others had been unable to do for him, Randolph would do for himself. "With the motives which I shall have for exertion," he told Governor Nicholas, "I hope much from my industry and perseverance."

Despite the initial misgivings of their families, Jane Hollins Nicholas, seventeen, and Thomas Jefferson Randolph, twenty-two, were married at Warren plantation, on March 6, 1815. The newlyweds moved into the third-floor Dome Room at Monticello, and Martha Randolph, to her surprise, found her daughter-in-law a charming addition to the family. Jane is "a lovely little woman," Martha told Elizabeth Trist a few weeks after the wedding, and her affection was reciprocated.

Martha, who did not attend the wedding, had yet to meet her son's new mother-in-law, but this was "not from any fault of mine," she told Mrs. Trist. "I shall certainly cultivate her acquaintance for the sake of her daughter, I may be an object of ridicule perhaps, but I trust never one of just cencure [*sic*]; and if undeserved . . . so much the worse for those who bestow it."

In-laws, Martha knew, could be difficult. Charles Bankhead's drinking, for instance, had become so well known that the neighbors were beginning to talk about it. Bankhead "has turn'd out to be a great sot," according to Mrs. Trist, "always frolicking and Carousing at the Taverns in the Neighbourhood poor Ann I feel for her." Ann's "has been a hard fate," Martha admitted; but, what-

ever became of her husband, she and her children "can never want a home."
They would always be welcome at Monticello. By now, Martha was thinking
of what would become of Ellen Randolph, who was eighteen. "I think sometimes she will never marry," Martha told a friend, "and indeed after her sister's
fate I almost *wish* she never may."

# Chapter 20

# The Realm of "Sobriety and Cool Reason"

In February 1815, two young gentlemen from Massachusetts rode in a carriage through the Albemarle wilderness—"miserable, barren country," one of them called it—en route to Monticello. The forest "had evidently been abandoned to nature," observed Francis Calley Gray, a recent graduate of Harvard College who had been John Quincy Adams's secretary when the latter was minister to Russia. The trees, while taller than New England's, Gray said, "were decaying from age, some were blasted, some uprooted by the wind and some appeared to have been twisted from their trunks by the violence of a hurricane."

The streams were frozen over, and, about eight miles east of Monticello, the driver had to break the ice to get the coach across Mechunk Creek. A horse, "drowned in attempting to pass," lay on the far bank. Somewhere along the way, the travelers met a band of bedraggled Virginian militiamen who had spent six months defending Norfolk against the British, "without winter clothing, exposed to three epidemics which desolated their camp, the ague and fever, the typhus, and the throat distemper." Discharged without pay, the men were heading home.

In time, the carriage bearing Calley and his traveling companion, George Ticknor, late of Dartmouth College, reached the base of South Mountain and began a rain-soaked ride up the "steep, savage hill," as Ticknor called it, "pensive and slow as Satan's ascent to Paradise."

At last reaching Monticello's door, Ticknor and Gray presented letters of introduction from John Adams, and in a few moments, Jefferson made his appearance. "He is quite tall, six feet, one or two inches," Gray noted, his "face streaked and speckled with red, [with] light grey eyes." Jefferson's hair was white, "his figure bony, long and with broad shoulders, a true Virginian." His shoes were "of very thin soft leather with pointed toes and heels ascending in a peak behind." He still wore knee breeches, with gray worsted stockings, a blue waistcoat, and a coat. His clothes, evidently produced on the plantation, were "of stiff thick cloth made of the wool of his own merinoes and badly manufactured."

The furnishings at Monticello were also less elegant that the New Englanders expected. Although the cherry and beech floor in the parlor was "polished as highly as if it were of fine mahogany," the chairs "had leather bottoms stuffed with hair, but the bottoms were completely worn through," with hair "sticking out in all directions." As Ticknor and Gray exchanged pleasantries with their host, a slave boarded up a broken window.

As in subsequent days, that evening was spent "in general conversation," and Ticknor had "seldom met a pleasanter party." Dinner "was always choice, and served in the French style," with bottles of wine decanted only after the meal was consumed and the dishes were removed. Martha Randolph and her daughters dined with the men but left the table at six and did not rejoin the men until a little before seven, when they arrived with a tea tray. The women

*The chairs "had leather bottoms stuffed with hair, but the bottoms were completely worn through." The parlor at Monticello.*

passed the rest of the evening with the men and "are obviously accustomed to join in the conversation, however high the topic may be." About half past ten, all retired to their rooms.

After breakfast on Ticknor and Gray's first morning at Monticello, Jefferson passed an hour in the library with his guests, pointing out, Gray recalled, "its principal treasures." They spent the next morning as well in the library, where Jefferson appeared in an especially expansive mood. Although he exuded "sobriety and cool reason" during most of Ticknor and Gray's visit, their host took a near juvenile delight in showing off his six-volume *Books of Kings* that included titillating accounts of royal scandals. These "seemed to be favorites with the philosopher," who pointed them out to Ticknor "with a satisfaction somewhat inconsistent with the measured gravity" with which he discussed most subjects.

Jefferson's exuberance may have reflected his response to good news he received at the time of the New Englanders' visit. On January 30, after nearly six months of sometimes caustic debate, the Congress had agreed to purchase the whole of Jefferson's library, which would mean a great windfall for its seller. The book dealer whom Jefferson had asked to appraise the collection assessed its value "at ten dollars for a folio, six for a quarto, three for an octavo, and one for a duodecimo," or just under $24,000 for all 6,487 volumes, a sum that both Jefferson and the Congress found acceptable.

Already Jefferson was planning to arrange them for transport. "This can be done only by myself, and admit of no help," he told Samuel Harrison Smith in February. Cataloguing the volumes would require Jefferson to "be constantly on my legs, and I must ask indulgence therefore to proceed only as my strength will admit."

In the spring, when Jefferson turned seventy-two, the collection, in sealed bookcases, arrived undamaged in Washington, where it formed the nucleus of what is today the Library of Congress. For a time, the books were stored on the third floor of Blodgett's Hotel, which then functioned as the temporary Capitol, at Seventh and E Streets, halfway between Jenkins Hill and the President's Mansion.

Jefferson then drew on the Treasury of the United States for full payment of $23,950. Of this sum, all but $10,580 went immediately to pay outstanding debts. A payment of $4,870 retired the debt to Kościuszko incurred six years earlier. These disbursements, after a few minor expenses, left Jefferson with $6,340 from the sale of a library that Gray, who had seen the best that Boston had to offer and had traveled throughout Europe, called "the most valuable in the world."

More good news—"GLORIOUS NEWS," the *National Intelligencer* called it—arrived at Monticello during Ticknor and Gray's visit. Jefferson and the rest of the household had gone to bed on the guests' last night when Jeff Randolph rode up from Charlottesville carrying a newspaper. Eager to share what he had learned, Randolph went immediately to his grandfather's chamber and requested entry, "but the old philosopher refused to open his door," Ticknor wrote, "saying he could wait until morning."

At breakfast, Jefferson learned that, on January 8, General Andrew Jackson's poorly provisioned army of Tennessee and Kentucky volunteers had defeated the British at the outskirts of New Orleans, saving a city that Jefferson feared might fall to the enemy, perhaps forever. Because of slow transatlantic communications, no one in America knew that, a week before, British and American commissioners had signed the Treaty of Ghent, ending the war, and that the battle had been unnecessary.

Necessary or not, the psychological effect of Jackson's smashing victory over the British was electric. "Old Hickory" was suddenly a great hero, and national pride was as high as it had been since Washington destroyed the British at Yorktown. Jefferson could take personal satisfaction, moreover, in knowing that the Louisiana Territory, soon to be rid of all foreign troops, was now securely American. "I sincerely congratulate you on the peace, and more especially on the éclat with which the war was closed," Jefferson wrote to Madison a few weeks later. "The affair of New Orleans was fraught with useful lessons to ourselves, our enemies, and our friends, and will powerfully influence our future relations with the nations of Europe. It will shew them that we mean to take no part in their wars, and count no odds when engaged in our own."

These lessons should be obvious to all. Jackson's volunteers had inflicted ten times as many casualties on the British troops as they had incurred. During the half-hour battle, only eight Americans were killed. One of the eight to fall at New Orleans was Isham Lewis, Jefferson's disgraced nephew. After escaping from jail in Kentucky in 1812, Lewis had taken a new name and, under this alias, enlisted in Jackson's army. Jefferson may never have learned of his death.

◇  ◇  ◇

One final occurrence during Ticknor and Gray's eventful visit to Monticello impressed them both. Every morning before breakfast, Jefferson would mount his horse and ride to the dam, mills, and canal he had constructed on the Rivanna over many years and at great expense. Sometimes Jefferson would inspect his works along the river in the afternoon as well, and after one such ride, he reported that ice was thick on the riverbank.

The following morning, when Jefferson had returned from yet another tour of inspection, he told Jeff Randolph "very quietly," in Ticknor's words, "that the dam had been carried away the night before." From his calm manner, both visitors supposed that the loss of the dam had been "an affair of small consequence." At worst, Gray assumed based upon Jefferson's demeanor, the loss would come to "one or two hundred dollars."

When Ticknor and Gray left Monticello, however, and passed through Charlottesville, they discovered that the townspeople could speak of little else. The event Jefferson had treated as hardly worthy of mention was in fact a calamity. "Mr. Jefferson's great dam was gone," Ticknor heard his neighbors say, "and it would cost $30,000 to rebuild it." Gray hoped that this sum was "a most wonderful miscalculation," but had no doubt that "the loss was serious."

Exactly how serious a blow is impossible to know, for if Jefferson did rebuild the dam, he recorded no expenditures for its repair in his highly detailed account books. If Jefferson did not repair the dam, and therefore lost whatever financial advantage he had gained by reducing the cost of getting his crops to market, this loss also is not reflected in his account books.

The absence of any record of the dam's destruction is fascinating for what it reveals about those account books and the mind of the man who compiled them. Jefferson was a meticulous record keeper his entire life. His account books begin on August 25, 1767, when he recorded the receipt of £10 s.9 from one "W. Bowan," and end only on June 7, 1826, four weeks before his death, when he entered a payment of $2.90 to a neighbor for cheese, $32.33 to a Charlottesville bookbinder, and $2 for "charity."

What is revealing about these records, considering their intricacy, the orderliness of their keeper's mind, his love of balance, and his knowledge of bookkeeping, is that he abandoned any attempt to balance credits and debits in 1770, a scant three years after the entries began. His record keeping seems to have performed a primarily psychological function rather than a financial one.

These minute entries, one following another, day after day, month after month, year after year, accumulating over a lifetime, as the sympathetic editors of his account books conclude, gave Jefferson the feeling that he exercised more control than he did, and thus "may actually have contributed to the disastrous legacy of debt that overwhelmed Jefferson's heirs after his death." This false sense of control, "combined with an optimistic nature that perpetually overestimated sources of income and underestimated expenses," prevented him from undertaking any meaningful financial planning until it was too late to matter.

That Jefferson did not enter into his account books any expenses he might have incurred in rebuilding his dam strongly suggests that he chose to do nothing about it. That he reacted to the calamity as calmly as he did and seems never to have mentioned it may also be revealing. It is as if the destruction that he witnessed that February morning never happened. For the decade of life left to him, this, all too often, would be Jefferson's preferred method of coping with misfortune. Sometimes, however, this would not be possible.

# Chapter 21

# "To Witness the Death of All Our Companions"

On the morning of August 7, 1815, Thomas Jefferson received word at Monticello that his only brother, fifty-nine-year-old Randolph Jefferson, had become seriously ill. Thomas Jefferson immediately set out for his brother's plantation, on the south side of the James River twenty miles below Monticello. That night, when he reached Scott's ferry, which would take him across the James, Jefferson "met the news of his [brother's] death," he told Wilson Cary Nicholas two days later, "and returned." Jefferson did not attend the burial and seems to have made no further comment on his brother's death.

What may seem a cold response would probably not have been regarded as such by men of his generation. A scion of Virginia's prerevolutionary gentry, Jefferson lived at a time when the death of loved ones, while painful, was an ever present reality. Children often died in infancy, and those who survived to adulthood and started their own families frequently experienced the death not only of children but also of spouses. Men typically lived into their middle to late fifties; women, after giving birth several times, often died in their thirties. When wives died, men found new ones. Women, like Jefferson's wife, often outlived their first husbands and then married again. Children raised at Monticello, unlike many of their contemporaries, knew their grandfather.

The reaction of Randolph Jefferson, four years earlier, to the news that their sister Martha Jefferson Carr had died seems typical. When Thomas Jefferson told him of Mrs. Carr's death, Randolph Jefferson let a month pass before he replied, saying he was "extremely sorry to hear of My sisters death and Would of bin over but it was not raly in my power but it is What we may all expect to come either later or sooner."

As Anglicans who found the emotionalism of the rising "dissenting" churches unappealing, members of the planter class also believed that any expressions of grief, especially on the part of gentlemen, should be restrained. Mourning was done privately, with a return to the normal activities of life made as quickly as possible. Prolonged grieving was considered morbid. For men like Jefferson, who were steeped in Enlightenment thought and tried to view the world as a scientist or philosopher would, reacting emotionally to the biological processes that led to the cessation of life was fundamentally irrational.

But even in the context of his time, Thomas Jefferson's response to the deaths of his loved ones seems unusual. By 1815, when his brother died, Jefferson had experienced the passing of his wife, five of their children, and two of their grandchildren, as well as the deaths of five of his siblings and many close friends. Still, he grappled not only with questions about how he should grieve but also about whether he should grieve at all.

These questions suggest that Jefferson entertained deep doubts about the validity of the emotions themselves. They also indicate the efforts that Jefferson took to minimize the pain of loss. This struggle against the agony of loss was a lifelong ordeal, and his reactions swung wildly between resolute refusal to acknowledge the pain that he endured, as with the death of his mother, and an utter surrender to it, as with that of his wife.

Nearly forty years earlier, when his mother, Jane Randolph Jefferson, had died, Jefferson entered a perfunctory mention of the fact in his account book, giving the event no more weight than he gave the fact that his mare Everalin had foaled the week before and that he had paid the slave named Ursula $3.75 the following day for eggs.

But shortly thereafter he also began to suffer from "paroxysms of the most excruciating pain," which lasted about six weeks and constituted one of the most protracted of his famous headaches. Five years later, when his wife, Martha, died, months passed before Jefferson emerged from the "stupor" that left him "as dead to the world as she whose loss occasioned it."

In 1804, when Jefferson was in his first term as president, and his daughter Maria Jefferson Eppes died at twenty-six, he acted in public as if he had experienced no loss at all. His refusal to observe any of the customary rituals of grief troubled other Washingtonians, including his friends. Neither "he nor his family put on mourning," Margaret Bayard Smith observed, "neither did he make any change in his social habits, but continued his dinner parties and received company as usual." In this, he "miscalculated the common feelings of humanity," which would have "approved rather than condemned his secluding himself for a while from society."

Jefferson may have pretended otherwise, but his grief at Maria's death had been "great indeed," as he told Governor John Page. Sometimes it seemed to him as if life consisted of little more than one loss followed by the next. By likening these losses to those on a battlefield, Jefferson may have revealed the extent to which he regarded his own struggle against grief as something like war:

> When you and I look back on the country over which we have passed, what a field of slaughter does it exhibit! Where are all the friends who entered it with us, under all the inspiring energies of health and hope? As if pursued by the havoc of war, they are strewed by the way, some earlier, some later, and scarce a few stragglers remain to count the numbers fallen, and to mark yet, by their own fall, the last footsteps of their party. Is it a desirable thing to bear up through the heat of action, to witness the death of all our companions, and merely be the last victim?

Increasingly, Jefferson doubted that mere endurance was desirable, and, on one of the few occasions when he indulged the hope of an afterlife, he expressed a longing for reunion with the many loved ones he had buried. There was some consolation, he told Page, in the fact that every "step shortens the distance we have to go; the end of the journey is in sight—the bed wherein we are to rest, and to rise in the midst of the friends we have lost!" But "whatever is to be our destiny, wisdom, as well as duty, dictates that we should acquiesce in the will of Him whose it is to give and take away, and be contented in the enjoyment of those who are still permitted to be with us."

In 1815, the year his brother died, Jefferson told John Adams, during an exchange of several letters on the subject, that he was unsure how to respond to loss because he could see little value in pain itself. "I think with you that it is a good world on the whole that it has been framed on a principle of benevolence, and more pleasure than pain dealt out to us," Jefferson wrote on April 8. There were "hypocondriac [*sic*] minds" that lived in a constant state of trepidation, but Jefferson always tried to "steer my bark with Hope in the head, leaving Fear astern." His hopes sometimes failed, "but not oftener than the forebodings of the gloomy." Even so, he wondered "for what good end the sensations of Grief could be intended." All other passions, "within proper bounds," served a discernible purpose. Because virtue lies "in a just equilibrium of all the passions [Jefferson wished] pathologists then would tell us what is the use of grief in the economy."

Adams, who did not regard himself as a scientist or philosopher, readily admitted that he found himself unable to "weigh Sensations and Reflections, Pleasures and Pains, Hopes and Fears in Money Scales." But Adams also had little doubt that the experience of grief and of suffering, generally, was essential to moral development. Grief leads men

> to reflect on the Vanity of human Wishes and Expectations; to learn the essential lesson of Resignation; to review their own Conduct toward the deceased; to correct any Errors or faults in their future Conduct towards their remaining friends and toward all Men; to recollect the Virtues of the Lost Friend and resolve to imitate them.

Grief leads men into "serious Reflection[,] sharpens the understanding and softens the heart," teaching patience and compassion, Adams wrote. But the meaning of grief cannot be understood, he concluded, without probing the meaning of evil. As grief "is a Pain," Adams wrote, "it stands in the Predicament of all other Evil and the great question Occurs what is the Origin and what the final cause of Evil."

Jefferson, who insisted throughout his life that such questions were "metaphysical," showed no interest in exploring the question further with Adams. Evil, as he saw it, was a spurious notion, promulgated by priests for their own aggrandizement. Defects of character, by contrast, resulted from inadequate education or from a disorder of the moral sense. Evil, viewed as a disorder of the moral sense, might in fact be physiological in origin, like disorders of any other sense, and could best be treated through a change of climate or diet, or a regimen of physical exercise, preferably performed out-of-doors.

Perhaps the only certain benefit from suffering the loss of loved ones, Jefferson told Adams in their last exchange on the subject, might best be understood in physiological terms as well: just as the gradual decay of our senses makes us less reluctant to die, so the loss of loved ones "prepares us to lose ourselves also without repugnance."

By the fall of 1815, Jefferson had decided that Charles Bankhead was so dangerous when drunk that something had to be done. If the man's need to drink was physiological in origin, as so many such disorders were, a cure could be found in medical attention and, perhaps, outdoor activity. On October 28, Jefferson wrote to tell Dr. John Bankhead that he was sending his son back to him "as a medical subject," accompanied by Ann and their children.

"Nothing less than his good, and the hope of restoring happiness to his family and friends & to yourself particularly could have induced me to the pain of this communication," Jefferson wrote. For a time, Charles Bankhead had stopped drinking, inspiring hope "of his being restored as a rational and valued member of the society of his friends." But a recent visit to Charlottesville had "damped these hopes." Bankhead had begun to go to taverns every day, returning in the evening "in a state approaching insanity."

On one such night, he "committed an assault on his wife of great violence [and] ordered her out of the room, forbidding her to enter it again & she was obliged to take refuge for the night in her mother's room. Nor was this a new thing." The next morning, he "would become repentant, and sincerely distressed, but recur again to the same excesses." In his remorse, he would talk of selling his property and moving away, though "his habits would follow him wherever he went, except under your roof, and we had too many proofs that his family would be safe no where else."

Jefferson implored Dr. Bankhead to keep the matter secret, because he had not told Tom Randolph how gravely Charles Bankhead's drinking endangered Ann and their children. Ann also was not to know that her father and her father-in-law were discussing the situation. "To this letter nobody is privy but my daughter and myself," Jefferson wrote, and for Ann to know of it "might increase [her uneasiness] and if known to Mr. Bankhead himself, might alienate him from us, which would add to the distresses of the case."

Jefferson told Dr. Bankhead he would happily defer to the physician's expertise concerning how best to treat this particular case, though, for exercise and recreation, he suggested a sport favored by many gentlemen. "The gun is a very enticing occupation," Jefferson wrote, "if once a fondness for it is acquired."

## Chapter 22

## *"The Eternal Preservation of . . . Republican Principles"*

On a cold Saturday morning in November 1815, Jefferson was writing to ask Martha Randolph to send his wolfskin pelisse and fur boots to him at Poplar Forest when he was interrupted "by a crowd of curious people come to see the house." Returning some minutes later, he added a postscript. He had been "most agreeably surprised" to find that the party he had assumed to be mere sightseers in fact consisted of General Andrew Jackson and his entourage en route from Tennessee to Washington.

Jackson was the most celebrated hero in America that season, destined, many felt, to succeed Washington, Adams, Jefferson, and Madison as president. Eleven months earlier, his rout of the British at New Orleans had made him famous, and controversial. An unschooled westerner who had grown rich from growing cotton, Jackson was also a fierce, impetuous character who had shot and killed a man back in Tennessee.

For a lawyer, Jackson also exhibited an astonishing contempt for the constitutional niceties to which Jefferson attached great importance. A defender of Aaron Burr, Jackson had come to Richmond in 1807 to denounce Jefferson's determination to bring Burr to justice, and the embargo, which Jackson considered an inexcusably weak response to the British capture of American seamen. "Mr. Jefferson can torture Aaron Burr," Jackson had said, "while England tortures our sailors."

If Jefferson still smarted from Jackson's attacks on him, he pretended otherwise. He welcomed his visitor to Poplar Forest and the next day, Jackson returned to invite Jefferson to a dinner in his honor in Lynchburg the following Tuesday.

When the big day came, the people of Lynchburg, having swept their streets for the occasion, held a parade. "A troop of horse, with many mounted citizens, headed by Major Lynch, proceeded early in the day to meet and escort our Hero to the town," the *Richmond Enquirer* reported. "The Artillery and

Rifle Companies, with their usual order and brilliancy, marched out beyond the hill to salute him as he advanced." When Jackson's party came into view, the soldiers fell in behind, and the parade moved grandly up the street. "Thomas Jefferson, Esq.," as the *Enquirer* called him, "added dignity to the procession."

That afternoon, in Lynchburg's largest tobacco warehouse, "a most sumptuous dinner was prepared and spread on tables sufficient for at least 300 seats." Any animosity between the former president and the future president was put aside for the occasion. "All was social conviviality," the *Enquirer* reported. Nearly thirty toasts gave voice to the "common emotions which every man felt, and was glad to utter," and a band played "Jefferson's March," which had been standard musical fare at patriotic gatherings since Jefferson's first inauguration fourteen years earlier. The "majority of the Gentlemen were rather too much elated on the occasion as you may suppose," one partygoer recalled, "for . . . there was 80 gallons of 6 dollar wine drank at the dinner that day."

Before the last of the drunken toasts were offered, Jefferson had taken his leave. By the time the revelers woke up with dry mouths and throbbing temples, Jackson had departed for Washington, and Jefferson was on his way to the Peaks of Otter in the Blue Ridge Mountains, half a day's journey west of Lynchburg. There, with a Ramsden's theodolite of 3½ I. radius, the amateur scientist measured the peaks, making one more contribution to Virginia's natural history and the nation's.

What Jefferson thought of Jackson was a matter of dispute in Jefferson's time and would remain so for the rest of their lives and beyond. The man who vanquished the British at New Orleans was a superb military leader, Jefferson conceded. Whether he was educationally or temperamentally suited for the presidency was another matter. Jackson's supporters would always claim that, as a fellow southern slaveholder and democrat, Jefferson would have supported their man, but the evidence for this assertion is not strong.

However engaging Jackson may have been, however valiant on the field of battle, this upstart also represented much that Jefferson distrusted in American political life and opposed: the consolidation of authority in the executive branch of government and a visceral desire for power itself, unrestrained by reason or by law. Jefferson had been committed to fighting against such despotism all his public life. But he had come to understand the problem differently in recent years, and the ingenious remedy that he proposed may yet prove his single most profound contribution to American political thought.

It was only in retirement that Jefferson gave these ideas full expression, and why they came together in his mind at this time seems evident. From the winter of 1815 through the summer of 1816, the Virginia General Assembly was debating the need for a new, publicly funded college and for a new state constitution that recognized the growing counties in the western part of the state. During these debates, Jefferson's views on both subjects were regularly solicited, and in his correspondence that season his thinking took mature form.

By 1815, Jefferson had come to agree with Benjamin Rush's view that America was fast becoming a republic in name only, where power may have been derived from the people, but where they possessed it "only on the days of their elections. After that it is the property of their rulers." The steady transfer of power from the local governments to the states and from the states to the federal government threatened to turn all the challenges of self-government—of what later generations would call democracy—into problems of administration. Self-government required the active participation of well-informed citizens. Problems of administration relied, instead, on a professional class of increasingly unaccountable government agents, with as little involvement as possible by the people themselves.

As this transfer of power took place, Jefferson believed that the capacity of ordinary people to govern themselves diminished and, over time, would disappear. The virtues developed by participation in government would atrophy until Americans were no longer fit to govern themselves. Losing any attachment to their liberties, the citizens would lack the will to resist their usurpation by ambitious men like Hamilton, Burr, and, yes, Jackson. The inevitable result would be the moral corruption of the American people, and despotism on the European model.

Jefferson's remedy was bold and, when recommendations similar to it are advanced today, still controversial. He wished to restructure American government so that all powers, except those that could be exercised only at the higher levels, were to remain at the fundamental unit he called "wards" or "ward republics." Based on the "hundreds" of Saxon Britain, these wards were to be no larger than five or six square miles. Smaller even than Virginia's county court system, the wards would become the most important units in the entire federal system, he told Governor John Tyler in 1810, because only within them could "the voice of the whole people [be] fairly, fully and peaceably expressed." There and there alone could policies be decided "by the common reason" of all citizens.

Only when the people were fully engaged in securing their own liberties, Jefferson argued, was republican government on the national or even continental scale possible. The way to have "good and safe government," Jefferson told State Senator Joseph C. Cabell of Virginia in 1814, "is not to trust it all to one, but to divide it among the many, distributing to every one exactly the functions he is competent to."

The national government should be entrusted with severely limited powers—chiefly, to regulate relations between the states and between the United States and foreign governments. State governments would be responsible for "what concerns the States generally," the counties with county affairs, and the wards with everything else. The wards, the counties, the states, and the union of states would form a "gradation of authorities," establishing a "system of fundamental balances and checks," preventing power from being consolidated at ever higher levels.

The wards would be entrusted with what was ultimately most vital to the survival of the republic itself: the education of children. Wards would fund, build, and run public primary schools where children would be taught subjects that would equip them to exercise their liberties responsibly. The establishment and administration of the schools also would provide an ongoing education in self-government for the parents. The notion that schools could be better run by "any other general authority of the government, than by the parents within each ward [is] a belief against all experience," Jefferson told Cabell in February 1816. Entrust the states with responsibility for education, and one might as well turn over to them "the management of all our farms, our mills, and our merchants' stores"—a policy that, of course, later generations of collectivists would endorse.

Jefferson's belief in wards was "not founded in views of education only," he told Governor Wilson Cary Nicholas on April 2, 1816, "but infinitely more as the means of a better administration of government, and the eternal preservation of its Republican principles." The operation of schools would be only one of the many responsibilities left to the wards. They would also retain authority for "the care of the poor, their roads, police, elections, the nomination of jurors, administration of justice in small cases, elementary exercises of militia." Under this system, each man would have a role to play so "that he is a participator in the government of affairs, not merely at an election at one day in the year, but every day."

In working out these ideas, Jefferson also solved, to his own satisfaction, one of the knottier problems with which theorists of republican government then wrestled: whether populous and geographically extensive countries could also be free and self-governing. They could, indeed, Jefferson decided, but only so long as local government flourished. As a "regularly organized power," the people in their wards would be able "to crush, regularly and peaceably, the usurpations of their unfaithful agents," uprooting tyranny before it could spread. By establishing ward government throughout the union, he concluded, "we shall be as republican as a large society can be."

It is in his correspondence on the subject of ward government that one of Jefferson's most frequently quoted and wildly misconstrued remarks appears. On July 12, 1816, in a response to Samuel Kercheval, a Virginia lawmaker who had solicited his opinion on written constitutions, Jefferson stated that, unlike some, he did not regard such documents with "sanctimonious reverence." Institutions

> must go hand in hand with progress of the human mind. As that becomes more developed, more enlightened, as new discoveries are made, new truths disclosed, and manners and opinions change with the change of circumstances, institutions must advance also, and keep pace with the times. We might as well require a man to wear still the coat which fitted him when a boy, as civilized society to remain ever under the regimen of their barbarous ancestors.

For years to come, this passage would become a favorite of those who favored an increasingly "flexible" interpretation of the U.S. Constitution and sought to enlist Jefferson, posthumously, in their efforts to expand federal power. To conscript Jefferson in this way, however, is to misread him completely. Jefferson was amenable to making the Virginia constitution more representative of the western counties, not because he believed it gave the state government in Richmond too little power, but because he believed it gave the state too much.

Despite Jefferson's attempts to locate the source of his ward republic ideas in the ancient history of Great Britain, where he had actually seen it operate most vigorously was in the New England townships. Their stiff resistance to his efforts to enforce the embargo taught him how fierce ordinary Americans could be when their liberties were threatened, and this was a lesson he did not forget.

He was forthright, moreover, in telling his fellow southerners that he had seen local government at its most vital not in their own states but in those of the North. Wards, "called townships in New England," he told Kercheval, "have proved themselves the wisest invention ever devised by the wit of man for the perfect exercise of self-government, and for its preservation."

Jefferson's belief in an expanded role for local government is a more radical notion than it might first appear, as Hannah Arendt, in *On Revolution*, would recognize one hundred and fifty years later. The flaw in the Constitution of the United States was that there was "no space reserved, no room left for the exercise of precisely those qualities which had been instrumental in building it," Arendt wrote. No one, at his time or since, "has perceived this seemingly inevitable flaw in the structure of the republic with greater clarity and with more passionate preoccupation," she noted, "than Jefferson." The revolution

> while it had given freedom to the people, had failed to provide a space where this freedom could be exercised. Only the representatives of the people, not the people themselves, had an opportunity to engage in those activities of "expressing, discussing and deciding," which in a positive sense are the activities of freedom.

To describe Jefferson during this period as an advocate of "states' rights," to borrow the language of a later period, is to understate the case. What Jefferson proposed was a radical decentralization of government itself. That his recommendations—on schools, on the division of government into units closest to the people themselves, on the necessity of restricting the power of the states and of the "foreign" branch—would be rejected does not mean they lacked merit.

Whether the United States is a better nation as a result of that rejection, or a worse one, is far from settled. This nation is certainly one in which power is exercised for the citizens rather than by them, and the results, to put the matter in as favorable a light as possible, are not all to the good.

But Jefferson was far from done with thinking about education and the need to inculcate virtue in young people. These were subjects that would occupy his mind for the rest of his life, to great and lasting effect. To what extent developments in his own household lent urgency to this task would be impossible to know, though domestic worries—especially the troubling behavior of Charles Bankhead—were also on Jefferson's mind in the fall of 1816, as the tulip poplars at Monticello turned from green to brown and the first cold rains fell.

# CHAPTER 23

## The Indulgent Patriarch

---

Jefferson cut short his fall visit to Poplar Forest in 1816, rushing back to Monticello to deal with difficulties caused by Bankhead's relapse into drunkenness.

For a time, Jefferson told Dr. Bankhead, Charles had resolved to remain sober and "stood his ground firmly." On the first of October, he had gone into town, where "all his resolution gave way" and he "went into full indulgence." Before the week was out, he had hired a driver to take him to Caroline County, presumably to dry out at his father's house. But when the driver stopped at Milton to feed his horses, Bankhead again "got so overpowered with liquor" that the driver brought him back to Monticello, where he was put to bed. For the next two days, the family managed to keep liquor from him "in the hope that he might cool and recover his resolution." On Saturday, October 5, however, Bankhead somehow got hold of a bottle, and drinking it "raised him from his languor." Energetic again, he promptly rode back to Charlottesville, returned at night, and "has been ever since in a state of strong intoxication, and the constant aberration of mind which you have probably witnessed."

When Jefferson was back at Poplar Forest, Martha wrote from Monticello to tell him that if Ann or the children were "much disturbed or endangered," Tom Randolph was prepared to "take at once the steps necessary for their protection, as circumstances may require."

The family had talked of committing Bankhead to the hospital for the insane in Williamsburg, but the madhouse "is but a temporary remedy," Martha said. After a few weeks there, "he would be returned with renewed health to torment his family the longer." Martha had begun to feel that the best solution might be to let her son-in-law drink himself to death. "I really think that the best way would be to hire a keeper to prevent his doing mischief," she told Jefferson, "and let him finish himself at once."

◇   ◇   ◇

The tension at Monticello could well have been inevitable in any large and prominent family struggling with debt and declining prospects, and Bankhead's drunkenness certainly made matters worse. But some of the strains developing within the household can be traced to Jefferson himself and the choices he had made, however well-intentioned. As the family discovered too late, there would be a price to pay—figuratively and literally—for the patriarch's generosity.

This was a man, after all, who had once been rich enough to buy, for himself and for those he loved, whatever he or they wanted: furniture, fine horses, fashionable clothes, musical instruments, books, and wine by the wagonload. Such habits can be hard to break, even for those who wish to break them, and there is no evidence that Jefferson ever wanted seriously to economize.

Because Jefferson had never remarried, the expensive gifts (and even small tokens of affection) that he might otherwise have lavished on a second Mrs. Jefferson were now bestowed on his only surviving child, her children, and his other grandchildren and great-grandchildren. Tom and Martha Randolph now had nine children living at home, and Martha, who was forty-four, would be pregnant again by the end of 1817. Charles and Ann Bankhead had three children, and Jeff and Jane Randolph had one, with a second to arrive the following July. Francis Eppes, the son of Jefferson's daughter Maria, also lived at Monticello during this period, making a total of eleven grandchildren and four great-grandchildren.

Rather than regard this growing family as a financial burden, Jefferson welcomed the opportunity to help raise the children, supervise their education, and surprise them with gifts. Tom and Martha Randolph's daughter, Virginia, who turned sixteen that summer, credited Jefferson with "all the small blessings and joyful surprises of my childish and girlish years." Jefferson's nature "was so eminently sympathetic," that, with those he loved, he could "enter into their feelings, anticipate their wishes, gratify their tastes, and surround them with an atmosphere of affection," as her own father could never do.

The previous summer, Virginia had begun to want a watch, "but knew the state of my father's finances promised no such indulgence." One afternoon, however, the mail arrived at Monticello with a small packet postmarked Philadelphia. Soon "an elegant lady's watch, with chain and seals, was in my hand, which trembled for very joy. My Bible came from him, my Shakespeare, my first writing-table, my first handsome writing-desk, my first Leghorn hat, my first silk-dress."

When Virginia began to ride horses, she was indifferent to the quality of the tack, and whether she used "an old saddle or broken bridle were matters of no moment." As soon as she began to show interest in the quality of her equipment, however, things changed. One sunny day, when she was standing in the portico, a man rode up to the door with "a beautiful lady's saddle and bridle before him. My heart bounded. These coveted articles were deposited at my feet. My grandfather came out of his room to tell me they were mine."

Another time, when one of the older granddaughters received a silk dress from an aunt, Virginia recalled that ten-year-old Cornelia "involuntarily expressed aloud some feelings which possessed her bosom on the occasion, by saying, 'I never had a silk dress in my life.'" The next day, "a silk dress came from Charlottesville to Cornelia and (to make the rest of us equally happy) also a pair of pretty dresses for Mary and myself." On another occasion, Jefferson saw Virginia tear a muslin dress on a broken windowpane. A few days later, he came to Virginia with a bundle in his hand.

"I have been mending your dress for you," he said.

Instead of the old one, however, she said, Jefferson presented her with "another beautiful dress."

In early 1816, Virginia decided that she wanted a guitar. She learned that a neighbor lady who owned one was moving west and was willing to sell the instrument, "but she asked so high a price that I never in my dreams aspired to its possession." One morning at breakfast, she spotted the guitar, "and grandpapa told me that if I would promise to learn to play on it I should have it." Virginia promised, and the guitar was hers.

That same spring, nineteen-year-old Ellen Randolph was visiting James and Dolley Madison at the President's House in Washington. Ellen needed spending money, but did not want to worry her "poor father." In January, Jefferson sent $100 to his business agent in Georgetown, asking him to establish a line of credit for Ellen to use "to any extent she may call for." Two weeks later, Jefferson renewed his note for $2,000 at the Bank of Virginia, effectively mortgaging his own grandchildren's futures to pay for all this largesse. The bill for these musical instruments, silk dresses, fancy saddles, and vacation trips would not come due, in a sense, for many years, when their grandfather died, and they inherited not wealth, of course, but debt.

One further consequence of Jefferson's generosity was that, over time, he came to supplant their own father in their affections. As Randolph's sympathetic biographer, William H. Gaines, Jr., has written, all of the children eventually

> felt far closer to [their grandfather] than they did to their preoccupied and taciturn sire, for he apparently did little to win the love of his offspring. Since he was a sensitive man, he must have realized that he did not stand first in his children's affections, and that realization, coupled with the knowledge that he could not provide for them, must have added to his unhappiness.

Randolph's jealousy was not the only reason that his relationship with his father-in-law suffered, though envy—of Jefferson's accomplishments, his self-assurance, his claim on Martha's affections, and now on those of his grandchildren—surely was a factor.

By 1817 or so, Randolph was spending less and less time at Monticello. He would eat breakfast there and then ride into the fields at Edgehill or Carlton,

*Jefferson's daughter played "a part in her children's affairs that should have been played by their father." Martha Jefferson Randolph.*

supervising the farms. Increasingly, however, he spent time by himself at Milton, where he owned a small house near the river, returning to Monticello only for dinner. Shortly after the meal, Randolph would excuse himself and retire for the night. When Randolph did speak, it was to grumble, in his "big grum voice," Edmund Bacon said, or yell at his children or, sometimes, at his wife. Randolph also began to drink heavily.

With Randolph gone much of the time, Gaines writes, Martha was forced "to take a part in her children's affairs that should have been played by their father." Just as Jefferson had served as mother as well as father to his children, now Martha acted as both father and mother—with Jefferson's help—to hers. In October 1818, when Nicholas Trist, Elizabeth Trist's eighteen-year-old grandson, wished to marry Virginia Randolph, who was seventeen, he went to Martha Randolph—the girl's mother—for permission, not to her father. With characteristic good sense but also, perhaps, speaking from unhappy experience, Martha told the would-be suitor that he and his intended were both too young to make a decision that would "decide the happiness, or wretchedness of [their] lives." (They would eventually marry, six years later, in September 1824.)

Roles and responsibilities at Monticello were not always what visitors expected. Here the "accomplished" women spoke as freely as the half-educated men. As George Ticknor and others discovered, Martha and her daughters spoke their minds, even upon matters that, on other plantations, were reserved for men only. At Monticello, women were encouraged to enter into serious conversation by Jefferson himself, who presided over dinner-table discussions like a firm but amiable professor, if not potentate. Throughout his retirement years, Jefferson's closest and most trusted adviser was clearly Martha, whose judgment he esteemed above that of most men.

Jefferson did not believe, however, that women should be involved in public life. He did not doubt that they were sufficiently intelligent or that they were capable of exercising authority. What troubled Jefferson was that participation in political life would require women to "mix promiscuously in the public meetings of men," as he told Samuel Kercheval in September 1816.

This prohibition against mixing "promiscuously," Jefferson explained, was "to prevent deprivation of morals and"—ironic, considering the realities of his own mixed-race household at Monticello—"ambiguity of issue."

# CHAPTER 24

# The "Yellow Children" of the Mountaintop

The presence of light-skinned slaves at Monticello, though taken for granted by Thomas Jefferson and his family, often surprised visitors. The household servants "have neither in their color nor their features a single trace of their origins, but they are the children of slave mothers and consequently slaves," the Duc de La Rochefoucauld-Liancourt observed in 1796, by which time Jefferson's preference for mulatto domestics was well established.

At least one of these house slaves looked so much like Jefferson himself, Jeff Randolph told the biographer Henry S. Randall, that "at some distance in the dusk the slave, dressed in the same way, might have been mistaken for Mr. Jefferson." On one occasion, Jeff said, a dinner guest "looked so startled as he raised his eyes from [Jefferson] to the servant behind him, that his discovery of the resemblance was ... perfectly obvious to all." Only Jefferson himself "never betrayed the least consciousness of the resemblance," Jeff Randolph said.

The existence of these "yellow children," as Jefferson's granddaughter Ellen Coolidge called them, appears not to have distressed the Randolphs except insofar as Jefferson was accused of being their father. In defending Jefferson against the charge of siring children by Sally Hemings, the family readily acknowledged that other white men, including his own close friends and relatives, routinely fathered children by the enslaved women at Monticello. By accusing these men of carousing at will with the slave women, family members unwittingly painted a picture of life at Monticello that is as lurid as that depicted by Jefferson's worst critics. If, from the accounts of members of his own household, Monticello seems a place where white men were free to prey on the enslaved black women, such an impression must owe less to the charges of those who hated Jefferson and had never been to Monticello than to those who loved him and lived there.

◇   ◇   ◇

Born in 1773, Sally Hemings was the youngest of fourteen children of Elizabeth (Betty) Hemings, a mulatto slave who belonged to John Wayles and was alleged to be his mistress. Wayles was also the father of the former Martha Wayles Skelton, Thomas Jefferson's wife. If Sally Hemings was indeed John Wayles's daughter, then she would have been the half-sister of Thomas Jefferson's beloved spouse.

Betty Hemings, her children, and their close relatives came to Monticello around 1776 as part of Martha Jefferson's inheritance from her father. There they worked as household servants and craftsmen, notable for their intellect, competence, and discretion. Sally's brother Peter Hemings, who possessed "great intelligence," in Jefferson's words, was Monticello's chief cook. Another brother, John Hemings, was a skilled carpenter.

A housekeeper and seamstress, Sally served in her girlhood as a maid to Maria Jefferson, accompanying Jefferson's younger daughter to Paris in 1787 and returning to Virginia with them two years later. Sally was "mighty near white," the slave Isaac Jefferson recalled, "very handsome" with "long straight hair down her back." She was "light colored," Jeff Randolph said, "and decidedly good looking."

Exactly how many children Sally Hemings bore over the course of her lifetime is a matter of spirited debate. Historians agree that four of her children, born between 1798 and 1808, grew to adulthood. A daughter, often referred to as Harriet I, was born in 1795 but died at two; a second daughter, unnamed, was born in 1799 but died in infancy. The children who grew up included son Beverley, born April 1, 1798; a second Harriet, born in May 1801; son Madison, born January 19, 1805; and son Eston, born May 21, 1808. About any other children, however, there is considerable dispute. For years, Jefferson's accusers claimed that Sally gave birth shortly after returning from Paris to a son supposedly named Tom. Sally would have been at most sixteen when she became pregnant with this child, who some researchers say grew up to be Thomas Woodson, a farmer in Ohio.

Thomas Woodson's descendants, claiming that he was sent away from Monticello as a child, have traced him to other Woodsons in Virginia and, in that way, to ownership by one of Thomas Jefferson's aunts. Documentary evidence placing Woodson at Monticello has never been found, however. In an 1873 interview with an Ohio newspaper, Sally's son Madison Hemings said that after his mother's return from Europe, she "gave birth to a child, of whom Thomas Jefferson was the father," but this child "lived but a short time." About a girl named Thenia, born at Monticello on December 7, 1799, there is also some debate. Some scholars have argued that she was Sally's daughter, others that she was Sally's niece, and still others that she was Sally's sister.

That it is impossible to know whose child Thenia was or whether a son named Tom ever existed suggests something of the sorrowfully disjointed lives of plantation slaves, when marriages were generally not recognized by law, when spouses could be torn apart at will, when oral tradition was all that children could rely on for knowledge of their origins, and when what would later be called blended families existed often by cruel necessity rather than choice.

At Monticello, moreover, Jefferson encouraged slaves to find partners "at home," rather than at other plantations, which increased the likelihood that cousins would marry. A consequence of encouraging such marriages was to interweave slave families so closely together that their genealogies became even more maddeningly convoluted than those of the old white Virginia families that owned them. What was said about the white Randolphs—that their family history resembled "a tangle of fish-hooks so ensnarled together that it was impossible to pick up one without pulling three or four others after it"—applied equally well to the black Hemingses.

When slave women were preyed upon by their masters' families and friends, as at many plantations, establishing paternity is almost impossible, at least without the benefit of science. Even then, as generations of Jeffersons, Randolphs, and Hemingses would discover two hundred years later, it can be difficult.

What no one disputes is that Sally's youngest child was Eston, born at Monticello in May 1808 when his mother was thirty-five and Jefferson was sixty-five. In all likelihood, Eston was conceived in late August 1807, when Thomas Jefferson was in his second term as president, Congress had adjourned, and he was back at Monticello.

This was a well-established pattern. A working politician who spent much of the year in Philadelphia and then in Washington, Jefferson would come home to Monticello for extended visits, and Sally would conceive; for much of her life, her pregnancies coincided with his visits. During each of these visits, he was in excellent health.

But in March 1809, when Jefferson returned to Monticello for good and his daughter, Martha Randolph, and several of her children also moved to Monticello, Sally's childbearing ceased.

◊　◊　◊

Thomas Jefferson seems never to have spoken, perhaps even privately, about the allegations that he was the father of Sally Hemings's children. Maintaining what he no doubt considered a dignified silence, Jefferson left the defense of his reputation to his friends and, especially, his family. This would present these advocates with a formidable challenge. The evidence, if examined with the scientific objectivity that Jefferson himself esteemed, pointed strongly toward Jefferson as the father of at least some, if not all, of these "yellow children." If Jefferson himself had been able to apply to this question the same dispassionate intelligence that he brought to bear on other matters, he would have conceded that his critics on this matter had good reason to reach the conclusions that they did.

As the maid who, according to Madison Hemings, "took care of [Jefferson's] chamber and wardrobe," Sally Hemings enjoyed an unusual level of access to her master. All four of her children who lived to adulthood were treated well and given their freedom. When Beverley and Harriet reached the age of twenty-one, they simply left Monticello and, rather than compel their return, Jefferson allowed them to go, unofficially releasing them to pass as white, which they did. Jefferson actually paid Harriet's stage fare, financing her departure. In his will, he granted Madison and Eston their freedom. Sally Hemings, inherited by Martha Randolph, was "given her time"—a nonbinding, informal emancipation—and released to live with her sons in Charlottesville.

Try as they might, Jefferson's defenders have never been able to explain these supposed coincidences. For many years, explanations were unnecessary, however, because the idea that Jefferson would have a sexual relationship with "the female attendant of his own pure children," as Ellen Randolph Coolidge put it, seemed ridiculous on its face. "There are such things, after all, as moral impossibilities," Coolidge told her husband, Joseph, in 1858. Jeff Randolph told his sister Ellen that as "a young man certain to know all that was going on behind the scenes," he "never saw or heard the smallest thing which could lead him to suspect that his grandfather's life was other than perfectly pure."

That Jefferson fathered a slave's children, Martha, Jeff, and Ellen would argue, was not only morally unimaginable but physically impossible, given the architecture and sleeping arrangements at Monticello. This argument, intriguing for what it reveals about Monticello and its maker's mind, deserves closer scrutiny. A three-story farmhouse designed to look like a one-floor villa, Monticello is a masterpiece of architectural deception, beginning with the way Jefferson concealed its workrooms, slave quarters, and other dependencies beneath the terraces and main house.

Even today, visitors are impressed by Jefferson's use of open space and natural light, by the ease with which one room opens into another, and by the effect of dividing rooms with all-glass French doors. Such devices convey the sense that life in this house is open and free, that nothing is hidden from view, and that, under its skylights, there are no secrets to be kept. Jefferson preferred octagonal rooms to square ones, Jack McLaughlin reminds us in his book on the architecture of Monticello, because octagons "eliminated dark corners."

This impression of openness and candor was an artful illusion. Monticello was, and is, a deceptive building, incorporating degrees of privacy unheard of in Virginia plantation houses in a structure that seems, at first glance, designed almost wholly for public use. This concern for domestic privacy can be difficult to distinguish from a need for secrecy, which is especially apparent in the design of Jefferson's personal quarters—and of the sleeping arrangements generally.

Although most of Monticello's first floor, with its expansive entrance hall,

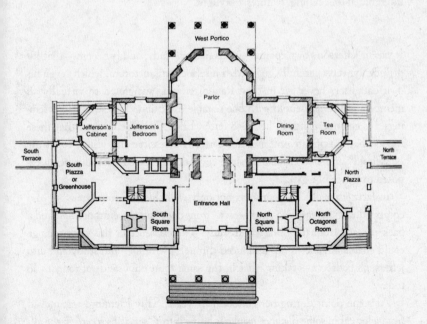

*No one "slept within sound of [Jefferson's] breathing." The floor plan of Monticello.*

parlor, and dining rooms, was very much a public space, it also included three bedrooms—Jefferson's, on the south side of the house, and two smaller guest bedrooms, on the north side, beyond the entrance hall and parlor. The rest of the family, that is, slept upstairs, and downstairs guests slept on the other side of the house. Jefferson's bedroom was thus sequestered from the bedrooms of his daughter and grandchildren and overnight guests.

Because Jefferson slept so far away from everyone else, one of Jeff Randolph's claims seems disingenuous. This is the argument that Jefferson and Sally Hemings could not have had a sexual relationship without being overheard. Randolph told Henry Randall, for example, that he "slept within sound of [Jefferson's] breathing at night." This is unlikely unless, as one critic has noted, the soft-spoken Jefferson "was a thunderous snorer." When Randolph lived at Monticello—well after Sally Hemings's childbearing years—he did not sleep near Jefferson's room, but in the Dome Room, two floors up. Because the only bedrooms other than Jefferson's on the first floor were on the other side of the house, no one slept "within sound of [Jefferson's] breathing." Nor did anyone sleep directly above Jefferson because, as any visitor can see, his bedroom, with its eighteen-foot ceiling, features a skylight.


It was in Jefferson's own rooms—in his library, study, and bedroom—that his privacy was most carefully guarded. This sanctum sanctorum, which "even his own daughters never sat in," Jeff Randolph said, was closed to virtually all members of the household with one notable exception. This was Sally Hemings, his chambermaid. In her 1858 letter, Ellen Coolidge claimed that these rooms "had no private entrance not perfectly accessible and visible to all the household" and that no female slave could have entered "without being exposed to the public gaze."

In fact, Jefferson's bedroom was not only well shielded from view but also equipped with at least two entrances: a "front door" off the entrance hall and a back passage from the library and study. The existence of this back passage could enable anyone to slip unnoticed through the library and study and into Jefferson's bedroom—taking, that is, the same route thousands of tourists do today.

At some point during her childbearing years, Sally Hemings was moved from a log cabin some distance from her house into a "servant's room" in the all-weather passageway that runs beneath it. "These porticles may not have been built specifically to facilitate Sally's nocturnal visits," Helen F. Leary has written in her admirably dispassionate investigation in *The National Genealogical Society Quarterly,* "but they certainly would have concealed them."

There was one additional means of access to Jefferson's *sanctum sanctorum.* This was a staircase, added around 1796, that led from the slave quarters under the terrace into a hallway adjacent to Jefferson library. Because of these architectural additions, Sally Hemings could easily have entered Jefferson's private chambers at any time of day or night, without being seen or heard.

Few male visitors to Monticello were as cautious as Jefferson, and it is to these friends and relations that his defenders, past and present, have been most eager to assign responsibility for "the yellow children." Around 1862, Edmund Bacon, Monticello's overseer for many years, said he knew who Harriet's father was (Bacon had seen the man "coming out of her mother's room many a morning") and that it was not Jefferson. Bacon failed to say more, however. Other defenders accused Randolph Jefferson, the president's younger brother, and Peter Carr, a nephew of Jefferson's who frequently visited Monticello.

This effort to point to someone other than Jefferson hit a snag in 1998, when the journal *Nature* published a widely reported analysis of the DNA of two descendants of Field Jefferson, an uncle of Thomas Jefferson; five descendants of a grandfather of Peter Carr; five descendants of Thomas Woodson; and one descendant of Eston Hemings.

The results of this comparison, while nowhere near as conclusive as newspaper and magazine accounts would indicate, nevertheless established several significant facts. The analysis indicated that the father of Eston Hemings was indeed a member of the Jefferson family. This did not, as some reports had it, prove that Thomas Jefferson was Eston's father, because, at the time Eston was conceived, about twenty-five male Jeffersons who could have been the father lived in Virginia and some of them visited Monticello. The analysis also revealed that Peter Carr could not have been the father of Eston Hemings and that Thomas Woodson was neither a Jefferson nor a Hemings.

Taking all the other nonscientific evidence into account, the researchers who conducted the DNA analysis concluded that the "simplest and most probable" conclusion was that Thomas Jefferson fathered Eston Hemings. Some months later, the Thomas Jefferson Foundation, which owns and operates Monticello, established a panel of its own to review the DNA research,

*South Dependencies at Monticello, site of Sally Hemings's "servant's room."*

citing "a high probability that Thomas Jefferson was the father of Eston Hemings and that he was perhaps the father of all six of Sally Hemings's children listed in Monticello records," meaning—besides Eston—both Harriets, Beverley, Madison and the unnamed daughter born in 1799.

This conclusion, it must be said, was not based on science, because only DNA traceable to Eston was tested. Strictly speaking, the DNA evidence revealed little or nothing about the identity of the father—or fathers—of Sally Hemings's other children. This, of course, leaves open the possibility that Sally Hemings might have borne children by more than one man. Sally's mother certainly did, as did her mother before her.

These women exercised little or no control of their bodies, and, if Jefferson's own grandchildren are to be believed, white men at Monticello took repeated advantage of them. That is the inescapable impression left by the family's attempts to find men other than Jefferson to blame for Sally Hemings's pregnancies. Jeff Randolph, for example, told Ellen Coolidge that he had overheard Peter Carr acknowledge, "with a laugh," fathering children by Sally Hemings, just as Samuel had fathered children by a sister of Sally's named Betty. Furthermore, Ellen Coolidge said, the sisters' "connection with the Carrs was perfectly notorious at Monticello." Ellen Coolidge claimed that all of Sally's children were sired by Peter Carr, whom she called "the most notorious good-natured Turk that ever was master of a black seraglio kept at other men's expense." Jeff Randolph even claimed to have confronted the Carrs about their misdeeds, reducing them to tears. Some aspects of this story might seem dubious, in light of the DNA evidence, but it is possible that Jeff Randolph believed the Carrs were responsible for Sally Hemings's pregnancies, and that the brothers did engage in sexual relations with slave women at Monticello.

With Peter Carr eliminated as the father of Eston Hemings, Jefferson's defenders since 1998 have focused their attention on Randolph Jefferson, who might seem a likely suspect. A widower when Eston Hemings was conceived, Randolph "used to come out among the black people, play the fiddle and dance half the night," according to Isaac Jefferson. Unfortunately for those who would blame Randolph Jefferson, there is no evidence that he was at Monticello when Sally became pregnant with Eston. Randolph Jefferson lived twenty miles south of Monticello, at his own plantation, and the only indication that he might have come to Monticello in the fall of 1807 is a casual invitation to visit at a time when Anna Scott Marks, Randolph Jefferson's twin sister, would be there. There is no evidence, however, that he did so.

Ellen Coolidge, who, of course, could not know what later DNA evidence would reveal about Eston's father, also pointed to other possible suspects, contributing to the picture of a plantation where white men, highborn and low, routinely had their way with slave women. Unnamed Irish laborers who worked on the house "were known to have had children of whom the mothers were black women," Ellen said. Finally, there were "dissipated young men in the neighborhood who sought the society of the mulatresses," but "were not anxious to establish any claim of paternity in the results of such associations."

If day laborers were allowed to prey on the slave women at Monticello, just how much license might Jefferson's peers have enjoyed? Jefferson, it must be remembered, was a gentleman, and gentlemen did not police the private behavior of their guests, or even speculate about it. This high-minded sentiment meant that gentlemen who were inclined to take advantage of their hosts' hospitality could do so with impunity.

Jefferson was also a generous host, which meant that he simply looked the other way when friends came to stay, and an atmosphere of laissez-faire prevailed. The working assumption seems to have been that whatever was the master's was also his guests', and whether or not the fastidious Jefferson intended it, his randier guests applied the principle to his human property—and there was little that even the members of Jefferson's own immediate family could do about it. To question their behavior would have been to question his. "What suited him," Henry Randall would write, "satisfied them."

It is clear, from almost every account, that Jefferson almost always urged visitors to stay overnight or longer, that he personally showed them around the plantation, and that he entertained them even more lavishly than he could afford. They would eat and drink, and then he would retire to his private chambers. After that, they were as free as their sense of honor and entitlement allowed them to be.

Just how free is revealed in stark and chilling specificity in the visits of Colonel Archibald Cary, a nephew of Jefferson's. When Colonel Cary was on his way, Jefferson would tell the slave Isaac when the colonel was to arrive and instruct him to open Monticello's three gates to allow the guest onto the property. When Isaac failed to get the gates open in time, Isaac said, "the Colonel soon as he git to the house look about for [me] and whip [me] with his horse-whip." Cary would also "walk straight into the kitchen and ax de cooks what they hab for dinner." If they didn't have what he wanted, he would wait "till it was cooked. Colonel Cary made freer at Monticello than he did at home; whip anybody." Cary—with Jefferson at home—"has given Isaac more whippings than he has fingers and toes." Jefferson, who was himself "very kind to servants," in Isaac's words, did not intervene when his houseguests were equally brutal.

He "has given Isaac more whippings than he has fingers and toes."
Isaac Jefferson, a Monticello slave.

That Cary was "a tall thin-visaged man jist like Mr. Jefferson" may also suggest that some of the slaves at Monticello who looked like their master might also have resembled this imperious and unbridled guest. Feeling no compunction about whipping the men, he hardly seems the kind of man who would have felt any scruples about forcing himself on the women.

The effect of this environment on Jefferson's daughter and granddaughters can only be imagined, but it is evident from their own recollections that the Sally Hemings scandal took its toll. It is also apparent that Jefferson—the only person at Monticello who "never betrayed the least consciousness" of the resemblance of the household slaves to himself—remained oblivious, if not insensitive, to the embarrassment and discomfort that it caused.

Only once that we know of did a family member raise the subject with Jefferson. Exactly when this occurred is unclear, and two slightly differing versions of the incident exist. One day, a visibly distraught Martha Randolph and a visitor, a family friend and Virginia congressman, William Burwell, entered the library at Monticello carrying a poem satirizing Jefferson's relationship with his "black Aspasia." Seeking some response that might put her mind at ease, Martha confronted her father with the poem.

In one of the two versions of the story, the "injured individual"—meaning Jefferson, not Martha—glanced at the poem, "only smiled" at its content, and appeared "not himself in the smallest degree annoyed." In the other version, upon reading the poem, Jefferson "broke into a hearty, clear laugh." Martha "looked a little crest-fallen, but as soon as the library door closed, joined heartily in the merriment."

In neither account of the incident did Jefferson offer any comfort to his daughter, and she never again mentioned the subject to him.

# Chapter 25

## "Something Very Great and Very New"

On May 5, 1817, the presence of three men in the Court Day crowd at Charlottesville, the *Richmond Enquirer* reported, attracted "the eager gaze of their Fellow Citizens." To create such an impression on Court Day was no small accomplishment, for this was a festive time when the judges who rode the circuit heard cases, and people from outlying farms and settlements rode into town, filling the streets.

The august trio consisted of Thomas Jefferson, James Madison, and James Monroe. Jefferson was already a legend. Madison, who had just completed his second term as president of the United States, could someday reach legendary status, too; and Monroe, sworn in just eight weeks earlier as Madison's successor, might have greatness in him as well.

They had come together on business that, at first glance, might well have seemed beneath their abilities. At Jefferson's prompting, Madison and Monroe were gathered for the first official meeting of the board of visitors of an obscure, nearly defunct private school originally named Albemarle Academy. At this meeting, the board of what from this day forward was to be called Central College took the bold step of voting to use the few assets the school had to buy land on the outskirts of town. On this land, they further voted to establish a new institution altogether, one that Jefferson hoped would be vastly more significant than Albemarle Academy or Central College. To that end, the board agreed to begin general fund-raising. Jefferson pledged $1,000 to the fund and presented sketches of what he would later call an "academical village."

As humble as these beginnings may have been, Central College represented in its earliest form the project to which Jefferson would devote much of his energy in the years to come. Since his earliest days in the House of Burgesses, he had dreamed of establishing in Virginia an institution of higher learning to rival Harvard College and the College of New Jersey at Princeton. This new institution would serve an ethical as well as academic function. The way to raise virtuous citizens was through education, and Virginia, the nation, and the world would be better for the upright, disinterested, and prudent young gentlemen this college would produce. Their moral senses would be refined as their intellects were developed.

As the New World's foremost exponent of the Enlightenment, Jefferson had taken upon himself the colossal task of launching this university, working with the materials at hand, however unpromising. Back in March 1814, Jefferson had been made a trustee of Albemarle Academy, established a decade earlier to teach the classics to the sons of county planters. Between the time of its founding and Jefferson's appointment to its board, however, the school had lost all of its students. In 1816, seeking a new start for the moribund institution and a name that reflected his grand ambitions for it, Jefferson obtained permission from the Virginia legislature to change its name from Albemarle Academy to Central College.

But, more important, Jefferson worked through sympathetic lawmakers in Richmond to persuade their colleagues to consider funding a new state college. His hope, obviously, was that Central College would be the logical recipient of the legislature's support and its financial backing.

Jefferson, who turned seventy-four a month before his meeting with Madison and Monroe in Charlottesville, plunged into this program with the zeal of a much younger man. Despite his painful wrist, he completed the architectural drawings that he had shared at the meeting and then sent them for review to William Thornton and Benjamin Latrobe, who had served as architects of the U.S. Capitol. With Monroe back in Washington and Madison at his plantation in Orange County, Jefferson soldiered on alone, proposing a curriculum and compiling lists of professors competent to teach it. From the start, he enjoyed the encouragement, if not the enthusiastic support, of the ever skeptical John Adams.

"I congratulate You and Madison and Monroe on your noble Employment in founding a University," Adams wrote on May 26. "From such a noble Tryumvirate, the World will expect something very great and very new. But if it contains any thing quite original, and very excellent, I fear the prejudices are too deeply rooted to suffer it to last long, though it may be accepted at first."

So far—this Jefferson did not tell Adams—the college had yet to meet with even tentative acceptance in Richmond, beyond approval of the name change. But what Jefferson wanted was indeed "something very great and very new": a university that would be wholly secular and utterly independent of any religious institution. An outpost of the Enlightenment, this university would be "so broad, so liberal, and modern," he told Joseph Priestley, "as to be worth patronizing with the public support." Whether the public would want to support such learning remained to be seen.

On June 23, 1817, the Central College board purchased a cornfield west of Charlottesville. Jefferson personally surveyed it, and within days, the ground was being prepared. By midsummer, $30,000 had been pledged in Albemarle alone, and the *Richmond Enquirer* pronounced it a "brilliant success."

Jefferson's design integrated classrooms and living spaces in a harmonious pattern that Latrobe called "entirely novel." It shunned the large, grand, and costly buildings preferred by older, European institutions in favor of parallel pavilions, apartments, and one-story dormitory rooms connected by a covered walkway. Laundries, privies, and other common areas would be built along these colonnades, with dining halls that Jefferson called "hotels" to be leased to innkeepers.

With his characteristic concern that not a minute be wasted, Jefferson wanted the first "hotel" rented to a French couple so the young scholars could learn the language of Diderot and D'Alembert while taking their meals. With a similar desire for efficiency, Jefferson ordered that the west pavilions be based on the Doric order, the east on the Ionic order, and, eventually, a central "Rotunda" on the Corinthian; this way, the buildings themselves could be used for teaching classical architecture.

The plan also allowed for the "academical village" to be built in stages as funds became available. In due course, the Rotunda, housing the library, could be built on the north end of the colonnades, connecting the whole. The south end, however, would remain "open to the horizon," as the architectural historian Hugh Howard has written in *Thomas Jefferson, Architect,* "just as Jefferson wanted the minds of the students and professors to be free and open to new ideas and possibilities."

As Jefferson developed his plans for the new university, he sought the counsel not only of Adams, Joseph Priestley, and Benjamin Rush, but also of the less well-known Thomas Cooper. London born and Oxford educated, Cooper was a radical in politics and a self-described "materialist" in religion who courted controversy wherever he went. A peculiar-looking specimen—barely five feet tall and given to corpulence in his later years—Cooper could be too hasty in his opinions for his own good, as even his friends admitted.

Cooper's sympathy for the French Revolution had made him highly unpopular in England, and in 1794, he sailed to America, settling in Pennsylvania, near Priestley and Rush. In 1800, his anti-Federalist political activities earned him a six-month prison sentence under the Sedition Act, but also brought him to Jefferson's attention. By 1811, when Cooper occupied the chair in natural philosophy and chemistry at Dickinson College, he and Jefferson corresponded frequently on philosophy, religion, the sciences, and education.

At the university, Jefferson told Cooper that he wished to "bring the whole circle of useful science under the direction of the smallest number of professors as possible," the first of whom, Jefferson hoped, would be Cooper himself. The young scholars would be taught mathematics, chemistry, anatomy, mineralogy, economics, and government.

Jefferson also offered the genuinely radical proposal that students not be instructed in theology or religion. Courses in ethics would be taught, but, Jefferson and Cooper agreed, there would be no professor of Divinity. The idea of purely secular education was new, though Jefferson insisted that the university would not be actively hostile to religion. It would be left to "every sect to provide, as they think fittest, the means of furthering instruction in their own peculiar tenets." Should the sects choose not to do so, this would be more than acceptable to Jefferson, who believed that church-controlled universities in Europe and in America had proved disastrous to science. To avoid such a calamity, Jefferson wanted to replace what he considered the obscurantism of the church with the precision of the Enlightenment.

In his belief that the controversial Cooper could be the first member of the faculty, Jefferson's usually astute political judgment faltered. Cooper had been even more outspoken in his criticism of orthodox Christianity than the diplomatic Jefferson had been, and in recent years, the broad-minded Anglican faith of Virginia's Tidewater gentry had given way, in numbers and in force, to the more censorious faith of the Baptists, Presbyterians, and other "dissenting" churches. These pious people regarded skeptics such as Cooper as of unsound character and feared their influence on the immortal souls of their impressionable charges. That these increasingly influential Protestants might oppose

Cooper and, by extension, the institution itself, Jefferson seems not to have anticipated or, if he did, he felt the principles involved too important to compromise.

Oblivious to these controversies or simply determined to prevail despite opposition, Jefferson praised Cooper to the other commissioners, writing to legislators in Richmond, and overseeing the preparation of the grounds at the cornfield. He rode to the site almost daily that summer, staying home only during the worst thunderstorms.

On October 6, 1817, only five months after Jefferson first presented his architectural sketches, the field west of Charlottesville was clogged with horses, carriages, dignitaries, and Albemarlians of the middlin' sort. As Madison stood nearby, President Monroe made a few remarks. Then, with what the *Richmond Enquirer* called "all the ceremony and solemnity due to such an occasion," he laid the cornerstone of the first pavilion at what would become the University of Virginia. Jefferson looked on proudly. Those who had not seen him in years were surprised that his hair had begun to go white.

In the months to come, he would preside over progress on several fronts. Buildings went up, and the legislature seemed to look favorably on the establishment of a new college. In February 1818, the lawmakers allocated $15,000 to establish this institution, and Governor James Preston appointed a special commission to select a politically acceptable site. Named to this commission, Jefferson clearly expected the funds to go to the university in Charlottesville, though whether the legislature would support the radically secular curriculum that he envisioned was far from certain.

The commission was to meet in the fall at a tavern at Rockfish Gap, in the Blue Ridge Mountains thirty miles west of Charlottesville. Despite a painful attack of rheumatism, Jefferson spent the spring drafting a report that drew on the results of the latest census to demonstrate that Charlottesville was at the precise center of the state in both geography and population and, therefore, was the only reasonable site for the new college.

In late July, Jefferson borrowed $100 from the Charlottesville storekeeper James Leitch, and he and Madison set off together on horseback, because the mountain roads to Rockfish Gap made travel by carriage impractical. Two days later, they arrived at the tavern. Presenting his report, Jefferson overwhelmed proponents of other sites with the rigor and detail of his argument and, when the question was called, Charlottesville received sixteen votes. Staunton and Lexington, the other candidates, received between them a total of five.

At Rockfish Gap, Jefferson also unveiled his plans for a curriculum, from which a "chair of divinity" was conspicuously absent. Such a professorship, he told his fellow commissioners, was prohibited "by the principles of our Constitution, which places all sects of religion on an equal footing," and "by the sentiments of the Legislature in favor of freedom of religion." If any of the commissioners found this aspect of Jefferson's plan objectionable, they held their fire, and Jefferson left Rockfish Gap in high spirits.

While Madison headed back to Montpelier, Jefferson rode on to Warm Springs, a resort near Staunton, the farthest west that his travels would ever take him. On the recommendation of well-meaning friends, he planned to spend three weeks at Warm Springs, bathing in the mineral waters to relieve his rheumatism.

For the first week, he found the experience "delicious," and soaked in the foul-smelling ninety-eight-degree waters three times a day. During the second week, however, a "large swelling" appeared on one of his buttocks, apparently the result of infection. The swelling increased "for several days past in size and hardness," he told Martha Randolph, preventing him from "sitting but on the corner of a chair." A second swelling soon developed on the other buttock, and before long Jefferson's entire backside was covered with boils so painful that he could not sit at all.

By this time, his strength was gone, which suggests blood poisoning, a common accompaniment to what Jefferson called an "eruptive complaint" of this kind. Jefferson believed the treatment that followed—"a concoction of mercury and sulfur"—only made his condition worse, bringing on the diarrhea that would afflict him for the rest of his life.

When Jefferson at last got back to Monticello in September, he had been reduced to "extreme weakness." His correspondence slowed to a trickle, and his planning for the college virtually ceased. For most of September, he was unable to get up at all, but by mid-October, he began to improve. "Within a few days," he reported on November 10, "I shall be able to get on my horse, to me that most sovereign of all doctors." This was wishful thinking. Jefferson would not ride again for another three weeks. By December 7, however, he was riding every day, "gathering flesh and strength."

For a time, Jefferson's health had been so compromised that rumors of his death circulated far and wide, and his family received sympathetic inquiries from every part of the country. In December, having ridden down from Montpelier to see for himself how their friend was faring, Madison was able to give Monroe an encouraging report.

"We found him substantially restored from his indisposition, with good appetite, and in the daily practice of taking exercise on horseback," Madison wrote on December 11. "All that remains of the effect produced by the mineral water, is a cutaneous affection of the most superficial kind which will probably soon disappear." Jefferson asked for no man's prayers.

# CHAPTER 26

# Struggling "All Our Lives with Debt & Difficulty"

During the long months during which Jefferson was planning his new college and recuperating from his illness, he came to a conclusion that might have served him well had he reached it years earlier. He now realized that, despite his interest in the theoretical aspects of agriculture, he was "an unskilled manager of my farms," and that it was time to turn to someone who might handle things better. By relinquishing supervision of the farms, he could also devote more time and energy to his fledgling university.

This realization marked a significant moment in Jefferson's life. It was perhaps his first admission—to others but also to himself—that such mastery as he once thought he exercised might well have been an illusion, and that reason alone was not sufficient for the successful management of life.

Under the best of circumstances, Jefferson now understood, he would never have been as diligent as the best farmers tended to be, and the period immediately following the War of 1812 was trying for the most single-minded Virginia planters. The spring of 1817 had been particularly difficult. A third of the entire state's wheat was destroyed by the Hessian fly, and prices fell in the face of competition from the fertile farmlands beyond the Blue Ridge.

During these years, Jefferson's corn, which fed both his slaves and his livestock, had done so poorly that he had to buy it from other farmers, who often had little to sell. The crop he had planted in the spring of 1817 failed also, and the livestock in the barns, stables, and pastures at Monticello sometimes seemed on the verge of starvation; once that spring, one of his mules collapsed and died on the road from Poplar Forest to Monticello, a victim of hunger and exhaustion.

The man into whose "better hands" Jefferson committed his farms was the one he trusted as he trusted few others. This was his grandson Jeff Randolph. Thomas Jefferson Randolph was twenty-four now and, at six feet, four inches, he stood taller than his grandfather, who stooped with age. Randolph's marriage to the former Jane Nicholas had proved a happy and fruitful one; their second child, Martha (Pat) Jefferson Randolph, named for her grandmother and great-grandmother, was born that summer. Randolph also had a home of his own now, four miles east of Monticello, on the other side of the Rivanna. He owned and worked acreage there as well as managed the farms at Monticello. As time went on, Randolph gradually assumed more responsibility for the farms at Poplar Forest, too, and would eventually take over there as well.

At first, Randolph became a kind of tenant farmer, working the land with eighty Monticello field hands and paying "a rent in kind such as [Jefferson] suggested himself," or in whatever commodity was at hand. His rent for the entire year of 1818, for example, took the form of 350 barrels of flour, ground from the wheat at the Monticello mill and shipped to Richmond. There his grandfather's business agent would sell it, crediting the profits to his accounts.

The summer of 1818 proved frustrating for both men. Severe drought left the Rivanna dry during much of August, which made shipping the flour to market difficult. When the boats did get the shipments to Richmond, the flour was found to be of poor quality, made from "smutted" wheat, the victim of excessive rains during the growing season. There was also rain in September, and some of Jefferson's flour was ruined as it sat on the docks before being taken to the warehouse. In November, Jefferson asked his business agent to hold on to the damaged wheat, so that he could determine whether it was from Monticello or Poplar Forest and ascertain "the responsible person." If the ruined flour had come from Monticello, Jefferson explained, "my grandson indemnifies me."

Jefferson, while diplomatic, was also demanding. As the recipient of his grandfather's trust, Randolph assumed a heavy burden that he sometimes resented. Day after day, he rose early, rode from plantation to plantation, supervising operations at his own farm as well as at Monticello, and returned home only after nightfall. Some days, he would be summoned to Poplar Forest or to Richmond, each of which was a day's ride away.

"I breakfasted in the winter by candle light and never came home untill dark," he recalled in his memoirs. Rain or snow "was not recognized as an excuse." Even if he was twenty-five miles from Albemarle County, "regardless of road or weather I always went home, fording or swimming in the night swollen bridgeless streams." Thankfully, he could "sleep any where eating any thing and never tiring." He attributed his "hardy temperament and indomitable will" not to his father but to his mother.

Jefferson demanded his grandson's presence, whenever possible, at Monticello. Impatient when Jeff spent time at his farm on the far side of the river, Jefferson prevailed upon him to move closer, and in 1817, Randolph settled his family in an unfinished farmhouse about a mile down the mountain from Monticello, which, even in summer, they could see through the trees. The Randolphs' new plantation, which abutted Monticello, was named Tufton by Martha Randolph for her friend Lady Caroline Tufton, whom she had known as a young girl at the convent school in Paris.

Life at Tufton was not nearly as elegant as at Monticello. Jane Randolph's sister Sarah Nicholas, who lived with the Randolphs at Tufton, said she would defy anyone "to find a worse" house, or a more poorly provisioned one. Sometimes, Sarah said, the Randolphs lacked "even the common comforts" of meat and firewood; one year, Jane had to cook all the seed peas just "to keep the family from starving." For a time, Jeff's two oldest daughters, Margaret and Pat, made do with "one or two frocks a week," and these were rarely laundered. "I remember full well how awfully dirty they were," Sarah wrote, "& how the flies congregated around Pat."

Jeff Randolph's life during his years as his grandfather's tenant farmer was not what he had imagined for himself, and, though he loved his grandfather, he sometimes thought about how his life might have been different. He had been raised in a household in which learning was esteemed and political office was an honorable calling. Tom Randolph, his father, had been educated at the University of Edinburgh, which at that time outranked even Oxford and Cambridge. Back in Virginia, however, Tom Randolph had managed his money too poorly "to retain anything for himself or his family," Jeff wrote in his memoirs. As a consequence, he had been "sent irregularly to inferior schools but never to college," and the moment he was needed on the farms, his schooling had abruptly ended.

Almost overnight, Jeff Randolph had gone from being a student, with all the privileges and prestige that students then enjoyed, and the opportunities that an education promised, to being a glorified farmhand. Eager "to make up for early deficiencies of education," he had tried to study on his own, "but was soon compelled to throw my books aside and devote myself, mind and body, and effects to the care of my grandfather and his affairs." Any hopes he might have entertained of being what he called a "professional" man—practicing law or medicine—had been jettisoned. Any dreams he had of entering political life were also abandoned, and later in life, he expressed his frustration and disappointment to his mother.

"My son," Martha Randolph replied, "if you have [sic] been professional or in public life, what would have become of us[?]"

Implicit in Martha's response was the recognition that Jeff Randolph was the only male in the household who could be trusted with the farms—that his own father was scarcely able to provide for himself, much less to look after the rest of the family's affairs, and that Charles Bankhead was incapable even of staying sober and controlling his temper.

If Jeff Randolph resented the fact that his own schooling had been cut short so his grandfather could devote his energies to establishing a university for the education of other young men, or if he even saw the irony, he never said so. But his lack of a college education would remain a sensitive subject, for which Jefferson offered no comfort.

Some years earlier, when Randolph had been a diligent student in Philadelphia, Rembrandt Peale had painted his portrait, which he presented as a gift to Jefferson. Jefferson hung the painting in the parlor at Monticello in the second tier, below those of Adams, Franklin, and Lafayette. Randolph—he recalled the moment in his memoirs—would never forget what his grandfather had said as the picture was displayed.

"Had you been educated," Jefferson told his grandson, "you would have been entitled to a place in the first—you'll always occupy the second."

During the closing months of 1818, Jeff Randolph planted yet another year's wheat, and his grandfather, at last recovered from the illness that had laid him low, could ride again. But decisions made many miles from the farm fields of Albemarle County gave the planters new cause for worry. Widely suspected of mismanaging its money, the Second Bank of the United States announced it could no longer honor the notes of its branches, which led to the economic panic that would soon grip the country. Banks up and down the eastern seaboard went under, businesses closed, and unemployment soared, especially in the new textile mills of the North. Below the Potomac, land prices collapsed, and landed gentry like the Randolphs suddenly faced new hardships.

Jefferson alone professed confidence, although he felt more vulnerable to forces beyond his control than he ever had before. With characteristic

*The combatants were "as bloody as butchers." Overseer Edmund Bacon.*

sangfroid, he reminded John Adams the following year that economic difficulties are but temporary occurrences "which like waves in a storm will pass under the ship."

Such fatalism characterized the Monticello household throughout this period, largely through Jefferson's influence. "God grant *we* may be enabled to weather the storm," Ellen Randolph told her mother the following year, "for ours is but a shattered bark to breast the waves which have overwhelmed so many goodly ships." There was no assurance of safe harbor, "for the race is not to the swift, nor the battle to the strong." Perhaps after "struggling all our lives with debt & difficulty," they would see good times return. When that happened, the family's story would stand as "proof of the capriciousness of fortune, who sometimes takes pleasure in elevating the long-depressed in the midst of the fall and ruin of her former favorites."

For now, however, their troubles continued, often in view of the public. In June 1818, the degraded state of affairs at Bankhead's plantation became general knowledge. In the case of *Commonwealth v. Farley*, the defendant was charged with "unlawful gambling & cards" at Carlton. The court decided that the plantation was "a place of public resort," but the record shows no further disposition of the case.

Bankhead, meanwhile, seemed to be getting in fights for the sheer sport of it, even when he was sober. One afternoon, when he had not been drinking, Bankhead asked Edmund Bacon to accompany him home from Charlottesville, but stopped his horse on the road back to Carlton. There he waited until William Fitzhugh Gordon, now an Albemarle lawyer, rode up in the company of a friend. Representing another party in a suit that involved Bankhead, Gordon had allegedly made some insulting comments about him in court, and Bankhead, seeking to avenge these insults, ordered the lawyer to dismount and fight, and threatened to shoot him if he refused.

Gordon "had hardly touched the ground," Bacon recalled years later, "before at it they went and I never in all my life saw such a fight." By the time Bacon and Gordon's friend separated the two combatants, they were "as bloody as butchers." Bankhead got the worst of it, Bacon said, with one eye badly injured, "and I think never did get entirely over the hurt."


Once, at a time when Jefferson was away, Bankhead started trouble at Monticello itself, and this time the episode could not be dismissed so lightly. It was night, and Bankhead had entered the candlelit dining room and ordered Burwell Colbert, the butler, to unlock the liquor cabinet. Seeing that Bankhead was drunk, Burwell refused, and Bankhead began shouting at him. Martha Randolph heard the commotion and, rather than summon her "excitable" husband, as Bacon recalled, she called for Bacon himself. Tom Randolph heard the uproar, however, and reached the dining room just as Bacon did. Bankhead now began to curse at Randolph.

Enraged, Randolph, who had also been drinking, picked up an iron poker that stood near the fireplace. He swung it at Bankhead, knocking him down "as quick as I ever saw a bullock fall," in Bacon's words. The blow "peeled the skin off one side of his forehead and face," and Bankhead's blood spilled onto the dining room floor. If it had been a square blow, instead of a glancing one, Bacon said, it would have killed him.

Years later, Jeff Randolph, who seems not to have been at Monticello that night, acknowledged that the episode had taken place, but dismissed it as a mere "row between two drunken men" who were "immediately reconciled."

It is possible, though it seems unlikely, that amiable relations between Bankhead and his father-in-law were quickly restored. Even if this were the case, the resentment between Bankhead and Jeff Randolph dating back several years continued to simmer. The Bankheads of Carlton and the Randolphs of Tufton had not been on speaking terms for some time, and in recent days there had been gossip about the two men in the saloons, slave quarters, and the plantation houses.

As the year 1819 arrived, people claimed they had heard Bankhead say he meant to harm his brother-in-law. What happened next would be impossible to conceal from Jefferson or anybody else.

# CHAPTER 27

# Blood in the Streets of Charlottesville

The harrowing events that Jefferson would never forget occurred on February 1. On that quiet morning, about the time he had returned from his garden and was catching up on his correspondence in his private chambers at Monticello, Charles Bankhead rode into Charlottesville and purchased a large knife.

This was not the first such weapon that Bankhead owned. He had bought several other knives in recent weeks, "ten or 12 of those Spanish knives in the course of a month," according to Elizabeth Trist. Each time he brought one home, Ann managed to find and hide it. Bankhead was rarely unarmed, in any case. Sometimes he carried pistols, and he almost never left home without "a knife as long as a dirk," according to Hetty Carr, a relative of the Randolphs.

February 1 was Court Day in Charlottesville, when cases were heard, horses and slaves were bought and sold, commoners engaged in wrestling matches, and on the outskirts of town, gentlemen raced their horses. Large sums were wagered on the outcomes of the races and the fights. Liquor flowed freely, and Bankhead, as usual, had spent time in the saloons. Jeff Randolph was in town, too, and had also been drinking.

Whether either man sought a confrontation or not, both knew that they were likely to meet and prepared for that eventuality. Randolph kept his horsewhip with him after he dismounted, and Bankhead carried a knife. Hetty Carr claimed that Bankhead had been threatening his brother-in-law, but not everything people said could be believed. Some days later, Bankhead claimed that Randolph had threatened him. No one knew quite what to believe. Slaves were spreading stories about their feuding masters, and some of these tales were getting back to the planters and their wives.

This much was certain. In recent days, Bankhead had written a "very insulting" letter, in Elizabeth Trist's words, to Randolph's wife. The letter has since been lost, so its contents cannot be known, but for Bankhead to have communicated at all with the wife of a man to whom he was not speaking constituted an offense in itself. Randolph surely regarded it as such and when the two men encountered each other outside the old brick courthouse, he did not disguise his feelings.

Bankhead was standing behind a wagon when he spotted Randolph walking past, carrying his whip. Bankhead stepped out from behind the wagon, grasped his knife, and stood in Randolph's path. Randolph stopped and demanded to know why Bankhead had written to his wife. Angry words followed.

Witnesses said that Randolph struck first, though he later denied it. Bankhead was the aggressor, the Monticello household believed, if only by forcing Randolph into a position in which he had to defend himself.

The crowd clustered around, and Bankhead closed in. Randolph backed away but kept his whip "playing near [his antagonist's] head," according to Hetty Carr. Bankhead brandished his knife, and Randolph "raised his whip to keep him off & struck him with the small end of it," Mrs. Carr said. Bankhead charged, thrusting with his knife, "which cut [Randolph's] coat to pieces." Falling backward, Randolph struck Bankhead with the whip, opening "a pretty considerable gash in the side of his head," Mrs. Trist said. Bankhead fell upon Randolph, stabbing him in the lower back and left arm.

The two struggled on the ground. Randolph struck Bankhead a "blessed providential blow" to the temple, as Randolph's wife, Jane, called it, which stunned Bankhead. Several men in the crowd separated the combatants and hustled Randolph—now nearly unconscious and losing "a great deal of blood," according to Mrs. Trist—into the backroom of Leitch's store. At least one physician followed, and word spread that two of Randolph's arteries had been severed and that he might bleed to death.

Although the records in *Commonwealth v. Bankhead* and *Commonwealth v. Randolph* are incomplete, this much can be determined from existing court documents, from the correspondence of the principals and their families, and from a later statement by Jeff Randolph.

As Randolph lay in the backroom of Leitch's store, Bankhead, whose injuries were not life-threatening, was detained and searched. The sheriff found two more knives on the prisoner and took him before Dabney Minor and John

M. Perry, Albemarle justices of the peace. The justices charged both Bankhead and Randolph, who was represented by a lawyer and family friend named Alexander Garrett, with breach of the peace.

A hearing was scheduled for a week later, on February 8, when witnesses would testify to what they had seen, enabling the court to determine whether additional charges should be filed against either man or both. The justices required Randolph to post bond of $600 and Bankhead to put up $1,000, half of which came from Eli Alexander, a friend. Bankhead was released on condition that he remain in the county unless given permission by the court to leave.

Meanwhile, messengers were dispatched from Leitch's store to tell friends and family that Randolph had been stabbed. One of these messengers was Little Phil, a slave who belonged to Jeff Randolph. The two had grown up together at Edgehill, and Phil was intelligent and resourceful and deeply devoted to his master. When Phil heard what had occurred, he rushed to the store. By the time he arrived, Randolph was feverish. Someone tried to help Randolph sit up, but he fainted. Moments later, when Randolph regained consciousness, Phil, with tears streaming down his face, was cradling him in his arms.

Phil was then sent to fetch Thomas Jefferson's physician, Thomas Watkins, which entailed "tracing the man on his rounds" until he found him. Phil caught up with him eighteen miles away in Fluvanna County, attending another patient. The patient's family refused to let the slave talk to the doctor, so Phil began shouting something about "murder." Dr. Watkins came to see what the trouble was. When he learned of Randolph's condition, he immediately set off and reached Leitch's store around eleven o'clock at night.

Alexander Garrett, meanwhile, had been dispatched to Monticello to notify Jefferson and, presumably, the combatants' wives. Jefferson had just completed his ride around the plantation when Garrett arrived.

"Dreadfully agitated" by the news, in Mrs. Carr's words, Jefferson ordered his horse to be brought back to the house and announced his intention of going to Charlottesville as soon as another mount could be made ready. Informed that Bankhead had been released to return to Carlton, Jefferson feared that the drunkard would go home and "wreak his vengeance on his wife." Perhaps fearing for the safety of all of the women of the Monticello household, Jefferson ordered them to stay home, which prevented them from going to Tufton or Carlton and offering comfort to Jane Randolph or Ann Bankhead.

Jefferson's horse was brought to the house and, over the objections of the women, he climbed back into the saddle and rode off into the darkness. He galloped past the returning messenger and reached Charlottesville "in a time that, over such ground, the boldest rider in Virginia, might, without suspicion to his courage, have pronounced appalling," Henry Randall wrote.

Shown into Leitch's backroom, Jefferson found his grandson still feverish and fighting for life. He dropped to his knees and began to sob. Recognizing his grandfather, Randolph wept as well.

Jefferson returned home that same night and dispatched several slaves with a litter, hoping that they would carry Randolph back to Monticello. Dr. Watkins said that the wounded man should stay in Charlottesville, however, under his care. Alexander Garrett rode up the mountain to reassure Jane Randolph that the doctor believed her husband would survive, provided his infection subsided. There was no reason to believe it would not do so. Watkins remained at Randolph's side, dressing his wounds, until nine the next morning.

The infection did indeed subside, but the injuries to Randolph's left arm were nonetheless serious. Randolph might lose the use of the arm, "a deplorable loss to any man," Jane's sister-in-law Sarah Nicholas reported, "but particularly so to a man of his industry and activity."

Garrett also invited Jane to stay at his house in Charlottesville, where Randolph would be taken as soon as he could be moved. On February 2, Randolph was taken to Garrett's where, six times over the next nine days, Watkins dressed his wounds and administered medicines, billing $50 for his services. For a time, Randolph suffered from a "severe colic," attributed to drinking "Apple water."

The hearing scheduled for February 8 did not take place, in part because Randolph was in no condition to appear, but also because Bankhead, after going back to Carlton, had fled to his father's house in Caroline County. This was no surprise, Randolph's lawyer reported. If there was any chance he might be sent to the penitentiary, Bankhead told Garrett, he would leave the county and forfeit the $500 he had posted.

The hearing was rescheduled for March 1. This delay frustrated the Randolphs and their friends, who wanted Bankhead to be punished and the charges against Randolph to be dropped. Cousin John Carr considered Bankhead "capable of anything nearly" and was "in high hopes he will get his neck broke." His execution would be "the only thing that would set his poor wife at liberty." Mary Patterson, one of the Nicholas in-laws, said she hoped the episode would persuade Bankhead's "unfortunate wife to comply with the wishes of her friends in separating from a creature whose presence must now excite horror and aversion." H. B. Trist, one of Elizabeth Trist's sons, could not fathom how "a woman of delicacy," brought up in a "most refined circle," could "get into bed with a drunk." Sarah Nicholas also thought "there must be something wrong with a woman who could live with such a beast," thinking it "almost entirely impossible for any one to love such a man."

But love him Ann did. Rebuffing invitations from family members to live at Monticello, she joined Bankhead in Caroline County. Several times she wrote to her parents, expressing her "great unhappiness at the event that took place" but insisting that Randolph "brought it on himself by commencing hostilities." Bankhead did not flee, she claimed. He had dutifully posted bond and merely gone to visit his father, as any man might have done.

A few days after the fight, a letter arrived at Monticello, addressed to Jefferson. "The course I now take in addressing you," Bankhead began, "is disapproved of by my wife whose judgment but rarely errs; she thinks your time & feelings have already been too much encroached upon & excited."

Bankhead, however, had decided that his own feelings took precedence over Jefferson's—and, apparently, over Ann's as well. Fearing that Jefferson believed the worst of him, Bankhead said that he wished to refute the charge that he had been planning to attack his brother-in-law. In fact, not "five minutes after the affray, when the minds of the people were warm and highly excited," Bankhead wrote, every single witness, "without the slightest variation in their testimony," told the authorities that Randolph "was the aggressor in the most unprovoked manner." By the time Bankhead could even draw his knife, his head "was laid open to the skull in two places."

Physical suffering was one thing, Bankhead said, but dishonor was far worse. "I can bear bodily pain I suspect with as much fortitude as most men, but the disgrace of having been horse-whiped in the presence of three or four hundred people would have sunk me into the dust and rendered me miserable for life." As a gentleman, Bankhead had had no choice but to strike back. Even Randolph's friend and lawyer, Alexander Garrett, told the sheriff that Randolph had threatened three weeks earlier to "horsewhip [Bankhead] on sight."

Garrett had warned Randolph that if he attacked Bankhead, "mischief would ensue."

Randolph's mistake, Bankhead wrote, was to listen to gossip—especially gossip from a slave. Had Randolph not believed "some slanderous tale told him by some poor negro, who I suppose thought to gain his favour by that step," Bankhead wrote, none of this would have happened. Randolph should have been "above receiving such intelligence from such a source," except after his mind "had been previously poisoned & prejudiced against me."

Had Randolph bothered to ask Bankhead about any of this, he would have gladly put matters to rest, "but it appears that he rashly prefered his horsewhip to any satisfaction that I could render." Bankhead closed on a high-minded note, however unconvincing. "I pray most sincerely and devoutly for his recovery," he concluded.

Jefferson did not reply.

Two weeks later, in a letter advising James Madison about the next meeting of the university's board, Jefferson closed by reporting that his grandson was "healing slowly" from wounds that Madison might have heard about, suffered in an "accident."

CHAPTER 28

*Fire, Sickness, Drought, and Storm*

In the first days of March 1819, Jefferson received a letter from Wilson Cary Nicholas, who, as Jeff Randolph's father-in-law, knew more about the events of February 1 than did James Madison.

"What, my Dear Sir, can be done to prevent the recurrence of a similar or more fatal misfortune than that which lately befell poor [Randolph]?" Nicholas asked. "I am in constant terror of that miserable man Bankhead perpetrating some dreadful deed or obliging some relation of his wife, her father or brother to kill him in their own defence." Bankhead's family "cannot be safe as long as they are in his power," Nicholas continued. "Something ought to be

*"I have for some time taken for granted that she would fall by [her husband's] hands." Ann Cary Randolph Bankhead.*

done. Most deeply do I feel for all connected with the parties, & bitterly lament that you should have such a source of affliction."

Jefferson wrote back that Randolph's "wounds are nearly healed," though the full use of his left arm was still in doubt. "With respect to Bankhead, there is much room to fear, and mostly for his wife. I have for some time taken for granted that she would fall by his hands." But Ann "is so attached to him that no persuasion has ever availed to induce her to separate and come to live with us, with her children."

By the end of February, court documents show that Albemarle County officials had gathered enough evidence to charge Bankhead with "stabbing and attempted murder." Bankhead failed to appear for the hearing scheduled for March 8, however, and Jefferson concluded that the accused had no intention of appearing at that hearing or any other. Bankhead had evidently decided that, by staying out of Albemarle, he could escape prosecution, and so far the sheriff had not tried to find him. Jefferson hoped that the scofflaw did not succeed in this effort to elude the authorities, since the penitentiary "is the only thing which can produce safety to others, or reformation to himself."

That Bankhead would ever be tried, convicted, and imprisoned seemed doubtful, Jefferson told Nicholas. Virginians could be scandalously nonchalant about enforcing the law, a discouraging trait in a people who prided themselves on their capacity for self-government. Expressing himself more in the language of Thomas Hobbes than that of Jean-Jacques Rousseau, Jefferson told Nicholas that a man in Randolph's position had no recourse but to defend himself, even if it meant killing his assailant. Unfortunately, "the execution of the law is so lenient in our country," Jefferson wrote, "that altho' it's provisions for personal safety are imperfect, enforcement of them is more so, and our citizens are, from this cause, left in a state of nature to save their own lives by taking that of another."

Jefferson and Nicholas were closely connected not only through the marriage of Jefferson's grandson to Nicholas's daughter. Both products of the College of William and Mary, both longtime residents of Albemarle County, they were also lifelong political allies and close friends. As a member of the Virginia legislature, Nicholas had supported Jefferson's efforts to establish religious liberty, and as a member of Congress when Jefferson was president, he had supported his friend's policies, including the hated embargo.

In 1817, after serving two terms as governor of Virginia, Nicholas retired because of ill health, but continued to help his friend. Nicholas was a supporter of the new college at Charlottesville, and as president of the Richmond branch of the Bank of the United States, he was now in a position to be very helpful indeed.

As well as expressing his indignation over Bankhead's attack on Randolph, Nicholas wrote on February 28 to recommend the services of a builder. He had become familiar with Arthur Brockenbrough's work on Richmond's new banks and thought the man might perform similar duties at Jefferson's college. From Nicholas's description, Jefferson replied that Brockenbrough was "exactly such a character as we greatly need for our Procter." He would eventually hire Brockenbrough for that position.

Nicholas tried to benefit Jefferson in other ways as well. In the fall of 1817, Jefferson wanted to borrow $6,000 from the Bank of the United States, and Nicholas—the bank's president—cosigned two separate notes of $3,000 each. These were approved. About six months later, in April 1818, when Nicholas wanted to borrow $20,000, also from the Bank of the United States, it was his turn to ask for Jefferson's signature. Nicholas assured Jefferson that he was worth at least $350,000 and would be easily able to repay the money. The loan would take the form of two $10,000 notes, plus interest of $1,200 per year. The notes would come due in the fall of 1819.

"You will do me the justice," he told Jefferson, "to believe that this request would not be made but under the most entire confidence that you can never suffer the slightest inconvenience from complying with it."

Signing the papers "in utter confidence," Jefferson sent them back to Richmond. The loans were approved, and Jefferson seems not to have given the matter further thought.

By the time of Nicholas's letter expressing concern about Bankhead and recommending Brockenbrough, what became known as the Panic of 1819 held Virginia and the rest of the country in its grip. The banks that remained open—including those in Richmond—began to restrict their lending, and that spring, the Bank of Virginia informed Jefferson that the $2,000 line of credit that he had renewed in the spring of 1816 was being reduced to only $1,700. This was one of five loans Jefferson now carried with Richmond banks, in addition to the two notes he had obtained on Nicholas's behalf through the Bank of the United States.

Such setbacks had begun to weigh heavily on Jefferson. As the months dragged by, that first day of February might have seemed an evil omen or, to one as free of superstition as Jefferson, at least a suitably dreadful beginning to what would prove a dismal year. Without reason, logic, or apparent purpose, there would be fire, sickness, drought, and storm, as one dispiriting calamity followed hard upon another: From February forward, Jefferson would try to summon the stoicism that had served him well in earlier years, seeking only to submit and endure, while maintaining a modicum of grace.

Unlike so many skills Jefferson had mastered through years of eager application, this was one he did not have to seek opportunities to practice. Increasingly, it seems, these opportunities sought him.

In March, the board of visitors of the University of Virginia elected Jefferson its first rector, and by the time the tulips bloomed at Monticello, the first two brick pavilions—housing and classrooms for the faculty—were being built. But when the other pavilions would be started no one knew, and work might have to cease at any moment. In an atmosphere of financial uncertainty, the Presbyterian and Baptist legislators in Richmond, lukewarm in their support for the university from the beginning, were less eager than ever to bankroll Jefferson's notions of liberal education.

At the second meeting of the board of visitors, at Madison's Montpelier, Jefferson was forced to defend his selection of Thomas Cooper as the university's first professor. Religious conservatives in the Virginia legislature were understandably displeased with Jefferson's choice of the outspoken skeptic to head the faculty, and the other board members were becoming uneasy about him, too. Pointing out that Cooper was "rather unpopular" with the clergy, Joseph C. Cabell warned Jefferson that the appointment could hurt the university's future funding. Perhaps so, Jefferson replied, but Cooper is "acknowledged by every enlightened man who knows him, to be the greatest man in America, in the powers of the mind, and in acquired information."

By late March, Jeff Randolph's injuries had healed sufficiently that he was able to ride his horse from Tufton to Monticello and had begun to supervise the farms again. He had even felt well enough to attend a ball in Charlottesville, Elizabeth Trist said, "but is crip[p]led in his left arm."

Charles Bankhead, meanwhile, had leased a farm in Caroline County with a former English sea captain named Joseph Miller and, by all evidence, was drinking again. This was not surprising, since Miller, in Jefferson's own words, was "the most skillful brewer" to have ever come to America. It was Miller who, in 1813, had helped Jefferson erect a still at Monticello. Bankhead evidently planned to stay in Caroline County, keeping Ann and their children with him. As soon as his wheat was harvested, he said he planned to move all his slaves from Carlton to his new farm.

April came, and for a brief but horrifying moment on the second Tuesday of the month, Jefferson feared that he might lose Monticello. That day, a fire of undetermined origin broke out in the north pavilion, threatening the entire structure. Jefferson, at seventy-five, insisted on joining the other men of the household in fighting the flames. H. B. Trist remembered the "wind blowing at a furious rate, towards the house," making it almost impossible to contain the blaze, which consumed part of the north pavilion. The flames raced along the wooden walkway to the south pavilion, near Jefferson's bedroom. Fortunately, Trist said, the wind changed direction "when the fire was raging with the greatest fury," and the frantic men were able to extinguish the blaze.

Jefferson fell during the commotion, peeling the skin from one of his shins. The injury was not serious, but mentions of it made the Washington newspapers. John Quincy Adams wrote to express his sympathy, and on May 10, Jefferson thanked him but insisted that the wound was of no consequence: "The bodily injury as well as that to my building were both slight. The former disappeared, and the latter will soon do so."

Jefferson's friends were not so blasé about the fire or the injury. "We seem to hear of nothing but hairbreadth escapes from Albemarle," Peggy Nicholas wrote to her sister Jane Randolph. "What a miracle Monticello was not burnt!"

After fire came drought, then disease. The summer of 1819 proved one of the hottest and driest anyone in Albemarle could remember. Crops wilted in the fields, and the Rivanna was so shallow that much of the flour milled from Jefferson's wheat could not be shipped to market in Richmond. The livestock suffered, too. Edmund Bacon urged Jefferson to buy new mules. The only two left at Monticello, Bacon wrote, "were about to give out." One had gone blind, and the other was "only able to work now & then."

It was also hot and dry at Poplar Forest, save for one night in early June when a horrendous hailstorm hit. "Your house appears to have been in the cen-

*"What a miracle Monticello was not burnt!" The mansion in disrepair.*

ter of it," Joel Yancey, the overseer, reported. Hailstones three inches in diameter crashed into the house, garden, and grounds, and almost all the windows in the house were "broken to atoms and the house is flooded." Until the glass could be replaced—stores in Lynchburg did not carry glass of that size—the house "is very much exposed."

How the slave cabins held up, Yancey did not say, but twice that month, disease swept through the slave population, decimating the Poplar Forest workforce. Yancey asked if Jefferson could spare some of the Monticello field hands to help harvest the Poplar Forest wheat. On June 25, Jefferson expressed "much concern with the deaths and sickness among our people" at Poplar Forest. Unfortunately, "here we are in worse condition." Sixteen slaves at Monticello were "laid up with the nervous fever," and two—a woman and a child—had died. The illness at Monticello "puts it out of my power to send you any help; for without all aid I can give my grandson he would lose his harvest."

On July 17, when Jefferson arrived at Poplar Forest, he saw for himself how much damage the storm had done. The windowpanes were not only shattered, as Yancey reported, but high winds had "done nearly the same mischief to the folding doors on one side of the dining room," according to Cornelia Randolph, who, with her sister Ellen, had accompanied their grandfather. "Nothing is left of the skylight but the sash." The skylight had been boarded up, which darkened the dining room, Ellen Randolph told their mother. The floors were "stained and moulded" from rain that had leaked into the house. The grounds showed signs not only of damage from the storm but also from neglect. Poplar Forest "looks rather more dismal than usual," Ellen said. The planks of the terrace had been ripped up "by the violence of the wind," and weeds "grow to the very door of the kitchen, as high as your head."

Hoping to relax, Jefferson instead found himself dealing with urgent and costly repairs to the house. He was also confronted with the sudden and serious illness of Burwell Colbert, the trusted butler who had made the trip to Poplar Forest with Jefferson and his granddaughters. Jefferson decided that Burwell suffered from a potentially fatal "stricture in the bowels" and set about, with his granddaughters' help, to treat the man himself. But this eager trio, Ellen told her mother, made up "as complete a tribe of ignoramuses as I do know, and I do not believe our three heads combined contain as much medical knowledge as would save a sparrow."

Unable to relieve Burwell's suffering, Jefferson finally contacted a real doctor, one William Steptoe. But Steptoe said he could not come to Poplar Forest and feared that he could be of little help even if he did pay a call because he lacked proper equipment. "My syringe," Steptoe said, "is so often lent and sent about the neighborhood that I am sorry to say I do not know who had it last."

Burwell's condition worsened until Jefferson became nearly as worried as he had been six months earlier, when Jeff Randolph had been wounded. "I never saw anybody so uneasy as Grandpapa," Ellen reported on July 28. That Burwell regained his health—he would live another thirty years—may have resulted more from the round-the-clock care of the carpenter John Hemings than from the efforts of Jefferson and his granddaughters. "Johnny is one of my favorites," Ellen told Virginia on August 4, "and more so, now than ever since I have witnessed his kind attentions to Burwell."

Then Jefferson himself fell ill. In early August, with the temperature outside reaching ninety-nine degrees, Jefferson was struck with "the severest attack of rheumatism I have ever experienced." Barely able to walk, his hands and feet swollen and in great pain, Jefferson had his limbs wrapped in flannel in hopes of easing his discomfort.

It was in this weakened condition that, on August 11, he received a letter from his friend Wilson Cary Nicholas. Jefferson read the letter and "*said* very little," Ellen Randolph told her mother, "but his countenance expressed a great deal."

The news from Nicholas was this. The first of the two $10,000 loans that Jefferson had cosigned in April 1818 had come due, and Nicholas had been unable to make his payments. The second loan would be due within the month, and he was delinquent there as well. The other officers of the Bank of the United States had determined—prematurely, Nicholas claimed—that he was insolvent and were calling in both loans. Although Nicholas was well aware that this news would be upsetting to Jefferson, he assured Jefferson that he need not worry. Despite what the other bankers might believe, Nicholas insisted that his assets exceeded his liabilities, and, given time, he would be able to pay his debts, with no inconvenience to his friend.

Jefferson was stunned. Despite Nicholas's assurances, Jefferson saw no reason to doubt the bankers' less optimistic assessment of the situation. And if they were correct, he faced an immediate and overwhelming financial crisis. If

*His bankruptcy was, for Jefferson, the "coup de grace." Wilson Cary Nicholas.*

Nicholas were indeed bankrupt, the bank would come after Jefferson for the money, which he did not have, and he knew only two ways to raise it. He could either sell off land, and land prices had collapsed, or he could go deeper into debt by taking out still more loans, and the banks had curtailed their lending.

Taking no comfort from his friend's bland reassurances, Jefferson wrote that day to Patrick Gibson, his business agent in Richmond. The news from Nicholas "falls on me like a clap of thunder," Jefferson wrote. Despite what he said, Nicholas was evidently bankrupt, and his claims that he could pay his debts provided his property "sells for anything like its value 6 years ago" were ludicrous. Distress sales in that part of Virginia were bringing prices "from 1/5 to 1/30th of what the same articles sold for a year ago." Jefferson needed to know, as soon as possible, all that Gibson could find out about Nicholas's financial condition and what Jefferson's options might be.

Jefferson also replied that day to Nicholas. His friend's letter had arrived when Jefferson was in great physical pain, he wrote, but its contents caused "affliction of another kind, very much on your account and not small on my own." Any requirement that Jefferson pay Nicholas's loans "would indeed close my course by a catastrophe I had never contemplated. But the comfort which supports me is the entire confidence I repose in your friendship to find some means of warding off this desperate calamity."

Nicholas reassured Jefferson that he was doing everything in his power to shield him from loss. He was seeking a sixty-day extension on his interest payments and asking for two years in which to pay the balance. Nicholas also expressed his remorse, and Jefferson, in his August 24 reply, tried to offer comfort.

"Have no uneasiness, dear Sir, for any part I bear in this painful business," Jefferson replied. "I know how well we are apt to be deluded by our calculations, and to be innocently led into error by them."

By this time, Jefferson had received official confirmation from J. B. Dandridge of the Bank of the United States of what Nicholas had told him a week earlier. The first of the two $10,000 notes that Jefferson had cosigned, due August 18, Dandridge wrote, "had been protested for nonpayment for which with interest you are held liable to the Bank of the United States." There was every reason to believe that Nicholas would default on the second loan as well. Meanwhile, Patrick Gibson reported that Nicholas was in much more dire straits than he had indicated. Far from solvent, Gibson had discovered that

Nicholas was more than $200,000 in debt. Even so, the bank gave Nicholas the sixty-day extension that he sought.

Jefferson, meanwhile, approached the bank with a proposition that he hoped would afford him more protection as well. He asked that the loans be renewed for a full year. In return, as further protection for the bank, Jefferson agreed to find an additional cosigner. Jefferson said he would deed over to this new cosigner land that would be worth at least $20,000. The deed was to be drawn up in such a way that the land would be security for the loan. In the event of default, the land became the property of the bank. Jefferson said he would arrange this transfer of property as soon as he returned to Monticello in three or four weeks. On September 2, the bank notified Jefferson that his proposal had been approved.

On September 13, Jefferson, his granddaughters, and a recovered Burwell Colbert left Poplar Forest for Monticello. They spent the night at an inn along the road and, before crossing the James River on the morning of September 14, paid a neighborly and, apparently, uneventful call upon Wilson Cary Nicholas at his riverfront plantation.

Back at Monticello, Jefferson found his new cosigner: Jeff Randolph.

On September 18, Jefferson deeded to his grandson 956 acres in Bedford County, and Randolph signed the loan documents. The acreage, Jefferson assured Randolph and the bank, was "amply sufficient for this debt." Given the precipitous and ongoing decline in the value of real property, it is impossible to say how Jefferson could have known the land's worth either at that moment or in coming years.

What can be said with certainty is this: just as Jefferson had been liable for the $20,000 when Nicholas defaulted, Randolph would now be liable should Jefferson default.

It was a custom of the family in Albemarle—"a sort of regulation imposed by his affection," Henry Randall wrote—that whenever one of the young women of the family returned after a visit elsewhere, she would pay her respects to Jefferson at Monticello before going to her own home.

Jane Randolph, Jeff Randolph's wife and Wilson Cary Nicholas's daughter, had been away when Jefferson came back from Poplar Forest. By the time she made her way up the mountain before going home to Tufton, she had learned of her father's bankruptcy. With some sense of what his insolvency might mean for Jefferson, she was worried about her father but also embarrassed for him. She did not know, however, that her own husband had now been ensnared in this web of debt.

Jane arrived at Monticello around dinnertime. Jefferson rarely left his study until the second dinner bell was rung, but today, having been told that Jane was on her way, he emerged as soon as the first bell rang.

"Has not Jane come?" he asked.

Hearing his voice, she hurried to meet him. "Instead of the usual hearty hand-shake and kiss," Randall wrote, "he folded her in his arms. His smile was radiant." They sat down to dinner, and throughout the meal, Jefferson spoke with his usual animation and good humor. "Neither then, nor on any subsequent occasion did he ever by a word or look make her aware that he was even conscious of the misfortune her father had brought upon him."

Although Jefferson tried to behave as if the Nicholas debacle did not worry him, Ellen Randolph suspected that Nicholas was less innocent than Jefferson seemed to think. Although she had always considered Nicholas to be "a man of the highest honor," Ellen told her mother that it was difficult to "reconcile his present situation with my ideas of honor" and impossible to believe that he could have been "ignorant of the precipice on which he stood." That he had involved Jefferson "in his ruin, merely to put off the evil day" was also hard to imagine. Such conduct "is worse than dishonorable," and for Ellen to believe him capable of it "would shake my general confidence in mankind."

For the present, however, "all my thoughts center on dear Grandfather; let his old age be secured from the storms which threaten us all, and I would willingly agree to abide their peltings. I am almost ready to fix my ideas of right and wrong on this single point; to believe every thing honorable which can save him—everything base, vile & dishonorable, that tends to obscure the evening of such a life."

That the close of Jefferson's life would be free of affliction seemed increasingly unlikely. By year's end, he was suffering mentally and physically. His rheumatism persisted well into October, when his miseries were compounded by severe constipation, or a "cholic which was attended with a stricture of the upper bowels," he reported to James Madison on October 18. This most recent affliction, which brought "great pain and immediate danger," turned out to be a precursor of the digestive difficulties that would afflict him for the rest of his life.

"Mr. Jefferson was very ill yesterday, his life even was in danger," H. B. Trist reported after visiting Jefferson on October 19. "His digestive powers which in general are so regular and good, failed him, and for two or three days a *passage* had been denied him by nature, consequently the old gentleman was taken very ill."

Trist hoped "for the good of his country that providence spare him for a score of years and another score for the sake of his family, and were it not asking too much for his own sake, for he deserves to live half a dozen ages of men." If longevity were bestowed "in proportion to correct conduct he would never die."

# CHAPTER 29

# A Philosophe's Faith

Throughout the fall of 1819, while ill and struggling to escape financial ruin, Jefferson was also quietly at work on a project that engaged his intellectual interests as few activities had in years, with the sole exception of the university. This was his summation, almost three decades in the making, of the life, character, and ethical system of Jesus of Nazareth. In it, Jefferson hoped to catalogue all he had concluded in his seventy-six years about the nature of what H. B. Trist had called "correct conduct."

Sequestered in his study, not telling even members of his family what he was working on, Jefferson labored for hours, cutting up New Testaments in Greek, Latin, French, and English. He then reassembled selected passages into what he considered a factual account of Jesus' life and an accurate presentation of his teaching. The result, Jefferson believed, could stand up to rigorous intellectual scrutiny as, he was convinced, the narratives of Matthew, Mark, Luke, and John could not.

Jefferson's desire to produce such a work could be traced to a time, years earlier, when he felt part of a small but highly influential fraternity of scientists and scholars—natural philosophers, they would have called themselves—of advanced views. Years earlier, when Jefferson first became active in the American Philosophical Society, his circle included such first-rate minds as Benjamin Franklin, David Rittenhouse, Joseph Priestley, and Benjamin Rush. These were men who looked favorably on the application of Enlightenment rationalism to all subjects, including religion and ethics. By 1819, however, all of these men had died—Franklin and Rittenhouse in the last decade of the previous century, Priestley in 1804, Rush in 1813.

Although Jefferson did not know it at the time, men of such liberal views, rare enough in their own day, would be rarer still in the censorious, more religiously conservative generation that followed. Priestley and Rush may have been the last of their line, which left Jefferson all but alone in his advocacy of reason, rather than revelation or ecclesiastical authority, as the source of truth in matters of religion. Among the few allies he had left was the outspoken, often abrasive Thomas Cooper, who had helped him develop the curriculum for the University of Virginia and shared Jefferson's belief that public education should be free of religious influence.

Jefferson's determination to apply reason to religion went back forty years before that, however. Unable, "from a very early part of my life," to accept the doctrine of the Trinity, Jefferson had fallen away from orthodox Christianity, even the latitudinarian variety practiced by the Anglicans of the Virginia gentry. "Question with boldness even the existence of a god," he urged one of his nephews in 1787, "because, if there be one, he must more approve the homage of reason, than that of blindfolded fear."

Jefferson himself seems not to have denied the existence of God, though—influenced by Voltaire, Helvétius, D'Alembert, Condorcet, and other figures of the French Enlightenment—his was Nature's God, a benevolent but detached Creator whose universe operated on strict, and scientifically knowable, laws. The basis for ethics, Jefferson also decided early in life, was not to be found in Holy Writ, but in the innate moral sense that exists in everyone, priest or plowman.

By the time Jefferson had become a figure on the national stage, his attitude toward religion was not only well known but, indeed, notorious. When his Federalist opponents in the hotly contested presidential campaign of 1800 accused him of plotting to "destroy religion, introduce immorality [and] loosen all the bounds of society," Jefferson nevertheless refused to rebut the charges. Religion, he believed, was a private matter between a man and his god, and religious division weakened the social harmony upon which the survival of the young republic's experiment in self-government depended.

Hoping to promote a Christianity that emphasized broadly acceptable ethical teachings, downplayed divisive matters of doctrine, and rendered his own skepticism palatable to the public, Jefferson, during his presidential years, approached first Priestley and then Rush about publishing works that depicted Jesus as a moral reformer rather than a miracle worker, a sage rather than a savior.

A chemist by training, Priestley was also a Nonconformist clergyman whose support for the French Revolution so outraged his neighbors that, in 1794, he was driven out of England. He was the author of *An History of the Corruptions of Christianity*, which Jefferson read in 1793, and *Socrates and Jesus Compared*, which he read ten years later. After leaving England, Priestley settled in Pennsylvania, in large part to be near Rush and Cooper, friends and fellow chemists. A Pennsylvania native educated in Scotland, Rush taught and practiced medicine in Philadelphia, served in the Continental Congress, and signed the Declaration of Independence. But as Jefferson would discover, neither Priestley nor Rush—who were closer in spirit to the Scottish Enlightenment than to that of the French—was as skeptical of orthodox Christian doctrine as he was.

Highly impressed by Priestley's *Socrates and Jesus Compared*, in 1803 Jefferson appealed to the author to expand the study, summarizing the teachings of all the major classical philosophers and demonstrating the ways in which their ethical teachings differed from those of Jesus. To encourage Priestley, Jefferson prepared what he called a "Syllabus" of such a work, which would establish that Epicurus, Epictetus, and other ancients had excelled in elucidating the duties that one owed to oneself—the importance of controlling the passions, for example—but said too little about "our duties to others." It was here, Jefferson said, that Jesus, "the most innocent, the most benevolent, the most eloquent and sublime character that has ever been exhibited to man," surpassed the ancient Greeks and Romans.

Jefferson wrote that because Jesus wrote nothing himself, the record of his teachings was left to "the most unlettered of men," whose works were then deliberately distorted by generations of opportunists who used Christianity to advance themselves and the church that employed them. This cabal of ambitious priests, Jefferson believed, had concocted the notions that Jesus was born of a virgin, that he claimed to be divine, that he could suspend the laws of nature, and that he rose from the dead.

Also in 1803, Jefferson sent a copy of his "Syllabus" to Rush, elaborating in the accompanying letter on his view that Jesus was a man like any other man, whose "parentage was obscure, his condition poor, and his education null." Jesus nevertheless made the most of his "natural endowments" to lead a life that was "correct and innocent." Over time, however, his simple teachings had been "mutilated, misstated and often [rendered] unintelligible." Once the "corruptions" were removed, his "sublime and benevolent" message would again shine forth.

To Jefferson's disappointment, Priestley questioned the project's premise, expressing amazement that anyone could deny that Jesus understood himself to be on a divine mission or that he claimed to be divine. This, Priestley wrote, was a notion "that I do not remember to have heard before." If Jesus had not claimed to be the Son of God and had not been considered divine by his followers, Priestley said, it would be impossible to account for Christianity's survival and spread. Rush's response, which arrived that same month, also disappointed Jefferson, for he likewise disputed Jefferson's conclusions about whether Jesus regarded himself as divine.

By the time of this correspondence with Priestley and Rush, Jefferson had decided to put his own religious beliefs in a written statement to share with family, with close friends, and with a few political allies. So, in 1804, when, as president of the United States, Jefferson was "overwhelmed with other business," he spent "one or two nights only" cutting out selected passages from two King James Bibles and pasting them in double columns on octavo pages. Undaunted by the challenges that vexed scholars before and after, Jefferson found the authentic sayings of Jesus, as he would tell John Adams ten years later, "as easily distinguishable as diamonds in the dunghill." The true teachings came wrapped "in so much ignorance, so much absurdity, so much untruth, charlatanism, and imposture," he told his former secretary William Short, that he found the work "obvious and easy." Later that year, Jefferson had the forty-six-page compilation privately published as "The Philosophy of Jesus of Nazareth," a copy of which he offered to send to Rush.

Again Jefferson was rebuffed, in much the same language and for almost identical reasons as Priestley and Rush had discouraged him the previous year. (Rush offered to review the work, provided, he told Jefferson, it "renders [Jesus's] *death* as well as his *life* necessary for the Restoration of Mankind.")

About this time, Jefferson abandoned the idea of sharing his religious views with anyone or seeking acceptance of them, either under his own name or through such intermediaries as Priestley or Rush. Why Jefferson decided against telling others what he believed is not altogether clear, but it seems likely that the cool response of these two trusted friends and powerful intellects decided the issue. If these men of the world could not accept his views, it was unrealistic to expect less broad-minded people to look on them with tolerance, much less favor. From now on, Jefferson would turn inward.

In the autumn of 1819, when he again took up the subject of Jesus' teachings, Jefferson kept his study secret, even from Martha Randolph. Beyond the cutting and pasting, not much is known about how Jefferson compiled *The Life and Morals of Jesus of Nazareth* or *The Jefferson Bible*, as it would be known after

1903, when it was published by the U.S. Government Printing Office and made available for the first time to the general public.

The result of his efforts, however, is obvious enough. *The Life and Morals of Jesus* is a biography, stripped of references that offended Jefferson's Enlightenment sensibilities. Beginning with the Gospel of Luke, Jefferson recorded Jesus's birth, though there would be no annunciation, no impregnation by the Holy Ghost, no shepherds, and no wise men. Jesus grew "in wisdom and stature," but not, as Luke had it, "in favor with God."

Jefferson's interest was in Jesus' public ministry, but here, too, Jefferson presented only those aspects of the Galilean rabbi's teachings that accorded with an eighteenth-century *philosophe*'s a priori notions of what such a ministry should involve. "If a moral lesson was embedded in a miracle," Edwin S. Gaustad has written in his study of Jefferson's religious life, "the lesson survived in Jeffersonian scripture, but the miracle did not."

Jefferson's Jesus went about preaching a simple message of universal benevolence, drove the moneychangers out of the Temple, and was condemned to die by Roman authorities. After Jesus was crucified, his followers put his corpse in a tomb, "rolled a great stone to the door of the sepulchre, and departed." Needless to say, Jesus did not rise from the dead.

The Jesus who was left when Jefferson finished his work in October 1819 bears a suspicious resemblance to Jefferson himself. Jefferson's Jesus is kindhearted, contemplative, democratic in his sympathies, quietly dismissive of tradition, and scornful of despots and priests.

Jesus, as Jefferson understood him, was not a world-historical revolutionary, however. This moral philosopher's mission in life was to give to others a set of estimable behavioral principles, although these were not especially original. "Do unto others as you would have them do unto you" was not a new piece of instruction. It is difficult to understand why the Roman and Jewish authorities would bother to put to death the inoffensive man of Jefferson's narrative. It is also difficult to imagine why, in this man's name, followers would give their lives and wars would be fought.

That Jefferson did not excise all passages dealing with sin, repentance, and judgment might suggest that he was no longer as satisfied as he once had been with Enlightenment rationalism, but this is a supposition. For most of Jefferson's life, he believed, with the French philosophes, that man was, by nature, good and capable of becoming progressively better, a view distinctly at odds with that of the early Christian church and the church of Jefferson's own time.

Jefferson's rationalism failed to acknowledge, much less account for, the existence of evil and had little to say about how to respond to it. Notions of man's fallen nature, of sin, and of the need for repentance played no part in the French Enlightenment's understanding of the human condition. The *philosophes* offered no better explanation for this most vexing social problem than to say that men often acted irrationally, but presented no means to make men act otherwise.

Jefferson's Jesus merely offers recommendations that wise men should ponder and, it was to be hoped, adopt in the conduct of their own lives. Whether they did so was, of course, left solely to their own discretion. They might, as rational men, examine these teachings and find them inadequate, inapplicable to their own situations, or in need of revision. That, after all, is the course of human progress, and the choice is the individual's to make.

It is not difficult to see how this ethical system could degenerate into a mere gentleman's code—as indeed, with many Christian slaveholders, it did. One is to treat all persons with kindness, whether they are highborn or low, educated or ignorant, free or enslaved, white, black, or red. One should also assume the best of others and refrain from questioning their motives. Self-restraint and a dignified consideration for others should govern our conduct; we should respect our fellow man enough to let him find his own way, in his own good time.

Reform of people and of institutions cannot be forced, as Jefferson had told Edward Coles in their correspondence about the best way to end slavery. Although sincerely opposed to slavery, Jefferson simply could not imagine a realistic way to end it. Under his code, one should seek the good but recognize that others might not share one's view of what the good is, as differing attitudes toward slavery made plain. In the end, one must be prepared to submit with grace to whatever life holds in store—a position convenient for the slaveholder, but less so for the slave.


On a personal rather than political or social level, Jefferson's ethical system might also have made it difficult for this deliberative gentleman to act with confidence in times of moral crisis. His code seems to have restrained him, for example, from inquiring into the conduct of such visitors as the notorious Colonel Archibald Cary, when they sexually exploited the women at Monticello. When the white men at Monticello cavorted at will with the women in the slave quarters, as Jefferson's family said was the case, they did so because the master, turning a blind eye, allowed the practice to go on. (That Jefferson kept a slave mistress of his own might also have inhibited him from restraining his friends, had he been inclined to do so.)

When the men in Jefferson's household, such as Charles Bankhead and Tom Randolph, drank too much, abused their wives, and tried to kill each other, Jefferson seems to have been capable of doing little more than looking with sympathy on those who bore the brunt of their attacks; he appears to have been unable to imagine ways to stop the violence and to act on them.

Jefferson's problem was the Enlightenment's. It is to Jefferson's great credit that his well-known democratic utterances were sincere. He did indeed believe that a plowman was no less qualified than a professor or a priest to form a proper response to a given moral dilemma. Jefferson genuinely believed that all men were equally free moral agents who functioned at their best as individuals, released from what he considered the shackles of religious dogma.

Even after his study of Jesus, Jefferson continued to regard ethics much as the French philosophes did: as a process by which the rational individual, gathering such facts as he can, seeks to identify the alternatives available to him in any situation and to select the one that seems the most reasonable, practical, and prudent. To put it differently, this rationalist understanding of the moral dimension of life, as historians of ethics have observed, is an exercise in the narrowing of options, based upon the application of abstract principles of right and wrong.

The authors of the four Gospels, however, approached ethics in a way that was distinctly at odds with that of Jefferson and the *philosophes*. Rather than attempting to limit one's options, the religious movement ignited by Jesus and spread by his followers—by those later regarded as saints—sought instead to expand people's sense of moral possibilities. They tried to do this, as they believed Jesus himself had done, through personal example, not through abstract reason.

At the heart of the religion of Jesus, which Jefferson found difficult to imagine and impossible to accept, was something very different from Enlightenment rationalism. To the early Christians, the meaningful life is not found through the prudent application of universally acceptable ethical principles, but in faithful, active, and even, as they defined it, joyful participation in the sufferings of the man they regarded as their savior, through sacrifice of self in service to others.

Jefferson had encountered examples of this understanding, had he recognized them for what they were. Edward Coles, for one, had a richer moral imagination than Jefferson and a capacity to act as well as to think. In April 1819, as Jefferson was about to begin his *Life and Morals of Jesus,* Coles, having rejected the older man's counsel, boarded his slaves on flatboats and accompanied them down the Ohio River, bound for the new state of Illinois.

One morning, he gathered them about him and announced that they were free and could continue with him to a new home or strike out on their own. "In breathless silence they stood before me, unable to utter a word," Coles recalled, "but with countenances beaming with expression which no words could convey, and which no language can now describe." In gratitude, they proceeded to Edwardsville, not far from St. Louis, helping Coles to get his own farm started and then settling on land of their own, which Coles had purchased for them. If Jefferson ever commented on what this erstwhile protégé—and future Illinois governor—had accomplished, his response is lost to history.

Unable as a young man to accept the idea of the Trinity, Jefferson had turned to other men who also found such doctrines incomprehensible and who rejected revelation and religious authority in favor of a more rational faith. Whether these influences led to his acceptance of the *philosophes'* understanding of ethics, or whether Jefferson found this view of ethics congenial because of his deep-seated need to escape into the refuge of abstraction, is impossible to know.

Rejecting as well the healings and the miracles ascribed to Jesus in the Gospels, his atonement for sin on the cross, and his resurrection, Jefferson assumed that the morality embodied in that life and death could flourish, as it were, in the abstract. When others took offense at Jefferson's attempt to render their faith more agreeable to his cosmopolitan sensibilities, he found their response difficult, perhaps impossible, to understand.

# CHAPTER 30

# *"We Shall Have Every Religious Man in Virginia Against Us"*

B y the time he had finished his *Life and Morals of Jesus,* Jefferson still suffered mightily in his legs, which he now wrapped routinely from the knee
to the toes to reduce the swelling. As 1819 drew to a close, these wraps provided warmth as well as relief. The temperatures at Monticello fell to five degrees in early February 1820, when a series of snowstorms blanketed the
mountain. By early spring, when melting snows turned the roads around Charlottesville into a quagmire, Jefferson, noting new and "suspicious symptoms" in
his legs, was content to stay at home and attend to university business through
the mails.

Once again, the appointment of Thomas Cooper to the faculty embroiled
the fledgling institution in controversy. Well aware that the University of Virginia might not open its doors for years, Cooper accepted a one-year appointment to the faculty of South Carolina College in Columbia. But news that
Cooper would eventually be employed in Charlottesville had already spread
throughout Virginia and, in January and February, the first major assault on
his appointment was mounted.

This attack came from a formidable force within the intellectual life of the
state and one who, though he believed that education required a religious
basis, had nevertheless supported the establishment of the university. This was
the Reverend John Holt Rice, founder of the first Presbyterian church in Richmond and editor of *The Virginia Evangelical and Literary Magazine.* Rice had obtained a copy of *The Memoirs of Dr. Joseph Priestley,* published in 1795, in which
Cooper had contributed his own observations on Priestley's life and work. As
a result of Priestley's liberalizing influence on the nation's intellectual life,
Cooper had written, ideas that once commanded unquestioned allegiance from
churchgoers could no longer be taken seriously. Thanks to Priestley and other
freethinkers, Cooper wrote, "the separate existence of the human soul, the free-

dom of the will, and the eternal duration of future punishment, like the doctrines of the Trinity and transubstantiation, may no longer be entitled to public discussion."

Such pronouncements might not have disturbed educated Anglicans in the circles in which Jefferson moved as a young man in Williamsburg, and they might well have found ready acceptance in the salons of Paris. But they offended a Virginia that was now more Presbyterian, Methodist, and Baptist than Episcopalian, Unitarian, or deist. Quoting Cooper's words in his magazine, Rice observed that the professor was "rash, dogmatical, and preemptory [*sic*]." His "prejudices appear to be violent; and all his liberality is reserved for his own party."

In March, Madison told Jefferson that he, too, had become "uneasy" about Cooper, and in April, Joseph C. Cabell, now a fellow member of the university board, warned Jefferson that if he continued to insist on Cooper, "we shall have every religious man in Virginia against us."

By this time, Cooper told Jefferson that his "feeling of security" in his appointment had been rattled. At sixty-one, heartily sick of controversy, Cooper offered to tender his resignation. On March 13, Jefferson assured Cooper that only the Presbyterian "priesthood" opposed his appointment. Because most Virginians were far too broad-minded to follow Rice's lead, Jefferson said, Cooper had no cause for concern.

By May, however, Jefferson's determination was weakening. On the sixteenth, he told two of the other board members that, although he personally had no desire to placate "these satellites of religious inquisition," others knew the current state of public opinion far better than he. Although Jefferson would regret "the irreparable loss of this professor," it might be prudent to quietly withdraw the board's support for Cooper's appointment.

In an apologetic note to Cooper, Jefferson blamed the "pulpit mountebanks." Cooper, in reply, regretted "the storm that has been raised on my account." Although he was disappointed by the failure of their efforts, Cooper said it was consolation enough to have enjoyed such support from "the first man" in the nation.

It is significant that at no time during the struggle to secure Cooper's services did Jefferson enlist the help of the University of Virginia's newest and most vocal champion in Richmond, whose views on religion and education were Jefferson's own but whose want of tact, self-control, and sound judgment made Jefferson increasingly leery of working with him.

This was Thomas Mann Randolph, Jr., Jefferson's son-in-law. In a turn of events unthinkable but for his formidable family connections, Randolph was now Virginia's governor. Given Randolph's irascible personality, his increasingly well-known financial difficulties, his weakness for hard liquor, and his lack of substantive accomplishment in any field of endeavor, he could not have gotten elected on merit alone.

What might dissuade others, however, never dissuaded him. Every few years, beginning in 1797, Randolph had insisted on seeking elective office, despite the fact that he was a poor public speaker, hated campaigning, and had been miserable during the four years he served in Congress. Randolph was twenty-nine when he left Congress. He was now fifty-one, and the financial problems that had begun early in his marriage and deepened during his years in Washington were severe. Although Martha Randolph believed that the farms at Edgehill required her husband's full attention, Randolph instead devoted the early spring of 1819 to campaigning for a seat in the Virginia House of Delegates, which, in April, he won. One story suggests how urgently he needed money. In the weeks after the balloting, he importuned Edmund Bacon to lend him $150. As collateral, Randolph offered one of the slave children at Edgehill, a little girl named Edy. When Bacon expressed reluctance, Randolph asked the overseer to "prevail upon your mother" to make the loan, and, in May, for $200, Randolph sold Bacon the child.

When the General Assembly convened in December 1819, one of its first duties was to elect a governor. Three names were put in nomination and, with the support of the delegates from the counties in the western part of the state, Randolph was elected to an office previously held by, among others, Patrick Henry, Benjamin Harrison, James Monroe, John Tyler, and, yes, Thomas Jefferson.

Although he confessed to some "anxiety about the exact performance of the manifold duties" of the office, Randolph seemed bold enough in his first substantive address, delivered in January 1820. Exhibiting what Jefferson called "zeal for the institution," the new governor stressed the importance of completing the University of Virginia and implored the General Assembly to appropriate the needed funds. In making the request, Randolph warned of the "vast waste . . . of native genius" to which any delay in the commencement of classes would surely contribute.

To frame the argument as Randolph did was not merely to appeal to the considerable pride of Virginians, though the speech surely had that effect. By warning that a failure to fund the college would squander the intellectual gifts of Virginia's younger generation, Governor Randolph signaled a significant shift in the role the university would play in American life. This change was a direct response to events outside Virginia that, Jefferson told Congressman John Holmes of Maine, in late April 1820, "like a fire-bell in the night, awakened and filled me with terror."

This "fire-bell in the night" was the Missouri Compromise.

On March 3, 1820, Congress accepted Missouri's petition for statehood with its proposed state constitution keeping slavery legal within its borders. To maintain a balance between free and slave states, Congress decided that Maine could come into the Union, too. The proviso that troubled Jefferson ordered that, after Missouri's admission, any new states north of 36 degrees, 30 feet, would be "forever free." To Jefferson, this act formalized the division of the nation into two hostile camps, slave and free, South and North, separated in the east by Mason and Dixon's line and in the west by the Ohio River.

As Jefferson knew, this division would further isolate the slaveholding South. The free states were becoming more densely populated, while the slave states were either losing population or, by failing to grow, nonetheless falling behind their northern neighbors. Home to a growing number of free laborers, the northern states were also becoming richer; the South was gaining population only in slaves, whose presence discouraged the immigration of white workers and, in the tobacco states, contributed to economic stagnation.

The political implications of these changes were profound. Each state was represented by two U.S. senators regardless of how many voters lived in it. But the number of votes in the House and in the electoral college was based on population. This meant that for the South to hold its own against the North and protect what a later generation would call states' rights, a slave state would have to be added with each new free state. Restricting slavery in the northern territories, of course, made the formation of new slave states increasingly difficult.

These developments put Jefferson, who had long argued that slavery should and would die, in an awkward position. He now found himself favoring the spread of slavery into the territories, which he had opposed earlier in his life.

Jefferson was also hoping for the creation of new slave states, if only to counter the growing political power of the North, which he viewed as a hotbed of recrudescent Federalism.

The most generous explanation for this change in thinking was Jefferson's own. He believed the northerners' agitation over slavery to be a "mere party trick," as he told Senator William Pinkney, of Maryland, on September 30, 1820. Northern advocates of "consolidation"—a term Jefferson used synonymously with "Federalism" and "monarchy" for a strong central government and a reduced role for the states—cared nothing about slaves or slavery. They were motivated, Jefferson maintained, by the desire for immediate political gain only. Their goal, Jefferson contended, was to use the slavery issue to divide the nation into two regional, irreversibly antagonistic parties. As Jefferson saw it, a conspiracy of the richest and most populous states sought to impose its will on the poorest and least populous, in hopes of replacing a government based on persuasion with one based on force. Jefferson had never ceased to fear a war between the races; now he had come to think that a war between the states was not only possible, but might even become necessary.

Although he had once been "among the most sanguine in believing our Union would be of long duration," he wrote to his former secretary William Short, on April 13, 1820, his own seventy-seventh birthday, he had now come to doubt it. Either ignorant of the risks they ran, or foolhardy in their disregard of them, the northern "consolidationists" were inciting so much "mutual & mortal hatred, as to render separation of [North and South] preferable to eternal discord," he said.

Such a rupture would represent nothing less, on the part of the generation in power, than "throwing away the fruits of their fathers sacrifices of life & fortune." The Missouri Compromise marked the "knell of the Union," he told Congressman Holmes. By every indication, all the sacrifice of "the generation of 1776, to acquire self-government and happiness" for their country, might soon be "thrown away by the unwise and unworthy passions of their sons," and Jefferson's only consolation was that he would "live not to weep over it."

Nowhere were the demographic changes reshaping American political life more evident than in Jefferson's Old Dominion. Throughout most of his life, Virginia had been the richest, most populous, and most powerful state in the

Union. But as the census of 1820 showed, Virginia now lagged behind New York and Pennsylvania in population. As *Niles' Weekly Register* reported, Virginia was slipping even more precipitously in terms of wealth.

If Virginia had any hope of regaining its position in the union, the *Richmond Enquirer* argued, it "must make up by the intelligence of her sons what she is losing in her census." Virginia needed to offer its young men an education comparable to that provided in the North, but founded on republican rather than consolidationist principles. She must prepare the South's future leaders intellectually for the stiff challenges ahead.

Many of Virginia's most promising young men were being educated at Harvard or Princeton, but these are "no longer proper for Southern or Western students," Jefferson told former Virginia congressman James Breckinridge in February 1821. "The signs of the time admonish us to call them home." Back in Virginia—presumably at his new college in Charlottesville—they could be educated in correct constitutional doctrine.

Jefferson had envisioned his "academical village" as a beacon of Enlightenment learning in the New World. By late 1820, however, he had come to regard the University of Virginia as an outpost of strict construction, fighting a rearguard action to determine how the U.S. Constitution was to be interpreted and applied. These may or may not have been mutually exclusive educational functions. But if they could not be reconciled, it was clear to Jefferson which should take precedence.

From this time forward, Jefferson began to speak with quasi-religious reverence for the constitutional doctrines he supported. Having labored mightily to prevent theological dogmatism from stifling intellectual inquiry within the university, Jefferson now began to use the language of the church itself—"heresy" and "orthodoxy"—when arguing against threats to his republican faith. Perhaps a February 17, 1825, letter to James Madison best expressed the evangelical fervor that he brought to the cause of strict construction and to the university's role in training disciples:

> It is in our seminary that the vestal flame is to be kept alive; from thence it is to spread anew over our own and the sister States. If we are true and vigilant in our trust, within a dozen or twenty years, a majority of our own legislators will be from one school, and many disciples will have carried its doctrines home with them to the several States.

# CHAPTER 32
## The "Hideous Evil" of Slavery

When the Virginia General Assembly reconvened in December 1820, Governor Randolph told the lawmakers that it was "impossible that the slave system would continue." Either Virginians would abolish it in their own way, or an end would be imposed by outsiders, but there was no avoiding the obvious fact that slavery was doomed. Then, introducing a scheme of emancipation that seems to have been similar to the one Jefferson himself drafted when he was a member of the House of Burgesses, Governor Randolph proposed the orderly manumission of a "fair proportion of slave youths" each year. These newly freed Negroes would be sent at taxpayers' expense to Hispaniola in the Caribbean, where free blacks already lived.

Any serious consideration that Randolph's proposal might have received did not survive the storm that resulted from the rest of his speech. For reasons known only to himself, Randolph then broached the subject of religion which, in the wake of the controversy over Thomas Cooper's ill-fated university appointment, proved needlessly inflammatory.

Giving voice to Jeffersonian deism at a time when evangelical Christianity was on the rise, Randolph said that he personally preferred "patient resignation for prayer, and silent admiration [to] labored praise or ceremonial worship." Others might recite prayers and creeds in churches, but Randolph favored the "persevering study of the attributes of the author and sovereign of nature, as they are unfolded in visible works and revealed further by the power of the human mind." (In a passage that surely proved embarrassing to the Monticello family five years later, Randolph also denounced lotteries as injurious to civic virtue.)

Presbyterians, Methodists, Baptists, and even some Anglicans were incensed, and ten days later, when Randolph stood for reelection to a second year in office, they mounted fierce opposition. Only after Samuel Blackburn, a supporter from Bath County in the west, reminded his fellow lawmakers that their duty was "not to elect a Bishop, a confessor, or a dervish, but a Governor," did Randolph retain his office.

But the damage had been done. The governor's plan to end slavery was promptly defeated, and from this time forward Randolph became morose and irrationally quarrelsome, until his behavior led to a near total breakdown in his relations with the legislature. He also began to show other signs of mental instability. At Christmas, Martha Randolph, who had remained with her father at Monticello during most of her husband's first term as governor, visited him at the Governor's House in Richmond. She "found everything in disorder," her daughter Harriet Randolph wrote, "windows unwashed carpets unshaken walls that had not seen a brush." The house her husband lived in, Martha said, had become "a scene of 'uncleanly desolation.'"

Because Jefferson believed that if slavery was to be abolished, it should be abolished by Virginians and not by a process imposed from the north, the disappointing defeat of his son-in-law's plan for emancipation was only one in a series of discouraging developments that year. Jefferson's health continued to decline—his rheumatism afflicted him almost every summer now—and the crops, Joel Yancey reported from Poplar Forest, "become more and more difficult each year." In the fall, Jefferson had taken his regular visit to his Bedford County retreat, though Ellen Randolph, who accompanied him, was "afraid he is getting too old for these long journeys."

When he returned to Monticello after two weeks at Poplar Forest, more bad news awaited him. On the morning of October 10, Wilson Cary Nicholas, Jeff Randolph's father-in-law and the friend whose loans Jefferson cosigned two years earlier, had died during a visit to the Randolphs at Tufton. Nicholas, who was fifty-nine, had been in poor health for some years, but his death was nonetheless a "very unexpected event to the family."

The body was taken up the mountain to Monticello and buried in the family graveyard. Jeff Randolph was "extremely affected at the funeral," according to Mrs. Trist. Nicholas "was one of Virginia's greatest men," Randolph would write in his memoirs. He was "a great listener, ever calm & dignified, never excited, in conversation concise clear forcible and impressive. His words fell upon the ear as those of wisdom, carrying conviction with them."

Now the burden of repaying $20,000 in loans—roughly four years of earnings from Jefferson's farms—fell on Jefferson; and should he die without paying the money back, the debt would pass to Jeff Randolph. The financial *"coup de grâce,"* as Jefferson called it, had fallen.

On October 20, ten days after the death of Wilson Cary Nicholas, Jefferson was seized with a sudden "spasmodic stricture of the ileum." Writing that day to Richard Rush, the U.S. ambassador to Great Britain, he acknowledged the "hideous evil" of slavery but insisted that southerners felt its horror more keenly than their northern neighbors, because it confronted them every day of their lives. Thanks to constant agitation from northern abolitionists, the slaves had been awakened to the freedoms denied them, and slaveholders consequently lived in constant and mounting fear of slave insurrections. Above the Potomac, ending slavery was a politically desirable goal; below the Potomac, Jefferson believed, the issue was becoming a matter of life and death.

No one could dispute the validity of slaves' claim to freedom. That they were right to feel as they did should not mean, however, that their owners must consent to be murdered in their beds. "We have the wolf by the ear, and we can neither hold him nor safely let him go," Jefferson told Congressman Holmes on April 22, 1820. "Justice is in one scale, and self-preservation in the other."

In early January 1821, Jefferson wrote in his autobiography, "Nothing is more certainly written in the book of fate than that [black slaves] are to be free. Nor is it less certain that the two races, equally free, cannot live in the same government. Nature, habit, opinion has drawn indelible lines of distinction between them." The states could "direct the process of emancipation and deportation peaceably and in such slow degree as that the evil will wear off insensibly," with black slave labor replaced by "free white laborers. If on the contrary, it is left to force itself, human nature must shudder at the prospect held up."

On the singularly sensitive matter of slavery, Jefferson and Adams had never corresponded, though they took up nearly every other issue of importance, private and public. But on January 22, 1821, Jefferson broached the subject, writing of "our anxieties in this corner" concerning Missouri and what Congress intended to do about it. The real question, for people in the states "afflicted with this unfortunate population," Jefferson wrote, is "Are our slaves to be presented with freedom and a dagger? For if Congress has a power to regulate the conditions of the inhabitants of the states, within the states, it will be but another exercise of that power to declare that all shall be free."

Adams expressed sympathy for the slaveholders and agreed that it was their problem to solve and not the federal government's or the northern states'. "Slavery in this Country I have seen hanging over it like a black cloud for half a Century," Adams wrote. If he were a mystic, he might even say he

had seen Armies of Negroes marching and countermarching in the air, shining in Armour. I have been so terrified with this Phenomenon that I constantly said in former times to the Southern Gentlemen, I cannot comprehend this object; I must leave it to you. I will vote for no measure against your judgements. What we are to see, *God* knows, and I leave it to him, and his agents in posterity.

# CHAPTER 33

# *"Ah, Jefferson!" "Ah, Lafayette!"*

On the morning of November 4, 1824, a coach drawn by four gray horses and accompanied by two carriages, a wagon, and a small military escort bowled smartly along the Three Notched Road, heading west toward Albemarle County. Stationed along the road, scouts on horseback alerted a uniformed troop of mounted men, 120 strong, at Boyd's Tavern. When the coach, "fleet as the wind," in Jeff Randolph's words, crossed into Albemarle, the waiting troops wheeled their mounts in a last-minute effort to form ranks. The coach pulled up to the tavern, and Randolph noted the time. At just after eleven A.M., Marie-Joseph-Paul-Yves-Roch-Gilbert du Motier de Lafayette—the Marquis de Lafayette—had arrived.

After he climbed down from the coach and received an official greeting from U.S. congressman William Cabell Rives, Lafayette was ushered into the tavern. Refreshments were served, and at noon, Lafayette was helped into an elegant landau dispatched by Jefferson, who waited at Monticello. Then Randolph and Rives, as members of the welcoming committee, climbed in, the wheels turned, and the landau started off.

With revolutionary banners waving, the procession made its way up the mountain road. All along, on either side, trees of red and gold stood out against the towering pines. Citizens who had gathered to watch the parade fell in behind and began the steep ascent. The military escort slipped through a gap in the woods and managed to make it to the front lawn of the house and reassemble before the guest of honor could arrive. A bugle signaled the procession's appearance, and, as if on cue, the crowd, now swelled to four hundred, formed itself into two semicircles that faced each other, with cavalry on one side, and everyone else on the other. The landau rolled to a stop, the crowd hushed, and hats were removed.

As a gouty Lafayette was helped down from the landau, Jefferson, who found it impossible to walk farther than his garden, emerged from the house and gingerly descended the steps. The old friends, forgetting their aches and pains, caught each other's eye and advanced. Randolph watched as his grandfather, "feeble with age," broke "into a shuffling quickened gait."

"Ah, Jefferson!" Lafayette called out.

"Ah, Lafayette!" his host replied, and "they threw themselves with tears into each others arms." From the onlookers, "not a sound escaped except an occasional sup[p]ressed sob."

The two old gentlemen turned and retired into the house, and, "in profound silence," Randolph said, the crowd dispersed.

Three decades had passed since Lafayette last laid eyes on Jefferson. Four decades had come and gone since Lafayette helped force the British to surrender at Yorktown and had last seen America itself. In the spring of 1824, eager to express the young republic's gratitude for the contribution that Lafayette made to its independence, President Monroe invited him back for this triumphant tour, which continued for more than a year.

Few of the acquaintances that Lafayette made in America proved as enduring as his friendship with Jefferson. In correspondence spanning their years of separation, they advised each other on politics and government, discussed philosophy, history, theology, and education, and, in recent years, shared news of their families and their health. More and more, they reminisced.

At Monticello, in contrast to New York, Boston, Philadelphia, and Washington, Lafayette wrote a few days after his arrival, "we are in a place where we can rest." Rest, for both men, was increasingly important. When Lafayette fought alongside the American colonists, he was a slender youth of nineteen. Now, at sixty-seven, he was "so much increased in bulk and changed in aspect that I should not have known him," wrote James Madison, who came to Monticello at sunset on the day Lafayette arrived.

Jefferson, of course, had changed, too. In 1789, when Lafayette last saw him, Jefferson was a vigorous forty-seven years old. In April, he would turn eighty-two. Although he exhibited "an extraordinary degree of health, vivacity and spirit" for a man his age, as Daniel Webster observed a month later, Jefferson's hearing had begun to falter, and "a number of voices in animated conversation confuses it."

Sometimes Jefferson's whole body seemed to be breaking down, though friends marveled at his energy and his resilience. Only two weeks before

Lafayette's arrival, he had suffered from an abscess on his jaw so painful he sub-sisted on fluids sucked through a straw. This did not prevent him, however, from continuing to devote his energies to the university and playing host to Lafayette and his party. "I have been received with much emotion by Mr. Jef-ferson," Lafayette wrote from Monticello. He found his friend "greatly aged after a separation of thirty-five years, but carrying his eighty-one years ad-mirably and enjoying the full vigor of his mind and soul." These mental facul-ties he "has consecrated to the building of a superb university."

At ten A.M. on the day after his arrival, Lafayette, Jefferson, and Madison rode in Jefferson's landau to the Central Hotel in Charlottesville. Again they were escorted by mounted troops and followed by townspeople. Local dignitaries of-fered speeches of welcome; at noon, the distinguished trio left the hotel for the university, which Jefferson was eager for Lafayette to see.

There would be no students to welcome them, however, and no professors, because the university had yet to open. This was in part Jefferson's doing. Oth-ers had wanted classes to have commenced by now, but Jefferson resisted. Once a faculty was hired, students were enrolled, and instruction had begun, Jeffer-son feared that salaries and other operating expenses would consume all avail-able funds, leaving little for the completion of the buildings he had designed.

Until 1819, when he hired Arthur Brockenbrough to take over these duties, Jefferson had personally supervised what proved to be one of the largest con-struction projects in America to that date. By the time of Lafayette's visit, ten pavilions for the housing of professors were ready, as were more than eighty dormitory rooms for students.

Work was slow and sporadic, however, as were attempts—after the Thomas Cooper fiasco—to assemble a faculty. Success in all of these endeav-ors depended upon the legislators who controlled the funding. A significant number of these legislators had always been hostile to the institution. Others regarded Jefferson as an increasingly impractical visionary, whose refusal to compromise on architectural plans they considered extravagant called to mind his determination to hire Cooper.

Lawmakers objected most passionately to Jefferson's proposed Rotunda, which would prove by far the university's costliest structure. Situated at the north end of the campus, this half-scale model of Rome's Pantheon was to be the university's centerpiece—a role chapels performed at other colleges—

linking the east and west pavilions. Its imposing dome was to house the library, with floors below for meetings and classrooms. As Jefferson told Madison in April 1822, one of the university's most stalwart supporters in the General Assembly "declared he would never vote another Dollar to the University but on condition that it not be applied to that building." ("That building" would not be completed until after Jefferson's death, at a cost, in 1826 dollars, of $60,000.)

Other legislators who might have looked favorably upon the university found themselves opposing anything that Governor Tom Randolph supported, and Jefferson's son-in-law had been one of the university's champions. He remained in office until December 1821, hanging on through three consecutive one-year terms, each more quarrelsome than the last. Randolph surely had a better education than most Virginians, as one exasperated member of the Governor's Council conceded, but he had "no useful sense at all." In his last years in office, the governor charged about "like a mad bull, cursing and denouncing" political adversaries, behavior that also did the cause of higher education no good.

With the support of Jefferson, Madison, and Monroe, the university nevertheless remained important to the majority of lawmakers. Like most farsighted Virginians, they agreed that a first-rate institution of higher learning, provided it was not too liberal, would help the Old Dominion regain past prominence.

Typical of the gentry, Martha Randolph looked forward to the day when Virginia "will again recover the high station she once held amongst her sister states," as she wrote in September 1822. "I see no reason why with equal advantages as to education, her sons may not again as in former times give lustre to the land of their birth, and that My dear father has had so great a share in restoring her to her lost glory, is a cordial to *my* heart, and I hope will be a solace to his declining years."

Already the university was an ornament to Virginia. By the time of Lafayette's visit, brick houses had gone up near the campus, "many of them in quite a handsome style," Martha reported. Three churches were under construction. Once classes started—in February 1825, she predicted—"we have every reason to believe that the society of the neighbourhood will be very good."

Martha's optimism was understandable. When, with Daniel Webster, George Ticknor of Harvard College visited the campus in December 1824, he called Jefferson's buildings "more beautiful than anything architectural in New

England, and more appropriate to a university than are to be found, perhaps, in the world."

When Lafayette, Jefferson, and Madison arrived at the university grounds shortly after noon on November 5, 1821, the terraces were lined with the ladies of the town, waving their handkerchiefs in welcome. After "the Hero of the Revolution and two of its Sages," as the *Charlottesville Central Gazette* described them, climbed the stairs to the unfinished Rotunda's six-columned portico, more speeches followed, and at three P.M., four hundred Virginia gentlemen and one fat Frenchman sat down inside the Dome Room and dined for the next six hours.

There were, of course, toasts. To one proclaiming "Thomas Jefferson and the Declaration of Independence—alike identified with the Cause of Liberty," Jefferson had prepared a response. Finding himself too weak to deliver it, he asked Valentine Southall, a highly esteemed local orator, to read it for him, and what followed was not only Jefferson's tribute to Lafayette, but also a farewell to his Albemarle neighbors.

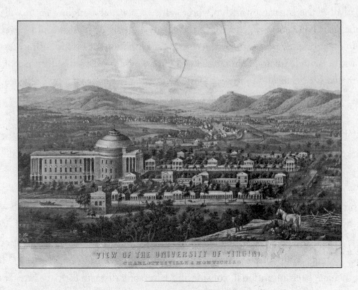

*"Something very great and very new." The University of Virginia, with Charlottesville and Monticello in the background.*

I will avail myself of this occasion, my beloved neighbors and friends, to thank you for the kindness which now, and at all times, I have received at your hands. Born and bred among your fathers, led by their partiality into the line of public life, I have labored in fellowship with them through that arduous struggle which, freeing us from foreign bondage, established us in the rights of self-government; rights which have blessed ourselves, and will bless, in their sequence, all the nations of the earth.

In this struggle, Southall read, "all did their utmost, and as none could do more, none had pretensions to superior merit." One man, however, did stand above the others. A Frenchman—here Lafayette, clasping Jefferson's hand, began to sob—"made our cause his own, as it was that of his native country also."

Jefferson's and Lafayette's names would forever be linked, but there was a difference: "I only held the nail," Jefferson proclaimed. "He drove it."

Then Jefferson made a final appeal for support of the university.

My friends, I am old, long in the disuse of making speeches, and without voice to utter them. In this feeble state [if I can] still contribute anything to advance the Institution within whose walls we are now mingling . . . it will be, as it has ever been, cheerfully and zealously bestowed. And could I live to see it once enjoy the patronage and cherishment of our public authorities with undivided voice, I should die without a doubt of the future fortunes of my native State, and in the consoling contemplation of the happy influence of this institution on its character, its virtue, its prosperity, and safety.

"Thomas Jefferson," James Dinsmore, a Monticello carpenter who now worked on the Rotunda, cried out, "founder of the University of Virginia!"

In predicting that classes would begin in February 1825, Martha Randolph was off by only one month. The long-awaited opening of the University of Virginia, on Monday, March 7, 1825, "appears to have been entirely unceremonious," Dumas Malone has written, "and could not have been impressive." This might have been intentional, considering Jefferson's distaste for pageantry, but there is no record to that effect. About thirty students began their studies—the number would triple by the fall—under five instructors, three recruited from the British Isles. A sixth, George Tucker, a William and Mary product who would teach moral philosophy, arrived in April. (An "orthodox" professor of law, committed to strict construction, still had not been found.)

Students could select their own courses of study, and choices of specialization were broader than those at most colleges. Jefferson soon discovered, however, that the young scholars were "not well enough prepared," he told Madison, and admission standards for some classes had to be lowered. Arriving from their plantations with horses, fowling pieces, and slaves who served as "body servants," these scions of the Virginia gentry were expected to conduct themselves honorably, as gentlemen.

In August, Jefferson reported happily to his granddaughter Ellen, who that spring had married Joseph Coolidge of Boston and now lived with him there, that the university "has been a model of good order and behavior, having never yet an occasion for the exercise of a single act of authority." The students were treated as adults, "under the guidance mainly of their own discretion."

This pleasing picture was not altogether accurate, whether Jefferson knew it or not. A few weeks earlier, in July, Cornelia Randolph had given Ellen a different account of university life. "There is a really shocking scandal afloat," Cornelia wrote. One young lady, "whom you may remember as a very bold impudent girl was missing one night & found at twelve o'clock in one of the dormitories of the students & it is said that it is not one but many that she visits, but really this is scandal of too black a dye to write."

# CHAPTER 34

# "More Than Patience Could Endure"

By the summer of 1825, such scandals as Cornelia passed on to her sister in Boston proved an amusing diversion for the young women of the increasingly hard-pressed Monticello household. By now, the family's financial difficulties were such common knowledge around Albemarle that friends and relatives talked openly about what should be done. Peggy Nicholas, Jeff Randolph's sister-in-law, suggested that the family close up half of the house at Monticello to save money, rent out the plantation lands, "and take the rent in Wood, Meat and Bread." Peggy's sister, Jane Randolph, considered opening a boardinghouse. Jeff Randolph talked of selling his land and living off wages from the management of his grandfather's farms. Jeff's sister Cornelia, meanwhile, wished she could support herself "instead of this unprofitable drudgery of keeping house here, but I suppose not until we sink entirely will it do for the grand daughters of Thomas Jefferson to take in work or keep a school."

Also that summer, the family was first confronted with the enormity of Tom Randolph's debts. The efforts of his presumptive heirs to avoid being ruined with him, moreover, resulted in deep and possibly irreparable family strife. For more than a year, Martha Randolph told Nicholas Trist in April, she had known enough of "the encreasing derangement" of her husband's affairs for them "to weigh heavily upon my spirits." Only in the last few months, however, had she become "aware of the extent of the ruin that awaits us from that quarter." Tom's debts by this time came to between $20,000 and $30,000—the equivalent of some five years' income from his plantations.

Several years earlier, much as his father-in-law had done, Tom Randolph had taken out a sizable loan from the Richmond branch of the Bank of the United States. As collateral, he had put up his most valuable asset: his house and plantation at Edgehill. But he also needed cosigners on the loan. One was Samuel Carr, a kinsman. The other was Jeff Randolph, his own son. Martha and Jeff Randolph had repeatedly urged Tom Randolph to seek "the immediate settlement of his affairs and the honest payment of his debts," in Martha's words, by selling his house, his land, and his slaves. There "are many ways in which a man of his experience and talents may support himself and a family," Martha said, and he and his family would always have a home at Monticello. Tom Randolph rebuffed their suggestions and, in May 1825, the bank called in his loan. Jeff Randolph, in response, took the unusual step, with Samuel Carr, of suing his father for possession of Edgehill.

Tom Randolph was enraged at what he considered a personal insult from an ungrateful son. In June, he told his friend Francis Gilmer that Jeff Randolph was guilty of "coldblooded avarice" and planned to turn Edgehill into a slave-breeding farm—an allegation for which no evidence can be found. Gilmer feared for the man's sanity. If Tom Randolph, "broke to atoms in mind, body, and estate," were to lose Edgehill and be "turned out to roam the world," he would "rave as wildly as Lear."

In fact, Randolph no longer lived at Edgehill. Increasingly, he spent his days alone at a small house at Milton, the port on the Rivanna east of Monticello, and visited Monticello only after dark, speaking to no one but Martha. After he learned of his son's lawsuit against him, he visited Monticello not at all.

In his despair, Randolph nevertheless reached out for sympathy to Jefferson, claiming that he had fallen prey to political enemies who, not content to spread lies about him, had ensnared his own son in their intrigues. "My ruin is inevitable," Randolph admitted, "but I am the victim of the avarice of one . . . encouraged by the vengeance of many." The "blind fury" of these enemies' attacks made it impossible to receive cooperation from bankers, without which he was doomed.

Jefferson implored Tom Randolph to cease brooding over his misfortunes, to submit gracefully to whatever fate held in store, and "to return & become a member of the family again," availing himself of "the soothing balm of their affections." He should take comfort, as Jefferson did, in "the resources of books."

By now, however, Jefferson himself was seeking relief in opiates.

Reliance upon opium was probably not unusual for a man at his age, in his time and place. As an anesthetic, opium had been a mainstay of medical practice for centuries and could be purchased in any apothecary in Jefferson's time. Plantation households typically kept both opium and laudanum—opium extract in brandy—for medicinal use. Opium's addictive properties seem not to have troubled practitioners of the day.

The evidence suggests, moreover, that the family had been familiar with opiates for many years. As early as 1803, Benjamin Rush recommended opium to ease Jefferson's diarrhea, and a recipe for "rye water," handwritten in Martha Randolph's copy of Dr. Robert Thomas's *Modern Practice of Medicine,* calls for laudanum with water and oil of vitriol, a form of sulfuric acid used to treat digestive ailments.

When Jefferson came to depend on opiates, however, he was under the care of Robley Dunglison, the University of Virginia's first professor of anatomy and medicine and, beginning in May 1825, Jefferson's personal physician. Dunglison arrived in Charlottesville none too soon. Jefferson's regular doctor, Andrew Kain, was leaving the area, and on May 17, Jefferson told Dunglison that "a chronical complaint which has been troublesome for some time has within a few days become too much to be longer unattended to." This was a prostate and bladder problem that made urination difficult and extremely painful.

Over the next several weeks, Dunglison came to Monticello at least fourteen times, relying heavily on opium to treat Jefferson's urinary difficulties as well as his diarrhea. Jefferson was clearly using opiates in pill form soon after becoming Dunglison's patient, for, in a letter to Jefferson dated July 18, 1825, the doctor recommended "50 drops of laudanum at bedtime, as you are deprived of your pills and the symptoms are exacerbated." Through August and September, when he was too weak to attend a dinner during Lafayette's return visit to Charlottesville, Jefferson regularly increased his dosages of opium at Dunglison's direction. By November, Jefferson reported that he would henceforth consider reliance on opium "to be my habitual state."

To what degree Jefferson was dependent upon opiates is hard to say. He was without doubt heavily medicated. But even when confined to a sofa, as he was for weeks, Jefferson still managed to devote his attention to university business, mostly through correspondence.

In a time of crisis, moreover, he could act. On the night of Friday, September 30, a small number of students gathered without permission on the university's Lawn, and, Jefferson said, became "animated with wine." Such "nightly disorders [had become] habitual with the students," Dunglison wrote, urging Jefferson to dispense with "the fallacy of placing any reliance on appeals to reason" with their young charges.

*Where "nightly disorders [had become] habitual with the students."*
*The University of Virginia Lawn.*

That night, a "rich fool," in Martha Randolph's words, tossed a bottle filled with urine through Professor George Long's window. Other students cursed the foreign-born faculty members and threatened to dunk them in the nearest pump. Order was restored, but on Saturday, October 1, a larger group of boys assembled, many of them wearing masks. When two professors came to investigate, they were pelted with brickbats. Each professor grabbed a student. One boy broke free, and the other struck his captor.

At a mandatory meeting on Sunday morning, the faculty stormed and threatened, but failed to induce any of the boys to snitch on the others. Showing greater solidarity, fifty students signed a letter accusing their teachers of falsehoods, and the two professors most closely involved in the fracas, saying they feared for their safety, resigned.

On Tuesday, Jefferson rode down to Charlottesville in his carriage and took his place in the Rotunda beside Madison and the other board members. The students filed in, and among those suspected of having assaulted their professors sat the nephew of one of Jefferson's own grandchildren. Jefferson rose to address the students but, by one version of events, he recognized this young face in the crowd and was too overcome to go on. In George Tucker's somewhat different account, an uncharacteristically passionate Jefferson seethed with anger.

"The shock which Mr. Jefferson felt when he, for the first time, discovered that the efforts of the last years of his life had been fouled and put in jeopardy by one of his family was more than his own patience could endure," Tucker recalled, "and he could not forbear from using, for the first time, the language of indignation and reproach."

All of the wrongdoers, including Jefferson's young kinsman, came forward to make themselves known. Expulsions, suspensions, and other punishments followed. Some rules were tightened, others relaxed. The professors agreed to return to their classrooms, and, with an uneasy truce proclaimed, classes resumed. By this time, however, embarrassing accounts of the "riot," as Jefferson called it, had traveled east to Richmond and as far north as Boston.

When Jefferson wrote to Ellen Coolidge on November 14, however, he insisted that it had all been for the best. The university, he said, had in truth benefited from the episode. "Every one is sensible," Jefferson wrote, "of the strength which the institution has derived from what appeared at first to threaten it's foundation."

# CHAPTER 35

# *"Take Care of Me When Dead . . ."*

On October 18, 1825, three weeks after the disturbances on the Lawn, Jefferson reported to Madison that everything "is going smoothly at the University. The students are attending their schools with more assiduity, and looking to their Professors with more respect," though some of the boys remain "somewhat in the pouts."

Jefferson was not feeling too well, either. A few days earlier, at Madison's suggestion, he had consented to sit for John H. I. Browere, a sculptor from New York who had developed his own system for making life masks. Worried by their eighty-two-year-old patriarch's declining health, the family at Monticello recommended against the sitting for fear that it would exhaust him. Madison insisted that the mask could be made "quickly . . . with little fatigue to the patient," and Jefferson "could not find it in his heart," Henry Randall wrote, "to refuse a man so trifling a favor, who had come so far."

Although Jefferson cared very deeply about how he would be remembered, he was not vain as politicians go. A revered figure about whom there was great public curiosity, he posed for the usual series of portraits over the course of his long career, but never with the eagerness of more conceited men. He agreed to sit for Browere as a courtesy to the artist, it seems clear, and because Madison asked him to, not because he craved another likeness of himself.

The sitting did not go smoothly. Feeling weak when Browere arrived, Jefferson allowed himself to be positioned on a sofa, sitting up, with an arm outstretched so he could grasp a chair for support. This posture in itself proved physically draining, because for weeks Jefferson had spent most of his waking hours lying down.

With his subject in place, the "vile plaisterer," as Jefferson's granddaughter Virginia Randolph called him, went to work. Browere anointed his subject's face, head, and throat with oil, and then applied layer after layer of thin grout, "which seems really like burying alive," Virginia said. These layers, when hardened, could be removed without discomfort. This part of the process would require no more than an hour. The removal of the materials would allow the sculptor to work with them alone, freeing the subject from his imprisonment.

That, anyway, was the plan. Evidently Browere miscalculated, for when the hour had elapsed, the grout was harder and drier than anticipated. He had also failed to put enough oil in the concoction "to prevent its adherence to the skin," Virginia said, and as a result, removing the plaster proved so "excessively painful" and so slow that "we expected Grand-papa to faint from exhaustion."

To remove the plaster, Browere produced a mallet and chisel, and began "to break it into pieces and cut off a piece at a time," Jefferson told Madison. "Those thumps of the mallet would have been sensible almost to a logger-head." Horrified by the spectacle, the family fled the room, leaving only the artist, his subject, and Burwell the butler.

Increasingly frustrated, Browere hammered away with increasing force and frequency until Jefferson was exhausted, "and there became real danger," he

*It seemed "the ears would separate from the head sooner than from the plaister."*
*Browere's life mask of Jefferson, October 1825.*

said, "that the ears would separate from the head sooner than from the plaister." By now, "patient [though] he always is in suffering," Virginia said, Jefferson could be heard sobbing.

He was also gasping for breath. Because of some defect in the arrangements made to permit the subject to breathe, Randall wrote, Jefferson "came near suffocation." Eager to attract the preoccupied artist's attention but unable to speak, Jefferson grabbed the chair on which his hand rested, lifted it as high as he could, and slammed it to the floor. The surprised sculptor's work-in-progress also fell with a clatter, and Burwell "sprang furiously forward," catching his master as he collapsed.

Hearing the commotion, the family rushed back into the room to find Jefferson in the arms of Burwell, "the fierce glare of [whose] African eye boded danger." Permitted "to pick up his fragments of plaster and carry them off," Browere remained at Monticello as his long-suffering subject's guest for at least that night, if not more.

Jefferson, though weary, managed to join the family at dinner, Virginia said, "with his usual cheerful spirits." The following day, Jefferson seemed physically no worse, but did appear "tormented by the chattering of the magpie who occasioned it all, & who still has had the impudence to advert to the scene as if it were a fit subject for his jests." Ever the gracious host, Jefferson regarded the unpleasant episode as a source of wry amusement, too—or let Browere think so. Nevertheless, a worn-out Jefferson told Madison, "I now bid adieu for ever to busts and even portraits."

This did not mean, however, that Jefferson had ceased to care about how he appeared in the eyes of his contemporaries or how history would judge him. He had always been proud and sensitive enough not to wish to appear either, and sufficiently self-conscious to protect his privacy. Unlike other politicians then and now, Jefferson authorized no campaign biography and offered no encouragement to writers who wished to tell his story. Secretive by nature, he felt nothing but "repugnance" toward revealing much about his personal life, he told the Philadelphia publisher Joseph Delaplaine in 1817. To divulge such information would "savor too much of vanity." (Jefferson's autobiography, as mentioned, is a largely impersonal account of the events of the Revolutionary years.)

Although Jefferson had no wish to leave much record of his private life, he worried that his public contributions to his country's achievement of its independence, to the survival of its experiment in self-government, and to the establishment of the University of Virginia would not be accurately recorded for future generations. He also cared deeply how Virginia's role in the Revolution would be remembered.

Jefferson understood, finally, the influence that he still wielded in his country's affairs, and he wished to exercise such authority wisely, with restraint. This determination to conduct himself in a manner that reflected well on him and on his native state would govern his actions in December when, for the final time, Jefferson sought to influence national policy.

At noon on December 6, 1825, John Quincy Adams delivered what would be the first annual presidential message to Congress. Written rather than presented in person, the message was reprinted—and lambasted—two days later in the *Richmond Enquirer*, the only newspaper that Jefferson still read.

In his message, Adams unveiled an ambitious program of internal improvements under the direction of the federal government. In the belief that the "general welfare" clause of the Constitution gave him the authority to do so, Adams wanted to build roads, dig canals, and establish a national astronomical observatory and a national university.

These proposals met with almost immediate resistance, not only from Virginia and the rest of the South but also from the North—especially from New York City, whose rising class of workingmen was suspicious of banks, corporate charters, and other special privileges conferred by Washington. Adams's call for an astronomical observatory to rival Europe's "lighthouses in the sky," as he put it, elicited ridicule above and below the Potomac.

Despite this initial opposition, however, the push for new roads and canals (if not for astronomical observatories) was gaining force throughout the country, as was the nationalist spirit that such programs represented. In October, with funds from the New York legislature, the Erie Canal was completed, and, in July, work on the Cumberland (or National) Road recommenced, to extend it from Wheeling, in what was then Virginia, into Ohio.

Still, projects such as Adams had proposed raised serious constitutional questions, even among members of the president's cabinet who questioned whether the program usurped powers properly reserved to the states. In the South, there was little doubt that it did. Senator Nathaniel Macon of North Carolina said that the president's program defied the limits to federal authority established years earlier, when, in the election of 1800, Jefferson's

Democratic-Republicans routed John Adams's Federalists. Now Adams's son dared "to claim all the power to the federal government," Macon said, that Jefferson's election had denied it.

Unfortunately for Adams, the uproar over his program of internal improvements coincided with developments in the Deep South that contributed to fears that the federal government was overstepping its rightful authority. That winter, Georgia's governor, George Troup, sought to remove the Creek Indians from lands that the tribe, with Adams's support, claimed as its own. Should Georgia persist in this effort to expel the Creeks, Adams said, he would send in federal forces to stop it.

Indignant Georgians responded in the same militant spirit. If Adams made good on his threat, they declared, they would take up arms against the federal troops—a vow that many Virginians applauded. There was also talk, in some quarters of the Old Dominion, of lending military support to the Georgians' cause. Such intervention by the federal government, many Virginians grumbled, smacked of tyranny and should be put down.

It was in this highly charged atmosphere that, on December 10, William Fitzhugh Gordon, one of Albemarle's representatives in the House of Delegates—the same William Fitzhugh Gordon who had fought Charles Bankhead on the road to Monticello—asked Jefferson how the Virginia legislature should respond to what many lawmakers considered a constitutional crisis. Over the next several days, Jefferson pondered the matter, concluding—as he told Madison on December 24—that the constitutional situation was indeed "desperate."

More than that, Jefferson took it upon himself to draft for the consideration of the Virginia General Assembly a formal objection to Adams's program that remains controversial to this day. This stirring, yet philosophically subtle manifesto, entitled a "solemn Declaration and Protest of the commonwealth of Virginia on the principles of the constitution of the US. of America and the violations of them," he submitted on Christmas Eve for Madison's response.

If Madison approved of the proclamation, he could forward it to Gordon "under the most sacred injunctions that it shall be used so that not a shadow of suspicion shall fall on you or myself." (In this, Jefferson hoped to operate under the cloak of anonymity, just as he and Madison had done nearly thirty years earlier when, in the Kentucky and Virginia Resolutions, they declared the Alien and Sedition Acts to be unconstitutional.) But if Madison disapproved of the document, "it shall be suppressed."

Virginia and her sister states, Jefferson's manifesto began, had "entered into a compact . . . called the Constitution of the US. of America," for the conduct of their relations with one another and with foreign powers, and for "certain other articles particularly specified." Lately, however, the federal branch had claimed "a right of enlarging its own powers by constructions, inferences and indefinite deductions, from those directly given." These claims the Virginia General Assembly hereby declared to be "usurpations" of the powers retained by the states, "mere interpolations into the compact, and direct infractions of it." The claim that the "general welfare" clause includes the authority for internal improvements is "false and unfounded," and those making that claim effectively asserted "a power to do whatever *they* may think or pretend, would promote the general welfare." Such an elastic view of the Constitution could lead to a federal government "without limitation of powers."

Here Jefferson's argument became more subtle and, in its political pragmatism, more supple. Knowing full well that Virginia's protest over internal improvements would be read at the same time that Georgia's threat to take up arms was on everyone's lips, Jefferson offered what, in his cover letter to Madison, he called an "olive branch" to hold out to the administration. If it was accepted, the Constitution "could be thus saved at a moderate sacrifice."

This olive branch consisted of the assurance that, while Virginians "will never voluntarily yield" rights not conferred on the federal government, they do not "raise the banner of disaffection, or of separation from their sister-states, co-parties with themselves to this compact." The significant point here is that Jefferson asserted Virginia's loyalty not to the federal union as a separate governmental entity but to the group of states that, taken together, composed it. Should any of those states at some future time wish to separate themselves from the federal union, the implication seems clear that they could do so.

Thus, while holding out the possibility of disunion, Jefferson nevertheless disavowed violent resistance—at least for now. Virginians, unlike Georgians, would not consider this infraction by the federal government as a warrant for armed resistance. Virginians refused "to make every difference of construction a ground of immediate rupture," which they would regard "as among the great calamities which could befall them, but not the greatest. There is one greater, submission to a government of unlimited powers." Only when the prospect of submission "shall become absolutely desperate" would Virginia resist.

Should the other states conclude that internal improvements were a proper function of the federal government, Virginians would "be patient and suffer much," confident that time, "ere it be too late," would persuade their fellows also of "the bitter consequences in which this usurpation will involve us."

Jefferson's manifesto further stated that "rather than separate from" the other states, Virginians would endure "every misfortune" short of "living under a government of unlimited powers." Virginians owed "every other sacrifice to ourselves, to our federal brethren, and to the world at large"—America, after all, was a model for all mankind—"to pursue with temper and perseverance the great experiment which shall prove that man is capable of living in society, governing itself by laws self-imposed, and securing to it's members the enjoyment of life, liberty, property and peace."

In due course, it was hoped, Americans would recall their government "to its original and legitimate principles," restoring it to the "rightful limits of self-government." Meanwhile, Virginians would "acquiesce under those acts of the federal branch of our government which we have declared to be usurpations, and against which, in point of right, we do protest as null and void, and never to be quoted as precedents of right."

Madison did not approve. On December 28, he wrote from Montpelier that Virginia should not take leadership, "or the appearance of it," on the issue. Yes, the program that Adams had proposed and Congress was now considering was unconstitutional. But "considering the prejudices which seem to have been excited of late [against] her," the time for Virginia to take the lead on this or any other issue had come and gone.

The New England states were by no means united on the issue of internal improvements, and New York, "where the power assumed by Congress has always been viewed with a degree of jealousy," might more persuasively take up the cause. Besides, John Bailey, a congressman from Massachusetts, had already proposed a constitutional amendment giving the federal government the authority Adams assumed, and, if adopted, this amendment could well render the whole issue moot.

Fairly or unfairly, Madison wrote, Virginia was increasingly viewed as an obstructionist force in national policy, and, as for Jefferson's "olive branch," the protest he proposed might have the effect of "irritating rather than subduing prejudices." The implied threat in Jefferson's manifesto, Madison said, was not only unwise but also futile. If the congressmen feel that their constituents are behind them—as, with respect to internal improvements, Madison suspected they were—"menace or defiance, will never deter them from their purposes."

And there, in a sense, the matter died. On January 2, 1826, Jefferson thanked Madison for his candid assessment of political realities and acknowledged that when he had written his manifesto "all was gloom." Subsequent events—opposition to internal improvements from other quarters, the introduction of Bailey's call for a constitutional amendment—made matters seem less dire and even, perhaps, hopeful. Jefferson's proclamation was, as he said, "suppressed," at least from the view of the Virginia legislators and from that of his other contemporaries.

In another sense, however, the matter did not die at all. Scholars through the years have studied this document, concluding almost to a man (and woman) that it reflects poorly on Jefferson. Its argument is evidence, they have written, of mental deterioration. It further indicates, they assert, that the magnanimity of spirit that had characterized him for so much of his life had disappeared. In place of devotion to the larger Empire of Reason that he had helped found, it is said, is a cramped, suspicious, and, above all, illiberal attachment to his native Virginia.

James Morton Smith, the editor of the Jefferson–Madison correspondence, has called the protest the work of an "agitated and impulsive octogenarian" whose unwarranted suspicion of federal power had led him to a "rabid defense of states' rights."

Leonard W. Levy, in *Jefferson and Civil Liberties,* argues that the "aged Jefferson had soured." His judgment had become "so smothered by localism," according to Levy, that he was now a mere "Southern apologist," a "crabbed and distrustful old man with little faith" in "the new nationalism or growing authority of the federal government."

Those who take this critical view fail to explain, however, in what way the fundamental hostility to overweening power that Jefferson expressed in his "solemn Declaration" differs from that articulated, much earlier, in the Declaration of Independence and in the Kentucky and Virginia Resolves, which they profess to approve. These critics also neglect to say why they regard the the earlier proclamations as enlightened and progressive yet consider the same sentiments, expressed half a century later, in Levy's words, "crabbed and distrustful."

Jefferson saw no contradiction, perhaps because none exists. Rulers derive their just powers from the consent of the governed, and the friends of self-government must remind their rulers of this fact whenever they forget it, as they always do. Jefferson reiterated these principles throughout his life, and it is surely evidence of their radicalism—and of Jefferson's timeless relevance—that they retain their power to offend even now.

In any case, his decision to suppress the manifesto is itself evidence that he was not quite the "soured" old man that his detractors claim. In deciding, as Madison suggested, that the issue could be resolved without threats, and that sufficient opposition to Adams's overreaching might yet emerge from outside Virginia to safeguard constitutional government (which proved to be the case when Adams's program collapsed), Jefferson was never more Jeffersonian. Once again, he chose to put faith in his countrymen and, as he had done so many times before in his long and eventful life, he put his hopes over his fears.

Jefferson was also pondering, at the time that he decided to suppress his manifesto, the role he had played in the great events of his time and how history would remember him. This subject would never be far from his thoughts as he entered the last year of his life.

Remarkably serene as financial problems engulfed him, saddened, but not inconsolably so, by the domestic disputes that cast such dark clouds over Monticello, Jefferson kept himself busy and productive as he looked toward his eighty-third birthday. He kept up the struggle of operating his university on the meager funding provided by a stingy legislature. He lobbied for completion of the buildings he had designed, and he continued his search for the ideal professor of law.

Jefferson also found time to correspond with old friends. He told John Adams on December 18, 1825, that, despite all the sadness and loss they had suffered, "the pleasures surely outweigh the pains of life." If he could be spared the physical afflictions of the last seven years, Jefferson said, he would be happy to live his life over again.

Jefferson and Madison remained in almost weekly contact that winter, chiefly on university business. On February 17, 1826, in a long letter that again addressed the problems of fund-raising and pondered what the future might hold for the fledgling institution they both loved, Jefferson took the occasion to express his respect and affection:

The friendship which has subsisted between us, now half a century, and the harmony of our political principles and pursuits, have been sources of constant happiness to me through that long period. And if I remove beyond the reach of attentions to the University, or beyond the bourne of life itself, as I soon must, it is a comfort to leave that institution under your care, and an assurance that they will neither be spared, nor ineffectual.

It was also a great comfort to believe that Madison would continue to defend

the course we have pursued for preserving, *in all their purity,* the blessings of self-government, which he had assisted too in acquiring for them. If ever the earth has beheld a system of administration conducted with a single and steadfast eye to the general interest and happiness of those committed to it . . . it is to that which our lives have been devoted.

Finally, having asked Madison to continue to work for the cause of the university and for that of human freedom—Jefferson regarded the two as synonymous—he made one final request. He asked Madison to safeguard his personal reputation as well: "To myself you have been a pillar of support through life. Take care of me when dead, and be assured that I shall leave with you my last affections."

# CHAPTER 36

## *"An Inspiration from the Realms of Bliss"*

The plan for his family's financial salvation came to Jefferson, Martha Randolph told Ellen Coolidge, "like an inspiration from the realms of bliss." One night in early January, Jefferson was lying awake "from painful thoughts," she wrote, when all suddenly became clear. As soon as the sun was up, he called Jeff Randolph to his side and unveiled the plan.

The family, Jefferson announced, could sponsor its own public lottery. With the Commonwealth's cooperation—legislative approval was required—they could sell tickets, offering as the prize some of the farmland they would otherwise be unable to sell. For the modest price of a single ticket—for perhaps as little as one dollar—the buyer would enjoy the chance to obtain land that he would ordinarily be unable to afford. The proceeds from ticket sales could be used for the household's living expenses and to pay debts. Jefferson thought that the family might be able to raise $60,000, which would enable them to live in comfort at Monticello, at least for the rest of Jefferson's life and Martha's.

The "immense advantage of the scheme," Martha told Ellen, was obvious. The money the family would make would allow Jefferson "to pay his debts,

*"For . . . the undisturbed possession of Monticello during his precious life."*
*Jefferson lottery ticket, 1826.*

[provide] a maintenance for the family, the means of educating the boys, and a home for my self and children that might be unprovided for, and tho not least, the undisturbed possession of Monticello during his precious life. All that would be ensured."

There was even a chance, or so Jefferson hoped, that the government might ultimately decide to burn all the tickets in a great patriotic bonfire, allowing the family to keep its land and the money. Any such arrangement, of course, would convert the entire transaction into a subsidy or sinecure for Jefferson. That this was precisely the sort of preferment he had always condemned as corrupt when granted by the British Crown did not dissuade Jefferson. Nor was he deterred by the fact that, throughout his public life, he had also opposed gambling in general and state-sanctioned lotteries in particular. (So, as governor, had Tom Randolph.)

That this lifelong rationalist chose to end his days not only promoting what was, at bottom, a game of chance, but also involving his family's financial future in its outcome was ironic, too. That he did so with no awareness of the apparent contradiction was, perhaps, a blessing.

The family's response to the prospect of such an unanticipated windfall as the lottery seemed to offer was as keen as Jefferson's. In December 1825, a loan of $3,950 came due, and the family had no way to pay it. Jeff Randolph was laboring heroically to support his household and his grandfather's on the earnings from the farms at Monticello and Tufton, but with crop prices depressed, this proved impossible.

With Tom Randolph living in seclusion at Milton, the farmland at Edgehill was neglected, so the family got little help from that quarter. Randolph's financial ruin explains his wife's reference, in her letter to Ellen Coolidge about the lottery, to "children that might be unprovided for." These were Martha and Tom Randolph's children, Jefferson's youngest grandchildren. There were six in all, ranging in age from ten to seventeen. Because their father was unable to support them, they lived with their mother at Monticello, as Jefferson's dependents.

Designed for beauty rather than for function, Monticello had always been expensive to maintain, and upkeep alone had become more than the family could afford. With its high ceilings, spacious public rooms, and expanses of glass windows, the house required enormous supplies of firewood in winter.

The roof, with its various levels of flat surfaces, collected water in shallow pools, so the ceilings seemed always to be leaking. Jefferson's beloved skylights leaked, too. Paint was peeling, and the cornices, balustrades, terraces, and other wooden surfaces had begun to rot. Even if the family could afford to buy all the building materials they would need to repair the disintegrating mansion, getting them up the mountain would have been prohibitively expensive.

Although the family felt a deep sentimental attachment to Monticello, they also knew how uncomfortable it could be and sometimes grumbled about its architect's sacrifice of comfort to aesthetics. They were understandably reluctant to suggest alterations, which would have been costly in any case. All but Jefferson himself lived upstairs, in rooms that were much more cramped than his and that could be reached only by climbing narrow staircases on which easy movement was impossible. (The wide staircases found in more conventional plantation houses Jefferson considered a waste of space.)

One of the few changes that anyone dared to make involved the placement of beds in specially designed alcoves, one of Jefferson's favorite architectural conceits. He believed that these, like narrow staircases, also saved space. Martha Randolph grew to dislike her "alcove" bed, however, and a few years earlier, in 1822, insisted upon turning the alcove in her room into a closet. When she mentioned the idea, Jefferson resisted mightily but, after several days of nagging, he eventually relented, Martha said, accepting her decision "in dignified *silence.*"

By 1826, however, the family was thinking of moving away from Monticello altogether. On more than one occasion, Martha spoke with Jeff Randolph about relocating the entire family, Grandpapa included, to Poplar Forest, and finding renters for the deteriorating architectural showcase. No one had the heart to broach the subject with Jefferson, however. Leaving Monticello would be "a most bitter sacrifice to us all," Martha told Ellen, "but nothing to the anguish of seeing My dear father turned out of his house and deprived in his old age of the few pleasures he was capable of enjoying." This prospect "made us recoil from the cruel task of proposing it to him."

They would not abandon Monticello if the lottery proved successful, of course, and Jefferson conducted himself as if success were assured. On January 20, he wrote to Joseph Cabell, who represented Albemarle in the Virginia Senate, notifying him that Jeff Randolph would be bringing "a subject of great importance" to the legislature's attention and asking Cabell to deal directly with Randolph on the matter. Jefferson then sent Randolph to Richmond to lobby for the lottery in person and waited eagerly at Monticello for news of his grandson's progress.

Although Jefferson said he anticipated little difficulty in securing the Virginia Assembly's support, he knew from a lifetime of dealing with legislators that nothing was certain and felt less secure about the lottery's prospects than he admitted. Lotteries had not always received legislative approval: often they were opposed on moral grounds, and, in a legislature in which there were more Presbyterians, Methodists, and Baptists than there had been in earlier times, some of the lawmakers would surely consider any lottery a form of gambling.

But this lottery "will injure no man," Jefferson said to Cabell in his almost pleading letter of January 20. Although Jefferson considered the plan "just," he understood that others might disagree. The undecided should consider the fact that the lottery, while harming no one, would benefit one old patriot and his family immensely. "To me," Jefferson admitted, "it is almost a question of life and death."

# CHAPTER 37

# "I Have Given My Whole Life to My Country"

It was while Jefferson was preoccupied with securing legislative approval for the lottery that Ann Bankhead came home to Monticello. For more than seven years, since shortly after her dissolute husband stabbed Jeff Randolph in 1819, she had been living with him near his parents' house in Caroline County. Her family had seen little of her during that time. Ann's eldest child and Thomas Jefferson's first great-grandchild, John Bankhead, was now sixteen, nearly a man. The next, Thomas Mann Randolph Bankhead, named for Ann's father, was away at school. This left only one child, a daughter, Ellen, still at home. And Ann, who turned thirty-five on January 23, was pregnant again.

Bankhead continued to drink, which may have played a role in Ann's decision to come back to Albemarle to have her baby. Bankhead himself had returned to Albemarle from time to time in the years since the arrest warrant was taken out against him, but he always managed to elude the authorities. This became easier with the passage of time, perhaps because officials of the county court simply lost interest in the case or because the Jefferson family saw little gain in pursuing it, and much embarrassment. The less attention Bankhead attracted, they seem to have concluded, the better for all concerned.

Martha Randolph had last seen Bankhead more than a year earlier, at the Albemarle home of a Mrs. Terrell, where he was "in one of his drunkest moods." Before two relatives "succeeded at last in carrying him home," Bankhead tried to shake hands with his mother-in-law, but when Martha drew back, he loudly accused the family "of unrelenting malice and persecution." This accusation prompted Martha to wonder what impression his performance might make on people who were not "fully acquainted with all the circumstances of the case," which suggests the neighborhood's ongoing curiosity about Bankhead's attack on Jeff Randolph and the family's sensitivity to gossip about it.

There was surely talk, out of heartfelt concern if nothing else, when Ann

Bankhead returned, apparently alone. Ann, the neighbors knew, was far advanced in pregnancy when reunited with her family, she was no longer young, and, like her maternal grandmother, she had always been delicate.

On January 30, probably at Tufton, Ann gave birth to a boy she named William Stuart Bankhead. When she did not recover as her family hoped, they brought her up the mountain to Monticello and put her in a first-floor room near Jefferson's private chambers. Four days later, on February 3, Sidney Nicholas wrote to Jeff Randolph, who was still in Richmond trying to rally support for the lottery. "Your sister Mrs. Bankhead is extremely ill and has been since the birth of her *boy*," Nicholas wrote. The family is "looking forward with great impatience to your return."

The family was also troubled that season with the ongoing quarrel between Jeff Randolph and his father, Tom Randolph, about Edgehill plantation and what, if anything, should be done with that underutilized and seriously encumbered property. This disagreement intensified early in the new year, when, over Tom Randolph's strenuous objections, Jeff Randolph and the estate's other trustees decided that Edgehill would go on the auction block.

Edgehill—"in the healthiest climate of the whole earth, sheltered by the mountains from the westerly winds of winters, and enjoying the cool breezes invariably descending from wooded crests on summer nights," an ad in the *Richmond Enquirer* would proclaim—had been Tom Randolph's largest asset for most of his life.

Several years earlier, seeking a bank loan, he had pledged the 1,950-acre plantation as collateral. In the spring of 1825, the bank called in the loan, and Jeff Randolph, as one of his father's cosigners and one of Edgehill's trustees, sued successfully for the right to liquidate the property. When Tom Randolph learned that his son planned to sell the farm in parcels, rather than as a whole, he was dumbfounded. To divide good farmland in such a way, Tom Randolph complained, would enable bidders to buy the estate for "almost nothing."

His confusion would soon turn to shock, however, then to suspicion, and, finally, to outrage. On January 6, 1826, Edgehill was sold at public auction. The winning bid for all five parcels was a surprisingly low $23,500, payable over three years. Edgehill's new owner, as Tom Randolph had begun to suspect might prove to be the case, was Jeff Randolph himself. The suspicion that the elder Randolph had been swindled by his own son was strengthened when, even before obtaining legal title to Edgehill, Jeff Randolph began to build a new two-story brick house on the property, which would replace his father's one-story frame house. Building so soon, Peggy Nicholas told Jane Randolph on July 23, 1827, "was a great impropriety."

In losing his real property, moreover, this ex–governor of Virginia and son-in-law of the former president of the United States also lost his right to hold office and even to vote. At this point in Tom Randolph's life, however, such losses seem to have meant little to him. What he still did care about, apparently, was his daughter Ann's health, and it had not improved.

On February 3, Jeff Randolph reported from the legislature that the lottery was facing stiffer resistance than he or his grandfather had anticipated. The main objection, voiced even by some family friends and longtime political allies, was that lotteries, as a form of gambling, fostered immorality. Opposition to them on moral grounds was "the policy of the state," Randolph said. In Jefferson's case, Randolph felt confident that such resistance could be overcome, however, and he encouraged his grandfather to remain optimistic.

This hostile reception humiliated Jefferson. "It is a part of my mortification

*Building the new house "was a great impropriety." Jeff Randolph's mansion at Edgehill.*

to perceive that I had so far overvalued myself as to have counted on [the lottery] with too much confidence," he wrote on February 9.

> I see in the failure of this hope, a deadly blast of all my peace of mind during my remaining days. You kindly encourage me to keep up my spirits; but, oppressed with disease, debility, age, and embarrassed affairs, this is difficult. For myself I should not regard a prostration of fortune, but I am overwhelmed at the prospect of the situation in which I may leave my family.

Jefferson could not have known this at the time, of course, but on February 8, the day before he wrote that gloomy letter, the lottery bill was introduced in the Virginia House of Delegates—and promptly tabled.

Three days after the lottery bill stalled in the Virginia legislature, Jefferson's mortification gave way to painful emotions of a different sort. That morning, Sidney Nicholas dispatched a note to Mary Randolph, at a neighbor's house, telling her that she "had better come down this morning for you will never see sister Ann[e] if you do not, there is no hope for her. Virginia ought to be told for she must know the worst soon, and grandpapa."

Because Jefferson was weakened by sickness, too, he had not been informed of the severity of Ann Bankhead's illness. This unhappy task fell to Dr. Dunglison.

"Mr. Jefferson was present in the adjoining apartment," Dunglison wrote in a memoir, "and when the announcement was made by me that little hope remained, that she was, indeed, past hope, it is impossible to imagine more poignant distress than was exhibited by him." When Jefferson entered the room where his granddaughter lay and found her, in his own words, "speechless and insensible," he began to weep and, Dunglison wrote, "abandoned himself to every evidence of intense grief."

At eleven o'clock on Sunday morning, February 11, Ann Randolph Bankhead died. By noon, Jefferson had composed himself sufficiently to write to Jeff Randolph: "Bad news . . . as to your sister. She expired about half an hour ago. . . . Heaven seems to be overwhelming us with every form of misfortune, and I expect your next will give me the *coup de grâce*. Your family are all well. Affectionately adieu."

◇　◇　◇

The family bore its grief with dignity. Although "in great distress," as Hetty Carr described her, Martha Randolph found the strength to welcome Charles Bankhead, who came to Monticello for his wife's burial. The younger Bankhead children came, too, and they would remain with the Randolphs after their father left.

"The natural consequence of our having the children was a reconciliation with the father," Martha told Ellen Coolidge, "and I must do him the justice to say that his conduct as it has come under my observation since our renewed intercourse, has been unexceptionable" in every situation in which "it was my sad fate to see him."

Martha even persuaded herself that for several months Bankhead had "abstained from the vice which has caused so much unhappiness in the family." She thought it only realistic, however, to assume that there might be "frequent relapses." Even these would not be too troublesome, however, because his character had been "much softened from physical causes," and his "intemperance no longer produces madness as it formerly did."

Martha also reported that Bankhead's "feelings are entirely kind to every member of the family." Perhaps it was fortunate that Jeff Randolph, still in Richmond on lottery business, was unable to return for his sister's burial.

Martha Randolph volunteered to raise the Bankhead children as her own, and Jeff Randolph expressed his eagerness to help care for his niece and nephew and their newborn brother. "You will not be surprised to hear that Ellen Bankhead and the poor little infant will live with me," Martha told Joseph Coolidge. As for his estranged brother-in-law, Jeff Randolph "determined at once to make up their differences and is very anxious to have little Thomas Bankhead."

Not every member of the Randolph family responded with such charity. Tom Randolph "has gone on since his daughters death more like a demon than ever," Jane Carr told Dabney Carr on February 27. Tormenting Martha by railing against their son, Tom Randolph forbade his children from ever visiting their aunt, uncle, and cousins at Tufton. The "very moment they cross the threshold" of Jeff Randolph's house, he would hold Martha responsible and snatch the children from her.

◇　◇　◇

In mid-February, the lottery's prospects brightened. Its increasingly vocal proponents in the Virginia legislature appealed to the other lawmakers' sympathy for Jefferson and managed, by a four-vote margin, to move the bill to both the House of Delegates and the Senate for floor votes. Cabell told Jefferson that it now seemed likely that the bill would pass, but strong opposition would influence the form of lottery that the legislature approved.

In fact, the proposal that Jeff Randolph submitted had already been modified. The plan to sell $60,000 worth of tickets was replaced by one stipulating that ticket revenues could not exceed the market value of the prize. The value of any land to be included in the prize, moreover, would be determined by an independent commission, not by Jefferson and his family. This would still benefit them, however, because the land would be assessed on the basis not of the depressed prices of Albemarle alone but of the more generous ones offered in more prosperous parts of the country. Jefferson would still be able to earn considerably more from the property than he would if the family were to try to sell it themselves locally.

The lottery bill that passed both the Senate and the House of Delegates on February 20 included one additional change, however. But it was not until his return from Richmond, probably in early March, that Jeff Randolph revealed to his grandfather the final condition to which he and the other proponents had agreed.

Unfortunately, the original idea of offering mere farmland as a prize had been deemed not attractive enough. For the lottery to be approved, Randolph said, something more valuable had to be added. That was Monticello itself— house, grounds, gardens, farms, and all.

When Jefferson heard this news, he "turned quite white," Hetty Carr said. For some moments, he sat silent. Jeff Randolph assured his grandfather that even if Monticello were lost in the lottery, he would be allowed to spend the rest of his days there and that it would also be Martha's to live in until her death. Then, and only then, would it pass out of the family.

Jefferson said that he needed "some time to think of it & to consult with Mrs. Randolph." Eventually, he gave his consent, agreeing, Mrs. Carr said, "as he would to anything that Jef[f] would propose."

Approval of the lottery, which had been so eagerly wished for, now cast an unexpected pall over the household. No matter what the lottery would mean financially, it would signal the end of the family's days at Monticello. "Fortune has persecuted us so unrelentingly," Cornelia Randolph wrote to Ellen Coolidge, "that even though at last she seems to give us one smile to excite hope, not one of us has spirits to feel it a promise of future good."

Jefferson's spirits proved more resilient than his family's, though they, too, came to view their situation somewhat more hopefully. There was good reason for this optimism. Their financial position did indeed improve, at least temporarily. By early March, when news of their plight had spread beyond Virginia, the newspapers were covering the lottery with approval, and officials in a number of cities began raising funds to give directly to the family.

Before the end of the year, the mayor of New York City sent $8,500, collected from his constituents. Philadelphia sent $5,000, and Baltimore contributed another $3,000. These efforts Jefferson discouraged, but not because he was too proud to accept charity, as some have assumed. Such well-intended programs, he feared, would divert attention, energy, and dollars from the lottery, reducing its chance of success. (Although he never knew it, this prediction proved accurate.)

Also by March, the women of the Monticello household were sufficiently encouraged that—ignoring the cost-conscious Jeff Randolph's protests against what he considered an extravagance—they ordered a new pianoforte, selected by the Coolidges in Boston. When the instrument arrived at Monticello, Jefferson was so impressed with "the cleanness and sweetness of the tone," Martha told Joseph Coolidge, that, as soon as the lottery money came in, he planned to purchase one for himself.

How his crippled fingers would ever play the pianoforte, Jefferson failed to say. That he seems to have thought he could accomplish such a feat is further evidence of the man's remarkable sense of possibility, which, while it might from time to time have wavered, would persist to the end.

The contributions that arrived from outside Virginia made him fret for the lottery's prospects, but nevertheless buoyed his spirits immensely. "I have spent three times as much money and given my whole life to my countrymen," he said, "and now they come forward, in the only way they can, to repay me and save an old servant from being turned like a dog out of doors." Not one cent of these contributions "is wrung from the tax-payer—it is the pure and unsolicited offering of love." This show of gratitude, Jefferson declared, would close "with a cloudless sun a long and serene day of life."

# CHAPTER 38

## *"Is It the Fourth?"*

O n March 16, 1826, "being of sound mind, and in my ordinary state of health," Thomas Jefferson made his will.

"Considering the insolvent state of the affairs of my friend and son-in-law Thomas Mann Randolph," he bequeathed Monticello and the rest of the Albemarle County land to Martha Randolph. For the rest of Tom Randolph's life, the will further stated, Martha's inheritance would remain under the control of three trustees—Jeff Randolph; Nicholas Trist, who had married Virginia Randolph in 1824; and Alexander Garrett, the chief financial officer of the university. The estate was to be administered "for the sole and separate use of Martha Randolph" and her heirs. Jeff Randolph would be the sole executor. Tom Randolph was to have no control over any inheritance.

Poplar Forest and the Bedford County land would go to Francis Eppes, Jefferson's twenty-four-year-old grandson by Maria Jefferson Eppes, who had

*The house leaked "not in one but a hundred places." Sitting room at Poplar Forest.*

lived there since shortly after his marriage in 1823. This would prove a bequest of dubious value. Eppes did not like living at Poplar Forest, which he found remote, uncomfortable as a residence, and unprofitable as a farm. (In June 1826, he would report to Jefferson that great rainstorms had washed away the topsoil of the farmland there, leaving little but clay, while the house itself had begun to leak "not in one but a hundred places." The plaster in the parlor "is so entirely wet every rain, that I begin to fear it will fall in. Large buckets of water pass through it. Your room is nearly as bad and the others leak more and more every rain.")

In a codicil written the day after he made his will, Jefferson disposed of items of personal property. His books, with a few exceptions, were to become part of the university library. His "gold-mounted walking staff" would go to James Madison. His silver watch would become Jeff Randolph's. Jefferson also requested that a gold watch be given to each of his grandchildren "who have not already received one from me." It had been Jefferson's practice to give the girls gold watches when they turned sixteen, the boys when they were twenty-one. The bequest meant that five new gold watches—no small expense—would have to be purchased.

Jefferson then turned his attention to the future status of three of his most valued slaves. Burwell Colbert, "my good, affectionate, and faithful servant," would receive his freedom and a gift of $300 "to buy necessities to commence his trade of painter and glazier, or to use otherwise, as he pleases."

Joe Fossett, the Monticello blacksmith, and John Hemings, the carpenter, would be freed one year after Jefferson's death. They would also be given their blacksmithing and carpentry tools, respectively. John Hemings would also receive the services of Madison and Eston Hemings, sons of Sally Hemings, as apprentices. When these two young men turned twenty-one, they, too, would be freed.

Jefferson further ordered that "a comfortable log-house" be built for each of the three older slaves, "on some part of my lands convenient to them with respect to the residence of their wives, and to Charlottesville, and the University," where he hoped they would find employment. Because Virginia law required that freed slaves leave the state within a year of their manumission, Jefferson petitioned the legislature to give these favored servants permission to remain in the state, which was granted.

Of Sally Hemings, who was now in her early fifties, Jefferson made no mention.

◇  ◇  ◇

About the time that Jefferson made his will, Jeff Randolph set off for Washington, Baltimore, Philadelphia, New York, and Boston. The goal was to build support for the lottery throughout the Northeast. The plan again had undergone alteration. Instead of selling an unlimited number of $1 tickets with a goal of raising $60,000—the plan that the Virginia legislature rejected—the family now spoke of printing 11,000 tickets, each of which would cost the purchaser $10. But because profits were not to exceed Monticello's market value, even when assessed nationally, it seems that the family never expected to sell all of the tickets, since they would not be able to keep the money had they raised even $60,000. The value of Monticello was unlikely to be two and a half times that of neighboring Edgehill, which had sold for $23,500, although, being the estate of Thomas Jefferson, Monticello could conceivably sell for more.

Clearly, much remained to be determined, and Randolph's trip north would presumably help answer a great many relevant questions. Not least of these was how much demand might exist for such a lottery and how receptive the officials of the major cities would prove to be. Their level of support would depend, of course, on what the country still thought of Thomas Jefferson, and this also was a matter about which the family could only guess.

Whatever else Randolph's trip accomplished, it did provide the occasion for the last exchange of letters between Jefferson and John Adams. On March 25, Jefferson informed his old friend that Randolph would soon arrive in Boston and "would think he had seen nothing were he to leave it without seeing you." Randolph wished to be able, "in the winter nights of old age," Jefferson wrote, "to recount to those around him what he has heard and learnt of the Heroic age preceding his birth, and which of the Argonauts particularly he was in time to have seen. . . . Gratify his ambition then by recieving his best bow, and my solicitude for your health by enabling him to bring me a favorable account of it."

On April 17, Adams wrote to say that he had indeed been visited by Randolph, whose height impressed the diminutive Bostonian. "How happens it that you Virginians are all sons of Anak?" Adams wrote. "We New Englanders are but Pygmies by the side of Mr. Randolph." After this pleasantry, Adams was his irascible old self again, observing that while theirs may well have been "a Heroic age," as Jefferson said, he saw little to recommend the present. "Public affairs," Adams wrote, "go on pretty much as usual: perpetual chicanery and rather more abuse than there used to be."

Referring to the duel between Henry Clay and Jefferson's cousin John Randolph of Roanoke—a duel precipitated by the kind of abuse he had just denounced—Adams expressed contempt for such practices. Dueling "ought not to be suffered in a republican Government. Our American Chivalry is the worst in the World. It has no Laws, no bounds, no definitions; it seems to be all a Caprice. My love to all your family, and best wishes for your health."

Adams's good wishes notwithstanding, Jefferson's health in May took a decided turn for the worse. The diarrhea that plagued him suddenly became more severe and, in early June, Dr. Dunglison treated Jefferson for what appears to have been a recurrence of the boils on his backside that first afflicted him almost ten years before.

On June 6, Jefferson was feeling well enough to make his final visit to Charlottesville, apparently on horseback. This trip was also, in all likelihood, Jefferson's last time in the saddle. He had been able to enjoy some exercise on his horse Old Eagle, himself "well stricken in years," according to Randall, throughout the winter and spring, though not without increasing difficulty. The horse would be led over from the stable and positioned at the south terrace. There, as Jefferson was lowered into the saddle, the horse waited "as immovable as a statue." The reins were placed in Jefferson's "crippled hands—as ineffectual as an infant's to curb his strength—and Old Eagle moved off with slow and stately gravity, as if perfectly conscious of the necessity of discretion in his movements." Jefferson resolutely refused to allow any of the slaves to accompany him, telling Martha he had "helped himself" since he was a child and was not about to change now.

By late June, when Jeff Randolph returned from the North, there was no longer any question of riding. Jefferson was visibly weaker and frailer than he had been only weeks before. The discouraging news that Randolph had made little progress on his trip could not have helped Jefferson regain his strength. For reasons that remain unclear, lottery tickets had still not even been offered for sale, and July 4, when the drawing was to be held, was fast approaching. Jefferson, once so optimistic about the lottery, began to worry again, especially for Martha Randolph, who was now ill, too.

"It was agony to leave her in the situation she is now in," he said, according to Jane Randolph. "She is sinking every day under the suffering she now endures; she is literally dying before my eyes." He pleaded with Jeff Randolph

*"She is sinking every day under the suffering she now endures." Martha Jefferson Randolph.*

never to leave his mother, and Randolph assured his grandfather that she would not be abandoned.

On June 26, Dunglison observed that his patient's various ailments were "making a decided impression on his bodily powers," and his "strength gradually diminished." After that, Jefferson would never again get out of bed. His diarrhea temporarily relented—his "evacuations became less numerous," Dunglison wrote—but it was nonetheless "manifest that his powers were failing." Jefferson's health now took priority over all other concerns, with one notable exception.

To the end, Jefferson worried about his place in history. Some months earlier, he had agreed to meet with Henry Lee, a son of the revolutionary war hero Light Horse Harry Lee. The elder Lee's *Memoirs of the War* had been critical of Jefferson's service as Virginia's wartime governor, and when he learned that the author's son was preparing a new edition of the work, Jefferson hoped to provide him with documents that would cast a more favorable light on that controversial episode.

On June 29, 1826, as Lee neared Charlottesville for the agreed-upon meeting, he learned that Jefferson's health was in serious and probably irreversible decline. Continuing toward Monticello, Lee climbed the mountain and, as he rode up to the house, "the anxiety and distress visible in the countenances of the servants, increased the gloom of my own forebodings," so that he entered "with no little agitation."

Martha Randolph greeted Lee but informed him that her father was too ill to receive him. When told of Lee's arrival, however, Jefferson asked Martha to show the visitor into the sickroom, which was hot and still on a summer afternoon, with flies buzzing about.

> There he was [Lee wrote] extended, feeble, prostrate; but the fine and clear expression of his countenance not all obscured. At the first glance he recognized me, and his hand and voice at once saluted me. The energy of his grasp, and the spirit of his conversation, were such as to make me hope he would yet rally—and that the superiority of mind over matter in his composition would preserve him yet longer.

Servants and family members came and went during Lee's visit, though Jefferson "kept the flies off himself, and seemed to decline assistance from his attendants." He apologized for his inability to help with Lee's book but said that, should he regain his strength, he would gladly share the documents he had promised.

Then they spoke of the weather—a summer storm had flooded the James River—and of the progress of the university. Once Jefferson "became so cheerful as to smile, even to laughing" at a whimsical remark Lee made. Jefferson also "alluded to the probability of his death—as a man would to the prospect of being caught in a shower—as an event not to be desired, but not to be feared."

Eager not to exhaust his host with further conversation, Lee attempted to leave, and Jefferson urged him to return another time. He also asked Lee to stay for dinner. When Lee replied that he would be honored to dine with the family when Jefferson was feeling better, Jefferson rebuked him.

"You *must* dine here," he said. "My sickness makes no difference."

Lee may have been the last person, other than Dunglison and members of the household, to see Jefferson alive.

◇  ◇  ◇

Before Henry Lee left Monticello, Martha Randolph told him of Jefferson's way of dealing with his failing health. His "plan was to fight old age off, by never admitting the approach of helplessness." Jefferson was so "exceedingly averse to giving trouble," Martha said, that he always insisted on doing as much for himself as possible.

By Friday, June 30, however, Jefferson gave up all pretense of taking care of himself. That day, Dunglison wrote in his journal, "the inflammation which first attacked [Jefferson's] bladder has now fallen on his bowels." Grandpapa was "most alarmingly weak," Virginia Randolph Trist observed, but "having resigned himself completely into the doctors hands, & suffering himself to be properly nursed," he comforted the rest of the household "in our present distress."

A routine was soon established. Martha Randolph remained at her father's bedside during the day, often with her son-in-law Nicholas Trist, and Dunglison was at Monticello "almost constantly." Jeff Randolph sat up with his grandfather at night. Virginia Trist and her sister Mary Randolph "go in whenever we can without being in the way." Household slaves, notably Burwell Colbert, were in constant attendance. At night, they brought pallets into the bedroom to be with their master as he slept.

On the morning of July 1, a Saturday, Jefferson awoke after a peaceful night's rest, but was "barely sensible," Jeff Randolph told his wife, giving "unequivocal indication of approaching dissolution." From this point forward, the family watched "from hour to hour to a close of the scene."

On July 2, "with intervals of wakefulness and consciousness," in Henry Randall's words, Jefferson found the strength to speak again. He told Martha of a gift for her in a pocketbook that could be found in a certain drawer that she was to look into after his death. He also spoke with each member of the family, urging them "to pursue virtue, be true and truthful," Jeff Randolph would recall. When eight-year-old George Wythe Randolph took in the confusing scene, Jefferson, managing a weak smile, said, "George does not understand what all this means."

Sometime during the day, Jefferson expressed a desire that James Madison succeed him as rector of the university. Jefferson said that he would not object to meeting with the Reverend Frederick Hatch, the Episcopal priest in Charlottesville who would officiate at the funeral, but as a "kind and good neighbor," not as a clergyman. He also ordered that his coffin be made.

◇　◇　◇

On several occasions, Jefferson had expressed a desire to live to see the Fourth of July, "to breathe his last," Ellen Coolidge recalled, "on that great day, the birthday of his country."

On the morning of July 3, when Nicholas Trist, fearing that Jefferson would not live another twenty-four hours and wishing not to disappoint, told him that the Fourth had already arrived, "an expression came over his countenance, which said, 'just as I wished.'" Sometime during the day, he roused himself again, uttered the words of the *Nunc dimittis* from Luke's Gospel—"Lord, now lettest thy servant depart in peace"—and rested again.

For the next several hours, Jefferson's pulse was barely perceptible. His arms and legs took on "the clamminess of death," in Trist's words. At around seven P.M., he awoke and, seeing Dunglison at his bedside, in a soft, somewhat indistinct voice, said, "Ah! Doctor, are you still here?"

Jefferson then asked, "Is it the Fourth?"

"It soon will be," Dunglison assured Jefferson, who drifted off again. Around eight P.M., the doctor told the family that Jefferson had perhaps fifteen minutes left to live; he lingered for another seventeen hours, evidently without pain.

At nine P.M., roused to take his laudanum, Jefferson protested, saying, "No, Doctor, nothing more," and slowly fell asleep. The lack of laudanum "caused his slumbers to be disturbed and dreamy," Jeff Randolph observed. Once that night, he sat up in his sleep and used his right hand, "as if writing on a tablet he held in the left," Nicholas Trist observed, and looking back on his days as Virginia's wartime governor, muttered something about "the Committee of Safety," saying it "ought to be warned."

Throughout the night, Trist, on a sofa near the bed, watched the hands of the clock, "which, it seemed to me, would never reach the point at which I wished to see them."

Midnight came, and the Fourth, a Tuesday, arrived. At four A.M., Jefferson awoke, summoning his house slaves "with a strong and clear voice," though what he said to them went unrecorded. "He did not speak again," Jeff Randolph would note.

At ten A.M., conscious again, Jefferson "fixed his eye intently upon me," Randolph recalled, "indicating some want, which most painfully, I could not understand." More sensitive to his master's wishes, Burwell Colbert noticed that Jefferson's head was not as elevated as he liked it to be and shifted the pillow. Jefferson relaxed.

At eleven A.M., Jefferson again looked to his grandson for help, moving his lips to indicate that his mouth was dry. Randolph applied a wet sponge to Jefferson's mouth, "which he sucked and appeared to relish—this was the last evidence he gave of consciousness."

Little more than an hour later, at fifteen minutes after twelve, Jefferson "ceased to breathe" and died peacefully. Randolph gently reached forward and "closed his eyes with my own hands."

Then, using a signal that Randolph and his wife had agreed upon, he draped a white sheet over a thornbush on Mulberry Row near the Monticello slave quarters. The display of this sheet, visible at Tufton, told Jane Randolph that the end had come.

Only a few hours later, John Adams, at ninety, lay near death at his house in Quincy, Massachusetts. As at Monticello, the dying man's family had also sat at his bedside night after night, with a physician nearby. Mostly, Adams slept; when awake, he lay with eyes closed, incapable of speech.

The story so often told about the nearly simultaneous deaths of the two old patriots and what one said about the other has become a part of American mythology. The tale is too good to be true, though not without a foundation in fact. Adams, like Jefferson, had been eager to survive until the Fourth of July, and when told that he had achieved his goal, Adams said, "It is a great day. It is a *good* day."

That morning, his family heard cannons fired in celebration, and around noon, shortly after Jefferson died, thunderclouds rolled over New England, bringing rain. At about one P.M., Adams roused himself and, according to his niece Louise Smith, managed to say the name "Thomas Jefferson," but whatever words might have followed that utterance were too indistinct to be understood. Later eulogists would claim that Adams ended his life with the moving, if misinformed, assertion "Thomas Jefferson still survives." Even if those were the words that Adams said, they would not be his last. These came later in the day when, short of breath, he whispered to his granddaughter, Susanna, "Help me, child! Help me."

Adams then fell silent and, shortly after six P.M., he died.

By early evening on the Fourth, the tolling of the courthouse bell brought the news of Thomas Jefferson's death to the people of Charlottesville. It cast a "gloom over every countenance," in the words of a family friend, Louise McIntyre. The townspeople could talk of little else; the students at the university hurriedly donned black crepe armbands.

Tom Randolph, who had not been to Monticello in weeks, either to comfort his wife as her father faced his final illness or to say goodbye to his father-in-law, now rode up the mountain. Upon his arrival, Dr. Dunglison reported, "a singular scene presented itself": noticing that Martha Randolph, while "in the deepest distress," did not weep, her husband began "taunting her for not shedding a tear."

Telling Dunglison that this failure to cry must be the result of a "morbid condition," Randolph asked the doctor to prescribe some treatment to induce tears. "Nothing as a matter of course could be done," Dunglison said, "but to enjoin quiet which she was not likely to obtain." Quiet was unlikely because

*At ten minutes to twelve, he "ceased to breathe."*
*Jefferson's deathbed at Monticello.*

*Jefferson's death cast a "gloom over every countenance."*
*George Wythe Randolph at his grandfather's grave.*

Randolph, in Mrs. McIntyre's words, "pretended to mourn exceedingly." Jeff Randolph considered this display hypocritical, accusing his father of "hating [Jefferson] in life [and] neglecting him in death."

At some point, Martha remembered that Jefferson had told her about a gift, and, in the pocketbook of the drawer he had mentioned, she found the following lines, composed by him and written in his own hand:

> Life's visions have vanished, its dreams are no more;
> Dear friends of my bosom, why bathed in tears?
> I go to my fathers, I welcome the shore
> Which crowns all my hopes or which buries my cares.
> Then farewell, my dear, my lov'd daughter, adieu!
> The last pang of life is in parting from you!
> Two seraphs await me long shrouded in death;
> I will bear them your love on my last parting breath.

In another drawer in Jefferson's room, the family found packages carefully labeled that contained locks of hair of his wife and of their daughter Maria—the "two seraphs" of his poem—and of both Lucy Elizabeths, the one who died in

1781 and the one who died in 1784. On one of these two packets appeared the words: "A lock of our first Lucy's hair, with some of my dear, dear wife's writing."

The family announced that a graveside funeral, at which the public was welcome, would be held on July 6, and businesses in Charlottesville closed for the day. The city fathers decided that a procession would form at the courthouse square at four P.M., to move en masse up the mountain and reach Monticello in time for the funeral, which was to begin at five.

Things did not go as planned. It rained, which discouraged turnout, and when a dispute arose over whether the students or the townspeople were to lead the procession, much time was lost. Some thirty or forty citizens, "becoming tired of the discussion," in the words of one of them, "turned our horses' heads to the mountain," and rode on. When this smaller detachment arrived, another quarrel threatened to delay the ceremonies. Tom Randolph thought that the Reverend Hatch should wait until the rest of the townspeople had arrived and, when Jeff Randolph disagreed, made a scene.

The younger Randolph prevailed and, standing before the coffin, which rested on narrow planks laid over the grave, read the burial service from the Book of Common Prayer. The coffin was lowered into the ground, the grave was filled up, and the family returned to the house. The townspeople started back down the mountain, where they met the official procession—about fifteen hundred strong—trudging through the rain. "They were sorely disappointed," a participant said, "and in some cases angered" to learn that the ceremonies were already over.

One young man who had arrived in time to witness the burial—one whose sensibility was so unlike Jefferson's as to signal the passing of one age and the dawn of another—was a morbidly sensitive seventeen-year-old student from Richmond who entertained his fellows with satirical verse.

This was Edgar Allan Poe.

Much of the country, learning that both Jefferson and Adams had died on the Fourth, mourned the passing of these last two giants of the Revolution. The *Richmond Enquirer* bordered its columns in black, and, by one account, the majority of the Virginia capital's people turned out for a solemn memorial parade.

In the weeks that followed, there were similar gatherings in Washington, Baltimore, Philadelphia, New York, and Boston.

Like many of his countrymen, President John Quincy Adams found the timing of the two patriots' deaths to be "visible and palpable marks of Divine favor." Daniel Webster, in an August 2 oration at Boston's Faneuil Hall, called it "striking and extraordinary" that

> on the day which has fast linked for ever their own fame with their country's glory, the heavens should open to receive them both at once. As their lives themselves were the gifts of Providence, who is not willing to recognize in their happy termination, as well as in their long continuance, proofs that our country and its benefactors are objects of His care?

Jefferson himself spoke about the significance of the day, although, as it were, from the grave. On June 24, ten days before his death, he had written to decline an invitation to join the residents of Washington, D.C., for their Independence Day celebration, citing "the sufferings of sickness."

In his letter, published in the *National Intelligencer* on July 4 and subsequently reprinted in newspapers throughout the nation, Jefferson implored his countrymen to remember that the day held meaning not only for Americans but for all mankind. He wanted their celebration to call the whole world "to burst the chains under which monkish ignorance and superstition" held them, and to trust instead in "the unbounded exercise of reason."

Americans in their experiment in self-government had shown the way, and now the future of all people, though it might be rocky, could also be one of unlimited advancement.

> All eyes are opened, or opening, to the rights of man. The general spread of the light of science has already laid open to every view the palpable truth, that the mass of mankind has not been born with saddles on their backs, nor a favored few booted and spurred, ready to ride them, legitimately, by the rights of man. These are grounds of hope for others. For ourselves, let the annual return of this day, forever refresh our recollections of these rights, and an undiminished devotion to them.

In August 1826, just weeks after Thomas Jefferson's death, Martha Randolph fled from Monticello to Boston, taking with her her two youngest children, George Wythe, eight, and Septimia Anne, twelve. Because she was no longer needed to help care for her father, Martha could at last leave the abusive Tom Randolph, something she may have been planning to do for months or, perhaps, years. She could also protect the children, whom their father had threatened to take from her.

The most that Tom Randolph knew of Martha's intentions was that she and the children were on a visit to Washington and would return. After a few weeks in Washington, however, they departed not for Monticello but for Boston. There they would live for the next two and a half years, initially with Martha's daughter Ellen Coolidge and her husband. Joseph Coolidge was a well-to-do merchant, but Martha, for reasons that are unclear, seems not to have shared in her son-in-law's prosperity, and soon found lodgings elsewhere. As early as January 1827, one of the Carrs reported, Martha was forced "to receive assistance from any one that can give it to her." She was unhappy in Boston, the result not only of economic deprivation but also of grief over her father's death and of her longing for Monticello. "I have lost all sensibility to pleasure or pain," she wrote to Jeff Randolph on March 2, 1827, and could no longer "comprehend the possibility of better days."

Had Martha remained in Virginia, she might have been unhappier still. On November 3, 1826, four months after Jefferson's death, Jeff Randolph announced in the *Charlottesville Central Gazette* an auction at Monticello of "the whole of the residue of the personal estate of Thomas Jefferson, dec., consisting of 130 VALUABLE NEGROES, Stock, Crop, &c. Household and Kitchen

Furniture." The slaves "are believed to be the most valuable for their number ever offered at one time in the State of Virginia."

Although the Randolphs still held out hope that the house and land would be disposed of through the lottery, they were willing, in the meantime, to sacrifice a great many of their belongings. These, according to the advertisement, included

> valuable historical and portrait paintings, busts of marble and plaister of distinguished individuals; one of marble of Thomas Jefferson, by Caracei, with the pedestal and truncated column on which it stands; a polygraph or copying instrument used by Thomas Jefferson, for the last twenty-five years; with various other articles curious and useful to men of business and private families.

The five-day sale began on January 15 when, despite extremely low temperatures, a large crowd turned out. As the forlorn family looked on, much of what they owned went under the gavel. Once fashionable furniture that Jefferson had purchased in Paris; prints and maps; wineglasses, teapots, chafing dishes, candlesticks, and punchbowls; saddles, bridles, and other items of tack; pitchforks and plows; horses, mules, cattle, and hogs were carted away by their

*EXECUTOR'S SALE.*

WILL be sold on the premises, on the first day of January, 1827, that well known and valuable estate called Poplar Forest, lying in the counties of Bedford and Campbell, the property of Thomas Jefferson, dec. within eight miles of Lynchburg and three of New London; also about 70 likely and valuable negroes, with stock, crops, &c. The terms of sale will be accommodating and made known previous to the day.

On the fifteenth of January, at Monticello, in the county of Albemarle; the whole of the residue of the personal property of Thomas Jefferson, dec., consisting of 130 valuable negroes, stock, crop, &c. household and kitchen furniture. The attention of the public is earnestly invited to this property. The negroes are believed to be the most valuable for their number ever offered at one time in the State of Virginia. The household furniture, many valuable historical and portrait paintings, busts of marble and plaister of distinguished individuals; one of marble of Thomas Jefferson, by Caracei, with the pedestal and truncated column on which it stands; a polygraph or copying instrument used by Thomas Jefferson, for the last twenty-five years; with various other articles curious and useful to men of business and private families. The terms of sale will be accommodating and made known previous to the day. The sales will be continued from day to day until completed. These sales being unavoidable, it is a sufficient guarantee to the public, that they will take place at the times and places appointed.

THOMAS J. RANDOLPH,

Nov. 3.    51—tds        Executor of Th. Jefferson, dec.

*"The whole of the residue of the personal property of Thomas Jefferson" for sale at auction.*
The Charlottesville Central Gazette, *November 3, 1826.*

new owners. (The paintings and busts were held back, despite Randolph's advertisment; these were shipped to Boston where Joseph Coolidge believed—mistakenly—that they would command higher prices. Most were then sent back to Virginia to gather dust.)

"Tell mama that the beds and linen have not been sold," Mary Randolph instructed Ellen Coolidge on January 25, "and that we thought it best to retain as many of the former . . . as would be necessary for the use of the family." Jefferson's bedroom furniture was also kept. Some of his clothes, also held back, were sent to storage at Edgehill.

The auction of slaves was an excruciating ordeal. The situation of Monticello's longtime blacksmith, Joe Fossett, and his family proved especially grim. Under the terms of Jefferson's will, Fossett was to receive his freedom on July 4, 1827, exactly one year after Jefferson's death. Fossett's wife, two adolescent daughters, and two infant sons, however, were sold to three different bidders, bringing the Randolphs $1,350.

Whether the breakup of the Fossett family was typical is impossible to say. Only thirty-four of the 130 slaves found buyers at the auction, with another thirty-three sold two years later, and historians do not know what happened to many of them, as individuals or as families. All but one were "sold to persons living in the state, many of them in this neighborhood or the adjoining counties . . . as much to their own wishes as they could be in leaving our estate," Mary Randolph told Ellen Coolidge.

When the slaves were led away by their new owners, Jeff Randolph was eager to wash his hands of "this dreadful business," as Mary called it. The "sale and dispersion of [the] slaves was a sad scene," Randolph wrote years later. "I had known all of them from childhood and had strong attachments to many. I was powerless to relieve them." They were "sold in families," Randolph insisted, though this was clearly not the case with the Fossetts.

Earnings from the auction enabled the Randolphs to retire $35,000 of their debts, but this still left the family more than $150,000 in arrears. Except for $20,000 given by Louisiana and South Carolina, contributions such as those sent the previous year by Baltimore, Philadelphia, and New York City ceased once Jefferson was dead.

By the time of the sale, the scant public enthusiasm for the lottery that survived Jefferson's death had vanished. Although some people might have been willing to buy lottery tickets to make Jefferson's final days less difficult, few showed interest in rescuing his descendants, and in April 1827, Randolph told James Madison that the lottery was "prostrate without the least hope of another revival." The idea was abandoned, leaving Randolph, as he told Dabney Carr, in "a perfect hell of trouble."

During the time Martha Randolph was in Boston, Tom Randolph had accepted a job helping survey the much disputed Georgia-Florida border, so this meant that for much of Martha's absence, her husband was also many miles from Monticello. Eventually, Martha wrote to him to admit that she had taken George Wythe and Septimia Anne with her to Boston and to tell him that, at fifty-four and in questionable health, she no longer had the strength or patience to live with him ever again.

Randolph wrote to Septimia, telling her that because of Martha's feelings, his hope "of spending some happy years yet" with his family had almost vanished. But he would never give up his children, he vowed, lest they be brought up "to disrespect and dislike" him. If Martha would not bring the children home voluntarily, he said, he would go to Boston and take them from her.

Informed of this threat, Joseph Coolidge told Jeff Randolph that Tom Randolph would be allowed to visit but only under strict supervision. He would "be received kindly," Coolidge said, but he "cannot compel the return of Mrs. R., and should he seriously attempt to possess himself of the children, they can be placed, for a time, with some friend at a distance, where he cannot discover them."

Tom Randolph never went to Boston. In June 1827, after several months in Georgia, he returned to Virginia. The following spring, a "rheumatic affection of the stomach," as he called it, destroyed his health, making further travel impossible. With funds "too low for any tavern," Randolph accepted an invitation from his elder daughters to move from Milton to Monticello, where, at his insistence, he lived alone in the north pavilion. There, as his health continued its slow dissolution, Randolph devoted himself to translating articles from European agricultural journals, which he hoped to publish for the benefit of American planters. These hopes came to nothing.

In May 1828, having learned that her husband was seriously ill, Martha also returned to Monticello. A reconciliation of sorts occurred, though they continued to live separately, with Martha moving back into the mansion and Tom remaining in the North Pavilion. In June, fearing the end was near, Randolph asked his "adored wife" to send for Jeff Randolph. When their son appeared, Tom Randolph "begged of him mutual forgiveness," declaring that "an *honester* man" did not exist. (Despite these efforts to make peace, Martha told Ellen Coolidge, Randolph retained "his propensity to *argue,*" even about "the injudicious arrangement of a pillow.")

On June 20, 1828, Thomas Mann Randolph, Jr., died at the age of sixty and was buried in the Monticello graveyard. The *Richmond Enquirer* acknowledged the former governor's intellectual attainments, which established Randolph as a man of the Enlightenment, critical of slavery, committed to public education, and dedicated to science. "He enjoyed every advantage which education could confer," the *Enquirer* observed, though the learning to be gleaned from books could not compensate for shortcomings of character. Had Randolph "possessed less irritability of temper and a larger acquaintance with the volume of men and things," he could have accomplished more in life and known less of failure and disappointment.

Monticello, which appeared desolate after Jefferson's death, seemed even more so during the years when Martha Randolph lived in Boston. The house fell to ruin, and a steady stream of sightseers tramped about the grounds, showing little respect for the family or the property. "It will grieve you very much to hear of the depredations that have been made at Monticello by the numerous parties who go to see the place," Virginia Trist told Ellen Coolidge in March 1827. "Mama's choicest flower roots have been carried off, one of her yellow jessamines, fig bushes [and] grape vines and everything and anything they fancied."

The "vulgar herd" that flocked to the place on Sundays behaved so badly, Virginia went on, that Jeff Randolph placed a notice in the *Charlottesville Gazette* asking visitors to refrain from stealing plants. Burwell Colbert, who looked after the grounds, said the vandalism became even worse after the notice appeared. The house and outbuildings fast became eyesores. Slave cabins were in "little heaps of ruin everywhere," Cornelia said, and Henry Gilpin, a Philadelphia lawyer who visited Monticello that year, described the mansion as "dark & much dilapidated with age & neglect." No monument had yet been placed over Jefferson's grave and, with "one or two exceptions," the graves were marked "by a board stuck in at the head with initials painted or cut in it."

*"Dark & much dilapidated with age & neglect." Monticello after the Randolphs sold it.*

In August 1828, Margaret Bayard Smith, who had last seen Monticello just after Jefferson retired from the presidency, paid a second visit.

> How different did it seem [she wrote] from what it did eighteen years ago! No kind friend with his gracious countenance stood in the Portico to welcome us, no train of domestics hastened with smiling alacrity to show us forward. All was silent. Ruin has already commenced its ravages—the inclosures, the terraces, the outer houses.

Met at the door by "a little negro girl poorly dressed," Mrs. Smith and her party found the entrance hall "once filled with busts and statues and natural curiosities to crowding, now empty! Bare walls and defaced floor, from then into the drawing room, once so gay and splendid, where walls were literally covered with pictures . . . bare and comfortless . . ."

Then Martha Randolph appeared, "with open arms and affectionate countenance," like "the spirit of the place, that had survived its body." Martha summoned the family, and Mrs. Smith counted fifteen members of the household, excluding the few remaining slaves. Besides Martha, there were four daughters, four sons, four grandchildren, son-in-law Nicholas Trist, and Nicholas's mother. Martha apologized that there were not enough chairs. "You will excuse all that is wanting," she said. "You know all that has passed."

◇  ◇  ◇

By the time of Mrs. Smith's visit, the family, after much anguish, had reached a decision. A few days earlier, on July 28, 1828, Jeff Randolph announced in the *Richmond Enquirer* the sale of his grandfather's lands in Bedford and Campbell Counties, the mills on the Rivanna, and, finally, "Monticello, in the County of Albemarle." (Later in the year, Francis Eppes found a buyer for Poplar Forest and, saying "good night Old Virginia," as he put it in a letter to Jeff Randolph in November, moved his wife and children to Florida.)

The family hoped to sell the house and adjacent farms at Monticello for between $15,000 and $20,000. If Randolph proved unable to find a buyer by September 29, the property would be offered at auction. In the meantime, they would all move to Edgehill. When September came and no one showed serious interest in buying Monticello, the auction was canceled, but the family moved nonetheless. Although Randolph fielded inquiries from would-be entrepreneurs eager to turn the property into an inn or boardinghouse, any such use, Cornelia declared, would be "like profaning a temple." She would "rather the weeds and wild animals which are fast taking possession of the grounds should grow and live in the house itself" than see Monticello "turned into a tavern." And so Monticello remained virtually unoccupied for the next two years.

On a snowy February day in 1830, Anne Newport Royall, a novelist and travel writer, visited Monticello, accompanied by a party of young men from Charlottesville. When no one answered their knock, Royall and her friends let themselves in. There, seated by the only fire in the house, they found "a great coarse Irish woman" who offered to show them around for fifty cents.

A bust of Jefferson still stood in the otherwise deserted entrance hall. The parlor was empty except for massive mirrors on either side of the door. Although Jefferson's bedroom was sealed off, the visitors glimpsed his bed through a window. On the third floor, Mrs. Royall's friends found a broken spinet among heaps of "coffee-urns, chinaware, glasses, globes, chairs and bedsteads." As the carriage began its descent, Mrs. Royall noticed a long, flat, bare patch of ground just southeast of the house. The plot "appeared to have been a garden," she observed, "but hardly a vestige of it remained."

In the summer of 1831, Jeff Randolph found a buyer for Monticello in James Barclay, a Charlottesville apothecary. The Randolphs agreed to sell the mansion and 522 adjacent acres for $7,000—about half of what they had hoped—plus a house Barclay owned in Charlottesville, worth $4,000. The Randolphs kept the cemetery.

The imminent sale, Cornelia Randolph told Ellen Coolidge on June 29, "is a blow to us particularly as we had been dreaming, almost hoping to return there to live." Martha called the loss of Monticello "a dreadful sacrifice, but the debts are letting the place go to ruin."

Barclay's purchase gave the Randolphs one additional, though minor, cause for concern. They feared that the new owner lacked refinement. "I am doubtful of Dr. Barclay's taste," Cornelia told Ellen, "& have some fear that he may disfigure that beautiful & sacred spot by some of that 'gingerbread work' which grandpapa used to hold in such contempt."

These fears soon gave way to more serious ones.

On the night of August 21, 1831, near the town of Jerusalem in Southampton County, Virginia, 140 miles southeast of Charlottesville, a slave named Nat

*"It will grieve you very much to hear of the depradations that have been made at Monticello." Jefferson's granddaughters Virginia Trist (left) to Ellen Coolidge (right), March 23, 1827.*

Turner and several cohorts broke into the home of Joseph Travis, Turner's owner, murdering Travis and his family in their sleep. Over the next thirty-six hours, Turner and some sixty to eighty followers—"a parcel of blood-thirsty wolves," in the words of the *Richmond Enquirer*—stabbed, shot, and beat to death nearly sixty whites, including twenty-four children. Over the next six weeks, as Turner eluded capture, terror gripped the Virginia countryside. In a wave of retribution, some two hundred blacks were murdered by white militia and mobs. Some of the slaughtered blacks' severed heads were displayed on poles as a warning to would-be insurrectionists.

In their panic, many planter families fled what the newspapers were calling "the black terror." On the road from Petersburg, Richmond's *Constitutional Whig* reported, "we found the whole country thoroughly alarmed; every man armed, the dwellings all deserted by the white inhabitants, and the farms most generally left in the possession of the blacks." Although far removed from the scene of the carnage, Albemarle whites recalled the terror of a decade earlier, when a slave named Gabriel led a similar revolt west of Richmond that targeted the arsenal in Fluvanna County, adjacent to Albemarle. Determined to prevent any such recurrence, white plantation owners organized their own slave patrols, which began to make nightly rounds throughout the county. Even the professors at the university were called upon for guard duty.

The events of the week before put everyone on edge, Cornelia Randolph told Ellen Coolidge on August 28. Cornelia, who considered slavery "unjust & tyrannical," had grown to loathe this "dreadful state of things where self defense makes men feel toward their fellow creatures as if they were bears & wolves & treat them accordingly."

The Randolphs themselves were not above treating slaves brutally. One example of this capacity for violence should suffice. In August 1833, as the fear aroused by Turner's rebellion still simmered, Martha Randolph and two of her daughters visited Richmond with one of their young house slaves, named Sally. When she stole a pair of stockings and Septimia's satin shoes, the family considered turning Sally over to the local police but decided that doing so "would give us a bad reputation."

Instead, they took matters into their own hands, which the family deemed amusing. "You will laugh to hear what disciplinarians we have turned out to be," Cornelia Randolph told Virginia Trist. Martha, Cornelia, and their host took Sally to the basement, where two of the women held her down, and Martha "inflicted the flagellation pretty severely." Although they found "nothing malignant or revengeful" about Sally, Martha thereafter hid the key to the medicine chest where poisons were kept.

To break free of a way of life that afforded one such power proved difficult, even for those who professed to disapprove of it. The Randolphs had become "accustomed to this state of things & attached to our own slaves," Cornelia admitted, "& as far as comfort and liking to old habits is concerned it suits me best."

Nevertheless, Turner's uprising led Jefferson's granddaughters to talk of leaving Virginia and throwing off the burden of slavery completely. In the process, they could also cast off the burden of slaves. Cornelia had "no more fervent prayer," she said, "than that we may be fairly rid of them." Mary Randolph told Ellen Coolidge that, although the family never entertained "an anxious thought about the present," the future looked bleak indeed "if some remedy is not applied in time." Whites in the Piedmont and Shenandoah Valley outnumbered blacks by three to one, and as long as this numerical superiority continued, Mary wrote, "the destruction of the conspirators at Southampton is more likely to operate for the present as a warning than as an incitement to rebellion." Even so, Mary hoped that her fellow Virginians would "keep their eyes open after the excitement of the present moment is over & until they have taken measures to remove the evil." Whether by "evil" Mary meant slavery, or merely slaves, she did not say.

Perhaps seeking absolution as well as safety, the women of the Monticello circle talked of moving to the utopian community of New Harmony, Indiana—they were unaware that this experiment in communal living had collapsed four years earlier—or to abolitionist Cincinnati. Cornelia feared, however, that Indiana and Ohio might prove too cold, and too distant from Monticello. "I do not think I should feel at home or happy anywhere but at Monticello," Cornelia told Ellen. "I want those familiar haunts, which alone seem to be home & which seem as if grandpapa was still there."

While the Randolphs could be wistful about Monticello, they also felt bitter. In July 1832, Meriwether Lewis Randolph, Cornelia's twenty-two-year-old brother, visited the property—now occupied by Dr. Barclay—and regretted having done so. "The prospect sickened me to the heart," Randolph wrote. "Every thing so changed. Corn growing to the verge of the Lawn." Except for "a *few* miserable looking, ghostlike trees, where the beautiful Scotch broom delighted the eye," only dead trees could be seen. "The savage burnt them," Randolph said. "At each turn you are insulted by a monument of the destroying hand of the Gothic barbarism."

If the Randolphs had not retained control of the cemetery, Barclay's plow would "have visited its walls & violated the sanctity of that soil which alone on this earth calls forth my admiration." Meriwether Lewis Randolph did not visit the house itself, he said, for that would have shown respect to its owner. He closed his account with an image that reflected more the sensibility of Edgar Allan Poe than that of Thomas Jefferson.

"I most sincerely pray," he wrote, "that before I leave the neighbourhood my eyes may be gladdened with the sight of the House wrapped in flames, and that every vestige of building be swept from the top of the Mountain."

Upon Tom Randolph's death, Jeff Randolph became the official as well as the de facto head of the sprawling Monticello-Edgehill family. At thirty-five, strong, pragmatic, and dutiful, Jeff Randolph had exercised responsibility for the family's finances for a decade. From the time he first became aware of his grandfather's debts, Randolph had been determined to pay them "to the last copper," as he would write in his memoirs, whether legally obligated to do so or not. He chose this course, he said, convinced that his own ambitions were less important than making sure "that a character like [Jefferson's] should not be tainted with having failed to comply with his obligations."

Throughout the 1830s, Randolph struggled to make payments, economizing when possible, selling land in Bedford and Campbell Counties, and restoring the farms in Albemarle to productivity. Instead of labor-intensive, soil-killing tobacco, Randolph planted clover, corn, and wheat; in time, he was able to produce three times more wheat per acre than his father and his grandfather had been able to do from the same fields.

Randolph also made money from less conventional enterprises. Employing his sisters as copyists, he edited the first collection of his grandfather's writings for commercial sale. Again employing his sisters (and, eventually, his mother), he opened a school for girls in one of the Edgehill dependencies—a school that would operate successfully for several decades.

And, steadily, he began to pay down his grandfather's debts. A precise record of his efforts in this direction is impossible to reconstruct, but in February 1833, he told Nicholas Trist that "no creditor has complained," and his success in pulling the family from the brink of bankruptcy continued throughout the next two decades. In November 1840, Randolph retired the debt to the heirs of his grandfather's friend Philip Mazzei, estimating that he had made payments on that one account alone of more than $13,000.

Randolph also kept the banks and other creditors satisfied without demanding great sacrifices from his family. Although they did not live as they had when Thomas Jefferson controlled the spending, they were nonetheless well provided for. "Meats, vegetables, milk and butter, and everything that a rich well managed farm can supply," Martha Randolph told Ellen Coolidge on June 20, 1834, "we have in abundance."

With Randolph's hard-won prosperity came a deepening respect from his Albemarle neighbors, respect based more upon his personal qualities than his distinguished lineage. Enjoying his newfound prestige, troubled by the slave uprising and his neighbors' reaction to it, Randolph, perhaps predictably, turned his attention to politics, which he had been reluctant to do in leaner times. In August 1831, he won a seat in the Virginia House of Delegates.

In January 1832, during his first term in that body, Randolph offered a plan for the gradual emancipation of Virginia's slaves very much like that favored by his father, when he was governor, and his grandfather. Under the plan that Jeff Randolph introduced, all children born to enslaved parents after July 4, 1840, would become the property of the state. When females reached the age of eighteen and males turned twenty-one, their services would be rented out by the state until enough money was raised to pay for their shipment out of the United States, presumably to Liberia. Then they would be free.

Basing his argument exclusively on expedience, which he found "better suited to the public mind," as he told his wife at the time, Randolph argued that Nat Turner's rebellion made adopting his plan or one like it imperative. Unless slavery was abolished, he told the other legislators, they faced an "appalling" future. Dissolution of the Union would be "inevitable in the fullness of time." Troops from the North would invade, and marching with them would be freed slaves "burning with enthusiasm for the liberation of their race." Was it not wise, "while the evil is still within our grasp, when we can gradually obliterate it," to do so now, and "prepare the way for better prospects [for] our children?"

Randolph's proposal ignited a vigorous debate in the Virginia legislature, with most lawmakers hotly opposing liberation in any form. During this debate, a new argument—unknown in Thomas Jefferson's day—was mounted.

Instead of agreeing that slavery was morally wrong but arguing, as Jefferson had, that conditions for abolition were not right, these legislators asserted that slavery was a positive good. Slavery, its proponents argued, was sanctioned by the Bible. Its virtues were demonstrated by the glories of slaveholding Greece and Rome, and its civic function attested to by the fact that plantation society produced Virginia's great leaders, including Jefferson himself.

This position found support among Virginia's best-educated and most articulate citizens. An influential book published in 1832, *Review of the Debates on the Abolition of Slavery in the Legislature of Virginia in the Winter of 1831 and 1832*, by Professor Thomas Roderick Dew of the College of William and Mary, stated a case for slavery on moral and cultural grounds that would find acceptance throughout the Tidewater region. Dew argued that slaves were the rightful property of an aristocratic class. An accomplished economist, he supported this argument by maintaining that slavery, far from being a liability, as Jefferson and most enlightened men of his generation held, was in fact an economic benefit.

Thoroughly repudiating Enlightenment ideas about inalienable rights, democratic liberties, and republican self-government, Dew rejected Jeffersonian idealism in favor of Hamiltonian realpolitik. "The great object of government," Dew concluded, "is the protection of property."

Invigorated by such notions, the Virginia legislature responded to Turner's rebellion and Randolph's proposal by cracking down harder to protect slaveholders and their interests. The existing slave code was made harsher, with additional restrictions on worship, speech, and travel of free as well as enslaved blacks. In time, the legislature would restrict the speech of free whites as well, prohibiting any discussion of slavery and its abolition.

When Jeff Randolph ran for reelection in April 1833, his opponents got their revenge, defeating him by sixty votes. He was "vilely traduced on the court-green as being guilty of every base act that man could be accused of," Jane Randolph told Sarah Nicholas. Although he would remain active in politics in coming years, his early antislavery efforts would always be held against him.

Even the trouble with Charles Bankhead was brought up by Randolph's political opponents, long after Bankhead himself had made his peace with the family and ceased to pose a threat to anybody but himself.

In June 1833, after years of poor health, Bankhead died at the age of forty-five. He had been "drunk for some days," according to Martha Randolph, and appeared at the home of his brother-in-law Benjamin Franklin Randolph, a

Richmond physician. There he suffered "an apoplectic fit," Dr. Randolph said, "after which he lived about two hours in a state of absolute insensibility from which it was impossible to rouse him."

The death of Martha Randolph three years later at Edgehill caused greater sadness. In October 1836, while preparing to visit the Coolidges in Boston, she suddenly fell ill with a severe headache accompanied by nausea. For much of her adult life, Martha had suffered from headaches similar to those that afflicted her father, and, since the illness "appeared to us to be one of her accustomed sick headaches," Ellen said, the family did nothing more "than apply the usual palliatives." But on Monday, October 8, 1836, the pain intensified, and the women of the household summoned Jeff Randolph to his mother's bedside. Martha managed to speak to him but "immediately after became sick," Ellen said, "heaved convulsively, fell forward into his arms and drew her last breath."

Martha Jefferson Randolph, dead at the age of sixty-four, was taken across the Rivanna and up the mountain to be buried at Monticello, "by her father's side," Ellen said. "In death she was not divided from him whom in life she had loved so dearly."

In the three decades following the death of Thomas Jefferson, Virginia entered a period of cultural decline. This decline, the result in large measure of the state's inability to free itself from the slave system, was noticeable in its early stages even while Jefferson lived. In August 1825, shortly after her arrival in Boston, Ellen Coolidge told her grandfather that seeing New England had given her "an idea of prosperity and improvement, such as I fear our Southern States cannot hope for, whilst the cancer of slavery eats into their hearts and diseases the whole body." Massachusetts, which lacked Virginia's abundant natural resources, is "at least a century [ahead of Virginia, and its inhabitants] are pressing forward in their course with a zeal and activity that I think must ensure success."

Six years later, in October 1833, after visiting New York's Hudson Valley, Ellen's brother Meriwether Lewis Randolph wrote of farms "in the highest state of cultivation," and of towns and cities "enjoying extensive commerce, & increasing in wealth & importance daily. In fact, an air of wealth, industry, prosperity & happiness [reigns] throughout the whole Country, entirely new to one from the sinking South."

By the late 1840s and early 1850s, Virginia's decline had become a matter of public comment, though little was done to arrest it. Before the Revolution, the *Richmond Enquirer* reported, Virginia "contained more wealth and a larger population than any other State of this Confederacy." By 1852, the Old Dominion, "from being first in wealth and political power, ranked below New York, Pennsylvania, Massachusetts and Ohio." These states, except for Massachusetts, were "literally chequered over with railroads and canals." (A somber "Address to the Farmers of Virginia" from the Virginia State Agricultural Society noted that the pride of Virginians ceased to be commendable "when it smothers up improvements in self-satisfaction.")

Intellectual life was almost nonexistent. Virginians published few newspapers and few books. Almost all literary works came from the North. The well-to-do refused to be taxed to pay for the education of their poorer neighbors, and the great majority of young people, white and black, received no formal schooling. A result was the almost complete absence of an educated middle class. There were only land-rich, cash-poor gentleman planters at the top, a somewhat larger group of lawyers, doctors, and merchants just below them, and then poor whites and free blacks at the bottom, followed by great numbers of slaves. Costly in itself, the presence of slaves discouraged the immigration of white laborers, denying Virginia much needed skills and enterprise.

With discussions of slavery prohibited, and the mails opened to confiscate abolitionist literature sent from the North, the entire society came to operate under censorship. Slavery, under increasing attack from the North, was passionately defended. The fear that slaves would be incited by northern abolitionists to rise up and kill the whites who owned them reached new levels of intensity. After October 1859, when John Brown raided the U.S. armory at Harpers Ferry to arm the slaves, even Virginians who had called themselves Unionists began reluctantly to call for secession.

Among these was Thomas Jefferson Randolph.


When Virginia seceded from the Union on April 25, 1861, Jeff Randolph was sixty-nine. He was far too old for military duty but served the Confederacy nonetheless, ordering and paying for an unnamed quantity of "Colt's six shooters of the navy size" which were sent to Edgehill for distribution to his Albemarle neighbors for their defense. Randolph sold war bonds. He also invested heavily in them. His youngest son, a second Meriwether Lewis Randolph, served as an aide to both General Thomas J. Stonewall Jackson and Robert E. Lee and, in his father's words, "escaped unscathed from twenty general actions" and a hundred skirmishes.

George Wythe Randolph, Jeff Randolph's brother, forty-three years old when the war came, also saw action. A former naval officer, George Wythe was one of three Virginia peace commissioners who went to Washington in April 1861 hoping to meet with President Lincoln and avert war. When this effort failed—the commissioners never got their meeting with Lincoln, and Fort Sumter was fired on before they left Washington—George Wythe gave up his law practice to fight for the Confederacy. He organized, financed, and led the Richmond Howitzers and personally oversaw the defense of Yorktown. In March 1862, he was named Confederate secretary of war. (Health problems and disagreements with President Jefferson Davis led to his resignation the following November.)

When the war ended, Jeff Randolph went to Washington, took the oath of loyalty to the United States, and returned to Virginia. Unlike much of the state, Albemarle had escaped the destruction that the war brought, and Randolph was able to devote himself once again to the farms at Edgehill.

In the fall of 1866 there appeared at Edgehill a visitor from Ohio. This was Israel Jefferson, who had been born a slave at Monticello on Christmas morning in 1797 and, as a small boy, lived in Washington and served as a postillion on the third president's coach. In Jefferson's retirement years, Israel had been a household slave at Monticello and, after Thomas Jefferson's death, performed other chores at Jeff Randolph's direction.

At the Monticello auction, Israel had been sold for $500 to Thomas Walker Gilmer, a friend of the Randolphs, but later managed to buy his own freedom for the same price that Gilmer had paid. It was when he registered as a free man at the Albemarle County Court House that he adopted the surname Jefferson because, he told a newspaperman many years later, "it would give me more dignity to be called after so eminent a man." After that, he moved to Cincinnati, where he worked as a waiter on a steamboat and then bought his own farm.

During Israel's return to Albemarle in 1866, he paid a call on Jeff Randolph, and the two men who had once been master and slave talked of former times. "He had grown old," Israel said of Randolph, "and was outwardly surrounded by the evidences of former ease and opulence gone to decay."

Randolph paid dearly for his decision to side with Virginia in the war, he told Israel. Selling and investing in war bonds, Randolph lost $80,000. Except for his house and his land, the war "stripped him of everything," Randolph said, "save one old, blind mule." He "lost all his servants and nearly all his personal property of every kind."

That this conversation between the former slave and his once "proud and haughty" master took place "within four miles of Monticello, where he was born and bred," Israel found significant. "Indeed," he said, "I then realized more than ever before, the great changes which time brings about in the affairs and circumstances of life."


In early 1871, after fifty-six years of marriage, Jeff Randolph's wife, the former Jane Nicholas, died at Edgehill and was buried at Monticello. Randolph was seventy-nine and suffering from time to time from an "alarming attack of palpitations of the heart," as his daughter Sarah Randolph described it. He nevertheless made one last foray into politics in the summer of 1872, serving as a Virginia delegate to the Democratic National Convention in Baltimore. A highlight of this otherwise uneventful gathering, according to the *Baltimore Sun*, occurred on July 9, "when the Hon. Jefferson Randolph came on the stage." Randolph's "towering figure, venerable appearance, and white locks made him an object of immediate interest, and he was soon surrounded."

The New York financier August Belmont made a long speech nominating Randolph to the largely honorary office of temporary chairman, leaving no doubt why. "I have the honor," Belmont intoned, "to propose to you as your temporary chairman a distinguished and venerable citizen of Virginia, a grandson of the patriot and statesman, Thomas Jefferson. It is an auspicious omen that a scion of the author of the Declaration of Independence is to inaugurate the struggle of the democracy for freedom and equality," with the rest of the oration quickly degenerating into the hoary clichés of campaign rhetoric.

The band struck up "Dixie," and the *Richmond Dispatch* reported that "the fine old gentleman" followed with a "brief and sensible," if otherwise forgettable, acceptance speech. In it, Randolph was characteristically modest, acknowledging the fact that he had been selected only because he was Thomas

*His "towering figure, venerable appearance, and white locks made him*
*an object of immediate interest." Thomas Jefferson Randolph.*

Jefferson's grandson. "I am aware," Randolph said, "that the very great honor conferred on me by this body is due to no personal merit of my own, but is a token of respect to the state from which I come, and a recognition of other circumstances."

He did not need to say what those "other circumstances" were.

Three years later, in September 1875, Jeff Randolph went to Hot Springs, Virginia, accompanied by his son Wilson Cary Nicholas Randolph, a physician. On the road back to Edgehill, their carriage broke down, slamming the old man against the side of the coach. For the rest of the way, according to the *Charlottesville Chronicle*, "he lay in his son's arms, suffering great pain and in a fainting condition." Once home, he asked to be positioned near a window that would allow him to look, for the last time, at Monticello.

On October 7, 1875, Thomas Jefferson Randolph died at eighty-three, the same age his grandfather had been when he died.

He, too, was buried in the Monticello graveyard.

# ACKNOWLEDGMENTS

With heartfelt gratitude to my editor, the superb Robert Loomis of Random House, and to Dana Isaacson, Cheryl Weinstein, and Porscha Burke, also of Random House; to Glen Hartley, my agent; to Christa Dierksheide, my archivist and researcher, without whom this book would not have been possible; and to Robin Cheslock, my copy editor.

Thanks as well to professors Peter Onuf, Phil Schwarz, and James Hall; to Daniel P. Jordan, president of the Thomas Jefferson Foundation, and his colleagues Jack Robertson and Wayne Mogielnicki; to Andrew Jackson O'Shaughnessy, Saunders Director of the International Center for Jefferson Studies, and his colleague Lucia Stanton; to Rebecca Dobyns of the Library of Virginia, Jeffrey Ruggles of the Virginia Historical Society, Octavia Starbuck of Thomas Jefferson's Poplar Forest; Skip Stockdon and David Kilmon of the Richmond Public Library; Edward Gaynor of Alderman Library at the University of Virginia; and to Stanley Craddock, Ron Gilmore, Bryan Clark Green, Bill Kauffman, S. J. Masty, Jon Newman of the Hodges Partnership, Kent Owen, Nancy Schoonmaker, Joe Slay, and Rick Britton.

Special thanks (forever) to my wife, Sally Curran, and to my sons, Ned and Tim.

NOTES

SOURCES

| | |
|---|---|
| *Adams-Jefferson Letters* | Lester J. Cappon, ed., *The Adams-Jefferson Letters* (Chapel Hill: University of North Carolina Press, 1988) |
| *Autobiography* | Thomas Jefferson, *The Autobiography of Thomas Jefferson* (New York: G. P. Putnam's Sons, 1980) |
| Brodie | Fawn M. Brodie, *Thomas Jefferson: An Intimate History* (New York: W. W. Norton, 1974) |
| *Domestic Life* | Sarah N. Randolph, *The Domestic Life of Thomas Jefferson* (Charlottesville: University of Virginia Press, 1978) |
| *Family Letters* | Edwin Morris Betts and James Adam Bear, Jr., ed., *The Family Letters of Thomas Jefferson* (Charlottesville: University of Virginia Press, 1986) |
| *Farm Book* | Edwin Morris Betts, ed., *Thomas Jefferson's Farm Book* (Charlottesville: University of Virginia Press, Thomas Jefferson Memorial Foundation, 1987) |
| *Jefferson at Monticello* | James A. Bear, Jr., ed., *Jefferson at Monticello* (Charlottesville: University of Virginia Press, 1967) |
| *Jefferson Himself* | Bernard Mayo, ed., *Jefferson Himself* (Charlottesville: University of Virginia Press, 1942) |
| *Jefferson Profile* | Saul K. Padover, ed., *A Jefferson Profile as Revealed in His Letters* (New York: John Day, 1956) |
| L. & B. | A. A. Lipscomb and A. F. Bergh eds., *The Writings of Thomas Jefferson*, 20 vols. (New York, 1930) |
| *Life of Thomas Jefferson* | Henry S. Randall, *The Life of Thomas Jefferson*, 3 vols. (New York: Derby & Jackson, 1858) |
| *Memoirs* | "Memoirs of Thomas Jefferson Randolph," ca. 1874, unpublished manuscript, Alderman Library, Special Collections, University of Virginia |
| *Memorandum Books* | *Jefferson's Memorandum Books*, 1767–1826, James A. Bear, Jr., and Lucia C. Stanton, eds., 2 vols., (Princeton, N.J.: Princeton University Press, 1997) |

| | |
|---|---|
| *Notes on the State of Virginia* | Thomas Jefferson, *Notes on the State of Virginia,* William Peden, ed. (New York, London: W. W. Norton & Co., 1982) |
| *Republic of Letters* | James Morton Smith, ed., *The Republic of Letters: The Correspondence Between Thomas Jefferson and James Madison,* 3 vols. (New York: W. W. Norton, 1995) |
| *Sage of Monticello* | Dumas Malone, *The Sage of Monticello,* vol. 6 of *Jefferson and His Time,* 6 vols. (Boston: Little, Brown and Company, 1981) |
| *Sworn on the Altar of God* | Edwin S. Gaustad, *Sworn on the Altar of God: A Religious Biography of Thomas Jefferson* (Grand Rapids, Mich.: William B. Eerdmans, 1996) |
| *Visitors to Monticello* | Merrill D. Peterson, ed., *Visitors to Monticello* (Charlottesville: University of Virginia Press, 1989) |

## Manuscript Collections

Albemarle County Court Records, Commonwealth Causes, Library of Virginia, Richmond

Joseph C. Cabell Papers, University of Virginia, Charlottesville

David Campbell Papers, Duke University Library, Durham, North Carolina

Carr-Cary Papers, University of Virginia, Charlottesville

Ellen W. Coolidge Papers, Alderman Library, University of Virginia, Charlottesville

Coolidge Collection, Massachusetts Historical Society, Boston

Edgehill-Randolph Papers, Alderman Library, University of Virginia, Charlottesville

Francis W. Gilmer Papers, Alderman Library, University of Virginia, Charlottesville

Gilmer Papers, Virginia Historical Society, Richmond

Grigsby Papers, Virginia Historical Society, Richmond

Hubard Family Papers, Southern Historical Collection, University of North Carolina at Chapel Hill

Thomas Jefferson Papers, Henry E. Huntington Library, San Marino, California

Thomas Jefferson Papers, Library of Congress, Washington, D.C.

Thomas Jefferson Papers, Alderman Library, University of Virginia, Charlottesville

Jefferson Additional Papers, Alderman Library, University of Virginia, Charlottesville

Randolph-Meikelham Papers, Alderman Library, University of Virginia, Charlottesville

James Monroe Papers, Library of Congress, Washington, D.C.

Randolph Papers, Duke University Library, Durham, North Carolina

Rare Virginia Pamphlets, Alderman Library, University of Virginia, Charlottesville

Nicholas P. Trist Papers, Southern Historical Collection, University of North Carolina at Chapel Hill

Elizabeth House Trist Papers, Virginia Historical Society, Richmond

Nicholas P. Trist Papers, Library of Congress, Washington, D.C.

## Epigraph

ix **"Nature intended illusions"** Sébastien-Roch-Nicolas Chamfort, *Products of the Perfected Civilization* (San Francisco: North Point Press, 1984), 123.

## Prologue *"I Shall Be for Ever at Ease"*

xv **"system of boils"** Thomas Jefferson to Martha Randolph, August 21, 1818, *Family Letters*, 426.

xvi **"even a young hare"** Peter J. Hatch, *The Gardens at Monticello* (Charlottesville: The Thomas Jefferson Memorial Foundation, 1992), 47.

xvii **"garden pharmacy"** John M. Holmes, *Thomas Jefferson Treats Himself: Herbs, Physic and Nutrition in Early America* (Fort Valley, Va.: Loft Press, 1997), 54.

xvii **"disorders of the head"** Ibid.

xvii **"expels wind"** Ibid.

xvii **"did not deliver"** Thomas Jefferson to Joel Yancey, January 17, 1819, *Farm Book*, 43.

xviii **"the barrel of apples"** Ibid.

xviii **"I consider the labor of a breeding woman"** Ibid.

xviii **"as in all other cases"** Ibid.

xx **"shivering and shrinking"** Thomas Jefferson to Charles Thomson, January 9, 1816, *Jefferson Profile*, 252.

xx **"How the right hand"** Thomas Jefferson to William Stephens Smith, *The Writings of Thomas Jefferson*, P. L. Ford., ed., 10 vols. (New York: G. P. Putnam's Sons, 1892–99), 4:325.

xx **"the only truths"** Thomas Jefferson to Nathaniel Macon, January 12, 1819, L. & B., 15:179.

xx **"with great pleasure"** Thomas Jefferson to John Adams, March 21, 1819, *Adams-Jefferson Letters*, 536.

xx **"slumber without fear"** Thomas Jefferson to Nathaniel Macon, January 12, 1819, L. & B., 15:179.

xxiii **"bread and butter"** Thomas Jefferson to Charles Pinckney, September 30, 1820, L. & B., 15:281.

xxiii **"manufacturing and navigating"** Ibid.

xxiii **"return to the embraces"** Ibid.

xxiii **seas looked stormy** Thomas Jefferson to John Adams, December 10, 1819, L. & B., 15:233.

xxiii **"live as long"** Thomas Jefferson to Elizabeth Trist, December 26, 1814, *Domestic Life*, 360.

xxiv **"I shall be for ever at ease"** Thomas Jefferson to Patrick Gibson, February 22, 1819, *Farm Book*, 335.

xxv **"all the neighbouring heights"** *Visitors to Monticello*, 22.

xxv **"are all atiptoe here"** Thomas Jefferson to John Adams, January 19, 1819, *Adams-Jefferson Letters*, 532.

xxvii **"the greatest of the God-sends"** Thomas Jefferson to Thomas Jefferson Randolph, February 8, 1826, *Jefferson Profile*, 342.

xxviii **"in a tone"** *Life of Thomas Jefferson*, 1:69.

xxviii **"with a clatter of hoofs"** Ibid.

## PART ONE  MORNING AND MIDDAY

### CHAPTER 1  *A Society of Would-be Country Squires*

4 **"dreary region"** Thomas Anburey, *Travels Through the Interior Parts of America*, 2 vols. (Boston: Houghton Mifflin, 1923) 2:195.

4 **"no proprietors"** Ibid., 190.

4 **"the wolves"** "Confessions of a Monticello Slave" in *Jefferson at Monticello*, 21.

4 **"doing their own work"** John Hammond Moore, *Albemarle: Jefferson's County, 1727–1976*, (Charlottesville: University of Virginia Press, 1976), 18.

5 **"very singular, striking"** Anburey, *Travels Through the Interior Parts of America*, 325.

5 **"horrible crash"** Ibid.

5 **"should seem"** Ibid.

5 **"making Virginia fences"** Ibid., 324.

5 **"red cast"** Ibid., 406.

6 **"whole counties"** *Notes on the State of Virginia*, 77.

6 **"are very frequent"** Anburey, *Travels Through the Interior Parts of America*, 412.

6 **"abandoned to gullies"** *Memoirs*, 50.

6 **"nine tenths"** Ibid.

6 **"sold it at low rates"** Ibid.

7 **"it not being"** Ibid., 13.

7 **"gouging, plucking"** David Hackett Fischer, *Albion's Seed: Four British Folkways in America* (New York: Oxford University Press, 1989), 737.

7 **"the better sort"** Ibid., 360.

### CHAPTER 2  *An Upcountry Prince*

8 **"handed up to a servant"** *Domestic Life*, 39.

8 **"weighing nearly"** *Life of Thomas Jefferson*, 1:13.

8 **"raise up"** Quoted in Henry Wiencek, *An Imperfect God* (New York: Farrar, Straus & Giroux, 2003), 31.

9 **"trace their pedigree"** *Autobiography*, 19.

9 **"having [Laurence] Sterne's word"** Thomas Jefferson to Thomas Adams, February 20, 1771, Ford, *Writings of Thomas Jefferson*, 1:388–89.

10 **"was burnt to the ground"** *Virginia Gazette*, February 22, 1770.

10 **"every paper"** Thomas Jefferson to John Page, *Life of Thomas Jefferson,* 1:59.

10 **"For his temerity"** John Chester Miller, *The Wolf by the Ears* (Charlottesville: University of Virginia Press, 1977), 4–5.

11 **"whom they admired"** Kenneth S. Lynn, *A Divided People* (Westport, Conn.: Greenwood Press, 1971), 70–71.

12 **"It is curious"** *Domestic Life,* 39.

12 **"rather deficient"** Ibid.

12 **"should be well dressed"** Brodie, 71.

13 **"Tom, I'll tell you how"** The Rev. Edgar Woods, *Albemarle County in Virginia* (Bridgewater, Va.: The Green Bookman, 1932), 237–38.

## Chapter 3 *The Education of a Philosopher*

14 **"as faultlessly"** *Life of Thomas Jefferson,* 1:69.

14 **"Devilsburg"** Thomas Jefferson to John Page, January 19, 1764, Ford, *Writings of Thomas Jefferson,* 1:13.

14 **"thrown into the society"** Thomas Jefferson to Thomas Jefferson Randolph, November 24, 1808, L. & B., 12:197–98.

15 **"enlarged and liberal"** *Autobiography,* 20.

15 **"his daily companion"** Ibid.

15 **"my first views"** Ibid.

15 **"the best Latin and Greek"** Thomas Jefferson to John Saunders, August 31, 1820, L. & B., 1:165.

15 **"to liberty and the natural"** Ibid.

15 **"compleat gentleman"** Dumas Malone, *Jefferson the Virginian* (Boston: Little, Brown, 1948), 77.

15 **"heard more good sense"** Thomas Jefferson to L. H. Girardin, January 15, 1815, L. & B., 14:231–32.

16 **"metaphysics"** See Daniel Boorstin, "The Perils of Metaphysics," *The Lost World of Thomas Jefferson* (Chicago and London: The University of Chicago Press, 1993), 128–39.

16 **"in my pocket"** Thomas Jefferson to John Page, December 25, 1762, L.& B., 4:1–5.

16 **"cursed rats"** Ibid.

16 **"jimmy-worked"** Ibid.

16 **"rats will be rats"** Ibid.

16 **"my opinion"** Ibid.

16 **"was the last stroke"** Ibid.

### Chapter 4 *The Young Revolutionary*

17 **"torrents"** Robert Douthat Meade, *Patrick Henry* (Philadelphia and New York: J. P. Lippincott, 1957), 1:174.

17 **"young hot"** Malone, *Jefferson the Virginian*, 94.

17 **"very indecent language"** *Journal of the House of Burgesses of Virginia, 1761–1765*, June 5, 1765.

17 **"splendid display"** *Autobiography*, 22.

### Chapter 5 *The Crucible of Revolution*

20 **"reputation for literature"** *Works of John Adams*, C. F. Adams, October 25, 1775, (Boston: 1956), 2:422.

20 **"sentiments of the day"** Thomas Jefferson to Henry Lee, May 8, 1825, L. & B., 16:118.

21 **"vehement philippic"** John Adams to Thomas Pickering, August 6, 1822, Adams, *Works of John Adams*, 2:512.

21 **"shall be compelled"** *Sworn on the Altar of God*, 67.

### Chapter 6 *"Whence He Might Contemplate the Whole Universe"*

24 **"grave and even cold"** *Visitors to Monticello*, 12.

24 **"no sooner spent"** Ibid.

24 **"it seems indeed"** Ibid., 13.

24 **"as good a husband"** Ibid., 17.

24 **"could not die happy"** *Jefferson at Monticello*, 100.

24 **"stupor of mind"** Thomas Jefferson to Chevalier François Jean de Chastellux, November 26, 1782, L. & B., 4:199.

### Chapter 7 *"The Hated Occupations of Politics"*

26 **"with real regret"** *Jefferson Himself*, 153.

26 **"young man of genius"** Ibid.

27 **"even your love to me"** Thomas Jefferson to Martha Randolph, April 4, 1790, *Family Letters*, 51.

27 **"as secondary"** Martha Randolph to Thomas Jefferson, April 25, 1790, *Family Letters*, 53.

27 **"wonder and mortification"** Thomas Jefferson to William Short, January 8, 1825, L. & B., 16:94.

27 **"preference"** Ibid.

27 **"those of European courts"** Ibid.

28 **"indecency"** Thomas Jefferson to Edmund Randolph, September 17, 1792, L. & B., 8:411.

28 **"be liberated"** Thomas Jefferson to Angelica Church, November 27, 1793, John Catanzariti, ed., *Papers of Thomas Jefferson* (Princeton, N.J.: Princeton University Press, 1997), 27:449.

28 **"a degree of degradation"** *Domestic Life,* 229.

28 **"little will be done"** Ibid.

28 **"very pretty"** Mary Jefferson to Thomas Jefferson, February 13, 1791, *Family Letters,* 72.

28 **"beautiful deep blue eyes"** Ibid.

28 **"your little namesake"** Martha Randolph to Thomas Jefferson, November 18, 1792, *Family Letters,* 106.

29 **"little inferior to his sister"** Martha Randolph to Thomas Jefferson, January 16, 1793, *Family Letters,* 109.

29 **"in a retirement I doat"** Thomas Jefferson to Edward Rutledge, November 30, 1795, L. & B., 9:313.

29 **"Monticello, according to its first plan"** *Visitors to Monticello,* 22.

29 **"had studied taste"** Ibid.

29 **"with the most pleasant mansions"** Ibid.

29 **"theory for [his] guide"** Ibid., 23.

29 **"accuse each other"** Ibid., 31.

29 **"will be only the president of a party"** Ibid.

29 **"the keenest pangs"** Ibid.

30 **"Men who have been intimate"** Thomas Jefferson to Edward Rutledge, June 24, 1797, L. & B., 9:411.

30 **"false, scandalous and malicious"** Melvin I. Urofsky, *A March of Liberty: A Constitutional History of the United States* (New York: Alfred A. Knopf, 1988), 172.

31 **"bastard"** Page Smith, *John Adams,* 2 vols. (Garden City, N.Y.: Doubleday & Co., 1962), 2:1028.

31 **"squibs, scoffs"** Ibid., 1002.

31 **"murder, robbery"** *Connecticut Courant,* September 15, 1800, quoted in Paul F. Boller, Jr., *Presidential Campaigns* (New York: Oxford University Press, 2004), 12.

31 **"cast into a bonfire"** Timothy Dwight, *The Duty of Americans at the Present Crisis* (New Haven, Conn: Thomas and Samuel Green, 1798), 20–21.

31 **"mockeries against God"** Ibid.

31 **"victims of legal prostitution"** Ibid.

31 **"passive and silent"** Thomas Jefferson, *The Anas,* L. & B., 1:451.

31 **"Here ends the 18th Century"** Charles Warren, *Jacobin and Junto* (Cambridge, Mass.: Harvard University Press, 1931), 158–59.

CHAPTER 8 *The Revolutionary Takes Command*

33 **"in plain cloth"** *Domestic Life,* 275–76.

33 **"wise and frugal government"** Jefferson, Inaugural Address, March 4, 1801, L. & B., 3:321.

33 **"and most returned"** Forrest McDonald, *The Presidency of Thomas Jefferson* (Lawrence: University Press of Kansas, 1976), 39.

34 **"peace, commerce"** Jefferson, Inaugural Address, March 4, 1801, L. & B., 3:321.

34 **"beyond the Constitution"** Thomas Jefferson to John Breckinridge, August 12, 1803, L. & B., 10:408–409.

34 **"fugitive occurrence"** Ibid.

34 **"metaphysical subtleties"** Ibid.

35 **"literary pursuit"** Gilbert Chinard, *Thomas Jefferson* (Ann Arbor: University of Michigan Press, 1957), 421.

35 **"information on the Indian tribes"** Ibid.

35 **"immense swarm"** Ibid.

35 **"in the full tide"** Hugh Garland, *The Life of John Randolph of Roanoke,* 2 vols. (New York: D. Appleton & Co., 1859), 1:198.

35 **"concubine"** *Richmond Recorder,* Library of Virginia, September 1, 1802.

35 **"Sally"** Ibid.

36 **"Dusky Sally"** Ellen W. Coolidge to Joseph Coolidge, October 24, 1858, Ellen W. Coolidge Papers, University of Virginia.

36 **"Black Sal"** Ibid.

36 **"decent"** Thomas Jefferson to Robert Livingstone, October 19, 1802, L. & B., 10:336.

36 **"to withdraw from society"** Thomas Jefferson to Mary Jefferson Eppes, March 3, 1802, *Family Letters,* 219.

36 **"requires that we"** Ibid.

36 **"a jog of the elbow"** Thomas Jefferson to Mary Jefferson Eppes, December 26, 1804, *Family Letters,* 295.

36 **"barely able to stand"** Thomas Jefferson to James Madison, April 9, 1804, *Republic of Letters,* 2:1304.

36 **"so disordered as to reject"** Ibid.

37 **"My evening prospects"** Thomas Jefferson to John Page, June 25, 1804, L. & B., 11:30–31.

38 **"the Barbarians of Tripoli"** Chinard, *Thomas Jefferson,* 443.

38 **"entangling alliances"** Jefferson, Inaugural Address, March 4, 1801, L. & B., 3:321.

39 **"silly bird"** Thomas Mann Randolph, Jr., to Thomas Jefferson, October 29, 1802, Jefferson Papers, Massachusetts Historical Society.

39 **"extraneous"** Thomas Jefferson to Thomas Mann Randolph, Jr., November 2, 1802, Jefferson Papers, Library of Congress.

39 **"lying two nights"** John W. Eppes to Thomas Jefferson, April 14, 1803, Edgehill-Randolph Papers, University of Virginia.

39 **"that lead and even steel"** *Annals of the Congress,* 9th Congress, 1st Session, December 2, 1805–April 21, 1806, 1104–1106.

39 **"cut each other's throats"** John Taylor to Wilson Cary Nicholas, June 26, 1806, Jefferson Papers, Library of Congress.

39 **"wife, and a family of children"** Thomas Jefferson to Thomas Mann Randolph, Jr., June 23, 1806, Edgehill-Randolph Papers, University of Virginia.

39 **"suppress all passion"** Ibid.

39 **"felt a preference"** Thomas Jefferson to Thomas Mann Randolph, Jr., February 19, 1807, Edgehill-Randolph Papers, University of Virginia.

40 **"that battery"** Thomas Jefferson to John Dickinson, December 19, 1801, L. & B., 10:301–302.

40 **"what laws are constitutional"** Thomas Jefferson to Abigail Adams, September 11, 1804, *Adams-Jefferson Letters,* 279.

40 **"would make the judiciary"** Ibid.

40 **"beyond all question"** Leonard W. Levy, *Jefferson and Civil Liberties: The Darker Side* (Chicago: Ivan R. Dee, 1963), 71.

CHAPTER 9 *"In a State of Almost Total Incapacity"*

41 **"since the battle of Lexington"** Thomas Jefferson to Pierre-Samuel du Pont de Nemours, July 14, 1807, L. & B., 9:274.

42 **"peaceable coercion"** Henry Adams, *History of the United States During the Administrations of Jefferson and Madison,* 2 vols. (Englewood Cliffs, N.J.: Prentice-Hall, 1963), 1:159.

42 **"experiment"** Thomas Jefferson to Albert Gallatin, May 20, 1808, Jefferson Papers, Library of Congress.

43 **"You give a bad account"** Thomas Jefferson to Ellen W. Randolph, February 23, 1808, *Family Letters,* 329.

43 **"never lived so comfortably"** Ibid.

43 **"remove the Embargo"** William A. Burwell to Thomas Jefferson, May 21, 1808, Jefferson Papers, Library of Congress.

44 **"blown off course"** Burton Spivak, *Jefferson's English Crisis* (Charlottesville: University of Virginia Press, 1979), 201.

44 **"suspicious"** Levy, *Jefferson and Civil Liberties,* 105.

44 **"Shall a man be refused"** Louis Martin Sears, *Jefferson and the Embargo* (New York: Octagon Books, 1966), 249.

44 **"How much longer"** Ibid., 103.

44 **"periodical head-aches"** John D. Battle, Jr., Ph.D., "The Periodical Headaches of Thomas Jefferson," *Cleveland Clinic Quarterly,* vol. 51, no. 3, Fall 1984, 531.

44 **"incapacitated"** Ibid., 532.

45 **"insensibility"** *Domestic Life,* 63.

45 **"only lying down occasionally"** Ibid.

45 **"stupor of mind"** Thomas Jefferson to Chevalier François Jean Chastellux, November 26, 1782, L. & B., 4:199.

45 **"as dead to the world"** Ibid.

45 **"very ill health"** Thomas Jefferson to James Madison, January 1, 1784, *Republic of Letters,* 1:290.

45 **"reading, writing"** Thomas Jefferson to William Short, March 1, 1784, *Cleveland Clinic.*

45 **"an attack"** Ibid.

45 **"the *almost constant headach[es]*"** Thomas Jefferson to Martha Randolph, June 23, 1791, *Family Letters,* 85.

45 **"the *drudgery of business*"** Ibid.

46 **"but a little moment"** Thomas Jefferson to Albert Gallatin, March 20, 1807, L. & B., 11:165.

46 **"shut up in a dark room"** Ibid., 166.

46 **"severe"** Ibid.

46 **"almost total incapacity"** Sears, *Jefferson and the Embargo,* 71.

46 **"entirely recovered"** Thomas Jefferson to Ellen W. Coolidge, April 12, 1808, Jefferson Papers, Massachusetts Historical Society.

46 **"too powerful"** Levy, *Jefferson and Civil Liberties,* 107.

46 **"by all means"** Ibid.

47 **"voting for detention"** Thomas Jefferson to Albert Gallatin, May 6, 1808, *Writings of Albert Gallatin,* Henry Adams, ed. (New York: Antiquarian Books, 1960), 1:386.

47 **"must legalize all *means*"** Thomas Jefferson to Albert Gallatin, August 11, 1808, L. & B., 12:122.

47 **"the most guilty"** Thomas Jefferson to Albert Gallatin, September 9, 1808, L. & B., 12:160.

47 **"Should we have"** Thomas Jefferson to James Brown, October 27, 1808, L. & B., 12:183.

48 **"a flea"** Forrest McDonald, *The American Presidency* (Lawrence: University Press of Kansas, 1994), 271.

48 **"begun as a means"** Levy, *Jefferson and Civil Liberties,* 105.

48 **"Go wretch"** Dumas Malone, *Jefferson the President: Second Term, 1805–1809* (Boston: Little, Brown, 1974), 5:606.

48 **"I find"** Thomas Jefferson to Ann Cary Randolph, June 7, 1807, *Family Letters,* 307–8.

49 **"perfectly lovely woman"** *Jefferson at Monticello,* 94.

49 **"active and useful"** *Domestic Life,* 341.

50 **"fine-looking man"** *Jefferson at Monticello,* 94.

50 **"I do not think"** Thomas Jefferson to Ann Cary Bankhead, November 8, 1808, *Family Letters,* 357.

50 **"a convenient acquisition"** Thomas Jefferson to Thomas Mann Randolph, Jr., November 22, 1808, Jefferson Papers, Library of Congress.

50 **"apt to live"** Thomas Jefferson to Thomas Jefferson Randolph, January 3, 1808, Jefferson Papers, Massachusetts Historical Society.

50 **"for his mathematics"** Thomas Jefferson to Dr. Caspar Wistar, October 12, 1808, Jefferson Papers, Library of Congress.

50 **"making acquaintances"** Ibid.

50 **"useful to him"** Ibid.

50 **"impatient of reproof"** Martha Randolph to Thomas Jefferson, July 15, 1808, *Family Letters,* 348.

51 **"enough of the Randolph character"** Martha Randolph to Thomas Jefferson, November 18, 1808, *Family Letters,* 359

51 **"I thought Congress"** Sears, *Jefferson and the Embargo,* 140.


# PART TWO LATE AFTERNOON AND SUNSET

### CHAPTER 10 *"A Prisoner Released from His Chains"*

55 **"in the benedictions"** *Republic of Letters,* 3:1561.

55 **"seemed in high spirits"** Ibid., 1562.

55 **"with a benevolent joy"** Ibid.

55 **"plain, unassuming citizen"** Ibid.

55 **"was excessive"** Ibid., 1563.

56 **"Am I too early?"** Margaret Bayard Smith, *The First Forty Years of Washington Society* (New York: Scribner's, 1906), 412.

56 **"You look so happy"** Ibid.

56 **"There's a good reason"** Ibid.

56 **"I am tired"** Thomas Jefferson to Martha Randolph, November 23, 1807, *Family Letters,* 315–16.

57 **"my family"** Thomas Jefferson to Pierre-Samuel du Pont de Nemours, March 2, 1809, *Jefferson Profile,* 179.

57 **"Having gained"** Ibid., 180.

57 **"examined my wardrobe"** *Memoirs,* 38.

57 **"pretty much loaded"** *Jefferson at Monticello,* 106.

58 **"costly wines"** Smith, *First Forty Years of Washington Society,* 391.

59 **"need not conclude"** *Sage of Monticello,* 34.

59 **"within the income"** Thomas Jefferson to Martha Randolph, February 27, 1809, *Family Letters,* 386.

59 **"Our lands"** Thomas Jefferson to Thomas Mann Randolph, Jr., January 5, 1808, *Family Letters,* 319.

59 **"to leave [it]"** Thomas Jefferson to Martha Randolph, February 6, 1808, *Family Letters,* 327.

59 **"My intervening nights"** Thomas Jefferson to unnamed "commission merchant," *Domestic Life,* 400.

60 **"beam of light"** Thomas Jefferson to Thaddeus Kościuszko, February 26, 1810, *Sage of Monticello,* 41.

60 **"of having added"** Thomas Jefferson to Monsieur le Comte Diodati, March 29, 1807, L. & B., 11:182.

60 **"I have now the gloomy prospect"** Thomas Jefferson to Martha Randolph, January 5, 1808, *Family Letters,* 319.

60 **"The impossibility of paying"** Martha Randolph to Thomas Jefferson, January 16, 1808, *Family Letters,* 322.

60 **"with never less"** Martha Randolph to Thomas Jefferson, February 17, 1809, *Family Letters,* 381–82.

61 **"My heart beats"** Ibid.

61 **"I look with infinite joy"** Thomas Jefferson to Thomas Mann Randolph, Jr., February 27, 1809, *Family Letters,* 385.

61 **"through as disagreeable"** Thomas Jefferson to James Madison, March 17, 1809, *Republic of Letters,* 3:1576.

61 **"as full"** *Jefferson at Monticello,* 107.

62 **"no inconvenience"** Thomas Jefferson to James Madison, March 17, 1809, *Republic of Letters,* 3:1576.

62 **"more confidence in my *vis vitae*"** Ibid.


CHAPTER 11 *"Elevated Above the Mass of Mankind"*

64 **"no seeds in the garden came up"** Thomas Jefferson to Thomas Jefferson Randolph, June 20, 1809, *Family Letters,* 393.

64 **"could not have been"** *Sage of Monticello,* 9.

65 **"produced from necessity"** Isham Lewis to Thomas Jefferson, April 27, 1809, Jefferson Papers, Massachusetts Historical Society.

65 **"promises of wealth"** Ibid.

65 **"in any useful pursuit"** Ibid.

65 **"in which I can propose to you"** Thomas Jefferson to Isham Lewis, May 1, 1809, *Jefferson Profile,* 186.

65 **"excellent dispositions"** Thomas Jefferson to Gideon Fitch, May 23, 1809, Jefferson Papers, Massachusetts Historical Society.

65 **"possessing qualities"** Thomas Jefferson to Seth Pease, May 23, 1809, Jefferson Papers.

65 **"without a friend or guardian"** Thomas Jefferson to Thomas Jefferson Randolph, November 24, 1808, *Family Letters,* 362–65.

66 **"incessantly studious"** Charles Willson Peale to Thomas Jefferson, January 17, 1809, Jefferson Papers, Library of Congress.

66 **"much contempt"** Charles Willson Peale to Thomas Jefferson, February 4, 1809, Edgehill-Randolph Papers, University of Virginia.

66 **"with some warmth"** Ibid.

66 **"filial affection"** Ibid.

67 **"with prudence and respectability"** Charles Willson Peale to Thomas Jefferson, November 12, 1808, Jefferson Papers, Library of Congress.

67 **"the bright fancy"** Thomas Jefferson to Benjamin Rush, January 3, 1808, *Jefferson Profile,* 167.

67 **"neglected education"** *Memoirs,* 41.

67 **"quite a sick family"** *Visitors to Monticello,* 46.

67 **"until they are almost worn out"** Ibid.

67 **"cast a gloom over our visit"** Ibid.

67 **"benignant smiles"** Ibid.

67 **"kind and cheerful manners"** Ibid.

68 **"sweet ladies' wine"** Ibid., 47.

68 **"excessive inflammation and pain"** Ibid., 51.

68 **"spots from which"** Ibid.

68 **"thick fog"** Ibid., 48.

68 **"you could scarcely believe"** Ibid.

68 **"the top of this mountain"** Ibid., 52.

68 **"little temples"** Ibid., 51.

68 **"after forty years"** Ibid., 52.

68 **"could hear its roaring"** Ibid.

68 **"philosophy and virtue"** Ibid., 54.

68 **"require a whole life"** Ibid., 52.

68 **"young man might doubt"** Ibid., 52.

68 **"But he seems"** Ibid.

68 **"It is in them he lives"** Ibid.

69 **"fear took from me"** Ibid., 50.

69 **"My dear madam"** Ibid., 50–51.

69 **"Grecian romance"** Ibid., 51.

69 **"gave the word"** Ibid., 53.

69 **"came panting"** Ibid.

69 **"What an amusement"** Ibid.

69 **"it is only with them"** Ibid.

CHAPTER 12 *"When I Expect to Settle My Grandchildren"*

71 **"the best dwelling"** S. Allen Chambers, Jr., *Poplar Forest and Thomas Jefferson* (Forest, Va.: Corporation for Thomas Jefferson's Poplar Forest, 1993), 74.

71 **"completely irrational plan"** Ibid., 30.

72 **"where I expect to settle"** Thomas Jefferson to Gideon Granger, September 20, 1810, Jefferson Papers, Library of Congress.

72 **"think of settling"** Thomas Jefferson to Martha Randolph, November 24, 1808, *Family Letters*, 366.

72 **"Those who labor"** *Notes on the State of Virginia*, 165.

72 **"Corruption of morals"** Ibid.

73 **"remain virtuous"** Thomas Jefferson to James Madison, December 20, 1787, *Republic of Letters*, 1:514.

73 **"to visit an idea"** Hugh Howard, *Thomas Jefferson, Architect: The Built Legacy of Our Third President* (New York: Rizzoli, 2003),115.

73 **"a geometry lesson"** Ibid., 119.

73 **"obsessed"** Roger G. Kennedy, "Poplar Forest: Jefferson's Quest for a True American Architecture," *Architectural Digest*, May 1992, 30.

73 **"Jefferson derived"** Ibid.

74 **"twenty-feet wide"** Howard, *Thomas Jefferson, Architect*, 120.

74 **"octagon 50 f. in diameter"** Ibid.

74 **"penetrates the circle"** Ibid., 127.

74 **"together with its attendant structures"** Ibid.

74 **"an idealized set of figures"** Ibid.

74 **"a totally impractical house"** Chambers, *Poplar Forest and Thomas Jefferson*, 37.

74 **"got so carried away"** Howard, *Thomas Jefferson, Architect*, 120.

74 **"flue steeply corbeled"** Ibid., 121.

74 **"is so pleased"** Thomas Jefferson to William A. Burwell, September 5, 1810, Jefferson Papers, Massachusetts Historical Society.

75 **"Nothing new has happened"** Thomas Jefferson to Ann Cary Bankhead, May 26, 1811, *Family Letters*, 400.

75 **"I fancy"** Elizabeth Trist to Catharine Wistar Bache, May 7, 1811, Papers of the American Philosophical Society.

75 **"it will not be"** Ibid.

75 **"I have seen him"** *Jefferson at Monticello*, 94.

76 **"total prostration"** Thomas Jefferson to Benjamin Rush, August 17, 1811, L. & B., 18:76.

76 **"forgotten much"** Ibid., 75.

76 **"old men"** Ibid., 76.

76 **"becoming a dotard"** Ibid.

76 **"My children have"** Mrs. Thomas Mann Randolph, Jr., to Elizabeth Trist, November 12, 1811, Edgehill-Randolph Papers, University of Virginia.

77 **"Our dear mother"** Peter Carr to Thomas Jefferson, August 31, 1811, Carr-Cary Papers, University of Virginia.

77 **"at last yielded"** Thomas Jefferson to Randolph Jefferson, September 6, 1811, *Thomas Jefferson and His Unknown Brother*, Bernard Mayo, ed. (Charlottesville: University of Virginia Press, 1981), 26.

CHAPTER 13 *"The Shock of an Earthquake"*

78 **"stopt, and doors"** *New York Evening Post,* December 21, 1811.

78 **"awful noise"** *Lorenzo Dow's Journal,* March 22, 1816, published by Joshua Martin, New Madrid, Territory of Missouri, 1849, p. 344–46. Quoted in "Firsthand Accounts of the New Madrid Earthquakes 1811–1812," http://comp.uark.edu~pjansma /nm2_accounts.pdf.

78 **"the complete saturation"** Ibid.

78 **"its waters gathering up"** Ibid.

78 **"fifteen to twenty feet"** Ibid.

78 **"the earth was horribly torn"** Ibid.

78 **"covered over"** Ibid.

78 **"and blood was every where"** George H. Crust, resident of Nelson County, N.Y., near Louisville, "Submitted by Floyd Croesey, great-grandchild of the author," www.hsv.com/genlintr/newMadrid.

78 **"were friendly"** Ibid.

79 **"a mysterious visitation"** *New York Evening Post,* December 21, 1811, from "Newspaper Accounts of the New Madrid Earthquake," www.rootsweb.com/monewmad/nm _history/paper5.htm.

79 **"The Comet"** *The Louisiana Gazette and Daily Advertiser,* December 21, 1811, from "Newspaper Accounts of the New Madrid Earthquake," www.rootsweb.com/monewmad /nm_history/paper5.htm.

79 **"a shock of an earthquake"** *Memorandum Books,* February 21, 1774, 1:369.

79 **"as violent"** Ibid., 370.

79 **"rather deficient in intellect"** *Domestic Life,* 39.

80 **"pugnacious humor"** Thomas Jefferson to John Adams, June 1, 1822, *Adams-Jefferson Letters,* 578.

80 **"metaphysical"** See Boorstin, "The Perils of Metaphysics," *The Lost World of Thomas Jefferson,* 128–39.

80 **"A person of perfect truth"** Thomas Jefferson to John Wayles Eppes, September 6, 1811, Jefferson Papers, Library of Congress.

81 **"a conqueror roaming"** Thomas Jefferson to Dr. Walter Jones, March 5, 1810, Ford, ed., *Writings of Thomas Jefferson,* 12:370.

82 **"request to be entered"** Boynton Merrill, Jr., *Jefferson's Nephews: A Frontier Tragedy* (Lexington: University Press of Kentucky, 1987), 295.

82 **"young man of excellent dispositions"** Thomas Jefferson to Gideon Fitch, May 23, 1809, Jefferson Papers, Massachusetts Historical Society.

CHAPTER 14 *Old Friends Reunited*

83 **"one continued tempest"** Boller, *Presidential Campaigns,* 12.

83 **"a half-breed Indian"** Ibid., 11.

83  "cast into a bonfire" Dwight, *Duty of Americans,* 20–21.

83  "chanting mockeries" Ibid.

83  "abuse and scandal" Ibid.

83  "to ruin and corrupt" Smith, *John Adams,* 2:1035.

84  "a moment of Melancholly" John Adams to Thomas Jefferson, March 24, 1801, *Adams-Jefferson Letters,* 264.

84  "the greatest Grief" Ibid.

84  "is not possible" Ibid.

84  "is in a state" Ibid.

85  "a hurried and agitated step" Edward Coles to Henry S. Randall, May 11, 1857, *Life of Thomas Jefferson,* 3:639.

85  "You have turned me out" Ibid., 640.

85  "I have not" Ibid.

85  "not one of a personal character" Ibid.

85  "a more accurate account" Ibid.

85  "Mr. Jefferson said" Ibid.

85  "That is enough for me" Thomas Jefferson to Benjamin Rush, December 5, 1811, L. & B., 13:115–16.

85  "an honest man" Ibid.

85  "defended him" Ibid.

85  "mine of learning and taste" Thomas Jefferson to John Adams, January 23, 1812, *Adams-Jefferson Letters,* 292–93.

85  "A letter from you" Thomas Jefferson to John Adams, January 21, 1812, *Adams-Jefferson Letters,* 291.

86  "Of the signers" Ibid., 292

86  "in the midst of my grandchildren" Ibid.

86  "No circumstances" Ibid.

86  "gruff, short" *The Works [of ] John Adams, second President of the United States,* with a life of the author, notes and illustrations by his grandson Charles Francis Adams (Boston: Little, Brown, 1856; edition: 1st AMS ed. [New York: AMS Press, 1971]), 1:616.

87  "severely flogged" Thomas Jefferson to Reuben Perry, April 16, 1812, *Farm Book,* 35.

87  "out of jail" Ibid.

87  "out of the state" Ibid.

88  "in Carpentry" Thomas Jefferson to Reuben Perry, September 3, 1812, *Farm Book,* 35.

89  "the great Outassete" Thomas Jefferson to John Adams, June 11, 1812, *Adams-Jefferson Letters,* 307.

89  "far advanced" Ibid.

89  "also felt an Interest" John Adams to Thomas Jefferson, June 18, 1812, *Adams-Jefferson Letters,* 310.

89  "in my boyish Rambles" Ibid.

89 **"went out to Service"** Ibid.

89 **"I remember the Time"** Ibid., 311.

89 **"will quiet the Indians"** Ibid.

90 **"English seductions"** Thomas Jefferson to John Adams, June 11, 1812, *Adams-Jefferson Letters*, 310.

90 **"doors of Congress will re-open"** Ibid.

## Chapter 15 *At War Again*

91 **"merely to keep"** Thomas Jefferson to James Madison, April 17, 1812, *Republic of Letters*, 3:1692.

91 **"will starve Great Britain"** Ibid.

92 **"Suffice it to say here"** *Sage of Monticello*, 123.

93 **"We spared nothing"** Thomas Jefferson to Alexander von Humboldt, December 6, 1813, *Jefferson Profile*, 225.

94 **"The confirmed brutalization"** Ibid.

94 **"We can indeed"** Thomas Jefferson to William Short, November 28, 1814, L. & B., 14:216.

94 **"would be unhappy for life"** Thomas Jefferson to Elizabeth Trist, May 10, 1813, Jefferson Papers, Massachusetts Historical Society.

94 **"He will be a great loss"** Ibid.

95 **"try another campaign"** Thomas Jefferson to Elizabeth Trist, February 10, 1814, Jefferson Papers, Massachusetts Historical Society.

95 **"impatient to risk"** Thomas Mann Randolph, Jr., to Joseph C. Cabell, December 29, 1813, Randolph Papers, Duke University Library.

96 **"wing of offices"** Thomas Jefferson to John W. Eppes, July 16, 1814, Henry E. Huntington Library, San Marino, Calif.

97 **"finest youth in Virginia"** William Fitzhugh Gordon to Mrs. Gordon, September 9, 1814, William Harris Gaines, *Thomas Mann Randolph* (Baton Rouge: Louisiana State University Press, 1966), 97.

97 **"with all his chivalry"** Ibid.

97 **"by force"** Thomas Mann Randolph, Jr., to Thomas Jefferson, March 8, 1814, Jefferson Papers, Library of Congress.

97 **"sometimes half again"** Gaines, *Thomas Mann Randolph*, 98.

97 **"have nothing in abundance"** Thomas Jefferson Randolph to Thomas Jefferson, September 9, 1814, *Family Letters*, 407.

## Chapter 16 *"This Enterprise Is for the Young"*

98 **"New Jerusalem"** "Edward Coles: An Agrarian on the Frontier," Kurt E. Leichtle, Ph.D. diss., University of Illinois at Chicago Circle, 19.

99 **"I never took up"** Edward Coles to Thomas Jefferson, July 14, 1814, *E. B. Wash-*

burne's *Edward Coles,* Clarence W. Alvord, ed., Collections of the Illinois State Historical Library, 1920, 15:22–24.

100 **"sentiments breathed through"** Thomas Jefferson to Edward Coles, August 25, 1814, *Life of Thomas Jefferson,* 3:643–45.

103 **"very sensibly"** Edward Coles to Thomas Jefferson, September 26, 1814, *E. B. Washburne's Edward Coles,* Clarence W. Alvord, ed., Collections of the Illinois State Historical Library, 1920, 15:28–30.

## Chapter 17 *"When I Reflect That God Is Just"*

105 **"Ethics & Natl Religion"** Thomas Jefferson to John W. Eppes, September 19, 1814, L. & B., 14:423.

105 **"moral sense"** Thomas Jefferson to Peter Carr, August 10, 1787, L. & B., 6:257.

105 **"soothsayers and necromancers"** Thomas Jefferson to Charles Clay, January 29, 1815, L. & B., 14:233.

105 **"bungling artist"** Thomas Jefferson to Thomas Law, June 13, 1814, L. & B., 14:142.

107 **"it must be any other"** *Notes on the State of Virginia,* 163.

107 **"as a free and independant people"** Ibid., 138.

107 **"deep rooted prejudices"** Ibid.

108 **"Truth advances"** Thomas Jefferson to Thomas Cooper, October 17, 1814, L. & B., 14:200.

108 **"unheroic but eminently prudent"** John Chester Miller, *The Wolf by the Ears* (Charlottesville: University of Virginia Press, 1991), 18.

108 **"Gothic"** Thomas Jefferson to Joseph Priestley, January 27, 1800, L. & B., 10:148.

109 **"I tremble for my country"** *Notes on the State of Virginia,* 163.

## Chapter 18 *A Library for "the American Statesman"*

110 **"destruction of the public library"** Thomas Jefferson to Samuel Harrison Smith, September 21, 1814, L. & B., 14:190.

110 **"turning over every book"** Ibid., 245.

110 **"such works relating to America"** Ibid.

110 **"the American statesman"** Ibid.

110 **"related to the duties"** Ibid.

111 **"at their own price"** Ibid.

111 **"not knowing myself"** Ibid.

111 **"by persons named by themselves"** Ibid.

111 **"convenient to the public"** Ibid.

111 **"days of peace and prosperity"** Ibid., 246.

111 **"would place it in Washington"** Ibid.

111 **"to amuse the time"** Ibid.

111 **"two years of embargo"** Thomas Jefferson to Archibald Robertson, April 25, 1817, *Farm Book,* 216.

112 **"for whatever he could get"** Thomas Jefferson to John Barnes, August 20, 1814, *Farm Book,* 214.

112 **"sell at all"** Ibid.

112 **"coming on us"** Thomas Jefferson to Elizabeth Trist, December 26, 1814, *Thomas Jefferson's Garden Book,* 526.

112 **"payable in a year"** *Memorandum Books,* January 1, 1815, 2:1305.

112 **"would report favorably"** James Madison to Thomas Jefferson, October 10, 1814, *Republic of Letters,* 3:1745.

## Chapter 19 *Jeff Randolph Takes a Wife*

113 **"found a lodestone"** Thomas Jefferson to Elizabeth Trist, February 1, 1814, Jefferson Papers, Coolidge Collection, Massachusetts Historical Society.

113 **"the attraction of the two bodies"** Ibid.

113 **"unfavorably impressed"** Joseph C. Vance, *Thomas Jefferson Randolph,* dissertation (University of Virginia, 1957), 39.

113 **"by others"** *Memoirs,* 41.

114 **"knew nothing of the affair"** All of the quotations concerning the ill feeling about Jane Nicholas are from the Statement by Mrs. Ann C. Bankhead, June 21, 1814, Papers of the Carr-Cary Family, University of Virginia.

114 **"vulgar looking woman"** Ibid.

115 **"confer on me"** Thomas Jefferson Randolph to Wilson Cary Nicholas, February 4, 1815, Edgehill-Randolph Papers, University of Virginia.

115 **"a lovely little woman"** Thomas Jefferson to Elizabeth Trist, May 31, 1815, Elizabeth House Trist Papers, Virginia Historical Society.

115 **"any fault of mine"** Ibid.

115 **"has turn'd out"** Elizabeth Trist to Catharine Wistar Bache, August 22, 1814, Papers of the American Philosophical Society.

115 **"a hard fate"** Ibid.

116 **"can never want a home"** Martha Randolph to Elizabeth Trist, May 31, 1815, Elizabeth House Trist Papers, Virginia Historical Society.

116 **"I think sometimes"** Ibid.

## Chapter 20 *The Realm of "Sobriety and Cool Reason"*

117 **"miserable, barren country"** *Visitors to Monticello,* 56.

117 **"abandoned to nature"** Ibid., 57.

117 **"were decaying from age"** Ibid.

117 **"drowned"** Ibid., 56.

117 **"without winter clothing"** Ibid.

117 **"steep, savage hill"** Ibid., 61.

117 **"He is quite tall"** Ibid., 57.

118 **"polished"** Ibid., 62.

118 **"leather bottoms"** Ibid., 57.

118 **"in general conversation"** Ibid., 63.

118 **"a pleasanter party"** Ibid.

118 **"in the French style"** Ibid., 64.

119 **"its principal treasures"** Ibid., 58.

119 **"sobriety and cool reason"** Ibid., 63.

119 **"seemed to be favorites"** Ibid.

119 **"at ten dollars"** *Sage of Monticello*, 176.

119 **"This can be done"** Thomas Jefferson to Samuel Harrison Smith, February 27, 1815, Jefferson Papers, Library of Congress.

119 **"on my legs"** Ibid.

120 **"GLORIOUS NEWS"** *Republic of Letters*, 2:1755.

120 **"but the old philosopher refused"** *Visitors to Monticello*, 65.

120 **"I sincerely congratulate you"** Thomas Jefferson to James Madison, March 23, 1815, *Republic of Letters*, 2:1763.

121 **"very quietly"** *Visitors to Monticello*, 60.

121 **"an affair of small consequence"** Ibid.

121 **"one or two hundred dollars"** Ibid.

121 **"Mr. Jefferson's great dam"** Ibid., 65.

121 **"a most wonderful miscalculation"** Ibid., 60.

121 **"W. Bowan"** *Memorandum Books*, August 18, 1767, 1:39.

121 **"charity"** *Memorandum Books*, June 1, 1826, 2:1417.

122 **"disastrous legacy"** *Memorandum Books*, 1:xix.

122 **"combined with an optimistic nature"** Ibid.


CHAPTER 21 *"To Witness the Death of All Our Companions"*

123 **"met the news"** Thomas Jefferson to Wilson Cary Nicholas, August 9, 1815, Thomas Jefferson Papers, Library of Congress.

123 **"extremely sorry"** Randolph Jefferson to Thomas Jefferson, October 6, 1811, Mayo, *Thomas Jefferson and His Unknown Brother*, 27.

124 **"paroxysms"** Thomas Jefferson to Thomas Cooper, October 27, 1808, L. & B., 12:180.

124 **"stupor"** Thomas Jefferson to the Chevalier François Jean Chastellux, November 26, 1782, L. & B., 4:199.

124 **"as dead to the world"** Ibid.

124 **"put on mourning"** Smith, *The First Forty Years of Washington Society*, 408.

125 **"great indeed"** Thomas Jefferson to Governor John Page, June 25, 1804, L. & B., 11:31.

125 **"When you and I"** Ibid., 31–32.

125 **"I think with you"** Thomas Jefferson to John Adams, April 8, 1816, *Adams-Jefferson Letters*, 467.

126 **"weigh Sensations"** John Adams to Thomas Jefferson, May 3, 1816, *Adams-Jefferson Letters*, 470.

126 **"the Vanity of human Wishes"** Ibid., 473.

126 **"metaphysical"** See Boorstin, "The Perils of Metaphysics," *The Lost World of Thomas Jefferson*, 128–39.

126 **"without repugnance"** Thomas Jefferson to John Adams, October 14, 1816, *Adams-Jefferson Letters*, 490.

127 **"as a medical subject"** Thomas Jefferson to John L. Bankhead, October 28, 1815, Jefferson Papers, University of Virginia.

127 **"Nothing less"** Ibid.

CHAPTER 22 *"The Eternal Preservation of . . . Republican Principles"*

128 **"by a crowd"** Thomas Jefferson to Martha Randolph, November 4, 1815, *Family Letters*, 411.

128 **"most agreeably surprised"** Ibid., 412.

128 **"torture Aaron Burr"** Burke Davis, *Old Hickory: A Life of Andrew Jackson* (New York: Dial Press, 1977), 57.

128 **"A troop of horse"** *Richmond Enquirer,* November 15, 1815, Library of Virginia.

129 **"majority of the Gentlemen"** Mary Pocahontas Hubard to Mrs. Susan Hubard, December 23, 1815, Hubard Family Papers, Southern Historical Collection, University of North Carolina at Chapel Hill.

130 **"only on the days"** Thomas Jefferson to Joseph Cabell, February 2, 1816, L. & B., 14:422.

130 **"wards," "ward republics"** Thomas Jefferson to Samuel Kercheval, July 12, 1816, L. & B., 15:38.

131 **"the whole people"** Ibid.

131 **"by the common reason"** Ibid.

131 **"good and safe government"** Thomas Jefferson to Joseph Cabell, February 2, 1816, L. & B., 14:421.

131 **"what concerns"** Ibid.

131 **"gradation of authorities"** Ibid., 422.

131 **"balances and checks"** Ibid.

131 **"any other general"** Ibid.

131 **"the management of all our farms"** Ibid., 421.

131 **"not founded"** Thomas Jefferson to Governor Wilson Cary Nicholas, April 2, 1816, L. & B., 14:454.

131  "the care of the poor" Thomas Jefferson to John Adams, October 28, 1813, L. & B., 13:400.

131  "participator in the government" Thomas Jefferson to Joseph Cabell, February 2, 1816, L. & B., 14:422.

132  "regularly organized power" Thomas Jefferson to Samuel Kercheval, September 5, 1816, L. & B., 15:71.

132  "we shall be as republican" Ibid.

132  "sanctimonious reverence" Thomas Jefferson to Samuel Kercheval, July 12, 1816, L. & B., 15:40.

133  "no space reserved" Hannah Arendt, *On Revolution* (New York: Viking Press, 1965), 234–35.

133  "expressing, discussing and deciding" Ibid., 238.

133  "foreign" Thomas Jefferson to Edward Livingston, April 4, 1824, L. & B., 16:23.

CHAPTER 23  *The Indulgent Patriarch*

134  "stood his ground firmly" Thomas Jefferson to John Bankhead, October 14, 1816, Edgehill-Randolph Papers, University of Virginia.

134  "much disturbed or endangered" Martha Randolph to Thomas Jefferson, November 20, 1816, *Family Letters,* 417.

135  "joyful surprises" Cornelia Randolph to Henry S. Randall, n.d., *Life of Thomas Jefferson,* 3:348.

135  "my father's finances" Ibid.

135  "an elegant lady's watch" Ibid., 348–49.

136  "an old saddle" Ibid., 348.

136  "lady's saddle and bridle" Ibid., 348–49.

136  "involuntarily expressed aloud" Virginia Randolph Trist to Nicholas P. Trist, May 26, 1839, *Life of Thomas Jefferson,* 3:350.

136  "mending your dress" Ibid.

136  "but she asked" Ibid., 351.

136  "poor father" Ellen R. Coolidge to Martha Randolph, January 31, 1816, Ellen R. Coolidge Papers, University of Virginia.

136  "to any extent" *Memorandum Books,* March 14, 1816, 2:1320.

137  "felt far closer" Gaines, *Thomas Mann Randolph,* 106.

138  "big grum voice" *Jefferson at Monticello,* 91.

138  "to take a part" Gaines, *Thomas Mann Randolph,* 105.

138  "decide the happiness" Martha Randolph to Nicholas Trist, September 18, 1818, Randolph Papers, University of Virginia.

138  "mix promiscuously" Thomas Jefferson to Samuel Kercheval, September 5, 1816, L. & B., 15:72.

CHAPTER 24 *The "Yellow Children" of the Mountaintop*

139 **"have neither in their color"** *Visitors to Monticello,* 30.

139 **"at some distance in the dusk"** Henry Randall to James Parton quoted in Fawn M. Brodie, *Thomas Jefferson: An Intimate History* (New York: Norton, 1974), 496.

139 **"looked so startled"** Ibid.

139 **"yellow children"** Ellen W. Coolidge to Joseph Coolidge, October 24, 1858, Ellen W. Coolidge Journal, Ellen W. Coolidge Papers, University of Virginia.

140 **"great intelligence"** "Peter Hemings Biography," Monticello.org.

140 **"mighty near white"** *Jefferson at Monticello,* 4.

140 **"light colored"** Randolph to James Parton, quoted in Brodie, 495.

140 **"gave birth to a child"** "Reminiscences of Madison Hemings," *Pike County* (Ohio) *Republican,* March 13, 1873; in Brodie, 473.

141 **"a tangle of fish-hooks"** Jonathan Daniels, *The Randolphs of Virginia* (Garden City, N.Y.: Doubleday & Co., 1972), 9.

142 **"took care of"** Brodie, 475.

142 **"the female attendant"** Ellen W. Coolidge to Joseph Coolidge, October 24, 1858, Ellen W. Coolidge Journal, Ellen W. Coolidge Papers, University of Virginia.

142 **"There are such things"** Ibid.

142 **"a young man"** Ibid.

143 **"eliminated dark corners"** Jack McLaughlin, *Jefferson and Monticello: The Biography of a Builder* (New York: Henry Holt, 1988), 254.

144 **"slept within sound"** Brodie, 495.

144 **"was a thunderous snorer"** Helen F. Leary, "Sally Hemings' Children: A Genealogical Analysis of the Evidence," *National Genealogical Society Quarterly,* September 2001, 205.

144 **"within sound of [Jefferson's] breathing"** Ellen W. Coolidge to Joseph Coolidge, October 24, 1858, Ellen W. Coolidge Papers, University of Virginia.

144 **"even his own daughters"** Thomas Jefferson Randolph, Broadside, "The Last Days of Thomas Jefferson," University of Virginia.

144 **"had no private entrance"** Ellen W. Coolidge to Joseph Coolidge, October 24, 1858, Ellen W. Coolidge Papers, University of Virginia.

144 **"porticles"** Leary, "Sally Hemings' Children," 206.

144 **"servant's room"** Ibid.

144 **"These porticles"** Ibid.

145 **"coming out of her mother's room"** *Jefferson at Monticello,* 102.

145 **"simplest and most probable"** "Thomas Jefferson and Sally Hemings: A Brief Account," statement from "Thomas Jefferson's Monticello," website of the Thomas Jefferson Memorial Foundation, Monticello, p. 2, www.monticello.org/plantation/ hemingscontro/hemings-jefferson_contro.html.

146 **"a high probability"** Ibid.

146 **"with a laugh"** Ellen W. Coolidge to Joseph Coolidge, October 24, 1858, Ellen W. Coolidge Papers, University of Virginia.

146 **"connection with the Carrs"** Brodie, 495.

146 **"good-natured Turk"** Ellen W. Coolidge to Joseph Coolidge, October 24, 1858, Ellen W. Coolidge Papers, University of Virginia.

147 **"used to come out"** *Jefferson at Monticello,* 22.

147 **"the mothers were black women"** Ellen W. Coolidge to Joseph Coolidge, October 24, 1858, Ellen W. Coolidge Papers, University of Virginia.

147 **"dissipated young men"** Ibid.

148 **"What suited him"** Brodie, 396.

148 **"the Colonel soon"** *Jefferson at Monticello,* 15–16.

148 **"has given Isaac more whippings"** Ibid., 15.

148 **"very kind to servants"** Ibid., 13.

149 **"a tall thin-visaged man"** Ibid., 16.

149 **"black Aspasia"** Ellen W. Coolidge memoir, quoted in Brodie, 370.

149 **"injured individual"** Ibid.

149 **"not himself in the smallest degree"** Ibid.

149 **"broke into a hearty, clear laugh"** *Life of Thomas Jefferson,* 3:119.

149 **"looked a little crest-fallen"** Ibid.

## Chapter 25 *"Something Very Great and Very New"*

150 **"the eager gaze"** *Republic of Letters,* 3:1777.

150 **"academical village"** Thomas Jefferson to Benjamin Henry Latrobe, August 3, 1817, Thomas Jefferson Papers, University of Virgina.

151 **"I congratulate You"** John Adams to Thomas Jefferson, May 26, 1817, *Adams-Jefferson Letters,* 518.

152 **"so broad, so liberal"** Thomas Jefferson to Joseph Priestley, January 18, 1800, L. & B., 10:140.

152 **"brilliant success"** *Richmond Enquirer,* July 19, 1817.

152 **"entirely novel"** Benjamin Latrobe to Thomas Jefferson, in Fiske Kimball, *Thomas Jefferson, Architect* (New York: Da Capo, 1968), 188.

152 **"hotels"** Thomas Jefferson to Board of Visitors, August 15, 1821, Cabell Papers, University of Virginia.

152 **"Rotunda"** Thomas Jefferson to James Madison, January 6, 1823, *Republic of Letters,* 3:1853.

152 **"open to the horizon"** Howard, *Thomas Jefferson, Architect,* 140.

153 **"bring the whole circle"** Thomas Jefferson to Thomas Cooper, August 25, 1814, L. & B., 14:174.

153 **"every sect to provide"** Thomas Jefferson, Resolution of October 7, 1822, to University Board, L. & B., 19:414.

154 **"all the ceremony"** *Richmond Enquirer,* October 10, 1817.

155 **"by the principles"** "Rockfish Report," Report of the Commissioners of the University of Virginia, August 4, 1818 (University of Virginia), 8.

155 **"by the sentiments"** Ibid., 4.

155 **"delicious"** Thomas Jefferson to Martha Randolph, August 21, 1818, *Family Letters,* 426.

155 **"large swelling"** Ibid.

155 **"for several days"** Ibid.

155 **"eruptive complaint"** Thomas Jefferson to Henry Dearborn, July 5, 1819, *Family Letters,* 427.

155 **"extreme weakness"** Thomas Jefferson to Joel Yancey, September 11, 1818, quoted in James A. Bear, Jr., "Medical Chronology of Thomas Jefferson," n.d., Thomas Jefferson Memorial Foundation, 668.

155 **"Within a few days"** Thomas Jefferson to John Barnes, November 10, 1818, in "Medical Chronology," 669.

155 **"gathering flesh and strength"** Thomas Jefferson to John Barnes, December 7, 1818, in "Medical Chronology," 670.

156 **"We found him"** James Madison to James Monroe, December 11, 1818, Monroe Papers, Library of Congress.

CHAPTER 26 *Struggling "All Our Lives with Debt & Difficulty"*

157 **"an unskilled manager"** Thomas Jefferson to John W. Eppes, n.d., *Domestic Life,* 364.

158 **"a rent in kind"** *Memoirs,* 47.

158 **"smutted"** Patrick Gibson to Thomas Jefferson, October 21, 1818, *Farm Book,* 219.

158 **"the responsible person"** Thomas Jefferson to Patrick Gibson, November 3, 1818, *Farm Book,* 219.

158 **"I breakfasted in the winter"** *Memoirs,* 48.

159 **"to find a worse"** Sarah E. Nicholas to Jane Randolph, February 12, 1841, Edgehill-Randolph Papers, University of Virginia.

159 **"to retain anything"** *Memoirs,* 22.

159 **"early deficiencies"** Ibid.

159 **"professional"** Ibid., 41.

160 **"My son"** Ibid.

160 **"Had you been educated"** Ibid., 40.

161 **"which like waves"** Thomas Jefferson to John Adams, December 10, 1819, L. & B., 15:233.

161 **"God grant *we*"** Ellen W. Randolph to Martha Jefferson Randolph, August 11, 1819, Ellen W. Coolidge Papers, University of Virginia.

161 **"unlawful gambling & cards"** Albemarle County Court Records, Commonwealth Causes, 1818–1819, *Commonwealth v. Farley,* Library of Virginia.

161 **"a place of public resort"** Ibid.

162  **"had hardly touched"** *Jefferson at Monticello,* 95.

162  **"excitable"** Ibid., 94.

162  **"as quick as I ever"** Ibid.

162  **"two drunken men"** "Last Days of Thomas Jefferson," Special Collections, University of Virginia.

CHAPTER 27  *Blood in the Streets of Charlottesville*

164  **"Spanish knives"** Elizabeth Trist to Nicholas P. Trist, February 3, 1819, Trist Papers, Library of Congress.

164  **"a knife as long as a dirk"** Hetty Carr to Dabney S. Carr, February 15, 1819, Carr-Cary Collection, University of Virginia.

164  **"very insulting"** Elizabeth Trist to Nicholas P. Trist, February 3, 1819, Nicholas P. Trist Papers, Library of Congress.

165  **"playing near"** Hetty Carr to Dabney S. Carr, February 15, 1819, Carr-Cary Collection, University of Virginia.

165  **"raised his whip"** Ibid.

165  **"which cut"** Ibid.

165  **"a pretty considerable gash"** Elizabeth Trist to Nicholas P. Trist, February 3, 1819, Trist Papers, Library of Congress.

165  **"blessed providential blow"** Elizabeth Trist to Nicholas P. Trist, February 7, 1819, Trist Papers, Library of Congress.

165  **"a great deal of blood"** Ibid.

166  **"tracing the man"** *Memoirs,* 5.

166  **"murder"** Ibid.

166  **"Dreadfully agitated"** Hetty Carr to Dabney S. Carr, February 15, 1819, Carr-Cary Collection, University of Virginia.

166  **"wreak his vengeance"** Elizabeth Trist to Nicholas P. Trist, February 3, 1819, Trist Papers, Library of Congress.

167  **"the boldest rider"** *Life of Thomas Jefferson,* 1:69.

167  **"a deplorable loss"** Peggy Nicholas to James Randolph, March 22, 1819, Edgehill-Randolph Papers, University of Virginia.

167  **"severe colic"** Alexander Garrett to John Hartwell Cocke, February 19, 1819, Cocke Papers, Shields Deposit, University of Virginia.

167  **"Apple water"** Ibid.

167  **"capable of anything nearly"** J. A. Carr to Dabney S. Carr, February 22, 1819, Carr-Cary Papers, University of Virginia.

168  **"unfortunate wife"** Mary B. Patterson to Sarah Nicholas, February 14, 1819, Edgehill-Randolph Papers, University of Virginia.

168  **"a woman of delicacy"** H. B. Trist to Nicholas P. Trist, February 19, 1819, Trist Papers, Library of Congress.

168 **"there must be something wrong"** Sarah Nicholas to Jane Randolph, March 11, 1819, Edgehill-Randolph Papers, University of Virginia.

168 **"great unhappiness"** Elizabeth Trist to Nicholas P. Trist, March 9, 1819, Nicholas P. Trist Papers, Library of Congress.

168 **"The course I now take"** Charles L. Bankhead to Thomas Jefferson, February 7, 1819, Thomas Jefferson Papers, Library of Congress.

168 **"five minutes after"** Ibid.

168 **"I can bear bodily pain"** Ibid.

168 **"horsewhip [Bankhead] on sight"** Ibid.

169 **"some slanderous tale"** Ibid.

169 **"healing slowly"** Thomas Jefferson to James Madison, February 19, 1819, *Republic of Letters,* 3:1807.

169 **"accident"** Ibid.

Chapter 28 *Fire, Sickness, Drought, and Storm*

170 **"What, my Dear Sir"** Wilson Cary Nicholas to Thomas Jefferson, February 28, 1819, The Thomas Jefferson Papers Series 1, General Correspondence, 1651–1827, Library of Congress, http://memory.loc.gov/cgi-bin/query/p?mtj=16:./temp/~ammem-e3rD::.

171 **"wounds are nearly"** Thomas Jefferson to Wilson Cary Nicholas, March 8, 1819, Thomas Jefferson Papers, Library of Congress.

171 **"stabbing and attempted murder"** Albemarle County Court Records, Commonwealth Causes, 1820–1821, *Commonwealth v. Bankhead,* Case 785, Library of Virginia.

171 **"the only thing"** Thomas Jefferson to Wilson Cary Nicholas, March 8, 1819, Thomas Jefferson Papers, Library of Congress.

171 **"the execution of the law"** Ibid.

172 **"exactly such a character"** Ibid.

172 **"You will do me the justice"** Wilson Cary Nicholas to Thomas Jefferson, April 19, 1818, Jefferson Papers, Library of Congress.

172 **"in utter confidence"** Thomas Jefferson to Wilson Cary Nicholas, May 1, 1818, Jefferson Papers, Library of Congress.

173 **"rather unpopular"** Joseph C. Cabell to Thomas Jefferson, February 22, 1819, Cabell Papers, University of Virginia.

173 **"every enlightened man"** Thomas Jefferson to Joseph C. Cabell, March 1, 1819, Cabell Papers, University of Virginia.

173 **"but is crip[p]led"** Elizabeth Trist to Nicholas P. Trist, March 9, 1819, Nicholas P. Trist Papers, Library of Congress.

174 **"the most skillful brewer"** Thomas Jefferson to Joseph Cabell, December 23, 1815, *Memorandum Books,* 2:1318.

174 **"wind blowing"** Hore B. Trist to Nicholas P. Trist, May 13, 1819, Nicholas P. Trist Papers, Library of Congress.

174 **"when the fire was raging"** Ibid.

174 **"The bodily injury"** Thomas Jefferson to John Quincy Adams, May 10, 1819, "Medical Chronology," 671.

174 **"We seem to hear of nothing"** Peggy Nicholas to Jane Randolph, April 10, 1819, Edgehill-Randolph Papers, University of Virginia.

174 **"were about to give out"** Joel Yancey to Thomas Jefferson, June 13, 1819, Jefferson Papers, Massachusetts Historical Society.

174 **"only able to work now & then"** Edmund Bacon to Thomas Jefferson, July 26, 1819, Jefferson Papers, University of Virginia.

174 **"Your house appears"** Joel Yancey to Thomas Jefferson, June 13, 1819, Jefferson Papers, Massachusetts Historical Society.

175 **"broken to atoms"** Ibid.

175 **"is very much exposed"** Ibid.

175 **"much concern"** Thomas Jefferson to Joel Yancey, June 25, 1819, Jefferson Papers, Massachusetts Historical Society.

176 **"the folding doors"** Cornelia Randolph to Virginia Randolph, July 18, 1819, Edgehill-Randolph Papers, University of Virginia.

176 **"stained and moulded"** Ellen W. Randolph to Martha Jefferson Randolph, June 8, 1819, Ellen W. Coolidge Papers, University of Virginia.

176 **"more dismal than usual"** Ibid.

176 **"stricture in the bowels"** Cornelia Randolph to Virginia Randolph, July 28, 1819, Edgehill-Randolph Papers, University of Virginia.

176 **"tribe of ignoramuses"** Ellen W. Randolph to Martha Randolph, July 28, 1819, Edgehill-Randolph Papers, University of Virginia.

176 **"My syringe"** William Steptoe to Thomas Jefferson, July 24, 1819, Jefferson Papers, Massachusetts Historical Society.

176 **"I never saw anybody"** Ellen W. Randolph to Martha Randolph, July 28, 1819, Edgehill-Randolph Papers, University of Virginia.

176 **"one of my favorites"** Ellen W. Randolph to Martha Randolph, August 4, 1819, Edgehill-Randolph Papers, University of Virginia.

176 **"attack of rheumatism"** Thomas Jefferson to Wilson Cary Nicholas, August 11, 1819, Jefferson Papers, Massachusetts Historical Society.

177 **"*said* very little"** Ellen W. Coolidge to Martha Randolph, August 24, 1819, Ellen W. Coolidge Correspondence, University of Virginia.

178 **"a clap of thunder"** Thomas Jefferson to Patrick Gibson, August 11, 1819, Jefferson Papers, Massachusetts Historical Society.

178 **"6 years ago"** Ibid.

178 **"from 1/5 to 1/30th"** Ibid.

178 **"affliction of another kind"** Thomas Jefferson to Wilson Cary Nicholas, August 11, 1819, Jefferson Papers, Library of Congress.

178 **"Have no uneasiness"** Thomas Jefferson to Wilson Cary Nicholas, August 24, 1819, Jefferson Papers, Library of Congress.

178 "had been protested" J. B. Dandridge to Thomas Jefferson, August 19, 1819, Coolidge Collection, University of Virginia.

179 "amply sufficient for this debt" Thomas Jefferson to Joseph Marx, August 24, 1819, Jefferson Papers, Library of Congress.

179 "a sort of regulation" *Life of Thomas Jefferson,* 3:533.

180 "Has not Jane come?" Ibid., 534.

180 "usual hearty hand-shake" Ibid.

180 "Neither then" Ibid.

180 "the highest honor" Ellen W. Coolidge to Martha Randolph, August 24, 1819, Ellen W. Coolidge Papers, University of Virginia.

180 "his present situation" Ibid.

180 "my general confidence" Ibid.

180 "all my thoughts" Ibid.

180 "cholic" Thomas Jefferson to James Madison, October 18, 1819, *Republic of Letters,* 3:1815.

180 "immediate danger" Ibid.

181 "very ill yesterday" H. B. Trist to Nicholas P. Trist, October 19, 1819, Nicholas P. Trist Papers, Library of Congress.

181 "for the good of his country" Ibid.

## Chapter 29 *A* Philosophe's *Faith*

182 "correct conduct" H. B. Trist to Nicholas P. Trist, October 19, 1819, Nicholas P. Trist Papers, Library of Congress.

183 "a very early part of my life" Thomas Jefferson to J.P.P. Derieux, July 25, 1788, quoted in *Jefferson's Excerpts from the Gospels,* Dickinson W. Adams, ed. (Princeton, N.J.: Princeton University Press, 1983), 5.

183 "Question with boldness" Thomas Jefferson to Peter Carr, August 10, 1787, L. & B., 6:258.

183 "destroy religion" The Rev. William Linn, quoted in Noble E. Cunningham, Jr., *In Pursuit of Reason: The Life of Thomas Jefferson* (Baton Rouge and Shreveport: Louisiana State University Press, 1987), 225.

184 "Syllabus" Thomas Jefferson to Benjamin Rush, April 21, 1803, L. & B., 10:381.

184 "our duties to others" Thomas Jefferson to Edward Dowse, Esq., April 19, 1803, L. & B., 10:377.

184 "the most innocent" Thomas Jefferson to Dr. Joseph Priestley, April 9, 1803, L. & B., 10:375.

184 "the most unlettered" Ibid.

184 "parentage was obscure" Thomas Jefferson to Benjamin Rush, April 21, 1803, L. & B., 10:383.

184 "natural endowments" and "correct and innocent" Ibid.

184 "mutilated" Ibid., 384.

184 "**sublime and benevolent**" Thomas Jefferson to Joseph Priestley, March 21, 1801, L. & B., 10:228.

184 "**that I do not remember**" *Sworn on the Altar of God*, 117.

185 "**overwhelmed with other business**" Thomas Jefferson to William Short, October 31, 1819, L. & B., 15:221.

185 "**one or two nights**" Ibid.

185 "**as easily distinguishable**" Thomas Jefferson to John Adams, October 12, 1813, *Adams-Jefferson Letters*, 384.

185 "**in so much ignorance**" Thomas Jefferson to William Short, April 13, 1820, L. & B., 15:245.

185 "**renders [Jesus's] death**" *Sworn on the Altar of God*, 120.

186 "**embedded in a miracle**" Ibid., 125.

189 "**In breathless silence**" Clarence W. Alvord, ed., *Governor Edward Coles*, (Springfield: Trustees of the Illinois State Historical Library, 1920), 44.

CHAPTER 30 *"We Shall Have Every Religious Man in Virginia Against Us"*

190 "**suspicious symptoms**" Thomas Jefferson to James Madison, February 16, 1820, *Republic of Letters*, 3:1822.

190 "**the separate existence**" *Sage of Monticello*, 376.

191 "**rash, dogmatical**" *Sworn on the Altar of God*, 176.

191 "**prejudices appear**" Ibid.

191 "**uneasy**" James Madison to Thomas Jefferson, March 6, 1819, *Republic of Letters*, 3:1808.

191 "**every religious man in Virginia**" W. H. Cabell to Joseph Cabell, March 21, 1820, Cabell Papers, University of Virginia.

191 "**priesthood**" *Sage of Monticello*, 377.

191 "**these satellites**" Thomas Jefferson to General Robert Taylor, May 16, 1820, L. & B., 15:254.

191 "**the irreparable loss**" Ibid., 256.

191 "**pulpit mountebanks**" Thomas Jefferson to Thomas Cooper, July 4, 1820, Jefferson Papers, University of Virginia.

191 "**the storm**" Thomas Jefferson to General Robert Taylor, May 16, 1820, L. & B., 15:254.

191 "**the first man**" Thomas Cooper to Thomas Jefferson, May 3, 1820, *Sage of Monticello*, 378.

192 "**prevail upon your mother**" Thomas Mann Randolph to Edmund Bacon, May 9, 1819, *Jefferson at Monticello*, 93.

192 "**exact performance**" Thomas Mann Randolph, Jr., "Message of Acceptance," December 11, 1819, *Journal of the House of Delegates*, 1819, 26–27.

192 "**zeal for the institution**" Thomas Jefferson to Thomas Mann Randolph, Jr., November 20, 1820, Jefferson Papers, Massachusetts Historical Society.

192–93 **"vast waste"** Gaines, *Thomas Mann Randolph,* 120.

193 **"a fire-bell in the night"** Thomas Jefferson to John Holmes, March 22, 1820, L. & B., 15:249.

## CHAPTER 31 *The Death Knell of the Union*

195 **"mere party trick"** Thomas Jefferson to Charles Pinckney, September 30, 1820, L. & B., 15:280.

195 **"consolidation"** Thomas Jefferson to Nathaniel Macon, November 23, 1821, L. & B., 15:341.

195 **"among the most sanguine"** Thomas Jefferson to William Short, April 13, 1820, L. & B., 15:247.

195 **"mutual & mortal"** Ibid., 248.

195 **"throwing away"** Ibid.

195 **"knell of the Union"** Thomas Jefferson to John C. Holmes, April 22, 1820, L. & B., 15:250.

195 **"the generation of 1776"** Ibid.

195 **"thrown away"** Ibid.

195 **"live not"** Ibid.

196 **"the intelligence of her sons"** *Richmond Enquirer,* January 3, 1822.

196 **"no longer proper"** Thomas Jefferson to John Taylor, February 14, 1821, Jefferson Papers, Library of Congress.

196 **"The signs of the time"** Ibid.

196 **"heresy"** Thomas Jefferson to Judge Spencer Roan, June 27, 1821, L. & B., 15:328.

196 **"orthodoxy"** *Autobiography,* 9.

196 **"It is in our seminary"** Thomas Jefferson to James Madison, February 17, 1826, *Republic of Letters,* 3:1965.

## CHAPTER 32 *The "Hideous Evil" of Slavery*

197 **"impossible"** Gaines, *Thomas Mann Randolph,* 125.

197 **"fair proportion"** Ibid.

197 **"patient resignation"** Ibid., 126.

197 **"persevering study"** Ibid.

198 **"not to elect"** Ibid., 127.

198 **"everything in disorder"** Harriet Randolph to Virginia Randolph, December 7, 1820, Edgehill-Randolph Papers, University of Virginia.

198 **"uncleanly desolation"** Ibid.

198 **"more and more difficult"** Joel Yancey to Thomas Jefferson, May 20, 1820, *Farm Book,* 221.

198 **"getting too old"** Ellen Wayles Coolidge to Martha Jefferson Randolph, September 13, 1820, Ellen W. Coolidge Papers, University of Virginia.

198 **"very unexpected"** Elizabeth Trist to Nicholas P. Trist, November 1, 1820, Nicholas P. Trist Papers, University of Virginia.

198 **"extremely affected"** Elizabeth Trist to Nicholas P. Trist, November 1, 1820, Southern Historical Collection, University of North Carolina.

198 **"Virginia's greatest men"** *Memoirs*, 42.

199 *"coup de grâce"* Thomas Jefferson to Edmund Bacon, February 21, 1826, Jefferson Collection, Massachusetts Historical Society.

199 **"spasmodic stricture"** Thomas Jefferson to William Short, October 31, 1820, L. & B., 15:219.

199 **"hideous evil"** Thomas Jefferson to Richard Rush, October 20, 1820, L. & B., 15:283.

199 **"the wolf by the ear"** Thomas Jefferson to John C. Holmes, April 22, 1820, L. & B., 15:249.

199 **"Nothing"** *Autobiography*, 62.

199 **"direct the process"** Ibid.

199 **"free white laborers"** Ibid.

199 **"our anxieties"** Thomas Jefferson to John Adams, January 22, 1821, *Adams-Jefferson Letters*, 569.

199 **"afflicted"** Ibid., 570.

200 **"Slavery in this Country"** John Adams to Thomas Jefferson, February 3, 1821, *Adams-Jefferson Letters*, 571.

## CHAPTER 33 *"Ah, Jefferson!" "Ah, Lafayette!"*

201 **"fleet as the wind"** *Memoirs*, 51.

202 **"feeble with age"** Ibid.

202 **"Ah, Jefferson!" "Ah, Lafayette!"** *Domestic Life*, 390.

202 **"they threw themselves"** *Memoirs*, 51.

202 **"not a sound"** Ibid.

202 **"in profound silence"** Ibid.

202 **"we are in a place"** *The Letters of Lafayette and Jefferson*, Gilbert Chinard, ed. (Baltimore: Johns Hopkins Press, 1929), 358.

202 **"increased in bulk"** James Madison to Dolley Madison, quoted in *Republic of Letters*, 3:1889.

202 **"an extraordinary degree"** *Visitors to Monticello*, 98.

202 **"a number of voices"** Ibid.

203 **"I have been received"** Olivier Bernier, *Lafayette: Hero of Two Worlds* (New York: E. P. Dutton, 1983), 295.

203 **"greatly aged"** Ibid.

204 **"declared he would"** Thomas Jefferson to James Madison, March 7, 1822, *Republic of Letters*, 3:1840.

204 **"no useful sense at all"** John Campbell to James Campbell, December 19, 1821, David Campbell Papers, Duke University Library.

204 **"like a mad bull"** John Campbell to Maria Campbell, January 1, 1822, David Campbell Papers, Duke University Library.

204 **"will again recover"** Martha Jefferson Randolph to Nicholas P. Trist, September 1, 1822, Nicholas P. Trist Papers, University of Virginia.

204 **"many of them"** Martha Randolph to Nicholas P. Trist, April 4, 1824, Nicholas P. Trist Papers, University of Virginia.

204 **"we have every reason"** Ibid.

204 **"more beautiful"** George Ticknor to W. H. Prescott, December 16, 1824, George Ticknor, *Life, Letters, and Journals*, 2 vols. (Boston: Houghton Mifflin Co., 1909), 1:348.

205 **"the Hero of the Revolution"** *Charlottesville Central Gazette*, quoted in *Richmond Enquirer*, November 5, 1824.

205 **"Thomas Jefferson and the Declaration of Independence"** *Life of Thomas Jefferson*, 3:504.

206 **"I will avail myself"** Ibid.

206 **"all did their utmost"** Ibid.

206 **"made our cause his own"** *Domestic Life*, 391.

206 **"I only held the nail"** Ibid.

206 **"My friends"** *Life of Thomas Jefferson*, 3:504.

206 **"Thomas Jefferson, founder"** Ibid.

206 **"entirely unceremonious"** *Sage of Monticello*, 422.

207 **"orthodox"** Thomas Jefferson to James Madison, March 22, 1825, *Republic of Letters*, 3:1930.

207 **"not well enough prepared"** Ibid.

207 **"has been a model"** Thomas Jefferson to Ellen W. Coolidge, August 27, 1825, *Family Letters*, 458.

207 **"a really shocking scandal"** Cornelia Randolph to Mrs. Joseph Coolidge, July 13, 1825, Ellen W. Coolidge Papers, University of Virginia.

CHAPTER 34 *"More Than Patience Could Endure"*

208 **"and take the rent"** Peggy Nicholas to Jane Randolph, April 25, 1825, Edgehill-Randolph Papers, University of Virginia.

208 **"instead of this unprofitable drudgery"** Cornelia Randolph to Mrs. Joseph Coolidge, November 24, 1825, Ellen W. Coolidge Papers, University of Virginia.

208 **"the encreasing derangement"** Martha Randolph to Nicholas P. Trist, April 4, 1824, Nicholas P. Trist Papers, University of Virginia.

208 **"aware of the extent"** Ibid.

209 **"the immediate settlement"** Ibid.

209 "are many ways" Ibid.

209 "coldblooded avarice" Thomas Mann Randolph, Jr., to Thomas Jefferson, July 8, 1825, Edgehill-Randolph Papers, University of Virginia.

209 "broke to atoms" Francis Walker Gilmer to Peachy R. Gilmer, June 19, 1825, Gilmer Papers, Virginia Historical Society.

209 "roam the world" Francis W. Gilmer to John Randolph, June 23, 1825, Gilmer Papers, Alderman Library, University of Virginia.

209 "as wildly as Lear" Ibid.

209 "My ruin is inevitable" Thomas Mann Randolph, Jr., to Thomas Jefferson, July 8, 1825, Edgehill-Randolph Papers, University of Virginia.

209 "return & become" Thomas Jefferson to Thomas Mann Randolph, July 5, 1825, Edgehill-Randolph Papers, University of Virginia.

210 "rye water" Holmes, *Thomas Jefferson Treats Himself,* 60–61.

210 "a chronical complaint" Thomas Jefferson to Dr. Robley Dunglison, May 17, 1825, *The Jefferson-Dunglison Letters,* John M. Dorsey, M.D., ed. (Charlottesville: University of Virginia Press, 1960), 13.

210 "50 drops" Robley Dunglison to Thomas Jefferson, July 18, 1825, Ibid., 37.

210 "to be my habitual state" Thomas Jefferson to Robley Dunglison, November 18, 1825, Thomas Jefferson Papers, University of Virginia.

210 "animated with wine" Thomas Jefferson to Joseph Coolidge, October 13, 1825, Ellen W. Coolidge Papers, University of Virginia.

210 "nightly disorders" *Life of Thomas Jefferson,* 3:518.

211 "rich fool" Martha Randolph to Ellen W. Coolidge, October 13, 1825, Ellen W. Coolidge Papers, University of Virginia.

212 "The shock" Martha Randolph to Ellen W. Coolidge, October 13, 1825, Ellen W. Coolidge Papers, University of Virginia.

212 "riot" *Life of Thomas Jefferson,* 3:518.

212 "Every one is sensible" Thomas Jefferson to Ellen W. Coolidge, November 14, 1825, *Family Letters,* 460.

## CHAPTER 35 *"Take Care of Me When Dead . . ."*

213 "is going smoothly" Thomas Jefferson to James Madison, October 18, 1825, *Republic of Letters,* 3:1942.

213 "fatigue to the patient" James Madison to Thomas Jefferson, October 14, 1825, *Republic of Letters,* 3:1943.

213 "could not find it" *Life of Thomas Jefferson,* 3:540.

213 "vile plaisterer" Virginia Randolph to Mrs. Joseph Coolidge, October 16, 1825, Ellen W. Coolidge Papers, University of Virginia.

213 "burying alive" Ibid.

214 "adherence to the skin" Ibid.

214 **"to break it into pieces"** Thomas Jefferson to James Madison, October 18, 1825, *Republic of Letters*, 3:1942.

214 **"thumps of the mallet"** Ibid.

214 **"real danger"** Ibid.

215 **"patient [though] he always is"** Virginia Randolph to Mrs. Joseph Coolidge, October 16, 1825, Ellen W. Coolidge Papers, University of Virginia.

215 **"came near suffocation"** *Life of Thomas Jefferson*, 3:540.

215 **"sprang furiously forward"** Ibid.

215 **"the fierce glare"** Ibid.

215 **"fragments of plaster"** Ibid.

215 **"cheerful spirits"** Virginia Randolph to Mrs. Joseph Coolidge, October 16, 1825, Ellen W. Coolidge Papers, University of Virginia.

215 **"tormented by the chattering"** Ibid.

215 **"I now bid adieu"** Thomas Jefferson to James Madison, October 18, 1825, *Republic of Letters*, 3:1942.

215 **"repugnance"** Thomas Jefferson to Joseph Delaplaine, April 12, 1817, L. & B., 19:246.

215 **"savor too much of vanity"** Ibid., 247.

216 **"general welfare"** Enclosure, Jefferson to Madison, December 24, 1825, *Republic of Letters*, 3:1944.

216 **"lighthouses in the sky"** *Sage of Monticello*, 437.

217 **"to claim all the power"** Norman K. Risjford, *The Old Republicans: Southern Conservatism in the Age of Jefferson* (New York: Columbia University Press, 1965), 258.

217 **"desperate"** Thomas Jefferson to James Madison, December 24, 1825, L. & B., 16:140.

217 **"solemn Declaration"** Enclosure, Jefferson to Madison, December 24, 1825, *Republic of Letters*, 3:1944–46.

217 **"under the most"** Ibid., 1944.

217 **"it shall be suppressed"** Ibid.

218 **"entered into a compact"** Ibid.

218 **"enlarging its own powers"** Ibid., 1945.

218 **"olive branch"** Ibid., 1943.

218 **"a moderate sacrifice"** Ibid., 1945.

218 **"voluntarily yield"** Ibid.

218 **"to make every difference"** Ibid., 1946.

219 **"or the appearance of it"** James Madison to Thomas Jefferson, December 28, 1825, *Republic of Letters*, 3:1947.

219 **"where the power assumed"** Ibid.

219 **"olive branch"** Ibid., 1943.

219 **"irritating rather than subduing"** James Madison to Thomas Jefferson, December 28, 1825, *Republic of Letters*, 3:1948.

220 **"menace or defiance"** Ibid.

220 **"all was gloom"** Thomas Jefferson to James Madison, January 2, 1826, *Republic of Letters,* 3:1961.

220 **"suppressed"** Thomas Jefferson to James Madison, December 28, 1825, *Republic of Letters,* 3:1944.

220 **"agitated and impulsive"** *Republic of Letters,* 3:1954.

220 **"aged Jefferson had soured"** Levy, *Jefferson and Civil Liberties,*149.

220 **"Southern apologist"** Ibid., 148.

220 **"solemn Declaration"** Enclosure, Jefferson to Madison, December 24, 1825, *Republic of Letters,* 3:1944.

220 **"crabbed and distrustful"** Levy, *Jefferson and Civil Liberties,* 149.

221 **"soured"** Ibid., 152.

221 **"the pleasures surely outweigh"** Thomas Jefferson to James Madison, December 18, 1825, *Adams-Jefferson Letters,* 3:612.

222 **"The friendship"** Thomas Jefferson to James Madison, February 17, 1826, *Republic of Letters,* 3:1966.

222 **"a pillar of support"** Ibid., 1967.

CHAPTER 36 *"An Inspiration from the Realms of Bliss"*

223 **"the realms of bliss"** Martha Jefferson to Ellen W. Coolidge, April 5, 1826, Ellen W. Coolidge Papers, University of Virginia.

223 **"immense advantage"** Ibid.

223 **"to pay his debts"** Ibid.

224 **"unprovided for"** Ibid.

225 **"alcove"** Martha Jefferson Randolph to Virginia Randolph, January 10, 1822, Southern Historical Collection, University of North Carolina.

225 **"in dignified *silence*"** Ibid.

225 **"a most bitter sacrifice"** Martha Jefferson Randolph to Ellen W. Coolidge, April 5, 1826, Ellen W. Coolidge Papers, University of Virginia.

225 **"made us recoil"** Ibid.

225 **"a subject of great importance"** Thomas Jefferson to Joseph Cabell, January 20, 1826, *Life of Thomas Jefferson,* 3:527.

226 **"will injure no man"** Ibid.

226 **"just"** Ibid.

226 **"To me"** Ibid.

CHAPTER 37 *"I Have Given My Whole Life to My Country"*

227 **"in one of his drunkest moods"** Martha Jefferson Randolph to Ellen W. Coolidge, September 11, 1825, Ellen W. Coolidge Papers, University of Virginia.

227 **"succeeded at last"** Ibid.

227 **"of unrelenting malice"** Ibid.

227 **"fully acquainted"** Ibid.

228 **"Your sister Mrs. Bankhead"** Sidney Nicholas to Thomas Jefferson Randolph, February 3, 1826, Edgehill-Randolph Papers, University of Virginia.

228 **"in the healthiest climate"** *Richmond Enquirer,* November 21, 1825.

228 **"almost nothing"** Thomas Mann Randolph, Jr., to Creed Taylor, October 29, 1825, Creed Taylor Papers, quoted in Gaines, *Thomas Mann Randolph,* 159.

229 **"was a great impropriety"** Peggy Nicholas to Jane Randolph, July 23, 1827, Edgehill-Randolph Papers, University of Virginia.

229 **"the policy of the state"** Thomas Jefferson Randolph to Thomas Jefferson, February 3, 1826, *Family Letters,* 467.

229 **"my mortification"** Thomas Jefferson to Thomas Jefferson Randolph, February 8, 1826, *Family Letters,* 469.

230 **"had better come"** Sidney Nicholas to Mary Randolph, February 11, 1826, Edgehill-Randolph Papers, University of Virginia.

230 **"Mr. Jefferson was present"** *Domestic Life,* 416.

230 **"Bad news"** Thomas Jefferson to Thomas Jefferson Randolph, February 11, 1826, *Domestic Life,* 416.

231 **"in great distress"** Hetty Carr to Dabney S. Carr, February 1, 1826, Carr-Cary Collection, University of Virginia.

231 **"The natural consequence"** Martha Jefferson Randolph to Joseph Coolidge, March 1, 1826, Ellen W. Coolidge Collection, University of Virginia.

231 **"abstained from the vice"** Ibid.

231 **"feelings are entirely kind"** Ibid.

231 **"You will not be surprised"** Ibid.

231 **"determined at once"** Ibid.

231 **"has gone on since"** Jane Margaret Carr to Dabney S. Carr, February 27, 1826, Carr-Cary Collection, University of Virginia.

231 **"cross the threshold"** Ibid.

232 **"turned quite white"** Hetty Carr to Dabney S. Carr, March 13, 1826, Carr-Cary Collection, University of Virginia.

232 **"some time to think of it"** Ibid.

232 **"as he would to anything"** Hetty Carr to Dabney S. Carr, March 10, 1826, Carr-Cary Collection, University of Virginia.

233 **"Fortune has persecuted us"** Cornelia Randolph to Ellen W. Coolidge, February 23, 1826, Ellen W. Coolidge Papers, University of Virginia.

233 **"the cleanness"** Martha Jefferson Randolph to Joseph Coolidge, April 5, 1826, Ellen W. Coolidge Papers, University of Virginia.

233 **"three times as much money"** *Life of Thomas Jefferson,* 3:537.

233 **"is wrung from the tax-payer"** Ibid.

233 **"serene day of life"** Thomas Jefferson to Thomas Jefferson Randolph, February 8, 1826, *Family Letters,* 469.

CHAPTER 38 *"Is It the Fourth?"*

234   **"being of sound mind"** Thomas Jefferson Will, *Life of Thomas Jefferson*, 3:665.

234   **"Considering the insolvent state"** Ibid.

235   **"not in one"** Francis Nayler Eppes to Thomas Jefferson, June 23, 1826, *Family Letters*.

235   **In a codicil** *Life of Thomas Jefferson*, 3:666.

235   **"on some part of my lands"** Ibid., 667.

236   **Jefferson informed** Thomas Jefferson to John Adams, March 25, 1826, *Adams-Jefferson Letters*, 614.

236   **On April 17, Adams wrote** John Adams to Thomas Jefferson, April 17, 1826, Ibid.

237   **"well stricken in years"** *Life of Thomas Jefferson*, 3:538.

237   **"as immovable as a statue"** Ibid.

237   **"crippled hands"** Ibid.

237   **"helped himself"** Ibid.

237   **"It was agony"** Jane Randolph to Cary Anne Smith, July 27, 1826, Edgehill-Randolph Papers, University of Virginia.

238   **"making a decided impression"** "Dr. Dunglison's Memorandum," *Life of Thomas Jefferson*, 3:548.

238   **"evacuations became less numerous"** Ibid.

238   **"his powers were failing"** Ibid.

239   **"the anxiety and distress"** *Visitors to Monticello*, 108.

239   **"There he was"** Ibid., 109.

239   **"kept the flies off himself"** Ibid., 110.

239   **"became so cheerful"** Ibid., 109.

239   **"You *must* dine here"** Ibid., 110.

240   **Martha Randolph told him** Ibid.

240   **"the inflammation"** Virginia Randolph Trist to Cornelia Randolph, June 30, 1826, Ellen W. Coolidge Papers, University of Virginia.

240   **"most alarmingly weak"** Ibid.

240   **"almost constantly"** Ibid.

240   **"whenever we can"** Virginia Randolph Trist to Cornelia Randolph, June 30, 1826, Edgehill-Randolph Papers, University of Virginia.

240   **"barely sensible"** Thomas Jefferson Randolph to Jane Randolph, July 2, 1826, Edgehill-Randolph Papers, University of Virginia.

240   **"from hour to hour"** Ibid.

240   **"with intervals of wakefulness"** "Dr. Dunglison's Memorandum," *Life of Thomas Jefferson*, 3:548.

240   **"to pursue virtue"** Thomas Jefferson Randolph to Henry Randall, n.d., *Life of Thomas Jefferson*, 3:544.

240   **"George does not understand"** Ibid.

240   **"kind and good neighbor"** Ibid., 543.

241 **"to breathe his last"** From 102-page volume containing notes and copies of letters to Henry S. Randall and others, 1856–1858, Ellen Wayles Coolidge, Ellen W. Coolidge Papers, University of Virginia, 10–11.

241 **"an expression came over"** *Life of Thomas Jefferson,* 3:546.

241 **"the clamminess of death"** Nicholas P. Trist to Joseph Coolidge, July 4, 1826, Ellen W. Coolidge Papers, University of Virginia.

241 **"Ah! Doctor"** "Dr. Dunglison's Memorandum," *Life of Thomas Jefferson,* 3:548.

241 **"No, Doctor"** Thomas Jefferson Randolph to Henry Randall, n.d., Ibid., 543.

241 **"caused his slumbers"** Ibid., 544.

241 **"as if writing"** Ibid., 546.

241 **"the Committee of Safety"** Thomas Jefferson Randolph to Randall, n.d., Ibid., 544.

241 **"which, it seemed to me"** Trist, quoted by Randall, Ibid., 546.

241 **"strong and clear voice"** Thomas Jefferson Randolph, quoted by Randall, Ibid., 544.

241 **"He did not speak again"** Ibid.

241 **"fixed his eye"** Ibid.

242 **"which he sucked"** Ibid.

242 **"ceased to breathe"** Ibid.

242 **"closed his eyes"** Ibid.

242 **"It is a great day"** David McCullough, *John Adams* (New York: Simon & Schuster, 2001), 646.

242 **"Thomas Jefferson"** Ibid.

242 **"Thomas Jefferson still survives"** Andrew Burstein, *American Jubilee* (New York: Knopf, 2001), 273.

242 **"Help me, child!"** McCullough, *John Adams,* 646.

243 **"gloom over every countenance"** Louise McIntyre to Jane M. Carr, July 6, 1826, Carr-Cary Papers, University of Virginia.

243 **"a singular scene"** "The Autobiographical Anas of Robley Dunglison," Samuel X. Radbill, ed. (Philadelphia: American Philosophical Society, 1963), 33.

243 **"pretended to mourn"** Louise McIntyre to Jane M. Carr, July 6, 1826, Carr-Cary Papers, University of Virginia.

244 **"hating [Jefferson] in life"** Thomas Jefferson Randolph to Dabney S. Carr, July 7, 1826, Carr-Cary Papers, University of Virginia.

244 **"Life's visions"** *Domestic Life,* 429.

245 **"our first Lucy's hair"** Ibid., 431.

245 **"becoming tired"** *Charlottesville Weekly Chronicle,* October 15, 1875.

245 **"sorely disappointed"** Ibid.

246 **"visible and palpable"** Marie Hecht, *John Quincy Adams* (New York: Macmillan, 1972), 437.

246 **"striking and extraordinary"** K. E. Shewmaker, *Daniel Webster: "The Completist Man"* (Hanover, N.H.: University Press of New England, 1990), 106.

246 **"the sufferings of sickness"** Thomas Jefferson to Robert C. Weightman, June 21, 1826, L. & B., 16:181.

246  **"to burst the chains"** Ibid.

246  **"the unbounded exercise"** Ibid.

246  **"All eyes are opened"** Ibid.

## EPILOGUE

247  **"to receive assistance"** Martha Jefferson Randolph to Thomas Jefferson Randolph, March 2, 1827, Edgehill-Randolph Papers, University of Virginia.

247  **"I have lost"** Ibid.

247  **"the whole of the residue"** *Charlottesville Central Gazette,* January 13, 1827.

248  **"valuable historical"** Ibid.

249  **"Tell mama"** Mary Randolph to Ellen W. Coolidge, January 25, 1827, Ellen W. Coolidge Papers, University of Virginia.

249  **"sold to persons"** Mary J. Randolph to Mrs. Joseph Coolidge, January 1, 1827, Ellen W. Coolidge Papers, University of Virginia.

249  **"this dreadful business"** Ibid.

249  **"sale and dispersion"** *Memoirs,* 54.

250  **"prostrate"** Thomas Jefferson Randolph to Dabney S. Carr, July 18, 1826, Carr-Cary Papers, University of Virginia.

250  **"a perfect hell"** Ibid.

250  **"some happy years yet"** Thomas Mann Randolph to Septimia Randolph, August 6, 1827, Randolph-Meikelham Papers, University of Virginia.

250  **"to disrespect and dislike"** Ibid.

250  **"be received kindly"** Joseph Coolidge to Thomas Jefferson Randolph, August 13, 1827, Edgehill-Randolph Papers, University of Virginia.

250  **"rheumatic affection"** Thomas Mann Randolph, Jr., to Nicholas P. Trist, March 11, 1827, Ellen W. Coolidge Papers, University of Virginia.

250  **"too low for any tavern"** Martha Randolph to Thomas Jefferson Randolph, February 29, 1828, Edgehill-Randolph Papers, University of Virginia.

251  **"adored wife"** Martha Randolph to Mrs. Joseph Coolidge, June [unclear], 1828, Ellen W. Coolidge Papers, University of Virginia.

251  **"mutual forgiveness"** Ibid.

251  **"an *honester* man"** Ibid.

251  **"his propensity to *argue*"** Ibid.

251  **"He enjoyed every advantage"** *Richmond Enquirer,* July 4, 1828.

251  **"It will grieve you"** Virginia Trist to Ellen W. Coolidge, March 23, 1827, Edgehill-Randolph Papers, University of Virginia.

251  **"little heaps of ruin"** Cornelia Randolph to Ellen W. Coolidge, July 6, 1828, quoted in Marc Leepson, *Saving Monticello* (New York: Free Press, 2001), 21.

251  **"dark & much dilapidated"** *Visitors to Monticello,* 111.

251  **"one or two exceptions"** Ibid., 112.

252 **"How different"** Smith, *First Forty Years of Washington Society,* 230.

252 **"once filled with busts"** Ibid., 230–31.

252 **"with open arms"** Ibid., 231.

252 **"You will excuse"** Ibid.

253 **"Monticello, in the County of Albemarle"** *Richmond Enquirer,* July 28, 1828.

253 **"good night Old Virginia"** Francis Eppes to Thomas Jefferson Randolph, November 6, 1828, Edgehill-Randolph Papers, University of Virginia.

253 **"profaning a temple"** Cornelia Randolph to Ellen W. Coolidge, July 6, 1828, quoted in Leepson, *Saving Monticello,* 21.

253 **"a great coarse Irish woman"** *Visitors to Monticello,* 116.

253 **"coffee-urns"** Ibid., 118.

253 **"appeared to have been a garden"** Ibid.

254 **"is a blow to us"** Cornelia Randolph to Mrs. Joseph Coolidge, June 29, 1831, Ellen W. Coolidge Papers, University of Virginia.

254 **"I am doubtful"** Cornelia Randolph to Mrs. Joseph Coolidge, August 28, 1831, Ellen W. Coolidge Papers, University of Virginia.

255 **"blood-thirsty wolves"** *Richmond Enquirer,* August 30, 1831.

255 **"the black terror"** Sally E. Hadden, *Slave Patrols: Law and Violence in Virginia and the Carolinas* (Cambridge, Mass.: Harvard University Press, 2001), 146.

255 **"thoroughly alarmed"** *The Constitutional Whig,* August 25, 1831, Richmond, Va., Library of Virginia.

255 **"unjust & tyrannical"** Cornelia Randolph to Mrs. Joseph Coolidge, August 28, 1831, Ellen W. Coolidge Papers, University of Virginia.

255 **"dreadful state of things"** Ibid.

255 **"You will laugh"** Cornelia Randolph to Virginia Trist, August 11, 1833, Southern Historical Collection, Nicholas P. Trist Papers, University of North Carolina at Chapel Hill.

256 **"this state of things"** Cornelia Randolph to Ellen W. Coolidge, August 28, 1831, Ellen W. Coolidge Papers, University of Virginia.

256 **"no more fervent prayer"** Ibid.

256 **"an anxious thought"** Mary Randolph to Ellen W. Coolidge, August 25, 1831, Ellen W. Coolidge Papers, University of Virginia.

256 **"the destruction of the conspirators"** Ibid.

256 **"keep their eyes open"** Ibid.

256 **"I do not think"** Cornelia Randolph to Ellen Coolidge, August 28, 1831, Ellen Coolidge, Correspondence, University of Virginia.

256 **"The prospect"** Lewis Randolph to Septimia Randolph, July 31, 1832, Randolph-Meikelham Papers, University of Virginia.

256 **"ghostlike trees"** Ibid.

257 **"The savage burnt them"** Ibid.

257 **"have visited its walls"** Ibid.

257   **"I most sincerely pray"** Ibid.

257   **"to the last copper"** *Memoirs,* 53.

257   **"that a character"** Ibid.

257   **"no creditor has complained"** Thomas Jefferson Randolph to Nicholas P. Trist, February 1, 1833, Nicholas P. Trist Papers, Library of Congress.

258   **"Meats, vegetables"** Martha Jefferson Randolph to Ellen Coolidge, June 20, 1834, Jefferson Additional Papers, University of Virginia.

258   **"better suited"** Thomas Jefferson Randolph to Jane Randolph, January 29, 1832, Edgehill-Randolph Papers, University of Virginia.

258   **"appalling"** Joseph Carroll Vance, "Thomas Jefferson Randolph," Ph.D. diss. (University of Virginia, 1957), 194.

258   **"inevitable"** Thomas Jefferson Randolph, "Speech in House of Delegates," January 20, 1832, in Rare Virginia Pamphlets, vol. 525, archived in University of Virginia Library.

258   **"burning with enthusiasm"** Ibid.

258   **"while the evil"** Ibid.

259   **"The great object"** W. E. Hemphill, M. W. Schlegel, and S. E. Engleberg, *Cavalier Commonwealth* (New York: McGraw-Hill, 1957), 228.

259   **"vilely traduced"** Jane Randolph to Sarah Nicholas, April 16, 1833, Edgehill-Randolph Papers, University of Virginia.

259   **"drunk for some days"** Martha Jefferson Randolph to Ellen W. Coolidge, June 23, 1833, Ellen W. Coolidge Papers, University of Virginia.

260   **"an apoplectic fit"** Ibid.

260   **"appeared to us"** Ellen W. Coolidge Journal, Ellen W. Coolidge Papers, University of Virginia.

260   **"immediately after"** Ibid.

260   **"by her father's side"** Ibid.

260   **"an idea of prosperity"** Ellen Coolidge to Thomas Jefferson, August 1, 1825, *Family Letters,* 454–55.

260   **"at least a century"** Ibid.

260   **"in the highest"** Lewis Randolph to Septimia Randolph, October 1, 1833, Randolph-Meikelham Papers, University of Virginia.

261   **"contained more wealth"** *Richmond Enquirer,* December 29, 1852.

261   **"when it smothers"** Quoted in Frederick Law Olmstead, *The Cotton Kingdom* (New York: Random House, 1984) 587.

261   **"Colt's six shooters"** George Wythe Randolph to Thomas Jefferson Randolph, March 4, 1861, Edgehill-Randolph Papers, University of Virginia.

262   **"escaped unscathed"** Vance, "Thomas Jefferson Randolph," 227.

262   **he told a newspaperman** The account that follows draws on "Life Among the Lowly," *The Pike County* (Ohio) *Republican,* December 25, 1873.

263   **"alarming attack"** Sarah N. Randolph to Hugh G. Grigsby, July 29, 1875, Grigsby Papers, Virginia Historical Society.

263 **"when the Hon. Jefferson Randolph"** *Baltimore Sun,* July 10, 1872.

263 **"I have the honor"** Ibid.

263 **"brief and sensible"** *Richmond Dispatch,* July 10, 1872.

264 **"I am aware"** Ibid.

264 **"he lay in his son's arms"** "A Memorial to Col. Thomas J. Randolph," reprinted as a pamphlet from the *Charlottesville Chronicle,* October 22, 1874, Virginia Historical Society.

# Index

# ILLUSTRATION CREDITS

148 Isaac Jefferson. Daguerreotype. © Tracy W. McGregor Library of American History, MSS 2041, Special Collections, University of Virginia Library.

161 Edmund Bacon. Daguerreotype. © Tracy W. McGregor Library of American History, MSS 5385-al, Special Collections, University of Virginia Library.

170 Ann Cary Randolph Bankhead. Bust by William John Coffee. © Monticello/The Thomas Jefferson Foundation, Inc.

175 Monticello, East Front. Photo by William Rhodes, 1870–1880. © Tracy W. McGregor Library of American History, MSS 798, Special Collections, University of Virginia Library.

177 Wilson Cary Nicholas. © Virginia Historical Society, Richmond, Virginia.

205 The University of Virginia, Charlottesville, and Monticello. © Tracy W. McGregor Library of American History, MSS 2535, Special Collections, University of Virginia Library.

211 Rotunda and Lawn from south. © Tracy W. McGregor Library of American History, Prints21442, Special Collections, University of Virginia Library.

214 "Thomas Jefferson," taken October 15, 1825, at Monticello, Virginia, by John Henri Isaac Browere (1790–1834), plaster bust, H: 26¼", W: 18½", D: 10½", N-241.40. Courtesy Fenimore Art Museum, Cooperstown, New York. Photo by Richard Walker.

223 Jefferson lottery ticket, 1826. © Monticello/The Thomas Jefferson Foundation, Inc.

229 Old House/Edgehill in Albemarle. © Tracy W. McGregor Library of American History, Prints File, Special Collections, University of Virginia Library.

234 Thomas Jefferson's Poplar Forest (interior). Courtesy of Thomas Jefferson's Poplar Forest.

238 Martha Jefferson Randolph. Portrait by Thomas Sully. © Monticello/The Thomas Jefferson Foundation, Inc.

243 Jefferson's bed chamber. © Monticello/The Thomas Jefferson Foundation, Inc.

244 Monticello graveyard with George W. Randolph, 1871. © Tracy W. McGregor Library of American History, MSS 9777-b, Special Collections, University of Virginia Library.

248 Executor's Sale Notice. *The Charlottesville Central Gazette,* November 3, 1826 © Monticello/The Thomas Jefferson Foundation, Inc.

252 Monticello, West Front. Photo by William Rhodes, 1870–1880. © Tracy W. McGregor Library of American History, MSS 798, Special Collections, University of Virginia Library.

254 Virginia Trist and Ellen Coolidge, March 23, 1827. © Monticello/The Thomas Jefferson Foundation, Inc.

264 Thomas Jefferson Randolph. From Barrington Vol. 1. © Tracy W. McGregor Library of American History, Prints File, Special Collections, University of Virginia Library.